PUBLIC BUDGETING AND FINANCIAL ADMINISTRATION IN DEVELOPING COUNTRIES

POLICY STUDIES AND DEVELOPING NATIONS

A Multi-Volume Treatise, Volume 3

Editor: Stuart S. Nagel, *Department of Political Science, University of Illinois*

Policy Studies and Developing Nations
(A Multi-Volume Treatise)

Edited by **Stuart S. Nagel**, *Department of Political Science, University of Illinois*

Volume 1.

Poverty Policy in Developing Countries

Edited by **Thomas R. DeGregori**, *University of Houston*
and **Harrell R. Rodgers, Jr.**, *University of Houston*

1994, 306 pp.
ISBN 1-55938-054-3

Volume 2.

Policy Reform and Developing Nations

Edited by **Stuart S. Nagel**, *University of Illinois*, **William Crotty**, *Northwestern University* and **James Scarritt**, *University of Colorado and Zambia University*

1996, 344 pp.
ISBN 1-55938-106-X

Volume 3.

Public Budgeting and Financial Administration in Developing Countries

Naomi Caiden, *California State University, Los Angeles*

1996, 320 pp.
ISBN 1-55938-190-6

Volume 4.

Human Rights and Developing Countries

Edited by **David Louis Cingranelli**
State University of New York at Binghamton

In preparation, Summer 1997
ISBN 0-7623-0036-1

Volume 5.

**Policy Analysis Concepts and Methods
An Institutional and Implementation Focus**

Edited by **Derick W. Brinkerhoff**, *University of Maryland*

In preparation, Summer 1997
ISBN 0-7623-0148-1

PUBLIC BUDGETING AND FINANCIAL ADMINISTRATION IN DEVELOPING COUNTRIES

Series Editor: STUART S. NAGEL
Department of Political Science
University of Illinois

Volume Editor: NAOMI CAIDEN
Department of Political Science
California State University, Los Angeles

VOLUME 3 • 1996

Emerald

United Kingdom – North America – Japan
India – Malaysia – China

Emerald Group Publishing Limited
Howard House, Wagon Lane, Bingley BD16 1WA, UK

Reprints and permission service
Contact: booksandseries@emeraldinsight.com

British Library Cataloguing in Publication Data
A catalogue record for this book is available from the British Library

ISBN: 978-1-55938-190-1

Printed and bound by CPI Group (UK) Ltd, Croydon, CR0 4YY

CONTENTS

LIST OF CONTRIBUTORS

William Allan	Fiscal Affairs Department International Monetary Fund
Naomi Caiden	Department of Political Science California State University, Los Angeles
Steven Chan	Department of Political Science University of Colorado, Boulder
Cal Clark	Department of Political Science Auburn University
Peter Dean	Department of Economic and Social Development United Nations
Martha de Melo	Transition and Macro Adjustment Division, World Bank
Jack Diamond	Budget and Expenditure Control Division International Monetary Fund
Joon Chien Doh	Nanyang Technological University, Singapore
Gundar J. King	Director Baltic Academic Centre Riga, Latvia
James Leigland	International Consulting Staff Institute of Public Administration

Jonathan N. Moyo	Department of Political and Administrative Studies University of Zimbabwe, Harare
Stephen B. Peterson	Harvard Institute for International Development Harvard University
David O. Porter	School of Management University of Alaska, Fairbanks
Katrina Sharkey	Economic Development Institute World Bank
Richard E. Zody	Institute for Public Management, Urban Affairs and Planning Virginia Polytechnic Institute and State University, Blacksburg, Virginia

INTRODUCTION

Naomi Caiden

Human inventions stand and fall by their utility for the tasks they are called upon to face. Budgeting and financial administration as we know them today were institutionalized during the nineteenth century in European countries to serve the needs for accountability and orderly management in the finances of emerging democratic states. Their concepts and practices were expanded in industrialized countries and transferred to and assimilated in developing countries, where they were further called upon to meet the demands of planning and development.

Now, toward the end of the twentieth century, budgeting and financial administration have taken on critical importance in the governance of all countries, while at the same time their capacity to fulfill expectations of them appears inadequate. The inability of prescription to meet implementation or to bring about desired outcomes is strikingly illustrated in many countries by intractable deficits, inability to bring about planned development, rampant corruption, failures in information and accountability, and loss of financial control in many governmental and quasi-governmental agencies and projects.

What has gone wrong? Have people failed to carry out the prescriptions for successful budgeting and financial administration through lack of understanding or lack of will? Or are the prescriptions themselves so ill-adapted to current realities that they are impossible to carry out or, even if implemented, would lead to undesirable outcomes? How might budgeting and financial administration be improved in developing countries?

The contributors to this book are all involved in relating prescription to practice, theory to reality, in budgeting and financial administration in developing countries. Their essays all seek to provide practical advice to administrators presently caught up in the fast-changing and unpredictable contemporary environment. Each touches on an aspect of budgeting or financial administration, but their work as a whole is not intended to form a comprehensive handbook or guide to the subject. Rather, the volume pinpoints salient issues confronting policymakers, in order to contribute to major current debates that center on the applicability and feasibility of policies grounded in predominant economic theories to practical day-to-day management of public finances in developing countries.

The reasons for this selective approach lie in three basic considerations. First, the subject of budgeting and financial administration is complex, sprawling, and poorly conceptualized. Second, the nature of developing countries is subject to considerable controversy. Third, the present environment is so uncertain and so difficult to interpret that policy prescriptions can no longer be regarded as definitive in nature.

THE NATURE OF BUDGETING AND FINANCIAL ADMINISTRATION

For nearly half a century, public budgeting has been defined and redefined, less to provide the term with greater precision than to recognize its expansion of function, both realized and innate. Budgeting was reconceptualized from a rather simple arrangement for financing the restricted agencies of government on an annual basis to an institution key, to the transformed nature of the public sector. In Schick's words, the capacity to budget became equivalent to the capacity to govern itself:

> Budgeting is essential to the effective operation of modern government. It has become the closest thing to a national command and control process, the means by which governments steer and finance their vast ambitions. It is no exaggeration to state that the capacity to govern depends on the capacity to budget....
>
> ...[G]overnment uses the budget to establish and pursue national objectives, to promote favorable economic conditions, to manage its diverse activities, to respond to the demands of citizens and groups, to assess past performance, and to plan for the future (1990, p. 1)

Financial administration, in contrast, remained a much more diffuse topic. Current texts give little indication of a unified conceptual framework. Rather, their contents pages are lists of activities or processes with few if any links among them. There is general agreement on the topics to be included under the heading of financial administration: for example, cash management, accounting, auditing, purchasing, inventory control, tax assessment and collection, fiscal forecasting. But few efforts seem to have been made to connect the topics together or to relate them to budgetary policy making.

Yet, the importance of financial administration is growing. Its increased significance may be understood by analyzing two different ways in which it may be related to budgeting. First, financial administration may be viewed as the activities involved in implementing a budget. As such, it is technical and subordinate, since the budget should comprise all necessary financial decisions (i.e., fiscal policy, taxation, expenditures); and from the point of its approval, all other activities should simply carry it out as it is written in an orderly, efficient, and responsible way.

This concept of financial administration assumes the regularity of the budget process, the feasibility of annual planning of revenues and expenditures, and a division between policy and administration such that the latter will not significantly alter or distort the expressed pronouncements of the former as enshrined in the budget document.

But in practice, things are not so simple, and the relationship between a budget and its realization is often far from exact. In conditions of economic volatility, the forecasting of revenues and expenditures is problematic, particularly where inflation is high and difficult to predict. Central budget authorities, whose budgets are vulnerable to disruption and which seek to use fiscal policy as a flexible instrument for economic guidance, monitor revenues and expenditures throughout the year, releasing or checking the flow of funds according to the immediate situation. Government agencies and parastatals often experience difficulties in controlling expenditures and forecasting needs, particularly where they are involved in project implementation, contracts, and negotiations of different kinds. Making the budget throughout the year, or repetitive budgeting, is not uncommon in many developing countries and demands an enhanced role for financial administration, as policy decisions affecting financial policy are no longer restricted to budget determination, and superficially neutral and technical financial administrative functions seriously affect revenue and expenditure outcomes.

Rather than financial administration therefore being regarded as simply the technical playing out or implementation of budgeting, budgeting might be regarded as one part of a larger subject of financial administration. If we retain the predominant cyclical view of financial administration, we might conceptualize it somewhat as follows:

THE BUDGET SYSTEM

ALLOCATES RESOURCES

Public expenditure planning	Programming funds Cash management Cost estimating
MOBILIZES RESOURCES	MANAGES AND IMPLEMENTS
Forecasting Fiscal policy making Assessment of revenues Revenue collection	Accounting Reporting Monitoring Auditing

EVALUATES

Of course, in practice all these activities are conducted simultaneously. Ideally, the cycle should capture an information and decision flow whereby the outcome of one function feeds into the others. In practice, linkages are probably fuzzier and more iterative, and certain functions may be poorly carried out or not carried out at all.

This concept of financial administration has been the guiding framework for this book, but not all its elements are represented. The major important subject omitted is revenue administration, not because it is not significant but because it constitutes a subject in its own right, and recent books that deal with it in detail are readily available (e.g., Bird and De Jantscher 1992). Other aspects are missing because of lack of up-to-date and reliable research on them. Financial administration is a difficult subject to research because it depends heavily on inside information: thus, what is available is often either prescriptive or propagandistic, and it is hard to find critical analyses of practice. It is therefore hoped that the appearance of this volume will stimulate studies of the various topics of financial administration. Meanwhile, even if the issues of *what* is to be studied and *how* it is to be studied may be resolved, the question arises of *where* it is to be studied and the validity of generalizations for any particular context.

THE NATURE OF DEVELOPING COUNTRIES

A major question that should concern us at the outset is whether issues of financial administration are the same in all places and at all times. Is it possible to generalize about financial administration—to set out rules, principles, criteria, frameworks, advice that are universal in their applicability? If so, there is really no subject of financial administration in developing countries, or at most it may only be defined in terms of problems of applying generally valid propositions to specific contexts. On the other hand, is it possible to conceptualize a specific set of policies, problems, and issues related to a defined context—that of "developing countries"—that is by its characteristic nature set off and separate from that of other kinds of countries? Which of these two approaches is more plausible in the case of financial administration?

When Wildavsky and I approached the subject of budgeting in the "developing countries" in the late 1960s, we were uneasy with the term. To us it appeared to have connotations of condescension and to suggest that these countries constituted a special case, where people could not be expected to implement the policies and administrative techniques suitable only for "advanced economies" or conversely (and paradoxically) were expected to implement such prescriptions as comprehensive economic planning and program planning which were actually rejected in Western industrialized countries. We felt that the major distinction among countries was not their level of development (a term subject to varying definitions) but their wealth or lack of it. We therefore settled on the term "poor countries," which contained its own imprecisions but had the merit of highlighting what we felt was perhaps the major qualitative variable accounting for the peculiar features of budgeting that we found with considerable regularity in these countries. Lack of complex functional redundancy, not culture or wisdom or even will or persistence, seemed to account for such phenomena as repetitive budgeting and budgetary disintegration (Caiden and Wildavsky 1980).

Now, more than 20 years later, the paradigm of development and developing countries is still germane. Can developing countries be clearly differentiated from developed ones in principle? Do they require special policies or technologies? Should they all follow a similar route to an identical future? *Which* countries fall under the rubric of "developing countries," and how do we know which they are?

One answer to these questions is to equate "development" with economic growth and to assume that all countries are subject to similar theories and prescriptions that, if followed, will lead to economic prosperity. People everywhere are assumed to respond to the same incentives, and investment will automatically result in economic growth given certain basic conditions such as free movement of capital and information, political stability, public investment in infrastructure and human resources, and absence of dysfunctional governmental initiatives. According to this perspective, all countries may be simply arranged on a continuum according to their per capita gross domestic product. In fact, the World Bank has for many years published a table of this kind, listing a number of indicators for each country and dividing them into categories.

It might thus be possible to differentiate policy prescriptions for these categories of countries, according to their standing in the table, to enable them to increase their per capita incomes, but though this approach has been tried in terms of sectoral policies, it does not seem to have been applied to issues of financial administration.

A different approach would be to emphasize the *change* component of the definition of development as "growth plus change," and to include those countries undergoing or striving to achieve change in their societies and economies. Such change need not necessarily be in a single preconceived direction. The objections to such a definition are that it embraces too many countries and lacks precision. But its merit is that it avoids preconceived deterministic lines of development and allows for greater choice in creating different models of development and relating prescriptions to differing contexts.

In fact, the terms "developing countries," "Third World," and even "poor countries" now include such widely varying contexts that it is difficult to group them together in a meaningful way or make meaningful generalizations about them. Any effort to be comprehensive would seem to be doomed to failure, while even selective comparisons are difficult to handle in view of the vast disparities among the nations in question.

To some degree, the uniformity of issues in financial administration and the relative lack of available research have come to the rescue. Without placing studies within a straitjacket of a single set of prescriptions or setting up definitive abstract criteria for denoting countries as either "developing" or "developed," we have chosen a variety of countries in which it has been possible to study salient issues. While an effort has been made to select countries from different continents, to include large as well as small countries, and also to include some more general chapters drawing on experience from a large number of examples, the countries chosen are by no means representative nor possibly even the most important. Major countries such as India or China have been omitted, while others, not usually included as "developing countries," such as Eastern European countries, have been included. Such choices are understandable, however, in view of the aim of the volume to discuss current issues of financial administration in the light of practical analysis wherever this is available.

THE NATURE OF THE ENVIRONMENT OF FINANCIAL ADMINISTRATION

The turbulent state of the global environment raises problems for budgeting and financial administration in developing countries, however these are defined. To the extent that financial administration is viewed as an entirely technical function, it might be thought it would be immune from environmental volatility, vulnerability, or uncertainty. Even then, however, its institutional stability might influence policy choices and implementation through such apparently neutral functions as revenue forecasting, expenditure estimating, regulation of cash flow, accounting conventions, investment criteria, foreign aid disbursements, and audit follow-up. But in practice, the interface between environment and financial administration is much more direct as it influences and is influenced by events and trends both within and outside government. Moreover, budgeting and financial administration cannot be entirely detached from policy concerns: they do not merely carry out policy but may also critically influence it by constraining some possibilities, facilitating others, and directly participating in decisions through the flow of information, substantive analysis, and responsiveness of processes.

Financial policymakers and administrators in developing countries work in an environment of increasing turbulence. The global economy, a more than ever interconnected system, is highly vulnerable to shocks and fluctuations. Its instability is furthered by the growing speed of communications, which magnifies disturbances as international markets react quickly to news and events. The pace of political change has quickened bringing its own uncertainties with the demise of communist regimes in the Soviet Union, Eastern Europe, and other countries, with the growth of fundamentalist political and religious movements in many countries, with the threatened breakup of many nations and states, and with increasing democratic pressures against authoritarian regimes.

Less obvious are the influences of fast growing populations and their concentration in urban centers, large migration movements including escalating numbers of refugees from various conflicts, and indeterminate movements of resources due to organized crime, hot money, illicit markets, and corruption. Uncertainties have also magnified as the result of changes in world environments concomitant with economic development, including the effects of such phenomena as depletion of forest cover and topsoil, loss of ecological balance, release of toxic and other wastes, pollution of air and water (including groundwater), and spread of old and new diseases. To these may be added the vagaries of climate and weather and possible scenarios of long-term, large-scale changes in global temperature and weather patterns.

The smaller and more vulnerable the country, the more it is likely to be affected by critical factors outside its control—for example, worldwide movements in prices for exports and imports, interest rates, economic swings in industrialized countries, and permeability of borders. Governments are called upon to develop policies to cope with the uncertainties of their position, deriving from both internal and external circumstances. To these have been added further pressures from international bodies, which in return for alleviation of debt problems (legacy of past policies) demand such measures as economic liberalization, privatization, deregulation, downsizing of government, greater governmental efficiency, and investment in infrastructure and human resources to create an environment in which private enterprise can compete in the international marketplace. Irrespective of the merits of such policies, there is no question that they increase the demands on financial administration, which is directly involved in implementing the changes they imply.

A primary issue is therefore the quality of financial administration and the need for its improvement. The areas are not difficult to list. They include:

- better revenue forecasting to provide adequate information about available resources in the short and long term;
- better revenue administration to ensure that all sums due are received and accounted for to cut down seepage and evasion;
- better expenditure estimation and stronger budget analysis to optimize use of funds;
- better monitoring of expenditures to prevent under- and overspending and to maximize returns on funds;
- better project evaluation to cut out wasteful projects;
- better capital budgeting and relating capital and current expenditures;
- stronger control of cash flow and disbursements;
- enforcement of accounting and reporting standards;
- good quality macroeconomic and sectoral analyses;
- use of financial and operational audits;
- public investment planning;
- use of financial and operational audits;
- better information on staffing, use of resources, and administrative efficiency generally; and
- better debt management.

These areas relate primarily to issues of information and control. They are relatively technical in nature, require extensive staff training, and their improvement may be aided considerably by use of computers. In many of them, manuals already exist, and while their implementation may require considerable effort, it is relatively noncontroversial.

Beyond this area of improvement of financial administrative processes lies a more value-laden area more closely related to policy concerns and issues. Within this area financial administration is more than a purely support function and is a direct participant in questions such as:

- What should be the relationship between capital and recurrent spending?
- What criteria should be considered in evaluating projects, and what should be their priority?
- What should be the balance between central control and agency (managerial) autonomy in decisions on expenditure?

- How should spending be apportioned throughout the year?
- What government enterprises and functions should be privatized and what procedures should be adopted?
- In which areas of spending should cuts be implemented and over what period?
- How should forecasts of revenues and expenditures be interpreted, and what changes should be made in their light?
- What use should be made of audit findings, and how should audits be conducted?
- What should be the relationship between planning and budgeting authorities?
- What measures should be adopted and maintained to contain corruption at all levels of government?
- How should fiscal policy be formulated, and how should its content be determined?

These and other questions impinge directly on core questions of public finance—the allocation, distribution, and stabilization of resources. They involve both policy and politics: What should be public and what private? Who gets and who pays? How much is there to be overall and for each function of government? They are directly concerned with the unstable, turbulent, and uncertain environment.

Financial administration may therefore be viewed as a continuum. At one end are relatively technical and noncontroversial elements whose good practice differs little whatever the environment. At the other are politically sensitive areas whose administration and alteration involve constant resolution of policy issues. This book is concerned with theory and practice at both ends of this continuum and in between.

We begin with the development of budgeting. Following a conceptual overview, Calvin Clark and Steven Chan apply the framework of budgetary development to a single country, Taiwan.

We then move on to issues of fiscal policy. Martha de Melo and Jack Diamond raise questions of the capability of governments in developing countries to choose their own fiscal policies: to balance variables such as budget deficits, inflation, debt, and economic growth in a deliberate fashion. Their contributions relate budgetary policies (within the control of policymakers) to the external environment (which is not). Their assumptions, approaches, and tools are those of economists, and to the extent their arguments rely on a conventional macroeconomic models, it is up to those who disagree to provide counter-models.

The third section is concerned with planning budgets. Bill Allan sets out the problems and potentialities of public expenditure planning and forecasting in developing countries. Stephen Peterson outlines the difficulties in achieving financial reform in Kenya. Katrina Sharkey explores new directions in public investment planning, within the context of recent World Bank initiatives, in the Caribbean.

The fourth section deals with issues in public expenditure management. Doh Joon Chien outlines the ways in which Singapore has adapted reforms stressing managerial decentralization, similar to those initiated in several industrialized countries, to its own context. Stephen Peterson re-examines the perennial question of the place of recurrent costs in operational, development, and capital budgets. Jonathan Moyo discusses problems in reforming public budgeting in Zimbabwe.

We have devoted a special section to the issue of privatization. James Leigland reports on the privatization of public enterprises in Asia, and David Porter and Gundar King discuss the factors impeding privatization in Latvia.

Finally, Peter Dean and Richard Zody provide general perspectives on accounting and auditing in developing countries.

REFERENCES

Schick, A. 1990. *The Capacity to Budget*. Washington, DC: Urban Institute.

Bird, R.M., and M.C. de Jantscher. 1992. *Improving Tax Administration in Developing Countries*. Washington, DC: International Monetary Fund.

Caiden, N., and A. Wildavsky. 1980. *Planning and Budgeting in Poor Countries*. New Brunswick, NJ: Transition Books.

PART I.

BUDGETING AND DEVELOPMENT

FROM HERE TO THERE AND BEYOND: CONCEPTS AND APPLICATIONS OF PUBLIC BUDGETING IN DEVELOPING COUNTRIES

Naomi Caiden

ABSTRACT

As governments moved from a primarily regulatory stance toward active intervention in economic and social matters, ideas about budgeting and financial administration developed from preoccupations with economy and accountability to encompass notions of efficient and effective management. With the growing trend toward structural adjustment and reliance on market mechanisms, emphasis has changed toward more flexible and integrated modes of public financial administration.

"No man is an island," wrote John Donne. So too, budgets, budgeting, and budgeters do not exist in isolation but are an integral part of their milieu and of the ideas and mores that characterize their times. Yet, texts on budgeting often give little hint of their intellectual moorings or even express awareness of their own specific and idiosyncratic context. It is as though

Policy Studies and Developing Nations, Volume 3, pages 3-17.

ISBN: 1-55938-190-6

budget processes and precepts are timeless and unvarying whatever the period. However, the history of public budgeting reveals the accepted practices of one age as the quaint curiosities of the next. Their proponents, like exponents of public budgeting today, not only took them seriously but saw little other direction as either feasible or desirable.

Any realistic analysis of the state of public financial management, especially as it is practiced in developing countries, demands perspective. We have to ask: Where are we *now* in relation to what is past and what is likely to transpire? Why do we do the things we do and propose the remedies we propose? In what ways were past ideas and practices of budgeting a product of their times? What is the validity of the ideas and circumstances that govern current prescriptions and processes? What are the salient features of contemporary public budgeting? In what direction are changes taking place? How should existing practices respond to a rapidly changing environment? And how may institutions and processes be influenced to achieve desirable outcomes?

This chapter traces the historical movement of ideas about public budgeting in the twentieth century. Its premise is that budgets are not simply technical tools, or easily manipulable clusters of classifications, processes, and institutions. The technical elements are closely related to ideas about the management of governmental systems and to the values these express. It follows that techniques and modes of organization of budgeting tend to differ in accordance with changing concepts of government management and dominant values in public life. The chapter also compares concepts of what budgeting *ought* to be with actual practices, and attempts to account for divergences between theory and practice by reference to responses of budgeters and managers to prevailing circumstances.

Public budgeting is an aspect, or even logical consequence, of the movement toward responsible and representative government. While its definitive beginning is open to argument, the flavor of budgeting in the nation-state is nineteenth century, and a useful point of departure or dividing line in the acceptability of budgeting as an idea is the end of the Napoleonic Wars in Europe (see Bruguierè 1969). The era of "pre-budgeting" financial administration is a subject on its own (see Caiden 1978, 1980, pp. 135-159). This chapter is concerned with currently accepted notions of budgeting as it emerged and developed in the twentieth century.

As governments in both industrialized and developing countries moved from a primarily regulatory stance toward active intervention in economic and social matters, ideas about budgeting and financial administration developed from preoccupations with economy and accountability to encompass notions of efficient and effective management. Predominant techniques of line-item budgeting were augmented by attempts to implement variants of program and performance budgeting (for a history of budget reform and the emergence of program budgeting, see Schick 1966). With the waning of government

Table 1.

	Role Of Government		
	Regulatory	*Development*	*Adjustment*
Budget Technique	Line item	Program Budgeting	Macropolicy and Medium term Investment Planning
Management Mode	Bureaucratic	Planning	Market
Expression of Values	Law and order Economy	Development	Efficiency

initiatives, particularly in the development planning area, and the growing trend toward structural adjustment and reliance on market mechanisms, the emphasis has moved toward more flexible and integrated modes of public financial administration. These trends are summarized in Table 1, which necessarily simplifies complex, variable, and overlapping developments. In real life, there are no sharp breaks between periods, and the ideas of one period often continue or are included in the next so that progression is cumulative. Moreover, ideas and practice tend to diverge, so that the characterizations of each stage are blurred rather than accurate. The summary representation of the table then should not be viewed as complete history but rather as an introductory "map" of the historical terrain, designed to guide and orient the reader in reviewing the contemporary scene.

REGULATORY BUDGETING

During the nineteenth century and the first third of the twentieth, the functions of national governments were relatively restricted. Traditional law and order and defense activities were gradually augmented by interventions in public health, construction of roads and railways, and conservation of natural resources. Several European countries saw the initiation of national pension schemes and other provisions for social welfare, but the variations even in industrialized countries were considerable, and in developing countries little if any provision existed. The role of government was perceived as primarily regulatory in nature, encompassing law and order activities, revenue raising, and regulation of industrial and commercial activities.

Budget processes reflected the concept of government. The first real budget in Europe, following the Napoleonic Wars in France, was created to ensure the exact funding of government activities for the coming year, in contrast to the previous haphazard paying out of monies. The principles were simple and formed a lasting basis for later elaborations (for the development of public budgeting during the nineteenth century, see Stourm 1909). Budgets should be annual and comprehensive (embracing all revenues and expenditures). They should be financed through annual appropriations authorized by a legislative body, and the correctness of spending according to those appropriations should be checked annually through audit when accounts were closed. The main characteristic of budgeting was its cyclical nature through which it exercised control over public expenditures.

Budgetary processes were essentially bureaucratic, reflecting more general theories of administration. They depended on a hierarchy of full-time neutral officials whose task was to implement the budget as passed, in as economical a fashion as possible, and to account for expenditures as stipulated. The assumption was that revenues would be allocated and spent on primarily administrative and well-defined tasks by full-time government officials working within government departments. The budget was a major instrument for centralized control by government. Of course, the realization of that control varied with the capability of national bureaucracies and the political capacity of governments: it was undoubtedly diluted in practice by corruption, incompetence, and political instability. But the concept—a centralized, bureaucratic control system—remained the dominant model for budgeting.

Its aim was the cheapest government possible. The goal of budgeting was economy, a sober contrast with the extravagance and profligacy of previous eras. The line item budget was well suited to this objective. Because it both appropriates and implements expenditures according to inputs, it facilitates "bean counting." Line item budgeting lists objects of expenditure (e.g., personnel, materials, fuel, travel, etc.) and estimates allocations of each of them for the coming year. The allocations must be spent according to the line items, except where special procedures allow transfers between them (or virement). It is also usual to list expenditures in each category for the previous year together with estimates of current year actual spending so that comparisons may be easily made with recent history. Increases out of the ordinary from year to year may be quickly spotted, and budgets may be cut down or questioned item by item. Control over the objects of expenditure is easily understood, and it is not surprising that line item budgeting is still the most practiced classification for budgets today.

The line item budget encourages incrementalism—relatively small and regular increases from year to year. Incrementalism is a useful way of making budgets, enabling governments to move cautiously, and reducing conflicts. Budgets tend to be built from below on the requests of ministries and agencies who may expect to receive allocations roughly in line with those of previous years. The incremental mode of budgeting appeared appropriate for stable governments with well-defined functions and established institutions.

Budgeting in developing countries followed the lines of that of the industrialized countries. Colonial governments were interested in governing their colonies as economically as possible. In Latin America, annual budgeting was augmented by control systems based on pre-audit, the certification of expenditures before spending, which often defeated their purpose by interposing a further layer of bureaucracy and encouraging corruption. As regulatory government gave way to developmental government, these traditional procedures were seen as a hindrance and outmoded.

BUDGETING FOR DEVELOPMENT

Although many governments in industrialized and developing countries had undertaken social and welfare activities earlier, from the 1930s governments began to take on a much stronger and more clearly defined role in accepting social and economic responsibilities for their citizenry. The cumulative effects of the 1930s depression, World War II, and post-war reconstruction transformed the guardian state into the welfare state, spearheaded by labor governments in Europe and followed by the United States in the 1960s, though not to the same degree. Keynesian macroeconomic theories, which placed national governments in the key position to influence economies to maintain conditions of high employment, price stability, and economic growth, filtered through into legislation and became assumptions of public life. In developing countries, newly independent governments as well as those of Latin America espoused economic development as an urgent necessity, with the state as the primary vehicle for effecting rapid and far-reaching economic and social transformation. In both developing and industrialized countries, wide-ranging public programs were initiated in such areas as urban development, regional planning, environmental protection, industrial policy, health, education, and social security and welfare.

The restricted role of government was abandoned in favor of a planning role. In the command economies of the Soviet Union and Eastern Europe, national economic planning embraced the whole economy, aspiring to the centralized allocation of all societal resources (for a description of budgeting in socialist planned economies, see Spulber 1990, pp. 109-128). Where it existed in industrialized countries, national planning was "indicative" or indirect in nature, relying on fiscal and monetary policies to "prime the pump" or damp down inflation. In developing countries, comprehensive economic planning became the norm. Medium-term national plans (for three-, five-, or other year terms) were formulated for both public and private sectors by central planning agencies. Planning was expected to perform a major coordinating role, to mobilize society, to accomplish development programs, and to bring about both growth and change.

Public administration too was expected to change as bureaucracies reoriented from regulatory to public welfare and developmental roles (although, of course, traditional functions continued and expanded). Broader forms of government action emerged, including a variety of kinds of public enterprises, intergovernmental fiscal systems, planning machinery, networks of grants and subsidies, external aid, and many types of entitlements. Although the patterns of organization, finances, and expenditures differed between industrialized and developing countries, the role conceived for government was little different in its assumptions. Public bureaucracies were expected to intervene to promote the public interest, protect the weaker elements of society, build the nation, steer the economy, safeguard democracy, and bring about a more just and prosperous society. Public administration was to be development administration.

While in industrialized countries the idea of development was muted, in developing countries it was a primary organizing concept. Development—often defined as growth plus change—was both process and goal, a general concept and a very real embodiment of specific governmental policies. The path to development was the subject of much theorizing, but in practical terms it invariably involved government programs, initiated, coordinated and implemented according to national plans, and institutionalized in a national planning apparatus.

Traditional budget systems in both industrialized and developing countries appeared inappropriate for the new interventionist role of government with its emphasis on planning and programs. Line item budgets, adapted to control of inputs within bureaucracies, did not provide the information needed by policymakers and managers and were particularly impervious to scrutiny by interested publics wishing to gain access to public resources. From its budget alone, no one could even figure out what a government organization *did*, let alone how well it did it, or how effective its programs and activities were. The annual perspective precluded and even impeded planning, which necessarily tried to make commitments beyond one year. The emphasis on economy seemed misplaced in face of urgent needs. If budgeting were to fulfill its potential and not to prove an intolerable hindrance on planning development, it would need to be recast.

Budget reform was not new (Schick 1966). As early as the turn of the century in the United States, efforts had been made to reclassify budgets according to government functions and activities as a means of achieving efficiency. This line of reasoning continued, concomitant with the "scientific management" movement, so that by the 1950s there was a well-developed theory of performance budgeting. Performance budgeting, like similar forms of management theory, broke activities down to their smallest units and analyzed their efficiency. Budgeting was in terms of activities, and the budget for each activity would be preceded by a short paragraph describing it. The reclassification would enable managers to build budgets on the basis of workload forecasts, to compare programs according to their relative efficiency, and to set standards (prescribed unit costs) for funding activities.

But the development paradigm demanded more from budgets than management of centralized organizations. Since budgeting was critical in determining program funding, it was essential that it should not be mere "bean counting" conducted routinely from year to year on incremental lines. Budgeting had to incorporate analytical techniques supporting the decision-making process of identifying and choosing optimal policies and programs. It had to also be linked to the planning process.

The solution, espoused by governments in a large number of countries and advocated by major international aid-giving organizations, was program budgeting. Program budgeting is a generic term for a specific reform that emerged in the United States during the 1960s labeled PPBS or Planning Programming Budgeting System. PPBS was a response to a number of factors that converged at that time: an expansion in governmental social programs, advocacy of national planning and policy making, popularity of ideas of public microeconomics, and availability of techniques of systems analysis. Whereas performance budgeting is essentially managerial in its thrust, concentrating on finding the most efficient ways of implement given objectives, program budgeting is analytical. It aims to transform the routines of budgeting into a regular appraisal of the relative value of programs which can be translated into allocation of funds. Instead of concentrating on inputs, or on the most efficient ways to undertake governmental activities, program budgeting is concerned with effectiveness: the societal impact of programs, the good they do, and the improvements they make to the general welfare.

Key to program budgeting is the concept of a program—a public policy objective together with the steps necessary to attain it. The first step in program budgeting is therefore to reclassify the budget in terms of programs. Note that programs do not necessarily follow organizational lines but take resources from wherever is appropriate. The planning element of program budgeting also mandates that program objectives stretch beyond a single year. The second step is to work out effectiveness measures for each program, measuring not only program *outputs* but also program *outcomes* (i.e., the extent to which objectives are attained). Budget analysis evaluates the relative worth and priority of programs; it chooses among objectives, not just the means to achieving them, on the basis of effectiveness data that is part of the budget submission. The final stage in program budgeting should be a realignment of government organization along program lines.

The popularity of program and performance budgeting lies rooted in a desire to improve budgeting and use it for policy-making purposes. The objective was to recast budgeting from an annual repetitive exercise to a tool for analysis of the effectiveness of government programs. The budget reforms would directly serve the goals of planning and development. In practice, the legion of difficulties involved in identifying logically viable programs, setting criteria of effectiveness across the range of widely differing government objectives, quantifying and measuring outcomes, and incorporating a long-term perspective led to adaptations of simpler and less ambitious forms. Program and performance budgeting in developing countries was distinguished from PPBS in the 1965 United Nations *Manual for Program and Performance Budgeting*, which recommended reorganizing budgets in terms of program structure, a system of accounts, fiscal management in line with the classification, and measurement of efficiency. These themes are also reflected in the International Monetary Fund's *Program Oriented Budgeting*. But the general concept has remained popular and symbolic of modernity and optimality in budgeting (Premchand 1983).

Critics might be divided into two groups. The first group believed that program budgeting was intrinsically impossible. Budgeting was essentially political in nature, and the choices to be made could only be resolved through political choices, not analysis. In addition, program budget advocates sought to rank effectiveness of programs on a common quantitative scale, whereas there was no common index of worth for public programs: one could not compare apples with oranges.

The second group of critics believed that program budgeting might be feasible and useful but not in the circumstances of developing countries, where it was too complex and expensive. It demanded large amounts of accurate and timely information, skilled and knowledgeable personnel, and sufficient flexible resources to move from program to program, and/or the possibility of augmenting resources to implement programs. In addition, program budgeting required sustained political commitment, a sound budgeting and accounting system in place, and a general level of stability and certainty to enable planning of public expenditures for a reasonable period of time.

Some would contend that program budgeting could succeed but that difficulties of implementation have been underestimated. They argue that an effective implementation strategy might bring about better results. Such a strategy would need to include strong political and top bureaucratic backing, training and education at all levels of the organization, efforts to collect information on a standardized basis, linkage of budgeting and accounting systems, gradual introduction of the new system using pilot programs, and a clear understanding at all stages of what is to be achieved (Dean 1989).

Meanwhile, dissatisfaction with the state of budgeting in developing countries continued during the 1970s and 1980s, and familiar criticisms were unabated despite continued reform efforts in line with the performance and program budgeting model (see Caiden and Wildavsky 1980; Lee 1992). In many countries, the "disappearing budget" remained characteristic: budgets were fragmented into many special funds and earmarked funds, sometimes restricting the general budget to only a small portion of expenditures. Public enterprises had an ambivalent relationship with the central budget: nominally independent and providing little information, they nevertheless expected subsidies to cover losses. Because of prevailing uncertainty, repetitive budgeting remained the norm in many countries—the budget was made throughout the year, sometimes even from month to month as forecasts of revenues and economic conditions changed. Rather than a rational analytical exercise, budget processes were a prolonged and frustrating game between central budget authorities and program agencies as each tried to pass their uncertainties to the other.

The most telling criticism against program budgeting, even where it had been introduced and was providing information, was that it was often not used for decision making, which followed an entirely different dynamic, governed by political priorities, donor opportunities and predilections, bureaucratic inertia and infighting, and dispersed power centers. Nor did program budgeting unite planning and budgeting (though several countries tried at least to bridge the organizational gap by combining them in one ministry), and planning often seemed more like an interest group bidding for a share of the budget than an overall controlling process.

Budgeting problems persisted. Where resources did become available, they were often squandered in a "boom and bust" pattern in the public no less than the private sector, leaving both decision-making processes and populations no better (or even worse) than they were before. High real deficits, debt crises, low growth rates, and loss of confidence in governments were the characteristics of the 1980s. Distorted budgets marked by corruption, lack of transparency and accountability, and perverse priorities (e.g., high military expenditures) bred cynicism about comprehensive budget reform and assisted attacks on national economic planning and development as well.

BUDGETING FOR STRUCTURAL ADJUSTMENT

During the 1970s, signs of trouble were already evident in slowing economic growth and economic volatility. In the 1980s, these trends became clearer and were reflected politically in Western industrialized countries in the election of conservative governments dedicated to a smaller role for government and deregulation of the private sector. In the Soviet Union and Eastern Europe, centralized economic direction and socialist planning were utterly discredited. Developing countries, to different degrees burdened by debt, adverse balance of payments problems, and budget deficits, were increasingly forced to turn to international lending institutions and accept their standards for budgetary rectitude.

Comprehensive economic planning lost its primacy of place as the mode of societal governance, although planning survived in title. The assumptions of planning were seen as less viable and its limitations as inherent. Planning techniques, it was alleged, could not cope with the complexity of economic change, could not make accurate forecasts, were too inflexible in fast changing conditions, and could not possibly respond to the multiple allocation decisions required in an effectively operating economy. Comprehensive economic planning appeared as an impediment, introducing distortions and preventing the market from making efficient decisions (see Agarwala 1985).

What was to take its place, and what values, theories of societal management, and budgetary techniques would emerge as predominant? During the 1980s, there was a major shift in emphasis: the primary place of governments in mobilizing and organizing national resources was conceived as giving way to that of markets. The mechanism through which this change was to take place was structural adjustment.

Structural adjustment has been defined as a cluster of policies designed to bring about a viable balance of payments situation (Riddell 1987). It summarizes a coherent set of policies espoused by international lending organizations confronting high levels of debt in many developing countries, which called for aid to assist them in meeting commitments they could not fulfill. While the International Monetary Fund extended loans for immediate stabilization problems, the World Bank extended structural adjustment loans and sector adjustment loans to assist economywide and sector policy reforms. The purposes of these policies, to quote *The Third Report on Adjustment Lending of the World Bank: Private and Public Resources for Growth*, is:

> to tackle macroeconomic difficulties, usually manifested in rising inflation and balance of payments problems, and to shift an economy to a new sustainable and poverty-reducing growth path. Typical adjustment policies are cuts in public spending, opening up to external or domestic competition, reforms in prices to allow them to reflect economic values, measures to improve government delivery of infrastructural and social services, and development of the institutions required to a well-functioning market economy, notably a sound financial system (World Bank 1992, p. 1).

Proponents of structural adjustment policies stress the need for a break with policies that in many countries had been responsible for high levels of debt, inflation, lack of investment, low growth rates, and distorted priorities. They link self-sustaining economic growth with removal of macroeconomic imbalances and price distortions. These core reforms are a necessary, though not sufficient, condition for "an effective transition to a sustainable poverty-reducing growth path" (p. 5). To smooth this path, policies promoting economic infrastructure, education, public health, and aid targeted to the most needy would also be required. Additional measures to promote good governance have been added in recent years. The record, while mixed, shows some encouraging signs, particularly in middle income countries that have received intensive adjustment lending (passim World Bank 1992).

Critics of structural adjustment contest the record and point to poor growth rates over the past decade. They cite reduced incomes, growing unemployment, and particular hardships suffered by the poor directly related to cuts in subsidies and public investment, depreciation of the currency, higher prices for basic necessities, and failure of wages to keep up. The basic assumptions of structural adjustment—that economic liberalization will bring about economic growth benefiting the whole society—is open to question in the light of prolonged recession in industrialized countries, the inequality such policies appear to encourage, and the subordination of other values to a market efficiency that may be on the one hand unattainable or on the other involve its own dysfunctions (see, e.g., Stewart 1991).

Our purpose here is less to debate the merits of structural adjustment than to trace its implications for public budgeting and financial administration in developing countries. Whereas the first two phases (regulation and development) were fairly closely associated with budget techniques, at least in theory if not in practice, the era of "adjustment" is less clearly identified with any single technique. Nevertheless, structural adjustment exerts a critical influence on budgeting, which is sufficient to demarcate it as a separate development, which has changed our frame of reference and vocabulary.

The first difference is the overt policy content of the reforms. Structural adjustment is not a neutral set of reforms but involves policy changes in budget priorities. Conditions for stabilization and strategic adjustment lending include detailed stipulations for such changes, important among which is downsizing the public sector. Downsizing reflects the change in the role of government from the primary actor in the development process to the provider of a framework conducive to political and economic stability, investment, and economic growth. Rather than behaving as an actor itself, government would restrict itself to providing an appropriate setting for the private sector, as bureaucratic and planning concepts of societal management should give way to the spontaneous working of the market. The private sector would take the lead in defining economic direction, that is, the goods and services to be produced and societal support (i.e., employment and distribution of income). Government budgets would need reorienting to reflect the changed priorities.

These priorities derive from a quest for efficiency in the sense of optimal use of resources. To productive efficiency—achieving the most output for a given input—is added the concept of market efficiency, which relates demand to supply through competition in a market place where individual consumers and suppliers signal information about costs and preferences to result in an optimal solution. The growing predominance of the value of market efficiency has a number of important implications for public budgeting in developing countries.

First, with the opening up of national economies to the international market place, countries are required to compete worldwide. The prices of the international economy are thus the prices that should determine the output of the national economy. Hence, government subsidies, export and import taxes, and other regulations are regarded as distortions, but their dismantling has serious budget repercussions.

Second, the use of efficiency as a criterion in budgetary decision making would bring about important changes in priorities. An obvious example is the use of cost-benefit analysis in determining projects. Another is the sorting out of activities between public and private sectors, where use of a strict "exclusion" principle would result in extensive privatization or the pricing of many public services. The criterion of efficiency applied to public enterprises requires them to deliver a competitive rate of return. Sub-national or local governments would be expected to pay their way, except where a case for spillovers or externalities is made. Use of strict efficiency criteria sets prices for government services and provides a climate for privatization, contracting out, and user fees. Serious review of existing budgets according to market efficiency criteria would require changes in their composition on both revenue and expenditure sides.

In practical terms, advocated changes in the role of government have brought about a changed emphasis in budgeting. Since governments are seen as providers of infrastructure and as setting a general framework for economic growth, interest has shifted from program budgeting (although efforts are still made to implement it) to medium-term investment programming through public investment programs and macroeconomic management. This shift in emphasis may also be linked with a more managerial model of public administration and public budgeting which is the basis for reform in recent years in several industrialized countries (see Caiden 1991; Goldman and Brashares 1991; Jonsson 1990; Keating and Rosalky 1990).

The management model attempts to combine sophisticated policy making and budgetary planning at the center with decentralized management in the departments, giving greater responsibility to managers in handling their own budgets. At the center, policymakers are involved in medium-term economic forecasting and macroeconomic policy making for a number of years and project the impact of changes in economic variables on budgetary estimates. In the departments, managers have increased flexibility to organize their resources to produce results. The two are tied together by specified results and strict budgetary limits, an emphasis on efficiency in operations backed by periodic reviews, and an integrated information system. There is a deliberate attempt to introduce the competitiveness, accounting conventions, and assumed managerial practices of the private sector into public financial management.

According to this model, policies are set at the center related to wider economic trends and adjusted according to economic fluctuations. Agency managers are given set objectives and made responsible for achieving them with allotted resources and in the most efficient manner possible at their discretion. The system is held together through the flow of information that transmits data regarding costs and results, enabling impacts to be assessed, priorities to be set, program adjustments to be made, and value-for-money audits to be conducted. Efficiency is achieved *through* managerial flexibility which rewards managers for results and penalizes them where they fall short. Accountability is improved because of the availability of accurate and relevant information and the capacity to enforce priorities. Resources and activities and income and expenditure are considered together, as a simultaneous equation, instead of apart, as separate zero sum games. The effectiveness of this model and its applicability or adaptability to developing countries is open to question, particularly since there has so far been little published systematic evaluation of results.

A more direct influence of strategic adjustment is the movement toward better "governance." In recent years, there has been a general recognition that even the best economic policy advice will be unavailing if governments lack the institutions to put it into effect (see Brautigan 1991). Budget systems and control of public expenditures are high on the list for reforms, which should include greater accountability and transparency, ethical conduct by public officials, rule of law, greater participation, and openness in decision making. Within this context should be noted integrated financial management system improvement, which includes the consolidation of numerous antiquated, conflictive, and inadequate laws into a single law governing public management; provisions and guidelines for budgeting allowing formulation of a realistic financial plan by those responsible for its implementation; an integrated accounting system to provide information needed by managers at all levels, an organized cash management system; independent and effective audit; and training systems for financial managers and audit. (Price 1990; Wesberry 1990).

THEORY AND PRACTICE

The conceptual road map to budgetary developments in this chapter is a guide to a general progression of ideas about budgeting. Each of the three concepts identified has its advocates and its critics. Regulatory budgeting is praised for its emphasis on accountability and condemned for over-bureaucratization, inflexibility, and lack of information. Program budgeting and its variants hold out the promise of greater rationality in resource allocation and improvement in program management but are criticized for lack of realism. Adjustment budgeting is seen as a means to correcting past dysfunctions and modernizing processes, at the same time as it is viewed as a mistaken set of policies inflicting great hardship on developing countries. This chapter has attempted to show that these developments do not exist in isolation but are linked to assumptions about governance and value systems.

But it is also important to realize that, influential as these concepts are, they do not necessarily determine budgetary behavior. The designs of those seeking to reform budgeting are not always or even often realized. The accountability of "regulatory" budgeting was frequently nonexistent. Reformers struggled to implement program budgeting with very mixed success. Those seeking to use budgeting to implement structural adjustment find it remarkably difficult to change priorities in the direction they desire. Instead, the literature is filled with the same complaints: repetitive budgeting, budgetary fragmentation, uncoordinated donor funding, inadequate O&M spending, excessive military budgets, unjustified subsidies, swollen ill-paid bureaucracies, games-playing between central budget agencies and program agencies, corruption and diversion of funds, and budget ceilings that become budget floors. Stories of successful budget reform seem few and far between.

Why the persistent gap between theories and practices? One reason probably lies in the political nature of budgeting—it is remarkably hard to take funds away from one recipient to give to another. Budgeting involves promises, conflicts, compromises, and political judgments: all of these take precedence over abstract concepts and reforms. Bureaucratic inertia is another reason for opposition to change, reinforcing budgetary dynamics in which the composition of expenditures itself tends to drive decision making, allowing little room for discretion.

Should one then be cynical about the prospects for future budgetary reform? Is the whole road map in the preceding pages a figment of the imagination, an intellectual construct, while the real world continues without reference to current fashions of budget reform or design?

To discount the influence of ideas is to discard an important part of history itself. Concepts of budgeting are influential because they affect not only what participants are doing but what they think they ought to be doing. Although the concepts may not affect processes and outcomes as directly as their proponents might like, they have an impact if only indirectly on assumptions, behavior, definition of problems, and the range of solutions seen as feasible.

Where then is the path of budgetary development currently leading? It is not easy to set out a blueprint for the future, but it would seem that emphasis is likely to be in the following directions. First, given the difficulties of reforming allocations through the budgetary process (though not necessarily through other means), attention is likely to move to administration rather than allocation—the hard and more mundane topics such as inventory control, productivity measures, cash flow management, fiscal forecasting, and so on. Second, there is likely to be a renewed emphasis on accountability, particularly aligning accounting and budgeting systems. Third, reform efforts themselves will probably come under scrutiny to include a more sophisticated application of theories of management of change. Finally, as people all over the world come to demand a greater say in their own lives, there will be a movement toward opening up budget institutions, including greater democratization, decentralization, more flexible service delivery, and greater individual choice.

REFERENCES

Agarwala, R. 1985. "Planning in Developing Countries." *Finance and Development* (March): 13-16.

Brautigan, D. 1991. "Governance and Economy: A Review." Policy Research Working Papers, Policy and Review Department (WPS 815), World Bank, December.

Bruguierè, M. 1969. *La Premiere Restauration et son Budget.* Geneva: Librairie Droz.

Caiden, G. 1991. *Administrative Reform Comes of Age.* Berlin: De Gruyter.

Caiden, N. 1978. "Patterns of Budgeting." *Public Administration Review* 38: 539-545.

________ . 1980. "Negative Financial Management: A Backward Look at Fiscal Stress." Pp. 135-159 in *Fiscal Stress and Public Policy*, edited by C. Levine and I. Rubin. Beverly Hills CA: Sage.

Caiden, N., and A. Wildavsky. 1980. *Planning and Budgeting in Poor Countries.* New Brunswick, NJ: Transaction Books.

Dean, P. 1989. *Government Budgeting in Developing Countries. London: Routledge.*

Goldman, F., and E. Brashares. 1991. "Performance and Accountability: Budget Reform in New Zealand." *Public Budgeting and Finance* 11 (Winter): 75-86.

Jonsson, G. 1990. "Government Accounting in Sweden." Pp. 275-292 in *Government Financial Management:Issues and Country Studies*, edited by A. Premchand. Washington, DC: International Monetary Fund.

Keating, M., and D. Rosalky. 1990. "Rolling Expenditure Plans: Australian Experience and Prognosis." Pp. 72-98 in *Government Financial Management: Issues and Country Studies*, edited by A. Premchand. Washington, DC: International Monetary Fund.

Lee, R.D., Jr. 1992. "Linkages Among Poverty, Development, and Budget Systems." *Public Budgeting and Finance* 12(1): 48-60.

Riddell, R.C. 1987. *Foreign Aid Reconsidered.* Washington, DC: Johns Hopkins.

Stewart, F. 1991. "Are Adjustment Policies in Africa Consistent With Long-Run Development Needs?" *Development Policy Review* 9: 413-436.

Premchand, A. 1983. *Government Budgeting and Expenditure Controls: Theory and Practice.* Washington, DC: International Monetary Fund.

Price, L. 1990. "The Reform of Public Financial Management in Bolivia and Argentina." Unpublished manuscript.

Schick, A. 1996. "The Road to PPB: The Stages of Budget Reform." *Public Administration Review* 26: 243-258.

Spulber, N. 1990. *Restructuring the Soviet Economy: In Search of the Market.* Ann Arbor: University of Michigan Press.

Stourm, R. 1909. *The Budget.* Paris: Alcan.

Wesberry, J.P., Jr. 1990. "Government Accounting and Financial Management in Latin American Countries." Pp. 345-374 in Government Financial Management: Issues and Country Studies, edited by A. Premchand. Washington, DC: International Monetary Fund.

World Bank. 1992. "Third Report on Adjustment Lending of the World Bank: Private and Public Resources for Growth." IDA/R92-29, World Bank, Washington, DC.

BUDGET TRANSFORMATIONS IN TAIWAN:

SOME DOGS THAT DID AND DID NOT BARK

Cal Clark and Steven Chan

ABSTRACT

Given Taiwan's very rapid economic growth during the postwar period, its experience in public finance might be valuable for other developing nations. This chapter then analyzes development in Taiwan in terms of Naomi Caiden's three-stage historical model of budgetary policies. Taiwan did progress through the "regulatory," "developmental," and "market adjustment" stages that Caiden described, although most recently it has moved back toward a strongly "developmental" policy. The key to Taiwan's success may lie in the fact that the "developmental" stage was fairly short, thus preventing the growth of a huge and inefficient political apparatus that would probably have stifled economic dynamism. Moreover, the public sector's direct ownership role in the economy was cut quite drastically during the "market adjustment" stage as the model would predict. The regime, however, was not content to put all its faith in the "magic of the marketplace." Rather, it took a leading role in promoting the structural adjustment of the economy away from labor-intensive industries. In addition,

Policy Studies and Developing Nations, Volume 3, pages 19-41.

ISBN: 1-55938-190-6

support for education and social services was gradually expanded during the "market adjustment" period. Furthermore, the government demonstrated that it could respond quickly to crises, as illustrated by its inspired management of the oil price explosion in the mid-1970s. In sum, the Taiwan experience indicates that both "state" and "market" have a positive role to play in development and that maintaining economic and political "flexibility" is perhaps the most important key to progress.

Taiwan has been one of the most successful developing countries in the world during the postwar era, at least in the economic realm. Since 1950, its real GNP growth rate has averaged 9 percent a year as its GNP per capita has skyrocketed almost a hundred fold from about $100 to a projected $10,000 at the end of 1992. In the process, it has been transformed from a poor agricultural society to a prosperous industrial one whose manufactured goods and exports have rapidly ascended the international product cycle from low quality light industry to heavy industry to high-tech production. Moreover, rapid economic growth has produced a rising standard of living; and unlike the normal situation of rapid growth exacerbating inequality, Taiwan's level of income inequality approximates that of the industrialized world. Finally, while Taiwan was ruled by an authoritarian regime for most of its history, very substantial democratization reforms transformed the polity in the late 1980s and early 1990s (Chan and Clark 1992; Cheng and Haggard 1992; Clark 1989b; Copper 1988; Galenson 1979; Gold 1986; Haggard 1990; Ho 1978; Hsiung 1981; Hwang 1991; Kuo 1983; Kuo, Ranis, and Fei 1981; Li 1988; Lin 1973; Myers 1984, 1987; Sutter 1988; Tien 1989; Wade 1990; Winckler and Greenhalgh 1988; Wu 1985).

Given Taiwan's successful economic transformation, its experience in public finance might be valuable for other developing nations. It is also interesting because, while this history follows the general three-stage model presented by Caiden in the introduction to this volume, there are important deviations from the model as well. Thus, to use the metaphor from the famous Sherlock Holmes story, some dogs barked and some did not. A consideration of how Taiwan fits the general model of historical stages in budget systems and strategies therefore should help illuminate this country's political economy and may have some broader implications for other nations that are currently attempting to follow Taiwan up the ladder of development.

In particular, the three general strategic orientations of emphasizing regulation, development, and structural adjustment can clearly be discerned, although there is a substantial degree of overlap and intermingling among them. However, Taiwan is now implementing another major reorientation that promises to take its strategic focus back to "development" and to reject decisively its longstanding fiscal conservatism that is also a central element of "structural adjustment." Second, the aggregate nature of the public sector has changed (or not changed) in several different ways. The overall size of the government has remained remarkably constant given the normal tendency for development to lead to a much larger role for government; there has been a gradual but steady shift in the government's spending priorities from "guns" toward "butter"; and the dominance of the industrial economy by the state sector in the 1950s was largely reversed by the early 1970s. Thus, specific changes in the public sector clearly did not follow any one pattern. Finally, budget transformations can also be a response to crisis. For Taiwan's export-dependent economy, the global surge in oil prices in the early 1970s created a horrendous challenge and threat. The government quickly responded with an inspired fiscal and public investment policy that both dampened inflation and restimulated the economy, even before the phrase "stagflation" became popular in the West. This chapter then explores these three aspects of budgetary transformation in Taiwan.

STAGES OF POLICY STRATEGY: BACK TO THE FUTURE?

As Caiden argues in her chapter in this volume, "From Here to There and Beyond," the principal "role of government" usually follows a three-stage developmental sequence over time: (1) a "regulatory" government primarily concerned with preserving stability ("law and order"), (2) a regime committed to promoting national "development" in terms of both economic growth and social equity which necessitates "planning" and fairly extensive intervention in the economy, and (3) a government which seeks "structural adjustment" by withdrawing from microeconomic initiatives in order to allow "market forces" to promote economic "efficiency."

These three general stages are clearly discernible for Taiwan government if its administration during the "Republic" era in China is added to its later history on Taiwan. However, there are significant overlaps among these stages; and much more importantly, the government has just initiated a very strong "developmental" effort after approximately 30 years of emphasizing "market adjustment."

Clearly, the state that was directed by the Nationalist (Kuomintang or KMT) Party in China, from its ascension to power in 1928 to its loss of the Chinese Civil War to the Communists in 1949, was primarily a "regulatory" one in the sense that throughout almost all this period it focused upon military and police matters. This is certainly understandable since the Nationalists were involved in almost continuous fighting—with warlords, communist rivals, and invading Japanese. While the Nationalists now have the image of being captured by China's economic elites, they were in reality far from the lackeys of landlords and capitalists. Rather, the Chiang Kai-shek government generally looked after its own interests (i.e., raising money to finance its military campaigns) in splendid isolation. For example, while the Kuomintang helped large business interests on its way to power, most of the time it engaged in nearly open extortion from the business sector (i.e., by forcing the purchase of bonds that would never be repaid). Moreover, its efforts at promoting economic development were centered on "bureaucratic capitalism" or structuring the economy around private or quasi-public monopolies controlled by leading officials. In the rural areas, the traditional social fabric was destroyed; and local leadership was assumed by "entrepreneurs" or "village bullies" whose primary goal was to profit from the escalating resources being extracted from the countryside (Coble 1980; Duara 1988; Eastman 1974; Fewsmith 1985).

Yet, this regulatory orientation was at sharp variance with the KMT's roots—a revolutionary nationalism that included a "developmental" commitment to promoting the "people's livelihood" based on Sun Yat-sen's Three Principles of the People. Whether the Nationalists ignored their proclaimed ideological goals because of their own venality or because of the financial exigencies of military conflict remains an open debate. However, for whatever reason, the result was a regulatory state that became increasingly authoritarian and corrupt over time (Botjer 1979; Coble 1980; Eastman 1974; Sheridan 1975; Tien 1972).

After the Nationalists evacuated their government to Taipei in 1949, they quickly moved, perhaps surprisingly, to become a developmental regime. The military remained strong, "Mainland Recovery" was the watchword, and a strongly coercive apparatus was instituted to maintain power—all hallmarks of a less than progressive regulatory state. Yet, at the same time, the Chiang Kai-shek regime made an equally strong commitment to promote economic development and popular development. This reorientation stemmed from a variety of reasons: (1) a recognition of the need to reform after the humiliating loss on the Mainland, (2) an attempt to build defense industries, (3) an appeal for popular support, and (4) American pressure (Clough 1978; Gold 1986).

The move to become a developmental state was reflected along several dimensions. First, the nature of the regime had to undergo a fundamental change. In particular, the push for rapid economic growth necessitated bringing a considerable number of technocrats, many of whom had been educated at American universities, into the top levels of what had been an essentially military regime (Ho 1987; Winckler 1988). Second, the government made a major investment in education and human capital development. Universal education through the sixth grade was introduced; and this education requirement was gradually expanded. The result was a literate and skilled workforce who both made rapid industrialization possible and experienced upward socioeconomic mobility (Huang 1984; Wei 1973). Third, in the economic realm per se there were two vital policy revolutions. One was a massive land reform which spurred production, thereby creating the resources necessary to finance the subsequent industrialization (Ho 1978; Lee 1971; Yang 1970). The other was establishing protectionist walls to stimulate "import substitution" industrialization in light consumer goods (Lin 1973; Ranis 1979).

Despite these substantial "developmental" policies though, significant aspects of the "regulatory" state remained prominent. In addition to the high priority given to military affairs and internal security noted above, three important policies (or in one case a nonpolicy) connoted a continued regulatory approach to the economy. First, the government responded to the hyperinflation of 1949-1950 with a strong and successful deflationary effort based on orthodox conservative monetary and fiscal policy (Kuo 1983; Li 1988; Lundberg 1979). Second, import-substitution recreated the "bureaucratic capitalism" of the interwar period because the state's strong control over the economy meant that the principal beneficiaries were managers of state corporations and private businessmen who had strong links to the regime (Gold 1986; Winckler 1988). Finally, the government provided little social welfare support at this time, clearly emphasizing "production" over "redistribution" to promote national well-being.

In many ways, Taiwan's "developmental" period was quite successful. The land reform turned out to be a textbook model of success; domestic light industries supplanted imports in just a few years, the education boom created a middle class within two-to-three decades, and the technocrats performed well. The system, however, contained the "seeds of its own destruction" (to quote the KMT's communist enemies). In particular, the domestic market soon became saturated which ended business expansion; and the technocrats became convinced that economic change was necessary. The technocrats and Taiwan's American advisers urged the "structural adjustment" to "market efficiency" by hitching Taiwan's economy to the international economy in the hope that the island's relatively skilled but low paid workforce could establish a "comparative advantage" in labor-intensive production. They were opposed by lower level bureaucrats who did not want to give up their power over the economy and military leaders who wanted to develop heavy defense industries. In the end, Chiang Kai-shek supported the technocrats; and Taiwan implemented "market adjustment" in the early 1960s (Kuo et al. 1981; Li 1988; Wade 1990).

The rest, as they say, is history. Taiwan rode an export boom, that was only briefly interrupted by the two oil crises of the 1970s, into prosperity. Exports soared, real growth averaged "double digits" for extended periods, the savings and investment rate soared to over 30 percent of GNP, unemployment averaged about 2 percent, the popular standard of living rose rapidly, in the 1980s an embarrassingly large trade deficit with the United States burgeoned, and in the late 1980s the small island (about the size of New Jersey) ranked second in the world with $70 billion to $80 billion in foreign currency reserves (Chan and Clark 1992; Clark 1989b; Galenson 1979; Haggard 1990; Hwang 1991;

Wade 1990). Thus, Taiwan has been cited with a good deal of justification as a prime example of successful market adjustment by neoclassical enthusiasts (Balassa 1981; Fei 1991; Galenson 1979; Li 1988; Linder 1986).

This can be considered a "market adjustment" along two very distinct dimensions. Economically, the role of the market became the leading factor in the economy; and Taiwan clearly became very competitive on world markets (Fei 1991). Socially and politically, in addition, the tremendous growth of Taiwan's economy after the early 1960s primarily involved the expansion of the private sector which was dominated by native Taiwanese (Islanders) who had few links with the Chiang Kai-shek government. Thus, something of a dual political and economic elite emerged; and business-government relations were described as "distant and cool" (Chu 1989; Gold 1986; Lam 1992; Winckler 1988).

This shift toward "market adjustment" was consistent with some of the continuing characteristics of the earlier "regulatory" regime, such as a relatively small government and conservative monetary and fiscal policies (see the next section). However, the regime also engaged in very considerable "developmental" initiatives to promote further structural adjustment. The oil crisis of 1973-1974 underlined the danger that Taiwan might be pricing itself out of its international niche of low-cost, labor-intensive production. Thus, the government adopted new policies to promote heavy and high-tech industries with much greater value-added. The heavy industry push, marked by the Ten Major Development Projects started in 1973, represented a strong return to a "developmental" approach since they were based on state corporations in steel and petrochemicals and huge government infrastructure projects (as well as an embarrassing failure to promote the automobile industry). The high-tech revolution though was much more consistent with "market adjustment" since it was led by highly entrepreneurial small firms (Arnold 1989; Chu 1989, 1991; Lam 1992; Wade 1990; Wu 1985).

A much more serious reversal of "market adjustment" occurred in response to the mounting pressures for structural adjustment in the late 1980s and early 1990s. By this time rapidly growing wages in Taiwan, mounting protectionism in the industrialized countries, and the growth of a "third wave" of NICs (newly industrializing countries) had put Taiwan's labor-intensive industries (e.g., textiles, shoes, plywood, low-tech electronics assembly) under intolerable pressure. Consequently, a large outflow of capital began (that in several years was greater than domestic investment)—first to the United States to evade protectionist walls and later to Southeast Asia and, quite ironically, to the People's Republic of China in search of cheap labor (Wu 1991).

In 1991, the government approved the Six-Year National Development Plan both to spur renewed domestic investment and to combat growing urban concentration and congestion. The plan projected expenditures of $303 billion over 1992-1996 with 34 percent being spent on transportation and communications, 12 percent each on energy development and on urban housing, 10 percent each on social welfare-security and on education and culture, and about 5 percent each on water development projects and on environmental protection. The plan involves dividing Taiwan into 18 regional development areas or "life circles" with comprehensive job opportunities, services, and housing available in each and includes massive infrastructure projects, investment in a variety of high-tech industries, and large-scale public planning. Furthermore, the motives for this are not just domestic. Rather, it appears to be an adjunct of Taiwan's recent "flexible diplomacy" campaign to upgrade its international status (Wang 1990) since many foreign nations are eager for their businesses to gain access to the lucrative projects.

This not only represents a huge "development" effort with massive social planning and government targeting of industries and subsidy of urban amenities, but it also is a decisive, if not revolutionary, rejection of Taiwan's fiscal conservatism (i.e., "regulatory" attitude toward governmental size and budget balances). The size of the plan, almost double the nation's 1990 GNP, means that it will inevitably involve huge increases in government spending, issuing massive amounts of government bonds (which are far more secure than those of the interwar republic), and large-scale international borrowing. Moreover, recent fears that pressures from underworld gangs will prevent an honest competition for many bids indicates another aspect of the breakdown of the "regulatory" state in Taiwan (Domes 1992; Liu 1991).

Taiwan, therefore, has followed the progression from "regulatory" to "developmental" to "market adjustment" strategies, although there were significant overlaps among and carryovers between these stages. The 1991 Six-Year National Development Plan is a reorientation of a far greater magnitude. While it was conceived as promoting development along "market-conforming" lines, it blatantly rejects "market adjustment" and gambles Taiwan's future on the ability of continued rapid growth to cover these massive expenditures. If the gamble works, it will elevate Taiwan to the ranks of the developed nations and perhaps suggest a new stage to Caiden's model. If it fails, future economic historians will speculate why the government repressed all the lessons which it might have learned from its four decades of economic success.

THE PUBLIC SECTOR: AN INTERMINGLING OF STASIS, EVOLUTION, AND REVOLUTION

The three-stage model of budgeting and public policy strategies implies that the general size of government should increase greatly from the "regulatory" to the "developmental" stage and then stabilize or even decrease slightly after the "market adjustment" phase is reached. For Taiwan, this sequence is

Table 1. Indicators of Government Size and Fiscal Policy

Year	*Government Budget % GNP*	*Government Workers % Workforce*	*Taxes% Personal Income*	*Budget Balance (million US$)*	*Direct Taxes % All Taxes*
1952	—	—	—	—	—
1953	—	—	—	—	—
1954	21.3	—	—	-4	24.4
1955	21.8	—	—	10	28.0
1956	22.0	—	—	-7	24.2
1957	22.2	—	—	8	23.4
1958	23.8	—	—	7	22.8
1959	**	—	—	**	**
1960	19.5	—	—	-2	22.1
1961	20.1	—	14.5	-1	24.0
1962	20.0	6.1	15.4	-9	21.6
1963	18.9	6.2	14.6	-15	20.9
1964	18.1	6.2	15.2	14	22.5
1965	19.9	6.3	15.7	25	22.1
1966	18.9	6.4	16.2	34	20.4
1967	21.1	6.3	16.4	23	19.5
1968	19.5	6.3	18.2	56	21.4
1969	21.3	6.3	19.9	79	23.2
1970	21.7	6.3	18.6	52	23.6
1971	20.8	6.4	17.8	63	25.4
1972	20.1	6.3	18.3	67	26.3
1973	19.5	6.2	19.0	256	26.2
1974	16.4	6.4	19.0	681	26.6
1975	21.6	6.6	20.1	200	28.3
1976	21.4	6.6	20.2	424	29.6
1977	23.4	6.4	20.0	35	31.0
1978	22.9	6.3	21.1	182	30.8
1979	21.3	6.3	21.9	908	32.1
1980	23.2	6.4	21.1	589	32.6
1981	24.6	6.6	20.4	122	35.2
1982	26.2	6.7	19.2	-69	38.0
1983	24.0	6.6	19.1	121	37.8
1984	22.5	6.5	18.5	166	36.8
1985	23.2	6.6	17.6	271	37.9
1986	22.5	6.5	16.2	94	38.9
1987	22.9	6.3	17.9	1,435	41.3
1988	24.0	6.4	19.8	3,521	45.1

Notes: **No data reported because definition of fiscal year changed in 1959.

Source: Chan and Clark (1992, appendexes).

anything but similar in different areas. The overall size of government changed very little, direct state ownership of industrial enterprises plummeted, and governmental budget priorities changed consistently but fairly gradually over the postwar era. Thus, several different dynamics were clearly at work which can be related to the stages of policy strategy described in the previous section.

Generally, economic development leads to a larger government as wealthier societies have more resources to invest in the public sector and to devote to the national welfare. The data in Table 1 on the general size of government in Taiwan definitely demonstrate that this generalization does not apply to the island. Rather, there was almost no change in the conventional measure of government size, the ratio of total government spending to GNP, between 1952 and 1988 when Taiwan's GNP per capita skyrocketed 40-fold from $150 to $6,000. This averaged about 21 percent to 22 percent during the 1950s, declined slightly to about 20 percent in the 1960s and 1970s as rapid growth outstripped government spending, and then rose slightly to 23 percent to 24 percent in the 1980s. Thus, Taiwan has maintained a "small" government. For example, its central government spending of 15.5 percent of GNP in 1987 was only half of the 31.5 percent that would be predicted for a country of its level of affluence (based on a regression of budget percent of GNP on GNP per capita for all reporting countries in World Bank 1988).

The other indicators included in Table 1 present a similar picture. Public employees as a percentage of the workforce increased very slightly from 6.2 percent in the early 1960s to 6.6 percent two decades later before slipping back to 6.4 percnet at the end of the 1980s. There was a significant increase in tax burden as a percentage of personal income from 15 percent in the early 1960s to 20 percent in the mid-1970s, but this ratio then declined by 1 or 2 percentage points. In addition, Taiwan has generally run a budget surplus (during the 1950s and early 1960s this was subsidized by large-scale American aid, see Jacoby 1966), providing another dimension of fiscal stability. There was significant change in another area of fiscal capability though—the ratio of direct taxes to total revenues which is often used as a measure of state strength since weaker governments rely more on easier-to-collect indirect taxes (Snider 1987). Taiwan's proportion of direct taxes remained fairly low at about 25 percent until the mid-1970s when it commenced a sharp rise to 45 percent in 1988. Thus, while overall government size hardly changed, the regime's fiscal capabilities evidently have been upgraded considerably.

The historical pattern is much different (and much more consistent with Caiden's model) in the data presented in Table 2 on the state's more direct intervention in the economy. In the "developmental" period of the 1950s, state ownership of productive forces was quite high, accounting for over half of industrial and manufacturing production. This very high figure might seem at odds with the regime's anti-communist ideology, but it represented historical happenstance—the seizing of Japanese assets after China regained Taiwan at the end of World War II—much more than an explicit strategy to use state ownership to promote development. In any event, the transition to the "market adjustment" strategy in the 1960s brought an immediate precipitous drop in state control over Taiwan's industry. In little more than a decade, the public

Table 2. State Economic Involvement and Impact

	State % Industrial Production	*State % Manufacturing Production*	*State % Investment*	*Real Government Spending Growth (%)*	*Real GNP Growth (%)*
1952	56.6	56.2	55.7	—	12.0
1953	55.9	55.9	43.4	—	9.3
1954	52.7	49.7	36.3	—	9.5
1955	51.1	48.7	47.6	10.9	8.1
1956	50.0	48.3	48.4	6.2	5.5
1957	51.3	48.7	54.3	8.5	7.3
1958	50.0	47.2	62.6	14.4	6.6
1959	48.7	45.2	53.1	**	7.8
1960	47.9	43.8	45.3	**	6.5
1961	48.2	45.3	41.8	10.1	6.8
1962	46.2	42.3	46.8	7.3	7.9
1963	44.8	40.6	36.0	3.2	9.4
1964	43.7	38.9	34.4	7.8	12.3
1965	41.3	36.8	31.3	22.0	11.0
1966	38.2	33.3	34.6	3.6	9.0
1967	34.7	28.8	37.5	23.4	10.6
1968	31.1	24.7	36.6	0.6	9.1
1969	29.4	22.7	41.8	19.3	9.1
1970	27.7	20.6	40.1	13.5	11.3
1971	22.9	15.3	40.4	8.3	13.0
1972	21.3	14.0	39.3	9.8	13.4
1973	21.1	13.8	34.7	9.1	12.8
1974	21.9	14.1	38.1	-15.0	1.2
1975	22.1	14.2	57.7	35.4	4.4
1976	22.5	15.2	53.3	14.4	13.7
1977	22.8	15.8	50.7	20.7	10.3
1978	21.5	14.9	45.0	11.9	14.0
1979	21.2	14.7	39.4	0.7	8.5
1980	20.9	14.5	48.5	16.7	7.1
1981	20.0	13.5	49.4	11.9	5.7
1982	20.1	13.3	53.6	10.2	3.4
1983	19.8	13.0	48.9	-1.0	8.0
1984	18.8	12.2	42.8	3.4	10.6
1985	18.8	12.0	46.7	8.4	5.1
1986	17.5	10.7	44.4	8.4	11.7
1987	17.3	10.5	40.9	4.1	11.9
1988	18.1	11.1	34.6	12.7	7.3

Note: **No data reported because definition of fiscal year changed in 1959.

Source: Chan and Clark (1992, appendices).

share of production was more than cut in half to about 20 percent of industrial and 15 percent of manufacturing output; and it has continued to decline very slowly since then despite massive investment in several state corporations in the heavy industry sector. Thus, a revolution has occurred in the state's direct control of production, just as the model of budget policy stages would imply.

The government's economic role appears larger and not necessarily declining when attention is turned to the more indirect influence exercised through investment as measured by the data on public investment (which includes investment by both the government and state corporations) in Table 2. State investment rate has been fairly high, ranging between 30 percent and 60 percent of total investment during the postwar era and averaging well over 40 percent. That state investment is so much higher than ownership is easily explained by the fact that it is concentrated in very expensive infrastructure and heavy industry projects. It has also been quite cyclical, being highest during the "developmental" 1950s and later during periods of economic downturn when it was evidently used as a countercyclical stimulus (see the next section). Thus, much of state investment during the "market adjustment" period may well have been helpful to the private sector.

Finally, a charting of the real growth in government spending against real GNP growth in the last two columns of Table 2 implies that it has been used to promote countercyclical adjustment. Thus, spending has been moderated at times of inflationary threats (the mid-1950s, the early and late 1970s, and the mid- to late 1980s) and expanded during times of economic stress (the mid-1970s and early 1980s). The one possible exception here—the 13 percent jump in real government spending in 1988 despite inflationary pressures from Taiwan's huge trade surplus—can be explained by the regime's attempts to counter the flight of foreign capital. Thus, macroeconomic policy seems to have been used fairly effectively to promote "market adjustment."

The final set of data in Table 3 focuses on Taiwan's budget priorities. Here, there has been a gradual evolution from the "regulatory" emphasis on "guns" to a developmental emphasis on "butter," although this transition did not start until the "market adjustment" period was well underway. In general, the growing attention to welfare has yet to be reversed as would be expected under "market adjustment." Nonetheless, some signs of the three-stage policy orientations can be discerned.

One hallmark of a "regulatory" state is a high emphasis on the security sector in state activities. This certainly was true of interwar China. Even after the move to Taiwan and the initiation of a "developmental" strategy, Taiwan certainly had every incentive to continue a strong defense in the 1950s and 1960s since it felt threatened by an invasion from the People's Republic of China which had the largest armed forces in the world. Therefore, it is not surprising that Taiwan did not decrease its defense burden significantly until much later than would have been predicted *a priori* from Caiden's model. Until the early 1970s, military expenditures consumed nearly 10 percent of GNP and about 4 percent of the island's population was under arms. During the 1970s and 1980s, this burden eased significantly with the defense spending/GNP ratio averaging 7 percent and the military participation ratio declining gradually but steadily to 2 percent. By 1988, defense spending had dropped to 5.2 percent

Table 3. Indicators of Policy Priorities

	Military Expenditure % GNP	*Military Personnel per 1000 Pop*	*% Budget for Economic Development*	*% Budget Education & Culture*	*% Budget Social Security & Welfare*	*Real Expenditure Per Primary Student (1981 NT$)*
1952	—	—	—	—	—	3296
1953	—	—	—	—	—	2904
1954	—	—	9.9	13.8	6.0	3468
1955	—	—	10.0	13.6	6.7	2962
1956	—	—	12.2	13.9	7.0	3671
1957	—	—	10.8	14.3	6.1	2729
1958	—	—	10.5	13.4	6.9	2784
1959	—	—	**	**	**	3225
1960	—	—	13.9	13.5	6.9	3045
1961	9.5	50.4	12.7	14.6	6.5	3366
1962	9.4	47.9	12.9	14.2	7.2	3501
1963	9.6	44.3	14.0	14.1	7.6	3689
1964	9.5	47.6	13.9	13.8	8.1	4057
1965	7.7	40.3	19.1	12.5	7.6	4470
1966	11.6	40.7	14.2	14.5	4.7	3668
1967	10.7	39.9	22.1	13.2	7.2	3815
1968	10.5	37.7	16.5	14.7	7.8	4781
1969	10.4	38.8	17.2	16.3	8.9	4981
1970	10.6	35.8	17.9	16.3	9.6	7217
1971	10.0	36.2	15.5	17.6	10.4	6992
1972	8.8	36.2	18.3	17.3	12.7	7503
1973	8.1	32.5	22.8	16.9	10.8	7861
1974	6.8	31.2	25.3	16.7	10.8	10153
1975	7.3	31.3	29.7	16.4	10.0	11179
1976	6.8	28.9	31.7	15.9	11.3	12665
1977	7.4	27.4	34.7	14.7	10.6	12022
1978	7.5	27.5	31.5	17.2	10.8	13002
1979	6.7	26.8	30.4	16.2	11.4	14790
1980	6.6	26.1	31.5	15.3	11.1	16728
1981	6.5	25.4	33.5	17.5	11.8	18353
1982	7.8	24.8	29.9	17.8	14.5	19377
1983	8.0	24.2	24.2	19.5	15.2	18927
1984	6.6	24.7	26.7	19.0	15.7	24385
1985	7.6	22.8	24.5	19.8	15.7	24552
1986	7.0	20.0	24.4	20.5	15.6	23477
1987	4.6	18.5	25.9	20.3	15.5	24714
1988	—	—	25.6	19.7	17.5	20224

Note: **No data reported because definition of fiscal year changed in 1959.

Source: Chan and Clark (1992, appendices).

of GNP, presaging a much more normal level of military outlays. Thus, while the effect was decidedly delayed by the special security threats facing Taiwan, in the end defense priority did decline in line with our expectations.

The declining emphasis on defense allowed higher priorities to be accorded economic development, education, and social security and welfare. These changes, as indicated in Table 3 by the share of total government spending in Taiwan accounted for by these three categories, increased gradually but quite significantly over the postwar period. Moreover, the phasing of these changes is exactly what the Caiden model would predict. The proportion of the budget devoted to economic development stayed fairly low and constant at about 10 percent for most of the "developmental" period. It then nearly doubled between the late 1950s and mid-1960s before jumping sharply from about a fifth to a third of governmental outlays between the early and late 1970s as the government intervened in the economy to try to offset the oil crisis. Finally, economic development's budget share declined somewhat over the 1980s to 25 percent.

In contrast, the priorities for education and culture and for social security and welfare did not appreciably increase until the end of the 1960s. The former rose very gradually from 13 percent to 14 percent to 16 percent to 17 percent during the 1970s and early 1980s to 20 percent in 1988, while the latter increased at a slightly more robust pace from 6 percent to 7 percent to 10 percent to 11 percent to 17.5 percent during the same time periods. Similarly but much more dramatically, real spending per primary school student remained almost constant during the 1950s but then really took off in the early 1960s, doubling between 1963 and 1972, doubling again by 1979, and doubling almost yet again by 1984. Thus, Taiwan focused first on stimulating economic development and only turned to boosting the priority of education and social spending later. However, after the government moved on to "market adjustment," there was no cut (and even a gradual increase) in the priority accorded to the realm of social spending; rather, it was economic development that saw its share of the budget go down.

BUDGETARY RESPONSE TO THE OIL CRISIS: AN ANTI-STAGFLATION STRATEGY THAT WORKED

Transformations of budget policy occur not only over long periods of time but can be responses aimed at managing short-term crisis situations. A government's ability to meet unexpected crises is vital to the long-term growth and stability of a society. This section then presents a case study of Taiwan's actions when a decade of export-led growth that averaged over 10 percent a year was threatened by the oil embargo and resulting price explosion of 1973-1974. As will be seen, the rapid and innovative budget transformations that were enacted mitigated the economic problems facing the island in surprisingly short order and laid the foundation for the country's continued economic dynamism.

Table 4. Taiwan's Economic Performance During Oil Crisis*

	1972	1973	1974	1975	1976	1977
Inflation						
Consumer Price Grth (%)	3.0	8.2	47.5	5.2	2.5	7.0
Wholesale Price Growth (%)	4.4	22.9	40.6	-5.1	2.8	2.8
Trade Performance						
Real Effective Export Rate (1980=100)	86.3	94.1	112.7	99.6	97.8	93.4
Real Export Growth (%)	37.0	24.3	-5.3	-7.8	45.8	7.7
Real Import Growth (%)	28.8	25.3	38.3	-16.6	21.0	5.2
Exports % GNP	38.0	41.9	39.2	34.7	44.5	43.6
Trade Balance (mil US$)	474	691	-1321	-643	567	850
Trade Balance % Exports	15.7	15.0	-24.2	-12.4	6.7	8.8
Economic Growth						
Real GNP Growth (%)	13.4	12.8	1.2	4.4	13.7	10.3
Rl Industrial Growth (%)	21.2	16.2	-4.5	9.5	23.3	13.3
Savings & Investment						
Real Savings Growth (%)	26.2	21.7	-7.5	-11.4	37.2	11.3
Real Investment Growth (%)	10.7	28.2	36.4	-18.7	14.4	1.2
Real Private Investment Growth (%)	15.0	38.0	29.2	-44.4	26.3	6.8
Real State Investment Growth (%)	16.3	12.9	49.9	23.0	5.7	-3.7
Savings % GNP	32.1	34.6	31.7	26.9	32.5	32.9
Investment % GDP	25.8	29.3	39.5	30.6	30.8	28.4
State % Investment	39.3	34.7	38.1	57.7	53.3	50.7
Real Foreign Investment Growth (%)	-28.5	63.0	-42.7	-39.0	13.5	8.8
Foreign Investment % Total Investment	6.3	7.9	3.3	2.5	2.5	2.7
Standard of Living						
Real Manufacturing Wage Increase (%)	4.2	1.1	-9.0	11.3	15.0	12.4
Income Ratio*	4.49	—	4.37	—	4.18	—
Food % Household Consumption	42.0	41.3	44.3	44.2	42.1	41.1
Fiscal & Monetary Policy						
Real Government Expenditure Growth (%)	9.8	9.4	-15.0	35.4	14.4	20.7
Government Expenditure % GNP	20.1	19.5	16.4	21.6	21.4	23.4
Budget Balance as % of Government Revenues	4.1	10.9	22.4	5.6	9.7	0.7
Money Supply Growth (%)	34.1	50.4	10.5	28.8	25.1	33.6

Note: *Ratio of income of richest to poorest fifths of population.

Sources: Chan and Clark (1992, appendices) and Kuo (1983, p. 307).

Taiwan certainly appeared to be a prime candidate for economic devastation. It imported almost all of its energy products; and as a highly trade-dependent economy, it was very vulnerable to global inflation and instability in international markets for its manufactured products. In particular, inflationary pressures threatened to destroy its ability to produce the cheap labor-intensive exports that were the staple underlying its rapid growth.

Table 4 certainly demonstrates that the surge in oil prices sent major shockwaves through Taiwan's economy. As would be expected, the oil price explosion created massive inflationary pressures. Both wholesale and consumer prices which had increased by under 5 percent a year for the preceding decade leaped to almost 30 percent average inflation for 1973-1974 with 1974 seeing increases in the 40 percent to 50 percent range, thus transmitting considerable inflationary pressure.

This had an immediate impact upon Taiwan's trade competitiveness as measured by Kuo's (1983, pp. 206-208) index of "the real effective exchange rate" (REER) which is based on relative prices and foreign exchange rates between Taiwan and its trade partners. Increases in this index thus indicate decreased trade competitiveness since this means that the prices of Taiwan's goods are rising in foreign markets. Taiwan's REER index for exports leaped by an astounding 30 percent from 86.3 in 1972 to 112.7 in 1974 (these index numbers are based on a value of 100 for 1980), indicating a tremendous decrease in trade competitiveness.

These changing relative prices put an immediate damper on Taiwan's export performance which had been outstanding in the early 1970s (e.g., real exports had grown by 30% annually during 1970-1973). First, exports declined in real terms by over 6 percent per year in 1974-1975, as the proportion of GNP being exported fell from 42 percent to 35 percent between 1973 and 1975. Second, the import bill of energy dependent Taiwan skyrocketed by 38 percent in real terms in 1974, creating a trade deficit of $1.3 billion (compared to a surplus of $0.7 billion in 1973) that equaled almost a quarter of total exports.

Poor performance in foreign trade in turn had a major adverse impact on the domestic economy as would certainly be expected in a country that exported 40 percent of its GNP. Real industrial production fell by 4.5 percent in 1974; and Taiwan's GNP growth dropped to a minuscule 1.2 percent that year. The economic downturn in turn undercut Taiwan's excellent record on savings and development. Real savings, which had grown by 20 percent a year in the early 1970s fell by 7.5 percent in 1974 and 11.4 percent in 1975. Furthermore, real foreign investment, which (while erratic) had averaged increases of 20 percent per year over the previous decade, fell precipitously by 40 percent annually in these two years, dropping from 8 percent to 2.5 percent of total investment. Despite the drop off in foreign capital, total private investment remained buoyant in 1974 (i.e., it grew by 29% vs. 38% in 1973) as domestic businessmen evidently tried to reinvest their profits to stay ahead of inflation. The effects of the deteriorating economy caught up with private sector investment with a vengeance in 1975 though, as it plummeted 44.5 percent in that year and led to an overall drop of 19 percent in total investment.

Not surprisingly, rapidly deteriorating economic performance hurt the popular standard of living as well. Real monthly wages in the manufacturing sector, which had grown by 4 percent in 1972, only increased 1 percent the next year and then fell sharply by 9 percent in 1974. Falling income would be expected to hurt the quality of life for the average citizen. For example, household spending on food actually increased from 41 percent to 44 percent of family budgets between 1973 and 1974, implying a significant drop in discretionary income. Unlike many developing countries, however, the poor did not have to bear a disproportionate share of the ill effects of the economic crisis since Taiwan's low ratio of the richest to the poorest fifths of the population actually decreased further from 4.5 to 4.2 between 1972 and 1976.

This externally-induced economic crisis produced a strong challenge to Taiwan; and the government responded quickly and actively to control it. In particular, four principal components of Taiwan's successful response can be delineated: (1) applying conservative fiscal measures to counter inflation, (2) managing inflationary pressures and psychology through a one-time major price increase, (3) using government spending and investment to reinvigorate the economy, thereby (4) enhancing international export competitiveness to stimulate another economic growth spurt (Clark 1989a).

Taiwan has always been highly sensitive to inflation and saw its containment of the hyperinflation during the early 1950s as a major reason for its economic success. Thus, the government's first reaction to the oil price explosion was to institute stabilization measures to dampen soaring prices. A major component of the stabilization program was a sharp increase in interest rates which proved quite successful in its deflationary aims of discouraging spending and promoting saving (Kuo 1983). The government also moved quickly in terms of monetary policy to control the inflationary pressures of the rapidly expanding money supply as its growth rate was cut back sharply from 50 percent in 1972 to 10.5 percent in 1973.

A major if not draconian reorientation in fiscal policy dampened the inflationary pressures as well. Real government expenditures which had grown by 9.5 percent in 1972 and 1973 were cut by 15 percent in 1974 as spending fell from 19.5 percent to 16.4 percent of GNP. This created a significant surplus in the government budget which rose as a proportion of total revenues from 4 percent in 1972 to 11 percent in 1973 to a high 22 percent in 1974. The government also tried to control inflation by managing price increases through the monopolies exercised by government corporations, such as the China Petroleum Corporation and the Taiwan Power Company. Initially, the highly profitable CPC tried to absorb the escalating oil prices, but when this proved impractical the government opted for a one-shot major price increase, including price hikes of 88 percent for oil products and 79 percent for electricity (Kuo 1983).

These measures, along with the stabilization of global energy prices, of course, proved highly successful in bringing inflation under control in Taiwan. While wholesale prices had increased by about 4 percent a month for the second half of 1973 and then leaped by 13 percent for each of the first two months of 1974, they actually fell slightly in every remaining month in 1974 and then dropped another 5 percent in 1975. Increases in consumer prices were somewhat higher, but they too were clearly under control by the end of 1974 (Kuo 1983).

The regime's response to the economic crisis went far beyond conservative stabilization policies, though. As sketched above, the inflationary surge had undermined the island's growth, investment, and export competitiveness. Thus, Taiwan faced the problems of inflation and recession simultaneously in a "stagflation" for which traditional Keynesian countercyclical remedies were clearly insufficient. The government evidently composed a sophisticated policy package that coupled its deflationary measures with targeted economic stimuli. The early 1970s had seen the beginning of the "Ten Major Development Projects" in heavy industry and infrastructure. Thus, their augmentation in the mid-1970s served several important purposes—providing a countercyclical stimulus to the economy, helping the structural transformation away from labor-intensive industry, and overcoming transportation and supply bottlenecks (Clark 1989a; Li 1988; Wade 1990). In addition, significant cuts were enacted in 1974 in income and commodity taxes and in customs duties to provide an economic stimulus (Li 1988; Ranis 1979).

In 1974, then, Taiwan simultaneously applied both the brake of fiscal conservatism and the accelerator of greatly increased public investment mostly by state corporations. State investment, which had grown by 10 percent annually in 1972-1973, was increased by 50 percent in real terms to offset drops in foreign investment and growing pressures on the private sector. By 1975, furthermore, the economic situation had changed considerably. Inflation had clearly been tamed, but the effects of the crisis were still quite evident in sluggish growth and export performance and in a disastrous drop of 44 percent in private investment. The government responded by removing the fiscal brake but keeping the investment accelerator pushed down. Government spending shot up by 37 percent in real terms, returning to its pre-crisis level of 21 percent of GNP, as the huge 1974 budgetary surplus of 22 percent of total revenues dropped to under 6 percent. The investment stimulus continued as well. Real state investment grew by 23 percent. Coupled with the precipitous drop in private investment, the state's share of total investment jumped to 58 percent from 38 percent the previous year, indicating that the state had assumed a major role in supporting future economic growth on the island.

This very successful stabilization and stimulation program then resulted in a considerable improvement in the competitive position of Taiwan's products in international trade. Taiwan's ability to move decisively and effectively against inflation meant that the country's prices stabilized more quickly than in most of its trade partners, thereby greatly increasing the competitiveness of its exports as the REER index dropped sharply from 112.7 in 1974 to 99.6 in 1975 and more slowly over the next two years to 93.4 in 1977—only slightly above what it had been in 1973.

Trade performance improved accordingly but in a slightly different pattern. Despite Taiwan's improved competitiveness in 1975, exports actually did worse than in the preceding year, falling by 8 percent in real terms as opposed to 5 percent in 1974, reflecting both the uncertain international market and a time lag before price changes affected trade. However, real imports were cut by nearly 17 percent which resulted in the trade deficit, expressed as a proportion of exports, being halved from 24 percent to 12 percent. Taiwan's major improvement in export competitiveness and stabilizing world markets came together in 1976 to create a remarkable trade resurgence. Exports shot up 46 percent in real terms, over twice the increase in imports, thereby restoring a healthy trade balance and moving up to 44.5 percent of GNP.

The recovery of foreign trade in turn stimulated a new spurt of economic growth. Real GNP growth shot up to "double digits" of 14 percent in 1976 and 10 percent in 1977, and real industrial production increased even faster. Savings and investment responded to the new growth spurt as well. Real savings jumped by 37 percent in 1976 and again surpassed 30 percent of GNP. Private domestic investment increased by 26 percent and foreign capital inflows by 13 percent as well. As a result of this economic rebound, real wages in manufacturing averaged increases of 13 percent during 1975-1971—by far the largest three-year spurt in the history of Taiwan. In response to the revived economy and growing private investment, the government cut back on its own stimulative activities and policies. The growth rate in real government expenditures was cut in half from the high of 37 percent in 1975; and its share of GNP stabilized at 22 percent to 23 percent. The cutbacks in state investment were even more pronounced as the regime seemed willing to allow the private sector to reassert economic leadership.

In sum, the strong external economic shock resulting from the OPEC revolution had only a fleeting impact upon Taiwan, unlike its more devastating consequences for many other countries in both the developed and especially the developing worlds. This occurred partly because Taiwan already had created a strong and expanding economic base that was able to absorb the shock. Considerable credit must be given to the Nationalist government, though, for responding with a sophisticated and subtle program. Even before the debate on "stagflation" had really commenced, the regime successfully blended deflationary and stimulative policies and fine-tuned the degree of government activities to rapidly changing macroeconomic conditions.

IMPLICATIONS

Taiwan has certainly had an enviable record in economic development that reflects both dynamic business entrepreneurship and state leadership in promoting economic transformations (Chan and Clark 1992; Clark 1989b;

Gold 1986; Haggard 1990; Hwang 1991; Wade 1990). In general outline, the island followed Caiden's three-stage model of how budgeting strategy changes in developing countries, but there are clear divergences as well. It is this combination of expected and unexpected patterns—or dogs that did and did not bark to use the Sherlock Holmes metaphor—that probably explains Taiwan's developmental success.

Taiwan progressed through the "regulatory," "developmental," and "market adjustment" stages that Caiden described. The key to Taiwan's success may lie in the fact that the "developmental" stage was fairly short, thus preventing the growth of a huge and inefficient political apparatus that would probably have stifled economic dynamism. In fact, one prominent dog that did not even yip was the almost constant size of the government in relation to the economy throughout the four decades under investigation. Moreover, the public sector's direct ownership role in the economy was cut quite drastically during the "market adjustment" stage, as the model would predict.

The Nationalist regime, however, was not content to put all its faith in the "magic of the marketplace." Rather, it took a leading role in promoting the structural adjustment of the economy away from labor-intensive industries by directly building a heavy industry base, regulating the activities of foreign multinational corporations, and creating a conducive environment for innovative firms in the high-tech industries (Chan and Clark 1992; Chu 1989; Haggard 1990; Haggard and Cheng 1987; Huang 1989; Wade 1990). In addition, because the government decreased its direct economic role, it was able to gradually expand its support of education and social services during the "market adjustment" period as well. Furthermore, the government demonstrated that it could respond quickly to crises, as illustrated by its inspired management of the oil price explosion in the mid-1970s. Finally, its recent move "back to the future" by taking on a strongly developmental role in the Six-Year National Development Plan indicates the beginning of a new stage, although it is too early to tell whether it will be for better or worse. In sum, the Taiwan experience indicates that both "state" and "market" have a positive role to play in development (Gilpin 1987) and that maintaining economic and political "flexibility" is perhaps the most important key to progress (Chan and Clark 1992).

This flexibility has been aided by a number of historical and institutional factors that tend to differentiate the Taiwan case from other developing and developed countries. As already mentioned, in the 1950s, massive and critical U.S. aid alleviated the defense burden and provided a much needed source of funds for social and economic reforms. Taiwan's rising export revenue and especially its expanding foreign currency reserve and the appreciating value of the new Taiwan dollar in the late 1980s gave the government the financial wherewithal to get "a bigger bang for its bucks." Naturally, the passing of the Cold War and the abatement of tension across the Taiwan Strait further created favorable conditions for changing spending priorities from "guns" to "butter." Therefore, these historical events or processes had provided greater policy space for the government.

This policy space has been greater in Taiwan in part because, until recently, various social and economic interest groups have been relatively weak in their ability to lobby government bureaucrats. And, again until very recently, electoral bidding and cycling have not exerted the sort of political pressure common in the United States for a continuously expanding budget (for both "guns" and "butter") and, at the same time, for government restraint on taxation. There has, therefore, been less of a "ratchet effect" in budgetary processes (whereby spending almost always goes up and rarely down), and there have been few "mandated programs" that introduce allocation rigidity in these processes. One is also reminded that Taiwan does not face the sort of institutional divisions between taxation and spending authorities, monetary and fiscal agencies, and federal and state/local governments (e.g., revenue-sharing schemes) that characterize the situation in the United States. In other words, almost unitary control of the fiscal and monetary levers (which, until recently, have included direct government control and operation of the banks) by the economic bureaucrats (relatively free from legislative oversight and electoral pressure) is a major reason for Taiwan's flexibility. To the extent that such institutional factors may not apply in other countries, their governments' ability to fine-tune the economy is reduced. Moreover, to the extent that these conditions are becoming less applicable to Taiwan itself due to the ongoing political liberalization of the island, its future budgetary processes are likely to become more politicized and the policy space for officials more constricted.

This implies, incidentally, a lamentable tradeoff between democratization and the economic capacities of a developmental state (for a somewhat different statement of this theory, see Olson 1982). Taiwan, therefore, may be moving back to a developmental orientation at precisely the moment when conventional theory would imply that it should be insulating the economy from the vagaries of domestic politics—thus providing another reason why the outcome of the Six-Year National Development Plan should be of more than passing interest and import.

REFERENCES

Arnold, W. 1989. "Bureaucratic Politics, State Capacity, and Taiwan's Automobile Industrial Policy." *Modern China* 15: 178-214.

Balassa, B. 1981. *The Newly Industrializing Countries in the World Economy.* New York: Pergamon.

Botjer, G.F. 1979. *A Short History of Nationalist China, 1919-1949.* New York: Putnam.

Chan, S., and C. Clark. 1992. *Flexibility, Foresight, and Fortuna in Taiwan's Development: Navigating Between Scylla and Charybdis.* London: Routledge.

Cheng, T.J., and S. Haggard. Eds. 1992. *Political Change in Taiwan*. Boulder, CO: Lynne Rienner.

Chu, Y.H. 1989. "State Structure and Economic Adjustment of the East Asian Newly Industrializing Countries." *International Organization* 43: 647-672.

———. 1991. "Industrial Change and Development in the East Asian NICs: A Case Study of the Automobile Industry in South Korea and Taiwan." Paper presented at the annual meeting of the American Political Science Association, Washington, DC, August 29-September 1.

Clark, C. 1989a. "External Shocks and Instability in Taiwan: The Dog That Didn't Bark." Pp. 173-197 in *Markets, Politics, and Change in the Global Economy*, edited by W.P. Avery and D.P. Rapkin. Boulder, CO: Lynne Rienner.

———. 1989b. *Taiwan's Development: Implications for Contending Political Economy Paradigms*. Westport, CT: Greenwood.

Clough, R.N. 1978. *Island China*. Cambridge, MA: Harvard University Press.

Coble, P.M. 1980. *The Shanghai Capitalists and the Nationalist Government, 1927-1937*. Cambridge, MA: Harvard University Press.

Copper, J.F. 1988. *A Quiet Revolution: Political Development in the Republic of China*. Washington, DC: Ethics and Public Policy Center.

Domes, J. 1992. "Taiwan in 1991: Searching for Political Consensus." *Asian Survey* 32: 42-49.

Duara, P. 1988. *Culture, Power, and the State: Rural North China, 1900-1942*. Stanford, CA: Stanford University Press.

Eastman, L.E. 1974. *The Abortive Revolution: China Under Nationalist Rule, 1927-1937*. Cambridge, MA: Harvard University Press.

Fei, J.C.H. 1991. "A Historical Perspective on Economic Modernization in the ROC." Pp. 97-110 in *Two Societies in Opposition: The Republic of China and the People's Republic of China After Forty Years*, edited by R.H. Myers. Stanford, CA: Hoover Institution Press.

Fewsmith, J. 1985. *Party, State, and Local Elites in Republican China: Merchant Organizations and Politics in Shanghai, 1890-1930*. Honolulu: University of Hawaii Press.

Galenson, W. Ed. 1979. *Economic Growth and Structural Change in Taiwan: The Postwar Experience of the Republic of China*. Ithaca, NY: Cornell University Press.

Gilpin, R. 1987. *The Political Economy of International Relations*. Princeton, NJ: Princeton University Press.

Gold, T.B. 1986. *State and Society in the Taiwan Miracle*. Armonk, NY: M.E. Sharpe.

Haggard, S. 1990. *Pathways From the Periphery: The Politics of Growth in the Newly Industrializing Countries*. Ithaca, NY: Cornell University Press.

Haggard, S., and T.J. Cheng. 1987. "State and Foreign Capital in the East Asian NICs." Pp. 84-135 in *The Political Economy of the New Asian Industrialism*, edited by F.C. Deyo. Ithaca, NY: Cornell University Press.

Ho, S.P.S. 1978. *Economic Development in Taiwan, 1860-1970*. New Haven, CT: Yale University Press.

———. 1987. "Economics, Economic Bureaucracy, and Taiwan's Economic Development." *Pacific Affairs* 60: 226-247.

Hsiung, J.C. Ed. 1981. *Contemporary Republic of China: The Taiwan Experience, 1950-1980*. New York: Praeger.

Huang, C. 1989. "The State and Foreign Investment: The Cases of Taiwan and Singapore." *Comparative Political Studies* 22: 93-121.

Huang, P.H. 1984. "Modernization of Education in the Republic of China Since 1949." Pp. 171-191 in *Chinese Modernization*, edited by Y.M. Shaw. San Francisco: Chinese Materials Center Publications.

Hwang, Y.D. 1991. *The Rise of a New World Economic Power: Postwar Taiwan*. New York: Greenwood.

Jacoby, N.H. 1966. *U.S. Aid to Taiwan: A Study of Foreign Aid, Self-Help, and Development.* New York: Praeger.

Kuo, S.W.Y. 1983. *The Taiwan Economy in Transition.* Boulder, CO: Westview.

Kuo, S.W.Y., G. Ranis, and J.C.H. Fei. 1981. *The Taiwan Success Story: Rapid Growth With Improved Income Distribution in the Republic of China.* Boulder, CO: Westview.

Lam, D.K.K. 1992. *Explaining Economic Development: A Case Study of State Policies Towards the Computer and Electronics Industry in Taiwan (1960-1980).* Unpublished Ph.D. dissertation, Carleton University, Ottawa, Ontario, Canada.

Lee, T.H. 1971. *Intersectoral Capital Flows in the Economic Development of Taiwan, 1895-1960.* Ithaca, NY: Cornell University Press.

Li, K.T. 1988. *The Evolution of Policy Behind Taiwan's Development Success.* New Haven: Yale University Press.

Lin, C.Y. 1973. *Industrialization in Taiwan, 1946-1972: Trade and Import Substitution Policies for Developing Countries.* New York: Praeger.

Linder, S.B. 1986. *The Pacific Century: Economic and Political Consequences of Asian-Pacific Dynamism.* Stanford, CA: Stanford University Press.

Liu, P. 1991. "A Plan in Search of Private Investment." *Free China Review* 41(6): 44-50.

Lundberg, E. 1979. "Fiscal and Monetary Policies." Pp. 261-307 in *Economic Growth and Structural Change in Taiwan: The Postwar Experience of the Republic of China*, edited by W. Galenson. Ithaca, NY: Cornell University Press.

Myers, R.H. 1984. "The Economic Transformation of the Republic of China on Taiwan." *China Quarterly* 99: 500-528.

________ . 1987. "Political Theory and Recent Political Developments in the Republic of China." *Asian Survey* 27: 1003-1022.

Olson, M. 1982. *The Rise and Decline of Nations: Economic Growth, Stagflation, and Social Rigidities.* New Haven, CT: Yale University Press.

Ranis, G. 1979. "Industrial Development." Pp. 206-262 in *Economic Growth and Structural Change in Taiwan: The Postwar Experience of the Republic of China*, edited by W. Galenson. Ithaca, NY: Cornell University Press.

Sheridan, J.E. 1975. *China in Disintegration: The Republican Era in Chinese History, 1912-1949.* New York: Free Press.

Snider, L.W. 1987. "Identifying the Elements of State Power." *Comparative Political Studies* 20: 314-356.

Sutter, R.G. 1988. *Taiwan: Entering the 21st Century.* Lanham, MD: University Press of America.

Tien, H.M. 1972. *Government and Politics in Kuomintang China, 1927-1937.* Stanford, CA: Stanford University Press.

________ . 1989. *The Great Transition: Political and Social Change in the Republic of China.* Stanford, CA: Hoover Institution Press.

Wade, R. 1990. *Governing the Market: Economic Theory and the Role of Government in East Asian Industrialization.* Princeton, NJ: Princeton University Press.

Wang, Y.S. Ed. 1990. *The Foreign Policy of the Republic of China on Taiwan: An Unorthodox Approach.* New York: Praeger.

Wei, Y. 1973. "Taiwan: A Modernizing Chinese Society." Pp. 435-505 in *Taiwan in Modern Times*, edited by P.K.T. Sih. New York: St. John's University Press.

Winckler, E.A. 1988. "Elite Political Struggle: 1945-1985." Pp. 151-171 in *Contending Approaches to the Political Economy of Taiwan*, edited by E.A. Winckler and S. Greenhalgh. Armonk, NY: M.E. Sharpe.

Winckler, E.A., and S. Greenhalgh. Eds. 1988. *Contending Approaches to the Political Economy of Taiwan.* Armonk, NY: M.E. Sharpe.

World Bank. 1988. *World Development Report, 1988*. Washington, DC: Oxford University Press.

Wu, Y.L. 1985. *Becoming an Industrialized Nation: ROC's Development on Taiwan*. New York: Praeger.

Wu, Y.S. 1991. "The Political Economy of Taiwan-Mainland Economic Relations." Paper presented at the conference on Permutations Across the Taiwan Strait, Texas A&M University College Station, TX, October 3-5.

Yang, M.M.C. 1970. *Socio-Economic Results of Land Reform in Taiwan*. Honolulu: East-West Center Press.

PART II.

ISSUES OF FISCAL POLICY

PART II

FISCAL STRESS AND STRUCTURAL ADJUSTMENT

Jack Diamond

ABSTRACT

This paper clarifies the meaning of fiscal stress and discusses how the concept applies to developing countries. The paper focuses on the approaches that have been adopted to accommodate fiscal stress in developing countries and their implications for longer-run structural adjustment. Specifically, it is argued that changes in the composition of government spending, as well as adaptations of budgetary procedures occasioned by fiscal stress, may have a negative short-run impact on the capacity of developing countries to adopt and sustain structural reforms.

The term "fiscal stress," although widely used throughout the last decade to describe fiscal problems, remains imprecise. There has been a tendency to use the term to describe symptoms rather than their cause and to concentrate on developed countries. But fiscal stress is also a fact of life in developing countries. There is now increasing concern that policies to cope with fiscal stress may

Policy Studies and Developing Nations, Volume 3, pages 45-68.

ISBN: 1-55938-190-6

have jeopardized the ability of these countries to undertake long-term structural reforms of their economies. This paper attempts to clarify the meaning of fiscal stress, and its application to developing countries. It then explores typical policy responses to fiscal stress, and how these responses have been reflected in the changing composition of expenditures and on the budgetary process. The final section examines the implications of these impacts for undertaking and sustaining structural adjustment reforms. The paper concludes with a brief review of the main elements that could form the basis for a strategy to improve the response to fiscal stress in developing countries.

THE ORIGINS OF FISCAL STRESS

Fiscal stress may be viewed as originating from a more generalized economic imbalance, represented by the saving-investment identity, or the resource constraint facing an economy. This identity states:

$$\text{Budget deficit} = (\text{private saving} - \text{private investment}) + (\text{current account deficit of the balance of payments}) \quad (1)$$

In an economy that has reached a level of activity commensurate with its productive capacity and has a given rate of saving, an increase in the deficit will result in either a reduction in investment (the "crowding out" problem) or an increase in the current account deficit of the balance of payments. Conversely, an increase in the balance of payments current account deficit due to some exogenous factor (e.g., an increase in petroleum prices), with no change in the savings rate, will necessitate a corresponding cut in private investment and/or the budget deficit to maintain equilibrium (see Bean and Buiter 1987). For the small, open developing economy, heavily dependent on imported inputs and exporting a small range of traditional staple exports, this line of causation is most probable.

For such economies, the severity of macroeconomic stress encountered may be described in four stages (see Schneider 1987). The first stage commences with a deterioration of the current account of the balance of payments. As long as international reserves are sufficient and foreign capital is forthcoming, this stage is unlikely to be perceived by the authorities as necessitating corrective action. The second stage is reached when the level of reserves falls to a point where the authorities feel compelled to stem the external deterioration through such measures as increasing import duties, introducing import surcharges, or even banning imports. Without any attempt to adjust domestically to this macroeconomic imbalance, the third stage will be reached where the authorities typically abandon the use of price to allocate foreign exchange and introduce administrative schemes to ration its ever-diminishing supply. When normal channels of trade financing are closed as the international community loses confidence in the country's repayment ability, the country may be regarded as having reached the fourth stage. Typically, only then is resistance to adjustment finally overcome.

The important repercussions of fiscal stress for the budgets of developing economies may be seen from Figure 1. Because of deterioration of the balance of payments current account, *taxes or other government receipts derived from exports* are likely to decline. The decline is likely to be compounded as foreign exchange becomes scarce and exports are diverted to the black market. Only at the later stages of fiscal stress, when the authorities are forced into some depreciation of the exchange rate, are receipts from this source likely to improve, depending on how badly export production is affected by unavailability of essential imported inputs.

In the early stages of fiscal stress, the revenue losses of *import taxes* from reduced import levels may be offset by the gains from the increased import duties and surcharges imposed to reduce imports. However, with increasing foreign exchange shortages, the base of these taxes will inevitably be compressed. The resulting revenue loss will be compounded by selective reductions in the level of imports and a bias toward low-duty and duty-exempt goods.

Income tax revenues may be expected to be comparatively buoyant throughout the different stages of macroeconomic stress. First, domestic manufacturing initially will benefit from the protection associated with increased import duties, although at later stages its production level may suffer due to the foreign exchange constraint. Second, relative buoyancy is magnified because many developing countries have extremely narrow tax nets which capture primarily those who benefit from this additional protection. Third, revenues will also benefit to the extent that the tax base is dependent on those with privileged access to foreign exchange and who reap the economic rents generated by the rationing of foreign exchange. Toward the later stages of macroeconomic stress, as domestic production is crippled by lack of foreign exchange, income tax revenues will necessarily contract.

Indirect taxes revenues (and to a certain extent *non-tax revenues*) may be expected to vary according to the effect of externally-induced macroeconomic stress on domestic production. At the early stages, domestic production is likely to be protected so that domestic sales tax revenues benefit from this increased protection. As foreign exchange availability and the supply of essential inputs declines, domestic production will slow down, and the base of indirect taxes will also increasingly contract.

Inflation is also likely to increase and to exert an important influence on revenues. (For a fuller discussion of the impact of inflation, see Mansfield 1980; Tanzi 1977.) On the one hand, revenues are likely to increase as a result of "bracket creep," which increases marginal direct tax rates in real terms. On the other hand, these gains may be offset by losses in the real value of revenues

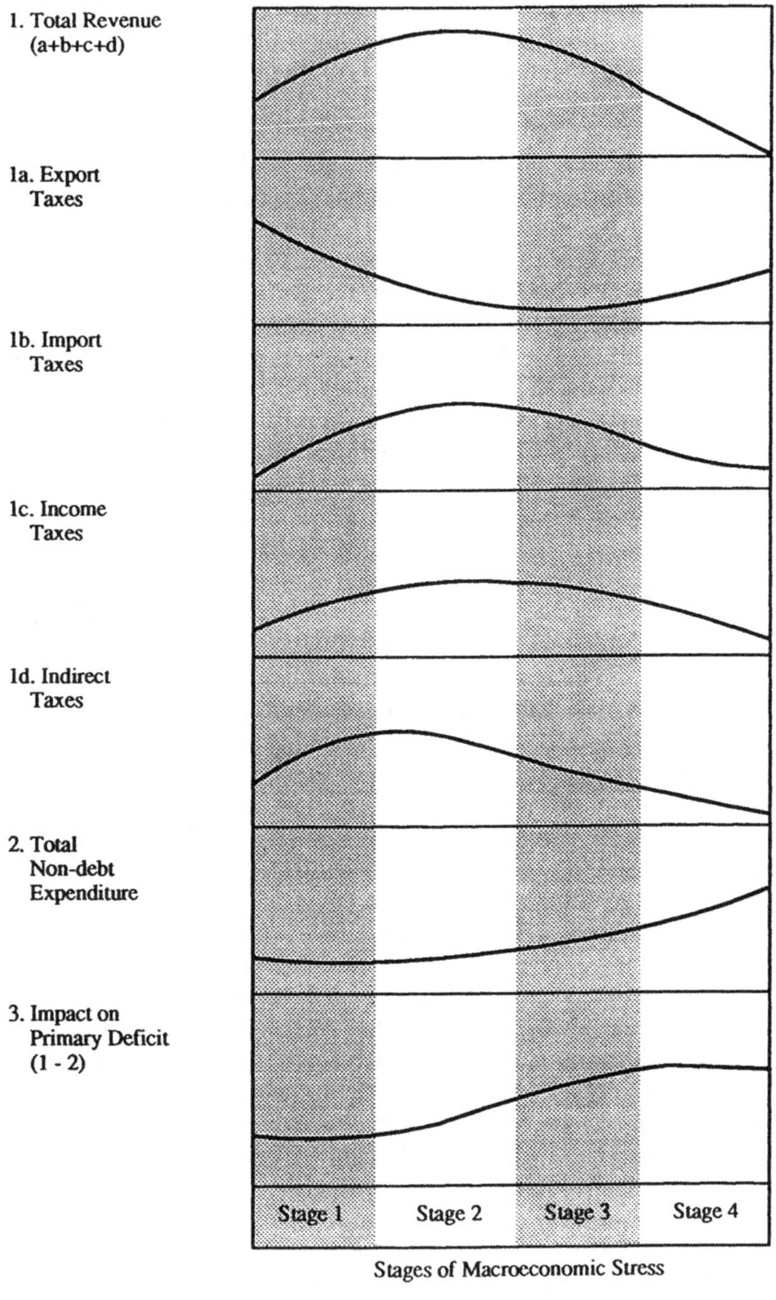

Figure 1. Stages of Macroeconomic and Fiscal Stress: Impact on Primary Deficit

due to collection lags and the existence of specific rather than ad valorem taxes. Thus, the net effect of inflation on revenues is likely to be determined largely by the rate and duration of inflation and the country's tax administrative capacity. The acknowledged weakness of tax administration in developing countries, and their consequent reliance on easily collected specific excises on mass consumption items, suggests the negative effects will predominate.

The combined effects on total revenue of these individual profiles indicates that after a possible initial increase an increasingly rapid decline in total revenues may be expected. It is, of course, difficult to give an exact picture without knowing the relative share of each tax in total revenues.

At the same time, the level and composition of expenditures are likely to change, depending on the severity of foreign exchange scarcity and the rate of inflation. Although the net impact is unpredictable, it is likely that, without discretionary action, the level of total nondebt service related spending will increase.

The combined revenue and nondebt expenditure effects are likely to increase the primary deficit (i.e., excluding interest payments). This widening gap will itself increase macroeconomic stress, leading to a vicious circle, so that the potential for fiscal stress appears to increase as the deficit increases.

In this environment, the options available to mitigate fiscal stress are either to reduce the deficit or finance it by printing money, running down foreign reserves, increasing borrowing, or domestic sale of its debt. Figure 2 portrays the most likely movement of each of these funding sources over the different stages of macroeconomic stress.

The printing of money at a faster rate than the demand for it at a given level of income initially creates excess cash balances in the hands of the public who, by reducing them through increased purchases, drive up the price level (i.e., expanding the money base leads to inflation, which in turn may feed back to the deficit).

Use of foreign reserves may be viewed as credit creation by the central bank. By running down reserves, the government may put off the inflationary effects of a deficit, although this strategy has obvious limits since reserves are finite. Even if this limit is not reached, the private sector's expectation that the limit is about to be reached may provoke capital flight and a balance of payments crisis. Moreover, running down reserves has the effect of appreciating the currency, making imports more attractive and exports less attractive, and reinforcing the negative impact on the balance of payments.

Foreign borrowing also appreciates the exchange rate, with negative impact on the current balance of payments. In any case, accumulation of more and more external debt will result in a negative impact on the trade balance and a heavier and heavier burden of debt service, with ultimate inability to borrow and external debt crisis.

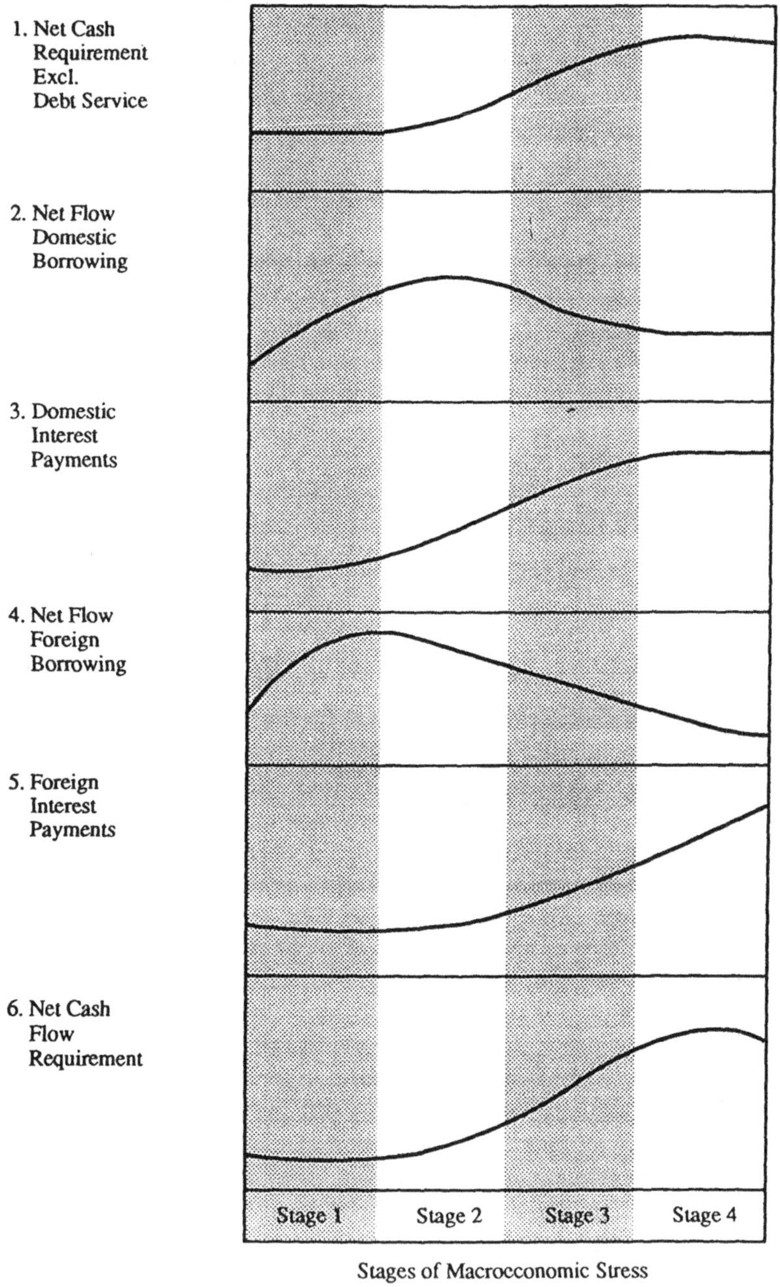

Figure 2. Stages of Macroeconomic and Fiscal Stress: Impact on Cash Flow

Finally, the government may *issue domestic debt*, but this strategy reduces credit that would be available to the private sector. The competition for credit is likely to increase interest rates, choking private sector investment and requiring increased interest payments. Even if interest rates are controlled, as is often the case in developing countries, this policy will lead to credit rationing and crowding out of private sector investment.

Net financing from domestic sources may be increased in Stages 1 and 2, but eventually the repayment of this lending reduces the net inflow, and the source of finance dries up as economic activity slows down. Similarly, foreign lending may be tapped at the early stages of macroeconomic stress, but the net inflow will also fall as repayments have to be made (at a depreciated exchange rate), and lenders become wary of extending further credit. In the final stages of fiscal stress, repayments and interest to finance the deficit will rise steeply, and governments will be forced to increase the stock of high-powered money, equivalent to credit creation by the central bank. It is the size of this inflationary financing which most accurately captures the degree of fiscal stress experienced by a country.

The scenario of increased deficits, higher inflation, exchange crises, external debt problems, and high real interest rates described a large part of the developing world in the 1980s. Many countries had already accumulated considerable foreign debt and run down their reserves and were faced with increasing inflation at a time when their economies were slowing down. The situation was aggravated by a number of adverse developments in the international environment, namely, the adoption of floating exchange rates among the major currencies, the large fluctuations in the world prices of commodities, sharp increases in real interest rates in international credit markets, and an extended period of slow growth in major export markets.

PATTERNS OF FISCAL STRESS

One approach to measuring the degree of fiscal stress is to examine the required time period in adjusting the budget to its resource constraint. Three cases may be distinguished. The first is a sudden *short-run* shock, one-time in nature, in which either receipts decline sharply or expenditures increase sharply. In a *cyclical* adjustment process, the budget follows a "boom-bust" cycle generating periodic fiscal stress. Finally, where growth rates of expenditures and receipts are so far apart that they can only be brought into line over a period of years to avoid imbalances in other parts of the economy, there is need for *long-run* structural adjustment. Each type of fiscal stress is associated with a different kind of economy and has generated a somewhat different response.

Short-Run Shocks

Small, open developing countries have been especially vulnerable to random shocks, such as the oil shocks of the 1970s. Their difficulty in accommodating these shocks may be due partly to a desire to build up social and physical infrastructure regardless of external circumstances; but it is also related to limited flexibility in financing government spending. They have thin financial markets, the tax base is usually narrow, and the constraints of the tax administration mean over-concentration on a few taxes, primarily those on foreign trade. These high commodity tax rates encourage the growth of black markets and smuggling, further contracting the tax base. The revenue system is thus very fragile and subject to wide swings as external conditions change. External financing is limited to official sources that depend critically on the economic state of the donor countries and their rate of growth.

Cyclical Fiscal Stress

The cyclical "boom-bust" type of fiscal stress begins with an upswing in the demand or prices of the country's exports. Since these exports also usually contribute substantial revenues to the government budget, either through direct state ownership or export taxes,[1] the increase in commodity prices unexpectedly lifts the budget's revenue constraint, and in many cases increases in government spending have exceeded revenues. A boom period follows with consequent inflationary pressure. Usually after some time, the demand for the country's exports declines, perhaps due to a recession in the importing countries, leading to an economic down-turn or "bust." As revenues fall, the country attempts to reverse the previous growth in government spending and experiences fiscal stress alongside budget-induced uncertainty. An upturn in demand for exports will set the cycle off again with two complicating factors. First, the cyclical process imparts a ratchet effect on expenditures so that adjustment in expenditures begins from a higher base. Second, countries are able to incur external debt during the boom, as foreign commercial banks eagerly lend on the security provided by commodity revenues. During the bust, nervous lenders are reluctant to make new loans, and net capital flows are reduced or even reversed. These countries are left with expanded external debt service commitments with substantially lower capital inflows. Contrary to the principle that debt should be used to smooth out such cycles, it tends to exacerbate them.

Omolehinwa and Roe (1989) illustrated the persistence of these boom and bust budgetary cycles in the case of Ghana, Kenya, and Nigeria, and Gupta and Miranda (1991) analyzed the ratchet effect on expenditures in the cases of Sri Lanka, Malaysia, and Kenya. Wider analyses of the policy reactions of various countries to different types of exogenous shocks are contained in Tanzi (1986) and Chu (1987).

The boom-bust trap is not unavoidable, and some countries have handled fluctuations in commodity prices quite successfully.[2] There have also been notable differences in the impact of cyclical influences not only on the level but also the composition of spending. In some cases, current expenditures responded to exogenous movements in export demand, and capital expenditures were maintained in the short-run; in others capital spending took the brunt of the adjustment and current expenditures remained above pre-boom levels (Gupta and Miranda 1991).

Structural Fiscal Stress

In advanced countries, structural fiscal stress has long been associated with the tendency for expenditures to grow faster than revenues. In the 1980s, a different kind of structural fiscal stress emerged in low- and middle-income countries, derived more specifically from the necessity of servicing a large and growing public debt. The debt problem in part arose from other types of fiscal stress described above.[3] These countries borrowed heavily in the late 1970s and early 1980s to finance consumption and domestic capital formation in the face of declining export prices and volumes. After 1980, official and private creditors and the countries themselves realized that the rate of public borrowing needed to be cut. As new disbursements dropped, most of the highly indebted countries responded to the cessation of lending by tightening their fiscal policies leading to debt-induced fiscal stress. This austerity helped them to avoid a general suspension of payments but was insufficient to solve their debt problem, in turn aggravated by higher real interest rates.[4] The continuing burden of servicing this overhang of debt has led to long-run fiscal stress which may be viewed as structural.

POLICY RESPONSES TO FISCAL STRESS

Fiscal stress has forced governments to make explicit a number of politically sensitive choices in resource allocation that were implicit in the choices made in more economically favorable times. First, decision makers face a tradeoff between inflation and unsatisfied public demands for goods and services. Second, fiscal stress opens up the debate on the "proper" size of government and the choice between public and private provision of goods and services. Third, recognition of the impossibility of meeting all demands for public services highlights the choice about the "right" composition of public spending. Fourth, the pressure on resources available to pay for government services raises questions about the "correct" means of paying for them. Ultimately, there is a choice between attempting to provide equal services to all citizens or only to those who can afford to pay for them.

It might be felt that persistent fiscal stress would bring about greater efficiency in the use of public resources, as governments were forced to examine priorities, make more optimal choices, cut waste in existing spending programs, and improve planning of future expenditures, thereby producing at least preconditions for structural adjustment reforms. Unfortunately, typical reactions of decision makers have generally resulted in less favorable outcomes.

In a world without politics and with perfect information, finding an optimal strategy for managing fiscal stress would be a relatively straightforward task. First, one would analyze the causes of a government's fiscal problems, including forecast of relevant trends, revenue raising capacity, and long-run demand for government services. Second, one would develop a list of priority rankings for all government programs, projects, and services so that high priority items could be retained or increased and low priority items could be reduced or terminated. Third, one would design an integrated strategy to generate new resources, improve productivity, and provide services so that revenue and expenditure sides of the budget could be neatly balanced at a sustainable level.

This comprehensive approach is little more than a pipe dream. A more typical approach is the adoption of short-run tactics and attempts to "muddle through." Table 1 identifies responses in three periods: the immediate short-run, short-run, and the longer-run.

Immediate short-run tactics to resist cutbacks typically involve the drawdown of existing fund surpluses, imaginative accounting, often involving interfund transfers, and increased borrowing to support increased operating deficits. All fail to confront the problem, and all are likely to make the ultimate adjustment greater.

Short-run cutback tactics usually involve a choice between spreading the pain of the cuts and cutting in a cost effective way. In the first approach, cuts would be distributed across government departments with equal probability of hurting all units. In the second, cuts would be allocated to minimize the loss in total government services as a whole. Typically, effectiveness loses out to "equity," since an across-the-board cuts approach tend to be easier to adopt and justify. More focused cuts tend to involve costly triage analysis and provoke resistance (see Doss and Wacht 1989). In practice, many of the short-run tactics employed are neither cost effective nor equitable (e.g., layoffs favoring length of service, hiring freezes, across-the-board cuts, average workload ratios).

Longer-run cutback strategies usually require practical solutions to a number of contradictions. First, it is common for voters to express their preference for lower public spending and lower taxation but to oppose cutbacks in programs which benefit them (see Citrin 1979). Second, there may be a conflict between macro targets, usually expressed as ceilings on total spending or limits on deficits, and micro decisions in the budget process, affecting specific departments and programs. Third, a number of implementation problems arise from the need to resolve conflicts between the ministry of finance, responsible

Table 1. The Sequence of Response to Fiscal Stress

Strategy	*Response Sequence*	*Time Period*	*Stage of Macroeconomic Stress*
Resist	• Ignore stress conditions • Take no action	Immediate Short-run	1
Smooth the Decline	• Moderate expenditure reduction in discretionary areas • Short-run across-the-board expenditure reductions in "less sensitive" areas • Existing revenue sources analyzed for increased potential	Short-run	2
	• Deeper program reduction: Across-the-board cuts Hiring and salary freezes Temporary employment reductions • Liabilities unfunded • Physical plant not maintained • New revenue sources sought	Medium-run	3
Adjust to the Decline	• Government plans longer-term measures to match revenues and expenditures, or reduce deficit • Specific program reduction and termination • Reorganization of service functions • Layoff employees • Privatization • Government implements longer term management plans. Service and program reorganization Rewards and employee incentives	Long-run	4

for macro budgeting and the setting of overall ceilings, and spending departments responsible for implementing those decisions, who tend to be the strongest advocates of their own services. The magnitude of the conflicts between them and the time and decision costs involved help explain delay in adopting structural adjustments in the budget and the attractiveness of the "muddling through" approach.

These typical reactions of decision makers to the new environment of austerity have obviously had a number of policy implications, particularly for the composition of government spending.

EMPIRICAL EVIDENCE ON EXPENDITURE CUTBACKS

Although the incidence of cutbacks on different types of expenditures has been the subject of some research, the picture is far from clear. There seems general consensus that social services (defined broadly to cover education, health, housing, social security, and welfare services) have been relatively protected (Hicks 1989; Hicks and Kubisch 1984; Meyers 1986) perhaps because of a bias toward recurrent expenditure associated with employment (Hicks and Kubisch 1984).

With respect to general public services and defense, the findings have been conflicting. Hafeez (1984) found that general administration and defense combined were the most vulnerable category of expenditure. But Meyers (1986) found that general public services had the greatest relative protection from cutbacks, and Hicks and Kubisch (1984) also found defense spending to be well protected, although Hicks (1989) found that in the period 1981-1984 this protection had declined.

There seems more general agreement that the economic functions of government spending seemed to bear the brunt of cutbacks. Hicks and Kubisch (1984) found infrastructure and productive sectors relatively vulnerable, with the highest frequency of cuts in transportation and communications. Meyers (1986) found that agriculture and transportation bore the greatest relative burden of expenditure cuts, although he noted large differences between countries.

The most dominant trend was one of dramatic relative growth in interest payments reflecting increased debt burdens while capital expenditures were compressed (Hafeez 1984; Hicks and Kubisch 1984; Meyers 1986). Hicks (1989) noted that, for his 1981-1984 sample of high debt countries, spending rose 21 percent while capital expenditure declined by 20 percent. In contrast, within current spending, wages and salaries were the most protected (Hafeez 1984; Hicks and Kubisch 1984), but Hicks (1989) found reduced wage expenditures. Hicks also found goods and services, an important category for operations and maintenance, lost out in their share of total spending, although they appeared to have exhibited some real growth. Of course, fiscal stress may not have been responsible for all these adjustments.

To differentiate normal adjustments to external environmental factors from those caused by fiscal stress, it is necessary to compare actual expenditures with what might be expected. The Heller/Diamond study (1990) used a comparison of international expenditure indexes from data of three-year averages centered around the years 1976, 1979, 1982, and 1985 to compare actual spending levels with those predicted from regression equations describing the principal determinants of each category of spending. They took the typical response in the base period using expenditure to GDP averages for 1975-1977, which might be considered perhaps a more normal environment than the periods which followed. Use of the structural coefficients in the base period and substitution of the changing environmental factors in subsequent periods allowed predictions of what expenditure levels might have been in the new environment if the expenditure response had been the same as in the base period. The comparison of actual levels with the predicted levels gave a measure of how actual expenditure levels deviated from what might have been expected in more normal times.

The derived indexes allow focus on two central questions: Has there been a change in the structural relationship between government expenditure shares and their underlying economic, social, and demographic determinants? Can a significant change be discerned in the expenditure priorities of a country?

The Heller/Diamond study highlighted regional differences in the response to global pressures on expenditure levels, which may be summarized as follows[5]:

a. In Africa and Asia, developing countries of Europe, and Western Hemisphere countries, social expenditures (education, health, and housing and community services) appeared to have been maintained and even increased their GDP share relative to what would be predicted. Exceptions appear to be social security and welfare expenditures in Africa that experienced a downward shift in the period, as did education expenditures in the developing countries of the European region. Also in the Middle Eastern countries, following the fall in oil prices after 1983, reduced priority was attached to health, social security, and welfare, which had however previously been very high.
b. In Africa and in developing European countries, there was a downward shift in general public services and defense spending, although in Asia the adjustment in these sectors was much less marked, without any systematic decline in their priority over the period.[6] In Western Hemisphere countries, an apparently higher priority was attached to outlays on defense. Middle Eastern countries displayed a sharp increase in defense expenditures after 1978 without any notable trend in general public administration.
c. In all regions, there was a squeeze on expenditures directed at the economic sectors. In Africa, this was most pronounced in transportation and communications. In Asia, the expenditure shares for roads, mining and manufacturing, and gas and electricity all declined relative to their predicted values, the only exception being the agricultural sector whose priority appeared to increase. After 1983 in the Middle Eastern countries, there was a notable decline in priority of economic services (particularly mining and manufacturing, gas and electricity, and roads). In Western Hemisphere countries, agriculture, gas and electricity, and transport sectors declined in priority.

d. The most pronounced trend was the increase in interest payments and the decline of capital spending. The results from the African region suggested a clear shift away from capital spending, which was mirrored to a lesser extent in Asia (particularly after 1978) and Europe. In Western Hemisphere countries, the move away from capital spending was reflected most in a lower than would be expected expenditure share on capital transfers, perhaps reflecting the more pronounced consolidation of public enterprises in the budgets of these countries. Only in the Middle East was there an increasing priority for fixed capital asset acquisition.
e. In Africa, there was a clear shift toward transfers and subsidies, which to a lesser extent is true also of Western Hemisphere countries. In Asian and European countries, the trend was less clear in contrast to the Middle Eastern countries which showed a sharp drop.
f. Wages and salaries appeared to have maintained their relative position in Africa, the Middle East, and Western Hemisphere countries. In Asia and Europe, there was some compression in this category.
g. Despite complaints about the neglect of operations and maintenance (O&M) expenditures, the trend in the "other current goods and services" category is unclear. For example, in complete contrast to expectations, in African countries there appears to have been a clear shift toward these expenditures whereas in Asia and Europe the reverse held true, especially after 1978. In Western Hemisphere countries, there was no clear trend, while in the Middle East there was increasing priority for outlays on other goods and services after 1978. The difficulty in interpreting these results most probably arises from problems in identifying O&M expenditures.

What is the significance of these regression results? If crisis management overrides rational choices and introduces a greater random element into the selection of expenditure cuts, one could expect the "normal" response to become less predictable, and it seems that the regression models explain less, particularly for economic services sector and capital spending between the mid-1970s to the mid-1980s. This disruption of the "normal" expenditure response is likely to affect both budgetary processes and the capacity to undertake long-run structural adjustment.

THE IMPACT ON BUDGETARY PROCESSES

Budget Formulation

Little has been written on budgetary responses to fiscal stress in developing countries. The first impression is that, as in advanced countries, there has been a top down approach, with emphasis on preparation and greater centralization. For example, those countries with adjustment programs under arrangements with the International Monetary Fund have necessarily integrated overall ceilings on the deficit, spending, and borrowing requirements into the budgetary process. There has been a clear trend away from ambitious multi-year development plans toward a more short-term view of government spending based on the need to meet financing targets. The growth of debt service payments has also increased the tendency for centralization.

However, although the imposition of overall limits has been attempted at the center, the absence of a pre-preparation budget phase has meant that the bottom-up approach continues. Both exercises are often carried out separately, with no mechanism to reconcile the centrally determined limits with the budget demands of the spending departments. Long delays result so that some countries have started their fiscal year without a budget. Because budget estimates are often initially unrealistic, large variations between the estimates and the actual outturns occur, requiring extensive use of supplementaries. Expenditure control becomes difficult and is compounded by poor accounting procedures and inordinate delays in the compilation of reports. The response of the central authorities is often to introduce additional, often ad hoc, control procedures. The spending agencies become alienated by the lack of consultation and find their management function undermined. The credibility of the whole budget process may be badly impaired.

Budget Execution

In advanced countries, the trend in budget execution has been toward broadening managerial flexibility, to promote managerial initiative and efficiency. There is no evidence that developing countries are following this trend. In fact, all indications are that the balance has tilted toward the central units and away from the spending agencies. One of the most noticeable side effects of crisis management is an excessive concentration of decision making at the center and, in the guise of greater control and accountability, a multiplication of central checks and controls. This has had two unfortunate effects. First, substituting verification controls for adequate policy control may be time consuming and wasteful of resources. Second, it has prevented the spending agencies from fully appreciating resource constraints and has eroded their management function. It is often felt that in many developing countries overcentralization has hindered their ability to manage fiscal stress.

Similarly, there is little evidence of improved cash management in developing countries. Poorly developed tax administrations find it difficult to impose taxes at source, and typically pay-as-you earn schemes are restricted to a small part of public sector employees. Many developing countries are characterized by poor accounting for the transfers to the rest of the public sector. The low level of administrative capacity in developing countries and deficient accounting have generally precluded the full implementation of control procedures. As a consequence, central agencies struggle to meet overall financing targets while spending agencies entrusted with check issuing powers build up balances in their accounts with advances from the central budget. Prolonged fiscal stress has made matters worse by forcing administrators to focus on expenditure control to the exclusion of other objectives, such as improving efficiency in cash management. In developing countries, this control has been concentrated on the last stages of the budget process rather than at the budget preparation and commitment stages. The payment process has become solely an instrument of control, as evidenced by the popularity of the use of cash limits. In some countries, in order to comply with these limits, checks issued are not permitted to be cashed, resulting in inordinate delays and/or underpayment to contractors. It is apparent that, to a great extent, budgetary procedures in developing countries have been undermined by crisis management, where decisions are made in a reactive rather than proactive fashion.

IMPLICATIONS FOR LONG-RUN STRUCTURAL ADJUSTMENT

Policies that help a country ease its fiscal stress may not necessarily help promote structural reforms. Although both types of policy should be complementary, in practice they often seem to conflict in the short-run. In a typical structural reform package, reforming the trade and exchange system usually involves a depreciation of the exchange rate with resulting extra costs to the budget for imported inputs and foreign debt service. This trend may be counteracted by increased revenues from foreign trade, but in heavily indebted countries where foreign interest payments are a large part of the budget, the net effect on the fiscal position may often be negative, at least in the short-run. Tariff reform usually involves lowering the level of effective protection granted to inefficient industries to encourage a better allocation of resources. But the lowering of average tariff rates is likely to result in a loss of revenue. Financial liberalization typically includes a rise in interest rates to encourage domestic savings. The indirect effect is to increase the costs of government domestic debt service.

In most developing countries with a large inefficient parastatal sector, structural reform requires some restructuring of public enterprises. Again, this may impose short-run costs on the budget. For example, commercialization or privatization of public enterprises has sometimes involved government in expensive initial restructuring or capitalization costs. Moreover, it may take enterprises some time to adjust to the increased costs incurred by combined effects of exchange rate flexibility, tariff reform, and interest rate liberalization.

In the meantime, there will be political pressure not to allow enterprises to adjust their prices immediately, increasing the need for budgetary support.

Finally, many developing countries suffer from high-debt burdens, and so structural reform often contains a debt rescheduling package as one of its preconditions. However, this has generally resulted in additional short-term costs to the budget, increasing the potential for fiscal stress. Governments may have to assume the debt of others (often not just those of the public sector or other levels of government) or settlement of arrears. In many cases, this exercise, combined with liberalization of the trade and exchange system, has implied substantial short-term foreign exchange losses for the central bank. Again, the budget suffers either through reduced profit remittances from the central bank or increased government transfers to the central bank to cover these losses.

In this conflict between short-term stabilization imperatives induced by fiscal stress and the longer-run objective of easing the budget constraint by structural reform, it is possible that the former may win out. The need for structural adjustment would seldom carry the same sense of urgency, its results would be less obvious and more gradual, and its reforms are likely to inflict visible damage on a few and bring less obvious benefits to the many.

Three features may illustrate how the management of fiscal stress may hamper structural adjustment: the types of spending cut, the manner in which expenditure cuts have been carried out, and the impediments policies have created to sustaining any structural reforms that have been introduced.[7]

Type of Expenditures Cut

Although the evidence is far from conclusive, it appears that stress-induced cuts in expenditure typically have fallen on operations and maintenance spending or delaying or cancelling capital projects rather than in cutting the wage bill, entitlements, or other consumer subsidies. This change in the composition of spending most probably diminishes economic growth in the rest of the economy.[8] Any slowing down in the economy's growth increases the potential for future fiscal stress, so making longer-term budgetary viability more difficult to sustain. Moreover, many structural reforms initially necessitate increased investment or capital transfers, and these will now be more difficult to carry out.

The Way Cuts Are Implemented

It may be argued it is not just the type of expenditure cuts that handicaps structural reforms but the manner in which they are implemented. Three typical approaches to cutting back expenditures in developing countries are strategies for reducing the wage bill, ways of containing transfers to lower levels of government, and adjusting the procedures used for controlling spending levels.

In many developing countries, the size of the wage bill has been tackled not by rationalizing the size and salary structure of the civil service but by hiring and salary freezes (for a contrary example, see Ghana in World Bank 1988). This policy may also attempt to protect the lowest income groups from the consequences of salary freezes, usually resulting in a narrowing of civil service pay differentials. The long-term consequence of such policies is to undermine the civil service, as the best people leave first, diluting the quality of administration, and weakening its capacity for implementing longer-term adjustment reforms.[9]

Another approach is to change the central government's relationship with lower levels of government and its transfers to them. In most developing countries, due to the narrow tax base and lack of tax administration capacity at the local level, the central government has always been required to cover the difference between local government revenues and expenditures. With a slow-down in the growth of the economy, this gap in local government finances has increased, while the ability of the central government to fill the gap has declined. To tackle this problem, central governments have increased the regulation of local government finance in a number of different ways (for a review of the European experience, see Meadows 1987). A common approach has been to exert downward pressure on local government spending by influencing the revenues accruing to them and constraining their borrowing activity. Another approach has been to reduce central government subsidization of local services by cutting transfers and allowing them to make up the difference from their own resources. A third, and more indirect approach, is to reassign responsibility for the provision of certain services between various levels of government, usually taking over the service at a higher level, often the central government, where the center has more direct control. All such tactics have generally been reinforced by an intensification of consultation between different levels of government, allowing for increased moral suasion. In sum, the impact of fiscal stress has been to encourage more centralized decision making and control over spending.

However, it is often claimed that decentralization is one of the best ways to ensure the government provides those services the public wants and to ensure the bureaucracy is motivated to provide them. Decentralization, it is argued, not only allows a regional variety of services to be provided, but one that is in line with local preferences. Proximity to the public and increased transparency of their actions is supposed to make local governments more responsive to public needs, which in turn are satisfied by smaller bureaucracies which are easier to administer efficiently. These potential gains of decentralization should not be over stressed in developing countries where decentralization may only open up more layers of corruption and absorb more scarce skills. But on balance, it could be argued that, in responding to fiscal stress, the longer-run allocative benefits of a more decentralized expenditure policy have been lost.

To restrain expenditures in the face of limited administrative capacity and a defective accounting system, many developing countries have adopted "fast fixes," like the imposition of aggregate cash limits. The result has often been the accumulation of substantial outstanding obligations due for payment by government which it has difficulty in discharging (see Diamond and Schiller 1987).

Arrears allow a government to exceed that level of resource absorption that the private sector would be willing to finance voluntarily either through taxation or domestic lending. This short-run effect will be offset in the longer-run by the rest of the economy limiting the resources it transfers to the government by holding back tax payments and other fees and charges. Indeed, there is danger of a complicated web of cross-arrears emerging, involving the government, the public enterprise sector, and the private sector, and possibly foreign official and commercial creditors. The disruption to normal business transactions that this may create, depending on the size of the arrears problem, may have a serious impact on the confidence of private enterprises and households. Private consumers and investors might anticipate increases in nominal tax rates, inflation, or more generally, a deterioration in the financial situation of the country over the medium term, with long-run consequences for economic growth.

Over time, and in the face of further arrears by the government, those economic agents providing goods and services to the government may begin to adjust their pricing and production behavior to take account of payment delays. Vendors dealing with government may begin to charge higher prices to make up for refinancing costs, impose a risk premium, and pay bribes to speed up the payment process. Thus, governments may have to pay prices above the market price and, with limited budgetary outlays, be forced to reduce the quantities of goods and services purchased. If the creation of arrears takes place at a very late stage of the expenditure process, it may increase the stock of outstanding checks beyond the normal check float and beyond the government's short-term capacity to honor them, thus directly promoting inflation. Since government checks are highly liquid, significant monetary effects may be expected. In some African countries, these checks have circulated at a discount and are the equivalent of an increase in broad money. If the demand for money does not grow at the same pace, eventually this will create pressure on prices and the balance of payments and add to the macroeconomic stress. Obviously, it is difficult to undertake longer-run structural reforms in such an environment.

Problems in Sustaining Adjustment

It may also be argued that fiscal stress weakens the ability of developing countries to *sustain* any structural reform once introduced. By magnifying existing administrative and procedural constraints to adjustment and by introducing a greater degree of uncertainty in fiscal planning, fiscal stress creates an environment inimical to maintaining policies of long-term structural adjustment.

An obvious institutional constraint arises because the bureaucracy, charged with implementing the structural reforms, would in many cases be negatively affected by them. Although the bureaucracy has been persistently targeted and although administrative functions often appear excessive and overstaffed to the outsider they are surprisingly resistant to cutbacks.[10] A number of obstacles to bureaucratic retrenchments are often encountered. Among them are the many statutory and other obligations that units may be required to discharge, political resistance to threatened programs and agencies, and lack of detailed knowledge of the inner workings of the spending departments by the central agencies. Unfortunately, this resistance to change puts a brake on other structural reforms. Unless the civil service is somehow restructured, preferably by reducing numbers and increasing average pay and differentials to attract needed skills, there is often little incentive administratively to undertake structural reforms in other areas. Crisis conditions of fiscal stress are unlikely to be the ideal environment for the introduction of a major reform of the civil service.

Even if the bureaucracy could see a net gain in supporting structural measures, the budgetary procedures it employs are often ill-equipped to deal with fiscal stress. For example, it is not unusual for foreign exchange budgets, usually formulated by the central bank, to be poorly coordinated with regular budgeting procedures at the ministry of finance. In many countries, there is evidence of equipment lying unutilized or construction not completed because of a lack of foreign exchange. The budgetary consequences of this lack of coordination are aggravated by a typical underestimation of the degree of adjustment required in the exchange rate in the process of adjustment. Similar inadequacies found in budgeting for domestic inputs in highly inflationary conditions make the budgetary process particularly vulnerable to the pressures of fiscal stress.

In part, the failure of budgetary procedures to support the sustainability of structural reforms arises from the crisis environment. In crisis management, immediate problems may be so compelling that managers focus solely on them and fail to develop capacity for a longer-term perspective.[11] In many reform programs, special organizations or units are set up and assigned responsibility for specific activities. These bypass government institutions that will have to assume responsibility for them in the long-run. While such units may be more effective at initiating reforms, it later becomes more difficult to sustain them.

Crisis management also tends to promote an authoritarian, technocratic, and centralized bias in management. This institutional response may be appropriate for the short-run problems originating in fiscal stress but not for structural adjustment, which requires the support of broader circles of policymakers. The negative effect of centralization on the management function of the spending departments is aggravated by the central units having to impose sudden and unanticipated changes in funding in a way that is most disruptive to the long-run budgetary process. The effect is to alienate further the spending agencies and undermine the credibility of the whole budgetary process.

TOWARD AN AGENDA FOR EASING FISCAL STRESS

It is important to tailor the strategy to deal with fiscal stress to the specific situation of each country and in particular to the type of fiscal stress that it is experiencing (i.e. short-run, cyclical, or structural).

Fiscal policy should be more closely integrated with overall macroeconomic strategy and should focus both on finding ways of increasing resources (e.g., structural changes in the tax system, greater reliance on user charges) and cutting expenditures (e.g., altering the mix between the public and private provision of services, greater commercialization of public enterprises to cut transfers to them). Whichever route is chosen, it is important that policymakers remind the public of the link between maintaining expenditure levels and increasing revenues and clarify the implications of these different approaches. If, as seems inevitable, it is decided that the growth in expenditures is to be reduced, a strategy must be devised to avoid the qualitative deterioration in the composition of expenditures which has characterized past periods of fiscal stress and jeopardized the development effort. In particular, countries should guard against the over reliance on cuts in operations and maintenance and capital spending which has been a complaint voiced about the ad hoc approach used in the past. At the same time, a number of issues common to many developing countries need to be addressed to reorient their budgetary systems so as to make them more capable of dealing with fiscal stress.

First, there is need to improve the balance between the central units and the spending agencies, excessive concentration of decision making at the center and a multiplication of central checks and controls. Second, there is a need to establish or re-establish long-term budgeting capability. The overwhelming concern with solutions to immediate crises has often undermined the effectiveness of budgetary procedures in dealing with fiscal stress. In particular, the overemphasis on the payment process as a means of control has meant neglect of more careful resource planning that would obviate the need for imposing cash limits and other increasing inefficient uses of resources. More attention should be placed on policy planning, and the introduction of multi-year rolling expenditure plans and cash management should be restored to its correct purpose of managing the government's finances.

Third, there is a need to develop more fully a financial information system for fiscal policymakers. This generally involves a redesign of accounting systems away from their traditional verification and recording function into more policy-oriented uses. Emphasis should be placed on providing timely and useful data for policy and control purposes.

Fourth, to promote more orderly financial management crises should be anticipated rather than resolved in crisis conditions. One approach is to develop detailed contingency plans. While large components of government spending, such as the wage bill, pensions, and debt service, cannot be cut, among remaining items, there is scope for assigning priorities, preferably with the collaboration of the spending departments involved. For example, it may be possible to distinguish among ongoing programs, expansion in selected programs, and new programs and projects. It should be possible to identify possible economies and plan for cuts on an ascending scale among these categories if the level of available resources turns out to be lower than programmed. In this way, the ministry of finance will be able to effect economies in an orderly manner with the minimum disruption to government programs as a whole.

Finally, it is important to differentiate inadequate institutional procedures from the manner in which administrators operate them. It is apparent that to a great extent procedures are being undermined by crisis management, partly associated with strains on the budgetary system because of extreme external conditions and related uncertainty imposing strains on the budgetary system. However, perhaps to a greater extent, the explanation lies in inadequate administrative skills that often preclude more imaginative and efficient longer-term approaches to fiscal stress management. To rectify this situation will require a heavy investment in training and technical assistance. It is gratifying to note that technical assistance, both multilateral and bilateral, has increased substantially in the past decade. Unfortunately, given the lengthy gestation period in implementing institutional reforms, its payoff in terms of easing fiscal stress has yet to be felt.

NOTES

1. A common intermediary situation is where the government operates marketing boards or stabilization funds. Typically, when world prices rose, these marketing boards did not raise the prices they paid to producers proportionately. For the case of Côte d'Ivoire, see Schiller (1989).

2. For example, Botswana, Cameroon, and Indonesia managed their boom revenues cautiously, easing adjustment in the downswing. See World Bank (1988, p. 73).

3. Tabellini (1985) argues from a sample of 48 non-oil developing countries that their inadequate fiscal adjustment to the 1979 shocks, in turn due to the easy availability of eurodollar loans, may have been an important cause of later external debt-servicing difficulties.

4. For example, by 1985 Argentina, Columbia, the Dominican Republic, Mexico, and the Philippines had all achieved a fiscal surplus if one excludes interest payments. However, there was a lot less improvement in the conventional deficit due to the burden of interest payments on foreign debt accumulated in the earlier fiscal expansion. For example, Argentinean interest payments on external debt were equivalent to 17.1 percent of current public revenues in 1985,

while in Mexico it was 12.9 percent. A more comprehensive view of these fiscal developments in Latin America can be found in Tanzi (1989b).

5. The following discussion is based on Heller and Diamond (1990, Table 4, p. 19, Table 8, p. 28) and is based on the averages of different regions. Within regions there are considerable inter-country differences in response which vary according to type of expenditure examined. It remains an open question whether the concept of a region employed here is the most significant one in differentiating expenditure patterns. For example, for certain types of expenditure, it may make more sense to differentiate the sub-Sahel from other parts of Africa.

6. The problem of identifying defense spending is not an easy one. In many developing countries, internal security and defense spending are often difficult to separate, and often spending on public order and safety is not separately identified but included under general administration. With these considerations in mind, this section deals with both categories.

7. For a comprehensive review of how reductions in the deficit can be largely cosmetic and qualitatively dubious, see Tanzi's discussion of the quality of fiscal adjustment (Tanzi 1989a).

8. Although, this is far from conclusive. For some evidence on the role of the composition of government spending on the growth of the economy, see Diamond (1990).

9. It has previously been noted that another approach, that of across-the-board cuts, although spreading the pain of adjusting to fiscal stress, is unlikely to be the most efficient means of cutting spending, tending to be disruptive and discriminatory, and so unlikely to aid structural adjustment.

10. As Tanzi has pointed out, "There is evidence, from some countries, that cuts in real wages have been accompanied by expansions in public sector employment" (1990, p. 16). This is largely a consequence of the government being viewed as the employer of last resort.

11. As Tanzi has pointed out, "A fundamental and common conflict that arises in adjustment programs is the one between the need to achieve quick results and the time necessary to develop, legislate, *and* implement sound policies: The need for quick results is often promoted by (a) the precariousness of the economic situation (rising inflation, exhausted foreign exchange reserves, building up arrears); (b) the fear that if changes are not made immediately, they will not be made; and (c) by arrangements with international institutions which are often time-constrained" (1990, p. 20). Unfortunately, if these structural issues are not addressed, they generally become more intractable.

REFERENCES

Bean, C.R., and W.H. Buiter. 1987. *The Plain Man's Guide to Fiscal and Financial Policy.* London: The Employment Institute.

Chu, K. 1987. "External Shocks and the Process of Fiscal Adjustment in a Small Open Developing Economy." WP/87/11, International Monetary Fund, Washington, DC.

Citrin, J. 1979. "Do People Want Something for Nothing: Public Opinion on Taxes and Government Spending." *National Tax Journal* 32 (Supplement): 113-130.

Diamond, J. 1990. "Government Expenditure and Growth." *Finance and Development* 27(4): 34-36.

Diamond, J., and C. Schiller. 1987. "Government Arrears in Fiscal Adjustment Programs." *Finanzarchiv* 45(2): 229-259.

Doss, C.B., and R.F. Wacht. 1989. *Fiscal Triage for Government.* Atlanta: Georgia State University Business Press.

Gupta, S., and K. Miranda. 1991. "Commodity Booms and Government Expenditure Responses." Unpublished paper, International Monetary Fund, Washington, DC.

Hafeez, S. 1984. "Patterns of Reduction in Sectoral Government Expenditures in Less Developed Countries: A Preliminary Investigation." Mimeo, CPD.

Heller, P.S., and J. Diamond. 1990. "International Comparisons of Government Expenditure Revisited: The Developing Countries, 1975-86." *Occasional Paper* No. 69, International Monetary Fund, Washington DC.

Hicks, N. 1989. "Expenditure Reductions in High-Debt Countries." *Finance and Development* 26 (March): 35-37.

Hicks, N., and A. Kubisch. 1984. "Cutting Government Expenditures in LDCs." *Finance and Development* 21(3): 37-39.

Levine, C.H. Ed. 1980. *Managing Fiscal Stress: The Crisis in the Public Sector*. Chatham, NJ: Chatham House.

Mansfield, C. 1980. "Tax Base Erosion During Inflation in a Controlled Economy: The Ghana Case." Unpublished paper, International Monetary Fund, Washington, DC.

Meadows, W.J. 1987. "The Response of Local Authorities to Central Government Incitement to Reduce Expenditure." Public Finance Foundation Discussion Paper No. 16.

Meyers, K. 1986. "A Reappraisal of the Sectoral Incidence of Government Expenditure Cutbacks." *CPD Discussion Paper* No. 1986-11.

Omelehinwa, E., and E.M. Roe. 1989. "Boom and Bust Budgeting: Repetitive Budgetary Processes in Nigeria, Kenya, and Ghana." *Public Budgeting and Finance* 9(2): 43-65.

Organization for Economic Cooperation and Development. 1988. "Measuring Performance and Allocating Resources." *OECD Public Management Studies* 5 (May): 1-8.

Schiller, C. 1989. "The Fiscal Role of Price Stabilization Funds: The Case of Côte d'Ivoire." *Journal of International Development* 1(3): 297-320.

Schneider, R.R. 1987. "Fiscal Adjustment Under Fund-Supported Adjustment Programs." Unpublished paper, International Monetary Fund, Washington, DC.

Tabellini, G. 1985. "Fiscal Policy Response to the External Shocks of 1979 in Selected Developing Countries: Theory and Facts." International Monetary Fund, DM/85/80.

Tanzi, V. 1977. "Inflation Lags in Collection, and the Real Value of Tax Revenue." *Staff Papers* 24(1): 154-167 (International Monetary Fund).

_______ . 1986. "Fiscal Policy Responses to Exogenous Shocks in Developing Countries." *American Economic Review* 76(2): 88-91.

_______ . 1989a. "Fiscal Policy, Growth, and the Design of Stabilization Programs." Pp. 13-32 in *Fiscal policy, Stabilization, and Growth in Developing Countries*, edited by M.I. Blejer and K.Y. Chu. Washington, DC: International Monetary Fund.

_______ . 1989b. "Fiscal Policy and Economic Reconstruction in Latin America." Working paper WP/89/94 pp. 1-33.

IMF. 1990. "Fiscal Issues in Adjustment Programs in Developing Countries." Development Studies Working Papers No. 26.

Terry, F. Ed. 1986. "Local Authority Budgeting Under Stress." Public Finance Foundation Discussion Paper No. 12.

Wolman, H. 1990. "Local Government Strategies to Cope With Fiscal Pressure." Pp. 231-248 in *Managing Fiscal Stress: The Crisis in the Public Sector*, edited by C.H. Levine and I. Rubin. Chatham, NJ: Chatham House.

World Bank. 1988. *World Development Report 1988*. New York: Oxford University Press.

FISCAL ASPECTS OF EXTERNAL DEBT

Martha de Melo

ABSTRACT

An external debt problem has a fiscal dimension that is less well known than its balance of payments dimension. This dimension manifests itself in the fiscal causes of debt accumulation, the fiscal consequences of the debt problem, and the fiscal options for managing the debt burden.

Large or persistent fiscal deficits have created pressures for exceptional external financing just as external shocks have. In either case, if the public sector contracts the external debt, it must repay it. The fiscal burden will vary according to the terms of financing and whether the public or private sector is the debtor. It is not predictable from other, more traditional debt burden indicators such as the ratio of external debt to GDP or the ratio of external debt service to exports.

The fiscal pressures, which are created when the debt is contracted by the public sector, can be dealt with in two stages. The first stage consists of a decision on the desired level of the fiscal deficit. For high-debt countries, the concept of a sustainable deficit, where debt levels are stabilized in real terms, is useful. Where budgetary pressures are strong, this may be the only realistic target. For other countries, it may be possible to move toward a desirable deficit, which reflects a socially-desired debt level. The second stage consists of a decision on the level and composition of budgetary revenues and expenditures for a given fiscal deficit. These decisions are complicated by a variety of fiscal feedback effects from deficit financing and debt-related institutional arrangements.

Policy Studies and Developing Nations, Volume 3, pages 69-89.

ISBN: 1-55938-190-6

The external debt crisis for many developing countries in the 1980s was largely associated with balance of payments problems and related trade and exchange rate policies. As important as these issues are, they tell only part of the story. The other part is told by fiscal policy. To highlight the fiscal dimension of the debt cycle, the fiscal aspects of external debt are considered here, including fiscal causes of an external debt buildup (Section 1), fiscal consequences of the debt problem (Section 2), fiscal options for managing the debt burden (Section 3), and fiscal feedback from traditional financing alternatives and institutional arrangements (Section 4). Section 5 provides a brief conclusion. The term "fiscal" will apply here to the budget of the central government administration, although the analysis could be extended to other parts of the public sector.

FISCAL CAUSES OF DEBT ACCUMULATION

Since the beginning of the debt crisis, considerable attention has been given to the role of external shocks in foreign debt accumulation (see Cuddington 1988 for a review of the causes of debt problems). Balassa (1986), Batista (1987), and Martone (1987), for example, explained foreign borrowing in terms of a variety of external shocks suffered by developing countries, including the 1973 and 1979 increases in the price of oil and the higher real interest rates and slower European economic growth that accompanied the 1979 price rise. Tanzi and Blejer (1986) and Balassa (1988) showed a strong statistical link between foreign borrowing and the budget deficit with pooled cross-country and time-series data, but general recognition that domestic factors were also responsible for the rapid accumulation of external debt lagged. Yet, debt resulting from poor domestic policies needs to be anticipated, since only with anticipation can it be effectively avoided.

One reason why the fiscal causes of debt accumulation received less attention was probably because the typical developed country, frequently used in exploring economic linkages, is characterized by less interdependence between the fiscal and external sectors than the typical developing country.[1] In developing countries, however, the fiscal-external sector link is relatively strong; and it works in both directions. For example, a decline in exports will lead to a drop in budgetary revenue from export or income taxes; and an increase in the price of imported intermediate goods, including oil, may lead to higher subsidies to public enterprises.[2] Working in the other direction, a large fiscal deficit will often lead to a deterioration in the balance of payments, since the use of contractionary monetary policy—and hence the ability to offset the effects of fiscal expansion on aggregate demand—is limited in developing countries. Further deterioration in the balance of payments may result from specific fiscal measures, such as export taxes, taken to reduce the deficit (see Tanzi 1987 for a discussion of this point).

A reasonable assessment of whether a debt buildup has been primarily due to balance of payments shocks can be obtained by looking at the evolution of the trade and finance components of the balance of payments. If the terms of trade, world export demand, and terms of external financing have remained neutral or favorable, one needs to look for domestic causes of external debt accumulation.

The domestic origin of the external debt buildup will often show up as an increase in the ratio of real imports to GDP, resulting from an expansion of public sector demand, an overvalued exchange rate, or a drop in the domestic supply of tradable goods (e.g., due to drought). Where public sector expansion occurs, it may require looking further at who is borrowing and what is being financed. For example, public enterprises may borrow heavily abroad to finance a large public investment program. Alternatively, they may borrow abroad to obtain foreign exchange destined for other government purposes. In the latter case, the fiscal authorities or the central bank will typically act as intermediary, on-lending in local currency and retaining the foreign exchange component. Also, large public enterprises (e.g., utilities) may borrow abroad to finance budgetary arrears to them or to other enterprises that are less credit worthy internationally. Thus, in some cases public enterprises may constitute the origin of a debt problem; in other cases, they may be serving only as a tool to solve a problem that lies elsewhere. Information on budgetary arrears and on the composition of public enterprise borrowing, showing whether enterprises are substituting foreign for domestic credit, can help sort out these questions.

FISCAL CONSEQUENCES OF EXTERNAL DEBT

The Budgetary Problem

Just as attention has switched from external shocks to fiscal deficits as the cause of external debt accumulation, recent studies have focused on "the budgetary problem" (the shortage of budgetary resources), as distinguished from "the foreign exchange problem" (the shortage of foreign exchange), as the consequence of external debt accumulation (see Dornbusch and Fisher 1985; Reisen and Van Trotsenburg 1988; Rodrik 1988).[3] The foreign exchange problem requires an improvement in the country's non-interest external current account deficit in order to generate the foreign exchange necessary to cover net financial transfers—that is, net capital plus net interest payments. The budgetary problem requires an improvement in the non-interest (or primary) fiscal deficit, through a transfer of domestic resources from the private to the public sector, in order to provide the local currency, budgetary counterpart to the government's external debt service obligation. The required transfer can

Table 1. Economic Characteristics of High-Debt Countries, 1985*

	Population (millions)	*Per Capita GNP ($)*	*Export Revenue (% GDP)*	*Budgetary Current Revenue (% GDP)*	*GDP Growth (1982-1986 Avg) (%)*	*Inflation (1982-1986 Avg) (%)*
Argentina	30.6	2120	16.0	11.2	0.2	390.4
Bolivia	6.4	490	12.2	7.7	-2.9	2711.5
Burkina Faso	7.9	150	26.6	12.8	6.8	3.1
Chile	12.1	1450	29.2	26.2	-0.1	21.3
Côte D'Ivoire	10.3	630	45.8	39.7	1.8	5.6
Dominican Republic	6.4	760	35.7	11.8	0.8	17.6
Ecuador	9.4	1150	20.8	17.1	2.1	29.4
Egypt	48.5	640	28.0	28.7	6.7	10.0
Greece	9.9	3620	23.6	20.6	1.5	20.2
Hungary	10.6	1940	50.4	36.7	1.5	5.3
Kenya	20.4	300	26.7	20.3	3.1	10.6
Korea	41.1	2160	38.1	17.2	8.5	4.2
Madagascar	10.2	240	14.5	13.3	1.0	17.0
Malawi	7.1	170	24.9	22.2	3.4	11.3
Mali	7.4	150	27.1	13.1	4.2	3.9
Mexico	78.5	2200	16.2	14.2	-0.5	68.3
Morocco	21.9	560	34.8	22.9	4.4	7.2
Niger	6.4	240	17.5	10.7	-1.1	3.4
Peru	19.4	1010	21.6	14.0	0.9	106.1
Philippines	55.8	570	24.4	11.2	-1.1	17.9
Portugal	10.2	1970	48.4	32.6	1.8	22.0
Senegal	6.6	370	33.1	18.8	4.3	9.6
Somalia	5.4	270	5.8	5.4	0.4	40.7
Sri Lanka	15.8	380	32.4	22.3	3.8	12.0
Sudan	21.9	280	19.9	10.5	-0.1	33.1
Tanzania	22.2	300	6.4	15.0	1.7	24.9
Tunisia	7.1	1190	36.5	30.7	2.8	8.2
Venezuela	17.3	3800	28.7	25.6	0.2	8.1
Zaire	30.7	160	45.0	19.0	1.2	52.5
Zambia	6.7	410	38.6	21.9	-0.7	33.4
Zimbabwe	8.4	640	27.6	27.8	2.1	12.7
Average	18.5	978.1	27.6	19.4	1.9	120.0
Without Argentina, Bolivia, and Peru						18.3

Note: * High-debt countries have population greater than 5 million and a ratio of external debt to GDP greater than 0.5.

Sources:	
Inflation	World Bank, implicit GDP deflator
Export Revenue	World Bank, (1990) export of goods and services, plus workers' remittances
Population	World Bank (1990)
GDP Growth	World Bank (1990)
Per Capita GNP	World Bank (1990)
Budgetary Revenue	IMF *Government Finance Statistics Yearbook* (1987) and country-specific data

Table 2. Economic Characteristics of Low-Debt Countries, 1985*

	Population (millions)	*Per Capita GNP ($)*	*Export Revenue (% GDP)*	*Budgetary Current Revenue (% GDP)*	*GDP Growth (1982-1986 Avg) (%)*	*Inflation (1982-1986 Avg) (%)*
Algeria	21.7	2550	24.6	37.6	3.9	4.4
Bangladesh	100.6	150	10.6	9.5	3.4	11.0
Brazil	135.6	1670	12.8	9.3	4.1	168.6
Cameroon	10.2	840	31.7	15.3	7.4	8.5
Colombia	28.4	1350	13.5	9.0	2.9	24.0
Ethiopia	42.3	110	11.7	22.8	0.8	3.3
Guatemala	8.0	1190	10.7	7.7	-1.2	15.2
India	765.1	290	7.3	13.6	5.1	7.5
Indonesia	163.4	520	23.7	20.4	3.1	7.3
Myanmar	36.9	190	11.3	13.6	4.6	1.7
Nepal	16.6	170	12.1	8.7	11.8	1.7
Nigeria	99.7	950	14.4	11.2	-0.8	8.0
Pakistan	96.2	340	19.5	16.0	6.6	7.5
Rwanda	6.0	280	10.0	12.2	2.5	4.4
Syria	10.5	1610	13.0	24.1	0.6	8.4
Thailand	51.7	810	27.4	15.7	5.3	2.3
Turkey	50.3	1080	24.8	16.8	5.5	36.5
Yemen	8.0	670	23.9	17.2	10.5	12.9
Yugoslavia	23.1	2060	36.1	5.3	1.1	58.5
Average	88.1	885.8	17.9	15.0	4.1	20.6
Without Brazil						12.4

Note: *Low-debt countries have population greater than 5 million and a ratio of external debt to GDP less than 0.5.

Sources:

Inflation	World Bank (1990), implicit GDP deflator
Export Revenue	World Bank (1990), export of goods and services, plus workers' remittances
Population	World Bank (1990)
GDP Growth	World Bank (1990)
Per Capita GNP	World Bank (1990)
Budgetary Revenue	IMF *Government Finance Statistics Yearbook* (1987) and country-specific data

be made by increasing revenues or reducing expenditures. It will need to be larger the higher budgetary external debt service is and the lower the increased revenues from activities financed by foreign borrowing are.

Budgetary and Other Characteristics of High-Debt Countries

Tables 1 and 2 highlight some economic characteristics of high-debt and low-debt countries, where high-debt countries are defined as having a total external debt to GDP ratio greater than 50 percent, and low-debt countries are defined as having an external debt to GDP ratio less than 50 percent. The role of exports and budgetary revenue are shown for one year, 1985, and GDP growth and inflation are shown for a five-year period, 1982-1986. The countries shown are limited to those with population greater than 5 million. The averages shown are unweighted.

The variation in country characteristics is quite wide on both tables, but on average GDP growth is substantially lower and inflation is higher in high-debt countries, suggesting that the excessive debt levels are at least partially responsible. One striking difference is the average ratio of exports to GDP, which is 28 percent for high-debt countries and only 18 percent for low-debt countries—suggesting that creditors put strong emphasis on their clients' foreign exchange liquidity. (Since smaller countries tend to be more open, it is not surprising that average population is lower in high-debt countries—19 million compared to 88 million.) The difference between Tables 1 and 2 in average government liquidity, as indicated by the ratio of budgetary current revenue to GDP, is far less—with central governments in high-debt countries mobilizing an average of 19 percent of GDP, compared to an average of 15 percent of GDP in low-debt countries. This difference is consistent with the point made above that most observers, including creditors, are more aware of and concerned about the foreign exchange problem than the budgetary problem.

The Fiscal Burden Arising From Debt Service

Traditionally, bankers as well as economists have looked at various ratio indicators of the external debt burden to assess a country's ability to service its debt. Two widely used indicators are total debt service to exports and total debt to GDP. The former is a good indicator of liquidity—that is, a country's current ability to accommodate the foreign exchange requirements of the existing debt on the agreed terms. The latter is a good indicator of solvency—that is, a country's future ability to pay off its debt claims, abstracting from the terms of borrowing. In recent years, preference has been expressed for the ratio of debt to exports as an indicator of both liquidity and solvency. (See Cohen 1988 for a recommended composite indicator of credit worthiness based on a weighted average of both the debt/GDP and debt/export ratios.) The variations in indicators are numerous, however, and include net debt to net wealth, real interest payments to GDP, and net financial transfers to GDP, defined as external debt service minus foreign loan disbursements.

None of these indicators measures the budgetary problem, which is a liquidity problem with respect to the domestic currency counterpart of the external debt. Yet, the shortage of budgetary resources suggests a need to include an explicit measure of fiscal burden among the indicators of a country's debt servicing capacity. This is expecially true since the external debt pressures on the budget are likely to contribute to the low growth and high inflation mentioned above. Typically, governments find it difficult to cut non-interest expenditures enough to release sufficient revenues for debt service payments. In the short-run, the budgetary problem is often resolved through monetization of the deficit, which leads to inflation and with it the aggravation of both the budgetary and foreign exchange problems.[4] Inflation may also lead to the heavy use of taxes on financial intermediation services, distorting financial markets and resulting in lower growth. And high inflation and low growth are major obstacles to regaining international creditworthiness (see Easterly 1989; Reisen and Van Trotsenburg 1988 for country-specific studies of these issues).

Table 3 shows a selection of debt burden indicators for the 31 high-debt countries identified in Table 1. The data are for one year only and should be interpreted as period-specific indicators only. The first three columns show the three ratios discussed above: total external debt to GDP, total external debt service to exports, and total external debt to exports. The last two columns show two additional indicators which measure the fiscal burden: the ratio of budgetary external debt service to budgetary current revenues and the ratio of external debt service on total public and publicly-guaranteed medium-and long-term (PPG) debt to budgetary current revenues. The budgetary external debt service ratio indicates the direct fiscal burden of the government's debt service obligations, and the PPG debt service ratio indicates the indirect or potential fiscal burden, as well as the direct budgetary payments on public medium- and long-term external debt.[5] There is substantial variation both among countries and between these indicators for any one country, although normally the PPG debt service ratio is substantially larger than the budgetary debt service ratio. Both ratios can be interpreted as the fiscal effort—in terms of extra revenue collection—required to finance the debt service.

There are two reasons why these fiscal measures are infrequently used in cross-country comparative analysis. As discussed earlier, the existence of the fiscal burden of external debt is less obvious than the existence of the foreign exchange burden. But also, fiscal data are less readily available on a cross-country basis than the debt, GDP, and exports data used for the other measures. Although some cross-country data on central government accounts are in principle available from the IMF's *Government Finance Statistics*, this publication does not distinguish external from domestic interest payments, nor does it provide data on debt amortization. Moreover, there is often a substantial time lag in the availability of the accounts. The data used here on budgetary debt service come from country-specific sources.

Table 3 shows the population-weighted and unweighted averages of each of the external debt burden indicators. The unweighted average gives more importance to smaller countries, and a comparison with the weighted average shows that smaller countries have slightly higher overall external debt ratios than larger countries but virtually the same debt service ratio. Smaller countries also have somewhat higher budgetary debt service ratios; however, the weighted and unweighted averages show the same PPG debt service ratio.

Table 3. External Debt Burden Indicators in High-Debt Countries, 1985 (Percent)

	(1) *External Debt /GDP*	(2) *Debt Service /Exports*	(3) *External Debt /Exports*	(4) *Budgetary Debt Service /Budgetary Revenue*	(5) *PPG Debt Service /Budgetary Revenue*
Argentina	77.4	59.3	485.4	22.0	31.4
Bolivia	80.3	47.9	660.1	6.2	55.4
Burkina Faso	50.6	11.8	190.0	15.7	19.0
Chile	127.4	45.8	436.6	7.6	26.6
Côte d'Ivoire	140.2	37.9	306.1	23.5	25.4
Dominican Republic	78.7	18.1	220.5	10.8	32.2
Ecuador	54.0	44.8	259.5	11.1	31.2
Egypt	84.7	26.2	302.4	4.7	21.8
Greece	55.9	30.3	236.9	13.7	29.9
Hungary	62.2	25.7	123.4	1.7	34.1
Kenya	73.6	43.1	276.0	18.1	29.8
Korea	54.3	26.4	142.4	6.5	32.1
Madagascar	105.0	32.9	722.0	34.3	35.9
Malawi	90.1	35.2	361.1	28.8	32.9
Mali	139.3	20.9	513.0	23.9	24.2
Mexico	52.5	52.2	323.8	13.1	35.3
Morocco	137.4	29.1	394.6	27.6	36.4
Niger	83.9	39.4	477.9	36.5	42.7
Peru	77.8	28.0	361.1	19.4	22.2
Philippines	80.9	30.9	331.9	12.2	34.0
Portugal	80.3	31.4	166.0	10.8	39.4
Senegal	93.9	19.1	284.1	22.9	19.5
Somalia	73.7	34.6	1279.0	34.5	37.1
Sri Lanka	59.2	15.5	182.7	11.0	18.2
Sudan	146.0	11.1	733.2	20.2	14.1
Tanzania	56.1	21.5	880.5	6.5	5.8
Tunisia	59.1	26.1	162.1	11.7	25.7
Venezuela	56.9	27.2	198.2	10.4	17.4
Zaire	134.2	18.6	298.3	47.9	41.1
Zambia	206.5	77.3	534.7	29.8	16.5
Zimbabwe	52.3	32.1	189.4	11.4	42.7
Average					
Unweighted	87.9	32.3	388.2	17.9	29.4
Population Weighted	82.6	33.4	361.6	16.1	29.4

Sources:	
Total External Debt	World Bank (1990)
GDP in Dollars	IMF *International Financial Statistics*
Exports	World Bank (1990), export of goods & services, plus workers' remittances
Debt Service	World Bank (1989-1990), interest and principle on total external debt
Budgetary Debt Service	Country-specific data
Budgetary Revenue	IMF *Government Finance Statistics Yearbook* (1987) and country-specific data
PPG Debt Service	World Bank (1989-1990), interest and principle on public/publicly guaranteed debt

These patterns are relatively easy to explain if one assumes that lenders are more concerned with the short-term liquidity measure, debt service to exports, than with the long-term solvency measure, external debt to GDP. This would mean that they would lend relatively more to smaller countries, which tend to be more open since their economies are less diversified. The higher budgetary ratio for smaller countries is consistent with their higher ratio of external debt to GDP.

A correlation matrix for the five measures of external debt burden in Table 3 shows that most pairwise correlations are positive but low. The highest correlation (0.53) is between the external debt to GDP ratio and the budgetary debt service ratio, which suggests that the external debt ratio might be the best proxy indicator of a budgetary problem in the absence of fiscal data. There is only a low positive correlation between the external debt service ratio on the one hand and the budgetary debt service ratio and the ratio of external debt to GDP on the other. The small negative correlation between the PPG debt service ratio and the two debt ratios suggests that the relative size of contingent fiscal liabilities cannot be assumed on the basis of overall debt levels.

In sum, the measures of external debt burden shown here reflect significantly different constraints—including differences in the terms of borrowing and the share of budgetary debt in total debt—and hence provide complementary rather than redundant information. In particular, the indicators of fiscal burden point to a budgetary problem which cannot be readily anticipated from the other three indicators.

FISCAL OPTIONS

The fiscal options in the face of an external debt overhang can be approached in two stages. The first stage involves a decision about the extent of financing versus adjustment, that is, about the size of the fiscal deficit. The second stage involves a decision about the level and composition of budgetary revenues and expenditures for a given deficit.

Financing Versus Adjustment

The central question in formulating the fiscal response to an external debt problem is deciding on the mix between adjustment and financing. There is, of course, a third option—namely, arrears and eventually default. This option is not explored here.

Financing entails the use of net foreign borrowing, net domestic borrowing, or direct monetization with their associated costs. Adjustment requires increases in revenues or reductions in expenditures affecting the primary (i.e., non-interest) deficit. A definitive answer to the question of the proper mix of options would require a detailed, dynamic general equilibrium model with implicit cost-benefit calculations for each option. Such a model is not feasible, so some simpler decision rules must be applied. Recommended decision criteria to guide the choice of financing versus adjustment have included:

- the domestic or international origin of the debt problem, with more adjustment appropriate if the origin is domestic (Khan and Knight 1983);
- the permanent or temporary character of the debt problem, with more adjustment appropriate if it is permanent (Khan and Knight 1983); and
- the country's preferences for current or future consumption, with more adjustment appropriate if it prefers future consumption (Bird 1982).

But there is no simple rule of thumb which can be used to arrive at the appropriate financing/adjustment mix.

In principle, the budget deficit level should be considered in the context of the deficit of the enlarged public sector—including the central bank, financial and nonfinancial public enterprises, and other extra-budgetary agencies or funds. Easterly (1989) shows, for example, that high-debt countries in crisis are characterized by continuing high deficits of the enlarged public sector, even though the budgetary primary deficits in these countries were reduced substantially.

Also, the budget deficit should be evaluated in the context of other macroeconomic policies and private sector behavior. Taylor (1988) discusses some of these linkages which depend on country-specific circumstances and which are frequently poorly understood. They include the possible complementarity of public and private investment, the possible contractionary effect of a devaluation on private sector demand, and the possible adverse distributional effects of reduced food subsidies or higher prices for publicly provided goods and services. If those considerations are kept in mind, and if all financing services are considered, the sustainable deficit approach and the desirable deficit approach can be used to arrive at the first stage decision. They are discussed in turn below.

The Sustainable Deficit Approach

In recent years, substantial attention has been given to defining a sustainable deficit for the government budget as a pragmatic approach to the financing/adjustment choice.[6] This approach can be interpreted as minimizing adjustment subject to feasible financing. The sustainable deficit says nothing about impact on economic growth; it simply indicates the maximum deficit consistent with target debt levels and a target inflation rate. It is formulated in terms of the primary deficit, where expenditures exclude interest payments.[7] The main idea is that a *sustainable* primary deficit occurs when initial levels of foreign and domestic debt are maintained and monetary financing is compatible with a target inflation rate. Its appeal is that it incorporates the decision criteria for how to finance as well as how much to finance.

The sustainable deficit is a convenient analytical tool in that it includes some of the fiscal feedback effects explained more fully in the following section. For example, as the real domestic interest rate rises, the decision rule calls for a reduction in domestic borrowing. Also, as export growth drops below the cost of foreign borrowing, the decision rule calls for a reduction in net foreign borrowing—limiting external debt servicing and hence the need for future real devaluations arising from the debt burden. By specifying the depressing effect of higher inflation on the demand for money (and hence seigniorage), it would also be possible to show the less than proportionate rise in allowable monetary financing with higher inflation.

Of course, the real world does not conform quite so neatly to simplifications. The sustainability criteria are only crude indicators and must be interpreted with caution. Real export growth, for example, should be defined in principle for net exports. This is particularly important for a country that is converting from primary product exports to manufactured exports, where the latter have a high import content. Also, expected growth rates and costs of borrowing should reflect likely medium- to long-term outcomes, rather than near-term potential or government targets. And money creation through the budget must be evaluated in the context of money creation through other means—namely increases in the central bank's net foreign assets and credit to public enterprises and the private sector. Thus, the simple formulation of a sustainable deficit applies to a steady state economy and ignores inevitable fluctuations.

The Desirable Deficit Approach

For many high-debt countries, the sustainable deficit approach may be the only realistic one—at least in the near future. For others, however, it may be possible to move toward a "desirable" deficit. Makin (1987) defines the "desirable" fiscal deficit by a "desirable" debt level—that is, one that permits government to undertake more activities than it could with no debt but that entails an acceptable level of debt service. The rules for setting the appropriate debt to GDP ratio cannot be precisely defined. However, Makin argues that the maintenance of a constant government debt to GDP ratio, regardless of its level, represents a neutral fiscal stance, which could be modified by prudent countercyclical adjustments.[8] Once the government debt to GDP target, Ω, has been chosen, the size of the desirable primary deficit can be set to keep it constant. It is similar to the previous expression for a sustainable deficit except that it does not take the existing debt level as the desirable one, hence the important role of an adjustment factor in establishing the targets for a debt repayment (buildup) rate.

There is no theoretical basis for choosing Ω; however, some important considerations can be identified. First, the proposed desirable debt level, which might be influenced by its historical level, should reflect a consensus among responsible government officials confirmed by legislative action. Second, as pointed out in the sustainable deficit approach, the ratio of central government debt to GDP should be seen in the context of (1) the debt ratios of public enterprises and the private sector and (2) private investment, and hence economic growth, which will be discouraged if higher overall public debt is accompanied by higher real interest rates or even partially anticipated tax increases. And third, the government debt ratio should ideally be set sufficiently low to keep the claim of debt servicing on government revenues at a comfortable level and to provide a comfortable margin in the securities markets for emergency use, in the case of natural disasters or major economic declines.

Once the appropriate debt ratio has been decided, the choice of financing by domestic or foreign borrowing must be made. There may be important considerations besides relative borrowing costs—including foreign credit availability and/or short-term foreign exchange needs—but costs are an important factor. In a fully integrated financial market—for example, in the United States—the nominal cost of borrowing by the government will be the domestic cost of risk-free funds, which should approximate the international borrowing rate adjusted by the expected nominal devaluation of the domestic currency relative to the debt-denominated currency. Thus, the choice of borrowing in the foreign versus the domestic market is irrelevant, if the actual devaluation equals the expected devaluation. At the other end of the financial liberalization continuum—for example, in many less developed countries—financial markets are strongly segmented and the costs of borrowing domestically and abroad may differ widely. In this latter case, cost minimization should be an important decision criterion in the choice of foreign versus domestic borrowing.

The costs of domestic borrowing can be calculated by taking a weighted average of the various debt instruments and their associated costs. The average foreign cost of borrowing is more complex but can be calculated by summing its three components—the weighted average cost of foreign borrowing expressed in a single currency such as U.S. dollars, the percent change in the local currency/$ nominal exchange rate, and the percent revaluation of dollar debt due to changes in cross-currency rates between the dollar and other debt-denominated currencies. The first component is a cash cost; the second and third components are accrued costs (or benefits), which must be taken into account in estimating the resource costs to the economy of foreign borrowing.

In sum, an assessment of relative borrowing costs in the future requires a judgment on likely movements in cross-currency exchange rates as well as likely movements in the country's own exchange rate vis-à-vis the major debt-denominated currency. It is perhaps because of the difficulty of these judgments that insufficient attention appears to be given to these costs comparisons in practice. A careful evaluation of the likely marginal costs of borrowing in domestic and foreign markets may, however, lead to useful shifts in the government's existing debt portfolio.

The Level and Composition of Budgetary Revenues and Expenditures

Once the deficit has been decided on, an infinite variety of levels and compositions of revenues and expenditures will be found compatible with it. For developing countries, it is not possible to generalize about optimum levels. Growth will depend more on the quality of the revenue and expenditure programs than their levels (World Bank 1988). Somewhat more can be said about the appropriate composition of revenues and expenditures—although the final choice will inevitably reflect social concerns, political acceptability, historical allocations, and implementation capacity, as well as efficiency and growth criteria. Nevertheless, some general principles have been accepted.

Revenue-raising can be achieved by increasing the tax rate, broadening the tax base, improving tax administration, and increasing user charges and other public sector prices. At the aggregate level, some insight into a country's revenue-raising potential can be obtained through cross-country information on tax/GDP ratios and tax buoyancy leading to rough rules of thumb. With respect to specific proposals, broadening the tax base and improving administration are preferred to increasing the tax rate, which may have negative incentives or lead to evasion (see Chelliah 1987). Also, there is some evidence that a revenue-neutral shift from import taxes and personal and corporate levies to sales or excise taxes may increase growth rates in developing countries (Skinner 1988). Cost recovery pricing of public services can be beneficial by providing appropriate signals for conservation and resource allocation; however, raising prices for revenue purposes alone can be problematic on the same grounds as higher tax rates.

Expenditure reduction can be achieved through improvements in organization, management, and operating efficiency. It can also be achieved through cuts in the government wage bill, which has become inflated in recent years in many countries as a result of the government role as residual employer (Gelb, Knight, and Sabot 1988). The need for efficiency argues for cuts in the public wage bill by reducing employment rather than the wage rate since adequate salaries are required to attract and motivate qualified staff (Nunberg 1988). Furthermore, subsidies and transfers established for social purposes can be better targeted, and general government non-wage administrative expenses can be closely monitored for need and effectiveness.

Beyond these principles, it is difficult to say whether rationalization of current and capital expenditures will lead to increased or decreased expenditure levels. Expenditure on operation, maintenance, and even rehabilitation of existing facilities is frequently more cost effective than net investment, although wasteful expenditures for these purposes can also occur. Public investment has been shown to help raise private sector investment and productivity, especially where it is in complementary areas such as infrastructure (Shah 1988). While cuts in unproductive public investment have been salutary, cuts in public investment with high rates of return have undoubtedly had adverse consequences for employment and growth, especially where private investment has lagged.

FISCAL FEEDBACK FROM FINANCING ARRANGEMENTS

Financing arrangements, including traditional deficit financing alternatives and debt-related institutional arrangements, provide secondary budgetary effects which need to be accounted for in budget formulation. Traditional financing alternatives are foreign borrowing, domestic borrowing, and monetary financing. (The use of international reserves and the sale of government assets to finance the budget are generally only available on an exceptional basis and hence are not considered here.) Debt-related institutional arrangements include foreign exchange risk schemes and debt rescheduling or conversion schemes. The fiscal feedback effects from these arrangements are often negative; thus, they need to be taken into account in addressing the budgetary problem associated with high external debt. The difficulty of estimating the ultimate impact, as distinguished from first round effects, should be recognized, however.

Traditional Financing Alternatives

Increased foreign borrowing by the government cycle will have an impact on the real exchange rate, which has secondary effects on the budget. The initial effect of foreign borrowing is to cause a real appreciation of the exchange rate relative to what it would otherwise be. The increase in the demand for domestic goods raises their prices but does not necessarily lead to a devaluation in the nominal exchange rate, since the foreign loan is available to finance additional imports. Following the loan disbursement, the subsequent external debt servicing causes a real depreciation of the exchange rate brought about by the excess demand for foreign exchange to carry out the transfer abroad. Both swings in the real exchange rate create changes in relative prices and can lead to a misallocation of resources, but the focus here is on the budgetary impact of the exchange rate movements.

The conditions under which a depreciation will have a negative secondary effect are suggested by Reisen (1988) and Rodrik (1988). They point out that, if the value of budgetary dollar (or other foreign currency) expenditures minus revenues is less than the net dollar capital inflow minus interest payments, a depreciation will reduce the need for domestic financing.[9] This condition could exist, for example, where the central government receives large revenues from mineral or agricultural commodity exports. However, where dollar expenditures minus revenues are greater than net dollar inflow minus interest payments, a real depreciation in the exchange rate generates a higher need for domestic financing. Under these circumstances, Rodrik suggests that increases in import tariffs—accompanied by export subsidies for the marginal producers—are an appropriate policy alternative to a real devaluation. This is so because tariffs both partially substitute for a real depreciation and raise revenue for the government. If sufficient foreign exchange is available for debt service payments, tariff equivalents could be substituted for quantitative restrictions—thus transferring resources from the private to the public sector without changing trade incentives.[10]

Increased domestic borrowing by the government to finance the local currency counterpart for debt service may also cause a secondary burden through a rise in domestic real interest rates and hence higher interest payments. The government may have to pay higher interest rates to persuade the general public to hold a larger quantity of government debt. Alternatively, the government may require selected lenders to provide funds at a fixed, below-market interest rate, creating for them an implicit tax. Typically, such lenders are public financial institutions which then have reduced funds to on-lend to the private sector; interest rates may increase or credit may be rationed. In either case, government borrowing is likely to result in a higher deficit since private investment will be crowded out, reducing growth and hence the tax base. Additional budgetary effects may result from differential taxation of borrowers and lenders. Under special circumstances, namely where potential workers' remittances or capital flight are being held abroad, these may be attracted by higher domestic interest rates, leading to an increase in the tax base. Such flows, however, will be heavily influenced by perceptions of political and economic stability and are not, in any case, a reliable source of financing.

Finally, excessive monetary financing of the deficit, leading to an inflation tax on money holdings, is likely also to entail negative fiscal feedback effects. Assuming the existence of explicit or implicit taxes on financial intermediation services, inflation contributes to a wedge between lending and deposit rates that undermines the tax base.[11] The high cost of borrowing "crowds out" investment and slows GDP growth (the alternative regime entailing interest subsidies and credit rationing will result in a misallocation of resources); and the low return on domestic financial savings reduces domestic intermediation and leads to capital flight, which in turn results in an erosion of the tax base and an aggravation of the foreign exchange problem.[12]

With single-digit inflation, negative effects from the inflation tax are relatively minor and may be more than compensated by the advantages of an additional tax handle, some flexibility in monetary policy, and the facilitation of changes in relative prices. With double-digit inflation, negative feedback effects appear to gain in importance—leading to a secondary burden which increasingly offsets the convenience of monetary financing. The effects of triple-digit inflation are unquestionably perverse. The inflation tax can also affect the budget in the following ways:

1. It has a negative effect on the primary deficit in that revenue loss from collection lags is typically not offset by revenue gains from bracket creep (the "Tanzi" effect); meanwhile, expenditures tend to rise in line with inflation.[13]
2. It leads to a drop in the demand for real money balances and hence an erosion of seigniorage, or noninflationary increases in the money supply, as a source of deficit financing.
3. If investors are risk-averse, the higher risk caused by higher volatility in relative prices under inflation can lead to reduced investment, and hence lower GDP and tax revenues.[14]
4. The authorities may attempt to dampen inflation by maintaining an overvalued exchange rate and increasing reserve requirements. In the first case, the overvalued exchange rate leads to a general need for high real interest rates to attract funds which might be otherwise held abroad as a result of capital flight (or failure of emigrant workers to remit). In the second case, the higher reserve requirements increase the above mentioned wedge between deposit and lending rates.

Debt-Related Institutional Arrangements

A variety of external-debt-related institutional arrangements affect the fiscal position. Such arrangements include (1) foreign exchange risk guarantee schemes meant to encourage foreign borrowing by public or private enterprises during a period of foreign exchange shortages, and (2) debt rescheduling and conversion schemes designed to alleviate external debt servicing obligations and reduce indebtedness.

Foreign exchange risk guarantee schemes are meant to facilitate, and often encourage, foreign borrowing by public enterprises or development banks by eliminating the risk of increased local currency costs for debt servicing due to changes in the exchange rate. They typically guarantee that external debt servicing can be made at the rate of exchange in effect at the time of the loan agreement. A premium may be charged for this guarantee, but it is usually less than the cost of the guarantee, which will depend on the nominal devaluation of the local currency vis-à-vis the debt-denominated foreign currency. An undervalued premium will lead to both over borrowing and an increasing fiscal burden, as budgetary expenditures are required to make up the difference between the local currency equivalents of the initial and current exchange rates.

Debt reschedulings will typically provide budgetary relief in the short-term; however, total budgetary external debt liabilities may increase if the rescheduling involves debt consolidation. Paris Club reschedulings on existing concessional terms may result not only in lower debt payments in the medium-term but effective debt reduction. London Club reschedulings normally do not entail debt reduction; however, extended maturities can provide important debt relief in the short-term. In either case, debt consolidation may occur and result, for example, in the reassignment of external debt liabilities away from public enterprises or other public agencies onto the budget. Such debt reassignments are made with a strong risk that the budget will not be able to collect the debt service from the previous debt owner.

Debt conversions may have a positive or negative budgetary impact. Although relatively small in comparison with the total amount of debt outstanding, the value of debt conversions affecting central government finances was nevertheless estimated at $15 billion to $20 billion in 1988 (World Bank 1989). The most popular debt conversion scheme is the debt-equity swap. Most debt-equity swaps are for equity in private firms, and these may involve substantial budgetary cost in the short-term when the budget serves as an intermediary. Where public debt is swapped for equity in public enterprises, there may be little or no immediate budgetary effect—only foregone future revenues to the extent that dividends to foreign equity holders will replace dividends claimed by the budget. Also popular are exit bonds, which provide debt or debt service reduction in exchange for some form of credit enhancement for existing debt. Such enhancement may decrease the government's liquidity (e.g., by blocking foreign assets) while reducing the direct budgetary burden associated with the original debt contract. Still another form of debt conversion is the buy back. Normally, a government will be prohibited by the terms of a loan from buying back its own debt; however, more than $600 million in direct buy backs took place in 1988—reducing longer-term debt service at the expense of a discounted fiscal payout in the short-term.[15] The effects of other types of debt conversions—such as debt-for-nature, debt-for-goods, or debt-for-exports—may entail only minimal up-front budgetary costs, although the cumulative effect will depend on the particular conversion scheme and the amount of debt reduction negotiated.

Aside from these international agreements on reschedulings and conversions, governments may engage in their own internal institutional arrangements for debt relief. Sometimes the central bank acts as a payment agent since it typically controls the country's foreign exchange reserves. However, ultimate responsibility for mobilizing the local currency counterpart to external debt servicing will fall to the budget, which may assume servicing responsibility even for private non-guaranteed external debt in order to preserve credit worthiness.

It is difficult to really know how much of a budgetary impact such arrangements have since they may result in a reduction in dividends from, or an increase in budgetary transfers to, the debtor agency—rather than to a direct assumption by the budget of the debt liabilities.

CONCLUSION

The purpose of this chapter has been to highlight the fiscal aspects of external debt. The fiscal problem is distinguished from external shocks as an important cause of the external debt buildup, and it is distinguished from the foreign exchange problem as a consequence of the debt burden.

The absolute levels of budget deficits are not particularly helpful in identifying countries experiencing a fiscal problem related to the debt overhang, because whether a given deficit level can be maintained depends on a number of economy-wide factors—including overall growth in gross domestic product, export growth, and interest rates on domestic and foreign debt. Ideally, one could capture all the relevant factors in a dynamic general equilibrium model of the economy; but in the real world, government officials may find it impractical to derive fiscal policy in this way. Thus, some intermediary approach is required which captures the most important aspects of macroeconomic structure and trends. The concepts of sustainable and desirable deficits can be useful in this process. Once the appropriate level of the deficit is agreed, the costs and limitations of alternative financing options—namely, external debt, domestic debt, and monetary financing approaches—can be explored.

ACKNOWLEDGMENT

I am grateful to Reza Firuzabadi for research assistance. The findings, interpretations, and conclusions expressed in this paper are entirely those of the author. They do not necessarily represent the views of the World Bank, its Executive Directors, or the countries they represent.

NOTES

1. A strong argument against a link between fiscal and external developments is provided by the "rational expectations" view that fiscal deficits do not increase aggregate demand since taxpayers increase their savings in anticipation of future tax liabilities. Few policy-oriented economists subscribe fully to this view, however.

2. Elsewhere in this volume, Jack Diamond also describes the initial build up of external public debt as a common response to fiscal stress arising from balance of payments problems.

3. As these papers point out, the distinction between the budgetary and the foreign exchange problems was a key feature of "transfer" theory, developed by Keynes and others in connection with German reparations after World War I.

4. Inflation may lead to a lag in fiscal revenues, the so-called "Tanzi effect" discussed further in this volume by Diamond, or to a lag in exchange rate adjustments and hence a decline in foreign exchange reserves.

5. In the typical case where the PPG debt service ratio exceeds the budgetary ratio, the excess is largely due to foreign borrowing by public enterprises. Such borrowing is usually a contingent liability of the budget and may provide an indirect burden on the budget in the form of subsidies or capital transfers required by the enterprise to repay the loan. In the few cases where the budgetary debt service ratio exceeds the PPG ratio, the former may include short-term debt or IMF debt (which PPG debt excludes), or the exchange rate used for conversion may differ from the average annual exchange rate used here.

6. Definitions of the sustainable deficit have been proposed by Branson (1988), Buiter (1986, 1988), Spaventa (1986), and Tanzi (1984). Anand and Van Wijnbergen (1987) provide a country application. Cohen (1985) and De Pinies (1989) define maximum sustainable foreign borrowing independently of other budgetary financing.

7. The following expression for the primary deficit of the government budget as a percent of GDP (d) can be derived from the government budget constraint:

$$d = b\,(\Delta y - r) + \beta x\,(\Delta x - (r^{\infty} + \Delta e) + m\,(p + s),$$

where Δy is real GDP growth; b is the ratio of domestic debt to GDP; β is the ratio of foreign debt to exports; x is the ratio of exports to GDP; Δx is real export growth; Δe is the change in the real exchange; r and r^{∞} are real domestic and international interest rates; m is the ratio of base money to GDP; p is the inflation rate; and s is the seigniorage rate, determined by the increase in the real demand for money. See De Melo (1990).

8. Considerable controversy surrounds the definition of a neutral fiscal stance. Most economists make some adjustment in the nominal deficit—if only for full employment—to arrive at a definition of neutral fiscal stance. Adjustments for inflation and capital spending have also been suggested but are not often made.

9. The assumption here is that foreign borrowing can be freely used. If it is tied to specific local cost projects or programs, the budgetary problem, in financial terms, can still occur because expenditures will have to increase to fully use the newly acquired loans.

10. A key assumption for these results is that public sector expenditures are socially valuable and, at the margin, more valuable than private expenditures.

11. Under perfect competition and assuming zero marginal costs of lending, the nominal lending rate, i_l, will equal the deposit rate, i_d, adjusted for the explicit and implicit tax rate on deposits, t: $i_l = (l + t)\, i_d$. Decomposing the nominal interest rates into their real and inflation-premium components ($i_l = r_l + p$ and $i_d = r_d + p$). Substituting terms, the real tax wedge can be defined as: $r_l - r_d = t\, r_d + t\, p$. Thus, the wedge is an increasing function of inflation, the real deposit rate, and the tax rate.

12. If confidence in government is weak, external borrowing may lead to capital flight even without inflation or other taxes on financial intermediation. Businesses and households may simply anticipate a devaluation to solve the foreign exchange problem and an increase in taxes to solve the budgetary problem.

13. The magnitude of the secondary burden on the budget from the differential effects of inflation on revenues and expenditures has been estimated by Aghevli and Khan (1978) for several countries.

14. By its nature, inflationary financing transfers private sector resources to the public sector through forced savings. Sometimes the shifts in income distribution resulting from inflation favor returns to capital and hence investment, which might offset the increased risk.

15. Where buy backs are initiated by non-government, largely private entities—for example, in exchange for debt to the central bank—the budget may not directly benefit at all from the discount, and it may have fiscal effects.

REFERENCES

Aghevli, B., and M. Khan. 1978. "Government Deficits and the Inflationary Process in Developing Countries." International Monetary Fund, *Staff Papers*.

Anand, R., and S. van Wijnbergen. 1989. Inflation and the Financing of Government Expenditure: in An Introductory Analysis with an application to Turkey *World Bank Economic Review*, 3: 17-38.

Balassa, B. 1986. "Policy Responses to Exogenous Shocks in Developing Countries." *The American Economic Review* 76: 75-83 (May).

———. 1988. "Public Finance and Economic Development." Policy Research Working Paper No. 31. World Bank Washington, DC.

Batista, P.N. 1987. "International Financial Flows to Brazil Since the Late 1960s: An Analysis of Debt Expansion and Payments Problems." World Bank Discussion Paper No. 7.

Bird, G. 1982. *The International Monetary System and the Less Developed Countries*. London: Macmillan.

Branson, W. 1988. Lecture notes for World Bank Seminar, October.

Buiter, W. 1986. "Macroeconomic Responses by Development Countries to Changes in External Economic Conditions." Mimeo National Bureau of Economic Research, Inc.

———. 1988. "Some Thoughts on the Role of Fiscal Policy in Stabilization and Structural Adjustment in Developing Countries." National Bureau of Economic Research Working Paper Series No. 2603.

Chelliah, R.J. 1987. "Growth-Oriented Adjustment Programs: Fiscal Policy Issues." In *Growth-Oriented Adjustment Programs*, edited by V. Corbo, Goldstein, and Khan. Washington, DC: International Monetary Fund.

Cohen, D. 1985. "How to Evaluate the Solvency of an Indebted Nation." *Economic Policy* 1 (November): 139-167.

———. 1988. "The Management of the Developing Countries' Debt: Guidelines and Applications to Brazil." *The World Bank Economic Review* 2(1): 77-103.

Cuddington, J. 1989. "The Extent and Causes of the Debt Servicing Crisis of the 1980s." In *Dealing with the Debt Crisis*. Washington, DC: World Bank, edited by Ishrat Husain and Ishrat Diwan.

De Melo, M. 1990. "Fiscal Adjustment in High-Debt Countries." *Ricerche Economiche* XLIV(2-3) pp. 251-272.

De Pinies, J. 1989. "Debt Sustainability and Overadjustment." *World Development* 17(1): 29-43.

Dornbusch, R., and S. Fischer. 1985. "The World Debt Problem: Origins and Prospects." *Journal of Development Planning* (16): 57-81.

Easterly, W. 1989. "Fiscal Adjustment and Deficit Financing During the Debt Crisis." Policy Research Working Paper No. 138. World Bank, Washington, D.C. (IMF).

Gelb, A., J. Knight, and R. Sabot. 1988. "Lewis Through a Looking Glass: Public Sector Employment, Rent-Seeking, and Economic Growth." World Bank Staff Working Paper No. 133.

International Monetary Fund. 1987. *Government Finance Statistics Yearbook, 1987*. Washington, D.C.

Khan, M., and M. Knight. 1983. "Sources of Payment Problems in LDCs." *Finance and Development*, 20(4): 2-5.

Makin, J. 1987. "Reducing the Deficit: Appropriate Targets and Effective Means." *U.S. Fiscal Policy: Its Effects at Home and Abroad*, Washington, DC: American Enterprise Institute.

Martone, C. 1987. "Macroeconomic Policies, Debt Accumulation, and Adjustment in Brazil, 1965-84." World Bank Discussion Paper No. 8.

Nunberg, B. 1988. "Public Sector Pay and Employment Reform." Policy Research Working Paper No. 113. World Book, Washington, D.C.

Reisen, H. 1988. "Public Developing Country Debt, External Competitiveness, and Required Fiscal Discipline." Mimeo OECD Development Centre.

Reisen, H., and A. van Trotsenburg. 1988. *Developing Country Debt: The Budgetary and Transfer Problem.* Paris: Development Centre Studies.

Rodrik, D. 1988. "The Welfare Economics of Debt Service." National Bureau of Economic Research, Inc., Working Paper No. 2655.

Shah, A. 1988. "Public Infrastructure and Private Sector Profitability and Productivity in Mexico." Policy Research Working Paper No. 100. World Bank, Washington, D.C.

Skinner, J. 1988. "Taxation and Output Growth in Africa." Policy Research Working Paper No. 73.

Spaventa, L. 1986. "The Growth of Public Debt: Sustainability, Fiscal Rules, and Monetary Rules." International Monetary Fund Working Paper No. 86/8. Washington, D.C.

Tanzi, V. 1984. "Is There a Limit to the Size of Fiscal Deficits in Developing Countries?" Pp. 139-152 in *Public Finance and Public Debt*, proceedings of the 40th Congress of the International Institute of Public Finance, Innsbruck.

———. 1987. "Fiscal Policy, Growth, and the Design of Stabilization Programs." WP/87/1, Fiscal Affairs Department. Washington, DC: International Monetary Fund.

Tanzi, V., and M. Blejer. 1986. "Public Debt and Fiscal Policy in Developing Countries." Washinton, DC: International Monetary Fund, Fiscal Affairs Department.

Taylor, L. 1988. "Fiscal Issues in Macroeconomic Stabilization." Policy Research Working Paper No. 34. Washington, D.C.

World Bank. 1988. *World Development Report, 1988*. Washington, DC: Author.

World Bank. 1990. *World Debt Tables, 1989-90*. Washington, DC: World Bank.

World Bank. 1990. *World Tables, 1990*. Washington, DC: World Bank.

PART III.

PLANNING BUDGETS

PUBLIC EXPENDITURE PLANNING AND FORECASTING

William Allan

ABSTRACT

The need to extend forecasts of expenditure and revenue beyond the annual budget timeframe and to use these forecasts as a basis for planning of public expenditures is now widely recognized. However, developing countries find it difficult to implement expenditure planning. This chapter outlines the origins of expenditure planning and examines the main issues involved in implementing it in developing countries.

The need to extend forecasts of expenditure and revenue beyond one year and to use these forecasts as a basis for planning of public expenditures is now widely recognized, but it has taken considerable time for these practices to become an effective part of public decision making. In developing countries (DCs), fiscal pressures, frequent conflict between central planning and the ministry of finance, and (in the case of many African DCs) lack of administrative resources have often made it difficult to implement them. This chapter outlines the origins of expenditure planning and examines the main issues to be faced in implementing it in DCs.

Policy Studies and Developing Nations, Volume 3, pages 93-113.

ISBN: 1-55938-190-6

EXPENDITURE PLANNING IN OECD COUNTRIES

Most OECD countries employ some form of multi-year forecasting of public expenditures. While in some the technique has become an integral part of the process of formulating the annual budget and is seen as a key instrument of expenditure control, in others the systems at least provide background information to assist in formulating annual budget policy.[1]

In 1961, a system of public expenditure surveys (PES) was initiated in the United Kingdom (United Kingdom 1961). Its main features were as follows:[2]

1. Rolling estimates for *all* public expenditures for a period covering the current budget year and four years ahead, later reduced to three;
2. Expenditure estimates in *constant prices*; and
3. Separation of expenditure estimates into "existing policy," including all elements necessary to maintain existing service levels and proposals for further spending.

The PES incorporated these elements in an annual cycle intended to complement the existing procedure of budget preparation and provide a basis for policy discussion to support parliamentary examination of the annual supply estimates (United Kingdom 1969a, 1969b; Henley 1989 provides a diagram illustrating the development of the PES and PEWP post-1988).

By the mid-1970s, it was generally acknowledged that the PES had failed to achieve one of its major objectives of controlling public expenditure and facilitating strategic choices between public and private use of resources. One problem was that constant price estimates meant that control was exercised over the volume of activity rather than cash outlays, requiring frequent resort to supplementary authorizations of spending to accommodate unanticipated price increases during the year. From the mid-1970s, cash limit controls were introduced to budget appropriations, and from the beginning of the 1980s forecasts were expressed in cash terms (see Else and Marshall 1979, pp. 52-59; Likierman 1988, pp. 72-79, 1990, pp. 311-314).

The introduction of cash limits was one of a range of initiatives introduced in the period from the late 1970s to the present to tighten control over spending and improve management in the public sector. Forecasting remains an important element of public expenditure management, which includes overall forecasts of public expenditure, detailed statistics, and separate departmental plans. These procedures allow a more timely examination of broad strategy and consistency with the government's medium-term financial strategy and immediate resource constraints (Henley 1989 describes the changes to the PEWP after 1988; developments in the FMI and Next Steps are summarized in Likierman 1990).

Development of rolling expenditure plans in Australia followed a very similar pattern in somewhat similar fiscal policy and public expenditure management conditions.[3] The government formally reviews and restates fiscal policy annually, and it is at this point that an updated set of forward estimates is available to the Expenditure Review Committee (a key committee of cabinet). The forward estimates are now completely integrated into the annual budget process. They are estimated in real terms, but strict cash limits are applied to the current year's budget appropriations.

Multi-year forecasting and financial planning are employed as at least a background to the annual estimates process in nearly all the OECD countries. These exercises have not always, however, helped the countries achieve their stated medium-term fiscal objectives. In the United States, where some form of forward estimates process has been practiced by the federal government since the early 1960s, the benefits of forecasting and setting medium-term fiscal targets has also not been very encouraging, despite specific legislation aimed at deficit reduction and spending control.

Expenditure planning may provide a better information base for expenditure control but by itself does not ensure that expenditure control objectives will be vigorously pursued. A study for the European Community (Von Hagen 1992) found that the application of long-term fiscal limits was not very strongly linked to fiscal performance in EC countries. The same study suggested that a budgeting process that gives the central ministries a dominance over the spending ministries and that limits the amendment powers of parliament is more likely to lead to strong fiscal discipline than in countries where the political power of the purse is more dispersed. It was concluded that fiscal constraints were only likely to be effective in countries where there was sufficient institutional strength to implement them effectively.

Expenditure Planning in Developing Economies

Expenditure planning in the sense described previously has not been widely applied in developing countries. The dominant tradition in most developing countries in the 1950s and 1960s was to use a development plan as the main vehicle for setting priorities and providing a perspective on public spending priorities for several (usually five) years ahead. Usually, the development plan focused mainly on capital investment projects and gave only a broad outline of recurrent spending of government in future years.

Development plans, however, usually coexisted with traditional line-item annual budgets, which were separately administered by a finance ministry. Since, as a rule, the finance ministry was relatively powerful and resources were in the end allocated through the budget, it was often the budget rather than the plan that determined actual spending in any one year. Development plans were of considerable importance, however, as vehicles for directing and encouraging capital investment. Aid donors generally expected recipient countries to have a development plan and that projects that they supported be included in the development plan. The planning office usually played an important role in negotiating project agreements. Support of projects after the development phase, however, depended on the budget—and these requirements placed considerable strains on the recurrent budget. A common complaint in many countries was that operations and maintenance expenditure from the budget was inadequate to meet the real needs of the projects.

From the late 1960s onward, development planning was regarded with increasing disfavor and various attempts were made to improve integration of budgeting and planning and to establish better control and direction of the public expenditure process. Efforts to improve the budget process in DCs, however, were not generally characterized by a continuous program of development and improvement but rather by surges of enthusiasm for particular techniques applied in the developed economies and too often a partial relapse into established routines. Efforts to include foreign aid into the overall expenditure planning process have generally been disappointing, and particularly for heavily aided countries, the availability of external aid for projects has continued to provide a "soft budget" option that allows departments to evade the discipline of the budget.

The application of program-oriented budgeting in the DCs provides a major illustration of this pattern. Program budgeting has, of course, had somewhat mixed reviews in the developed economies, but its application has been even more difficult in the DC context. Many DCs now have established program budget structures, which in principle allow them to focus more clearly on setting budget priorities. In fact, however, most of them lack the administrative and political capacity to use the program structure for more effective priority setting, and budget decisions remain incremental and driven by short-term fiscal pressures rather than by medium-term plans.

Budget reforms in recent times must also be considered in the context of very strong pressures for fiscal restraint as a key instrument for controlling inflation. In industrialized countries, programs of economic adjustment instituted by the national governments have proved to be a powerful stimulus for establishing more effective budget processes.

In DCs, however, the link between structural adjustment processes and budget reform has been much less assured; and, indeed, on some aspects the two processes appear to have been in conflict rather than mutually supportive. Two prominent differences between DC and industrialized country experience in this respect are, first, that political support for structural adjustment has been much less coherent in DCs than in the industrial country examples cited. Second, the DCs generally have a much weaker administrative capacity to absorb or support the prolonged process that has proved necessary to implement such major and technically complex institutional changes.

Medium-term expenditure forecasting and planning has perhaps proved particularly difficult to introduce in the context of a major structural adjustment program in DCs. Structural adjustment programs supported by International Monetary Fund and World Bank resources in these countries have usually been introduced after significant deterioration in budget and expenditure control systems. In some cases, the budget has significant elements of underestimation in expenditures and overestimation of revenues, though the main parameters are agreed with Fund staff. More generally, there are strong pressures—for political reasons or because there are commitments that are not properly reflected in the estimates—to increase spending during the year, and the administration has limited capacity to adjust expenditures when there is a revenue shortfall. The net result is that the finance ministry has to resort to restricting cash allocations and payments during the year in order to meet the fiscal and domestic credit targets set in the program.

In this kind of environment, it is very difficult to promote medium-term expenditure planning as a feasible means of improving budgeting. Increasingly these issues are being recognized in IMF- and World Bank-supported structural adjustment programs. Expenditure forecasting and planning has, in several cases, been identified as one of a range of institutional improvements in public expenditure management (structural benchmarks) that need to be established under the policy framework paper (PFP) agreed between the IMF, the World Bank, and the country in receipt of structural adjustment lending.[4]

It remains true, however, that programs of technical assistance to help achieve these improvements have a mixed record, monitoring and evaluation of these programs is ad hoc, and there is no generally agreed strategy on how to achieve sustainable improvements of public expenditure management systems or what elements of these programs should be given highest priority. (For a discussion of TA programs in the area of public expenditure management in the context of structural adjustment lending by the IMF and World Bank, see Nunberg 1990; Wallace 1990). The questions are still open as to what role promotion of medium-term expenditure planning should play in achieving structural adjustment targets and if there is any strategy of general applicability that can be applied to develop such systems in DCs.

A few DCs have made sustained attempts to introduce forms of medium-term expenditure planning, though none have achieved a fully operational system comparable to those of the United Kingdom or Australia. Possibly the most successful example is that of Botswana (a brief description of the links between planning, expenditure planning, and the annual budget is given in Stevens 1985), which has consistently set its budgets in a medium-term framework for many years. The medium-term projections are used as a basis for setting recurrent budget ceilings at an early stage of annual budget preparation. Botswana has, however, had the advantage of a strong revenue base and has been able to use its resources to create a strong administration;

the application of expenditure planning techniques have been less successful in many other DCs.

Kenya is another country that has made a sustained effort to develop a forward estimates process. It has used a forward budget as part of its public expenditure management system since 1973. The forward budget was originally intended to serve as a bridge between the five-year development plan and the annual budget. At the beginning of each new five-year planning period, expenditure ceilings were established for each ministry for the first two budget years of the National Development Plan. Treasury then called for forward budget estimates from ministries which have to be consistent with the ceilings. The forward estimates covered five years in the year of plan preparation and three years in other years. The first year is the basis of the budget for the forthcoming year, and the projections for later years became (after revision) the basis of budget ceilings for successive budget years. This rolling expenditure planning process continues in a similar form—though since the mid-1970s the plans deal with broad policy issues and no longer provide the basis for the forward estimates.

For a number of reasons, the system has not worked precisely as intended and has not yet proved a particularly effective instrument for managing public expenditures. Roe (1986) has characterized the main problem as loose overall expenditure control—the expenditure ceilings set in the forward budgets effectively became a floor from which to negotiate higher budget provisions rather than a strict limit on expenditure. The problem was compounded by the way in which treasury focused on items of expenditure (such as travel) rather than programs in order to reduce the initial bids of departments. This combination of techniques introduced inefficiencies into ministry programs without achieving aggregate control. Kenya has experienced continuing problems in reducing its fiscal imbalance and achieving structural adjustment targets up to the present time. Notwithstanding these difficulties, the forward budget has become an established feature of its expenditure management system and is being further strengthened in the context of increased efforts to reduce the fiscal deficit.[5]

Papua New Guinea provides another example of a major effort by a DC to integrate medium-term planning with the budget process. The system, which was initiated in 1978, was in some respects modeled on the PES of the United Kingdom, but it also attempted to link expenditure plans to the stated political objectives of the government by establishing expenditure ceilings for specific objectives (e.g., rural development). Projects were assigned to the objective to which they were most closely related ("strategic objective") and appraised in the annual budget process against other similar projects competing for the share of the overall expenditure ceiling for new initiatives allocated to that objective. Consistent sectoral plans were to be achieved by means of "policy hearings" which reviewed the program for a sector against all objectives for that sector and were intended, in principle, to give expenditure guidelines for ministries to prepare projects for inclusion in future years of the expenditure plan.

The process operated within an overall macroeconomic framework in which control of public spending was seen as the main instrument for maintaining the exchange rate and controlling inflation. In the initial years, the system did effectively maintain control over public spending. Various political pressures and the administrative burden of maintaining the system, however, led to its eventual replacement by a more general planning and annual budgeting process. Two key weaknesses of the system were its overt linkages to political objectives (which, of course, changed) and the failure to establish sectoral programs that extended much beyond the annual budget.[6]

Modified forms of expenditure planning have been adopted in many DCs, though no evidence has yet been compiled to demonstrate whether or not these efforts have contributed greatly to improved expenditure management. One area where the World Bank has, for some time, given considerable emphasis is the need to improve investment programming. The outcome for many countries has been the development of a public sector investment program (PSIP) which is, in intention at least, an expenditure plan for the investment component of the budget. In many cases, however, the PSIP is more of a "wish list" of projects seeking financing than a carefully designed strategy of investment. Links between the PSIP and recurrent spending generally remain unsatisfactory, and inevitably conflicts emerge between implementation of the PSIP and the achievement of structural adjustment targets (see Lacey 1989 for discussion of various initiatives of the World Bank in this area).

THE MAIN ELEMENTS OF EXPENDITURE PLANNING

It is clear from the experience outlined previously that, however persuasive the rationale for adopting expenditure planning, actually achieving the benefits claimed for such a system is very difficult in practice. Particularly in developing countries, there are many basic constraints that need to be addressed—or that may simply make such a system not feasible in a practical timeframe. In all countries, the questions must be asked whether the proposed system has enough political support and whether there are enough incentives for decision makers to use the additional information effectively to improve budget decisions. Technical fixes in the field of expenditure management have not had a happy history in the absence of such support.

It is a matter for judgment, however, whether these factors constitute an absolute barrier to introducing measures to improve planning of public expenditures. Political support can be gained over time, and it is invariably necessary to undertake a sustained program of training and awareness raising to introduce technical innovations to such basic administrative processes as those of budgeting. It can be added that the demonstrable effectiveness of these techniques in countries such as the United Kingdom and Australia and the general contemporary acceptance of the critical role of public expenditure control in macroeconomic management provide a more amenable environment for implementing such measures than has existed in the past.

The main points to stress are that introduction of expenditure planning requires a clear appreciation of the rationale for establishing such a system, an evaluation of each element of expenditure planning in relation to the constraints that apply in the particular country, and a commitment to improving public expenditure management.

The Rationale for Expenditure Planning

Public expenditure planning is a natural extension of annual budgeting which has the primary aims of improving both control over the aggregate level of public spending and the allocation of resources to particular activities.[7] Its serves these objectives mainly by:

- providing better information on the medium-term costs of current expenditure policies and thereby giving greater scope to initiate changes in budget policy that will take more than one year to implement; and
- revealing links between capital expenditures and future recurrent costs and thereby facilitating analysis of the impact of public investments on the budget over the medium-term.

An important distinction should be drawn between the needs of the Western industrialized countries and the DCs in terms of these objectives. A major feature in industrialized countries is the very high proportion of expenditures in the form of standing appropriations for social security or unemployment benefit entitlements. Control through an annual budget process is thus limited both in terms of the time horizon and the scope of expenditures covered by annual appropriation. In principle, an expenditure plan should give an opportunity to review the whole range of expenditures, but it remains an open question whether expenditure planning has had a major impact on entitlements policies.

DCs in general do not have major social security commitments. Many, however, have great difficulty in ensuring that the future recurrent costs of capital developments are taken into account—and thereby give rise to problems of recurrent expenditure control. These problems are often exacerbated by a donor focus on individual capital projects combined with a lack of coordination among donors. Expenditure planning for DCs, therefore, needs to be designed particularly to deal with coordination of capital and recurrent budgets and integration of foreign assistance into the budget process.

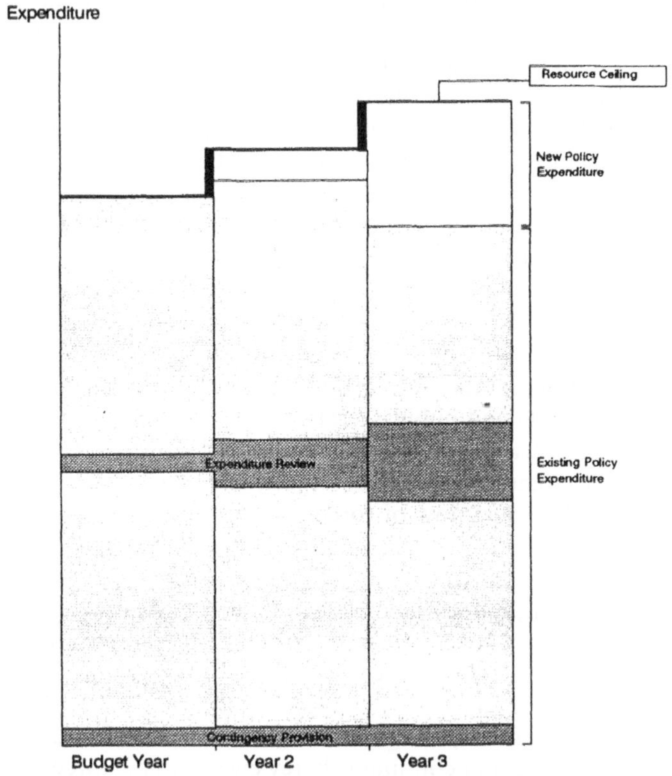

Figure 1. The Main Elements of Public Expenditure Planning

The relative emphasis given to control and allocation (planning) objectives has also been the subject of some debate. While improved planning and allocation were seen initially as a major reason for expenditure planning, the objective of aggregate control has become increasingly dominant. In the OECD countries, this emphasis has been offset to some extent by the increasing flexibility given to spending ministries in allocating resources within their cash ceilings.

The various elements that must be considered in detailed design of an expenditure planning system are discussed in turn. A number of these elements are illustrated in Figure 1.

The Macroeconomic Framework

One of the basic aims of expenditure planning is to improve the aggregate control of expenditure as an integral part of macroeconomic management. Control of the size of the budget deficit and ensuring that it is financed from noninflationary sources are key instruments in fighting inflation. An explicit macroeconomic framework is thus an essential feature of an expenditure planning system. This framework involves some form of formal forecasting to help assess the main economic and fiscal parameters for expenditure planning over the medium- and short-term, a fiscal reporting system to monitor actual fiscal performance against planned, and a process of review to reassess the economic and fiscal environment and adjust the budget in light of changed circumstances. The starting point for expenditure planning is a realistic appraisal of resources likely to be available to the government in the light of the following main factors:

- Assessment of likely BOP, inflation, and economic growth over the forecast period (usually three to five years);
- Policies on acceptable rate of growth of domestic credit and its share between private and public sector;
- Policies on external borrowing and expected growth of foreign exchange earnings to finance future debt service; and
- For DCs, expected flow of foreign grants and policies on aid and aid dependency.

These forecasts and policy analyses will be the basis of an estimate of the revenues and sustainable borrowing that could be generated for the government over the forecast period. This concept is shown in Figure 1 as the expenditure planning "resource ceiling."

Industrialized countries, in general, have well-established systems and institutions to prepare and continuously review economic forecasts. The IMF and the World Bank, in consultation with the authorities, use such a framework as a basic element of structural adjustment programs, but the DCs themselves have not always been able to develop their own institutional capacity (or policy resolve) to maintain or extend this framework for internal decision making. Creating a strong institutional and technical basis for macroeconomic policy formulation and implementation is an essential prerequisite to introducing expenditure planning.

Coverage of the Expenditure Plan

Since the main macroeconomic concern is with the extent of public sector borrowing and inflationary financing of the deficit, it is desirable that the total public sector deficit (often called the public sector borrowing requirement—or PSBR) be considered as the main target variable at the highest planning level. In principle, therefore, the whole public sector should be considered in the expenditure plan. Two main considerations affect the application of this in practice, however. First, there are important qualitative differences between different elements of the public sector. In particular, the public enterprise sector requires different treatment from central and local budget-supported organizations—at least to the extent that its operations are conducted on a commercial basis. Second, the appropriate coverage of an expenditure plan depends on the structure of government. In federal systems, the central government can plan its own expenditures—including any transfers to lower levels of government—but detailed planning of expenditures by state or provincial governments must be done by government at that level.

Transactions covered by expenditure planning should also provide a clear picture of the macroeconomic impact of the public sector. Some of the main considerations[8] are as follows:

- Quasi-fiscal operations carried out by the banking system should be considered as part of the fiscal deficit.
- Contingent liabilities as a result of government guarantees need to be considered explicitly as potential future expenditures.
- Special (extra-budgetary) funds should be consolidated with the budget for expenditure planning purposes.
- Tax expenditures should, as far as possible, be explicitly estimated and policies on these considered alongside budget expenditures within the overall macroeconomic framework—though, in practice, it is extremely difficult to include these in the budget process.

The key point is that public expenditure planning should not be concerned solely with planning the legally defined central government budget. It is, of course, necessary to plan for each legal entity or policy area encompassed by the public sector, but these individual plans should be related to an overall framework covering all relevant public sector transactions.

Classification of Expenditures

Transactions need to be appropriately classified to enable analysis of their macroeconomic impact. Industrialized countries invariably have comprehensive budget classifications that permit analysis from a variety of perspectives as well as meeting administrative needs. Many developing countries, however, either have significant weaknesses in their classifications (particularly in the development budget) or do not use the data adequately for fiscal analysis. In the former case, it will be necessary to revise the classification of budget and other relevant fiscal transactions. The IMF *Manual on Government Finance Statistics* (1986) provides a standard analytical classification of budget transactions. Many elements of this may be adopted directly in the basic classification of the budget—though the budget classification has to satisfy administrative requirements as well as a range of analytical needs. Clearly, computerization of public accounting records will facilitate the generation of a variety of reports to meet these various purposes.

Policy Basis of Expenditures

It is vital that the policy justifying particular levels of expenditure in each sector and agency be specified as explicitly as possible. Figure 1 illustrates the basic distinction between *existing policy* and *new policy*. Projections of expenditure should invariably be based, in the first instance, on estimating the costs of continuing existing policies and then the difference between those estimates and the resource ceiling will indicate the scope for introducing new policy (which in some circumstances may be negative—requiring adoption of policies to reduce the real level of government spending).

Existing policy estimates are based, first, on assumptions about price, wage movements, and economic growth over the expenditure planning period. Second, the estimates depend on specific policies governing each area of expenditure. In many cases, policies are not specified in sufficient detail to allow precise costing. Some programs, moreover, may have specific authority that elapses during the plan period, but there may be an implicit agreement that the programs will continue. Thus, there are often considerable areas of disagreement over what constitutes existing policy. The expenditure planning process, however, provides a forum whereby these disagreements can be resolved. Once the process is well established, the main specific policy concerns should be with the estimates for the year added on each plan rollover and with programs requiring fresh authority during the expenditure plan period.

A number of other policy-related characteristics should also be identified as clearly as possible. One important aspect is the level of discretion available to decision makers within the planning timeframe. Many standing appropriations (e.g., for unemployment benefits) (a) can only be changed by changing the underlying legislation, and (b) are strongly subject to cyclical variation. Other expenditures may have policy commitments which may be subject to review during the forecast period. It is important to identify the policy status of different types of expenditure and categorize these appropriately for decision making.

A major benefit of introducing expenditure planning, therefore, should be that policies are more clearly stated, and discussion of existing policy estimates should be less time consuming and focused on areas where policy is not clear. The process should lead to a sharper definition of existing policies and allow more consideration of specific areas of policy review and new policy expenditure proposals.

Correspondingly, more effort can also be devoted to evaluating new policy proposals and setting priorities for implementing these within the resources forecast to be available. For DCs, much new policy will be based on the PSIP. It is important, however, that new policy not be conceived entirely in the same terms as the traditional "recurrent" and "development" budgets. One of the continuing difficulties of public investment in the DCs is the inadequate provision of recurrent operations and maintenance expenditure necessary to maintain new assets. Formulation of PSIPs in the context of medium-term expenditure plans, where these are feasible, should help to overcome these difficulties. Where expenditure planning is not feasible, successful implementation of PSIPs also seems unlikely. Despite widespread advocacy of program budgeting in DCs, it is very common for budget estimates to be presented with neither policy status nor program clearly defined; usually, there are insufficient skilled administrative resources to apply these techniques in a sustained way.

Prices, Inflation, and Cash Limits

Of course, estimates of future expenditure, particularly for several years ahead, are highly subject to changes in assumed prices, wages, and the level of economic activity. Since the budget itself is a major determinant of changes in these variables, the basis of estimating and the way in which the budget appropriations are allowed to change with actual changes in these parameters are of key importance in fiscal policy.

In an ideal budget model, estimates would be prepared on the basis of quantities of inputs required for each program and the estimated price for each input. The treasury would provide standard sets of assumptions for prices and wage rates to be applied to each sector—and might make provision separately for expected changes during the plan period. As prices change during the plan, additional funds would be appropriated to maintain the budget level of service. In the event, however, that it becomes necessary to restrict public spending as part of macroeconomic policy to combat inflation, priorities for spending should be reviewed, and the volume of lower priority services reduced.

This type of "volume planning" model was the basis of the original formulation of expenditure planning in the United Kingdom. The failure to adjust volume parameters quickly enough to reduce aggregate spending, however, became the basis for introducing cash limits as one of the principal instruments for controlling aggregate spending. Cash limits involve setting a cash ceiling on the amount to be spent in the plan period with the implication that any variation in prices beyond those embodied in the estimates be absorbed by changes in volume of service (see Wright 1977). The advantage of the technique is that it provides a clear signal of responsibility for adjustment to individual ministries—volume planning in contrast allows ministries to assume that the burden of adjustment will be borne in other "lower priority" areas. It has been effective in controlling moderate levels of inflation, such as those experienced in the United Kingdom and Australia. Such broadbrush methods cannot be applied successfully, however, when inflation is very high or relative rates of inflation vary widely between sectors.

Expenditure Review

The budget and expenditure planning system should also include some form of review of expenditures to enable the efficiency and effectiveness of programs to be examined and appropriate adjustments to be made. In Figure 1, this aspect of expenditure planning is illustrated as part of existing policy expenditure with an additional portion being designated as under review each year.

A variety of approaches are used to review the continuing expenditures of government. Review of expenditure programs, of course, is an integral feature of program-type budget reforms and was particularly emphasized in so-called zero base budgeting. Even prior to such innovations, reviews of specific areas of expenditure—prompted in some cases by audit or political pressure—have been essential features of any budget system. Reforms in recent years have emphasized the need for such reviews to be regular rather than ad hoc. The need for structural adjustment in many countries has also given an added emphasis to the review process.

A recent example of a systematic review process that is integrated with expenditure planning is provided by the Swedish budget process which requires all agencies to provide an in-depth report of their activities and the results achieved once over a rolling three-year cycle so as to encourage more intensive examination of existing policies in a timeframe that allows policies and expenditure plans to be adjusted (see Jonsson 1990). External reviews of expenditure, such as the U.K. Efficiency Unit, have been introduced in several countries as part of a general policy of streamlining government. Such efficiency scrutinies along Rayner lines have resulted in significant reductions in public expenditure and have pointed to areas where efficiency could be improved. High level political support for undertaking scrutinies and implementing their recommendations is essential, however. It has also been the general experience that actual savings are substantially less (and take longer to achieve) than the estimates of the initial scrutiny study.[9] Possibly because of the need for sustained political support, the techniques have not been applied to any extent in DCs.

Contingencies

Expenditure planning, like any planning, has to deal with an uncertain future. Many of the assumptions underlying the plan projections will prove to be inaccurate, and unforeseen events with revenue or expenditure implications will occur. An essential feature of expenditure planning, therefore, is that provision should be made for contingencies. Management of risk and uncertainty should be built into the public expenditure management process in a formal way through adoption of appropriate procedures, explicit assessment of uncertainty and risk, and explicit monitoring and control of those elements of the budget deemed to be most uncertain. Several different aspects of dealing with uncertainty need to be distinguished.

Contingency Mechanisms

An essential step in contingency planning is to ensure that an administrative framework is available for dealing with events that may not be predictable in time but are sure to happen at some time. An obvious example is a natural disaster in areas prone to earthquake, hurricane, or other periodic natural occurrences. The appropriate response is to establish an organization with basic capabilities for dealing with these events when they do occur. At a more general level, many countries give the executive the authority to undertake expenditure without prior legislative approval for genuinely unforeseen and unavoidable expenditures. Of course, such expenditures must be approved ex post by the legislature. Neither of these mechanisms require, of necessity, a specific reserve fund to meet contingencies. Actual expenses may be met by adjusting expenditures or revenues elsewhere—and, in the case of natural disasters, some resources may be provided by external donors.

Contingency Reserves

Some countries, however, do make a formal provision of funds for contingencies both in the forward estimates and the annual budget. In the former case, the reserve fund will inevitably tend to be somewhat flexible and provide scope for new policies as well as contingency provisions.

Formal reserves run the danger of being seen as an avenue for a variety of new spending initiatives during the year. Where reserves are used, therefore, it is critical that the amount provided be related to specific types of contingency, that clear criteria be set for use of funds, and that access to the reserve be controlled strictly according to these criteria. Administration of reserves often proves very difficult in DCs.

Contingent Liabilities

A particular contingency that poses problems for many countries is the possible liability to central government that may arise from the issue of guarantees to public corporations or lower levels of government. These liabilities are often administered in an ad hoc way, with no systematic records or explicit estimates of possible payments that may have to be made. Some countries levy charges on the recipient for issue of guarantees.

Several steps are suggested for dealing appropriately with liabilities arising from issue of guarantees:

1. The initial issue of guarantees should be controlled and properly registered. The issue of a guarantee should be examined in the same way as other forms of budgetary support.
2. An explicit probabilistic estimate of payments against the guarantee should be made and this provision included in the forward estimates as a component of a general contingency reserve.
3. A schedule of all future liabilities for each month of the budget year and for each year of the forward estimates should be maintained and actual payments monitored during the year.

Provision of a contingency reserve would, of course, be subject to the conditions outlined above to ensure proper control—and it may be that actual payments are best met by compensatory budget adjustments, along the lines of the Australian system. Explicit estimation of expected payments and explicit monitoring of potential claims, however, should be embodied in the central government budget process.

Core Programs

Even if contingency reserves are maintained, the amounts provided are often inadequate to handle major unexpected demands on expenditure. The possibility of a large disruption to expenditure programs during the year should, therefore, be included as an integral part of expenditure planning.

A common recommendation—often by the World Bank in relation to PSIPs—is that core programs be identified and protected as far as possible from budget reductions. While it is clearly desirable to adopt such a practice in DCs, however, there are often difficulties in drawing up a priority list that has full political support. Moreover, the administrative mechanisms, in some cases, may not draw sufficiently clear distinctions (say in issuing expenditure warrants) to ensure that the priorities are observed in practice. Application of the principle of "core programs" requires that all details of the way it is to be applied be made explicit.

Windfalls

Not all contingencies have a negative impact on the budget balance. Revenues may be higher than estimated (particularly if conservative revenue estimating procedures are used as an implicit contingency reserve mechanism), or estimated contingency payments may not eventuate. It is equally important for overall expenditure control that plans be in place for such windfalls as well as for unforeseen additional pressures on the deficit. It is important that additional one-time resources do not lead to unacceptable long-term increases in recurrent costs and that the normal budget procedures for priority setting are observed for any expenditure proposal.

One obvious avenue for using such gains is for repayment of debt. Alternatively, the funds could be applied to the highest priority investment among the non-core projects. The basic requirement, therefore, is that the authorities have a clear listing of priorities for use of funds (including debt reduction) in the event that additional resources become available during the year.

Organizational Aspects

Expenditure planning is radically different from "economic planning" or "development planning." The function is much more an extension of annual budgeting and expenditure management than an attempt to provide an overall blueprint for national economic and social development. Essentially, it aims to provide the fiscal framework within which individual ministries and the private sector can develop specific development programs. It follows that the primary organizational responsibility for expenditure planning should lie in the ministry responsible for annual budget preparation. It should not be assigned to a ministry of planning—where, as is often the case in DCs, the planning function is separated from finance/treasury functions.

What should be the continuing functions of a planning ministry or agency under an expenditure planning system? In some DCs, there is a reluctance to dismantle the paraphernalia of medium-term planning, which provides the main rationale for the existence of the planning organization as a separate entity. The most productive use of the planning units is likely to be in coordinating preparation of medium-term PSIPs—provided these are consistent with the overall macroeconomic and expenditure planning framework. A number of DCs are focusing their planning efforts in this direction, and in many cases, the ministries of finance and planning are being combined.

Time Horizon

What should be the appropriate time horizon for an expenditure plan? There appears to be little in favor of extending the forward estimates more than two or so years beyond the budget year. This timeframe gives an idea of continuing costs and links successive budget years effectively. It may indeed be argued that one additional year may be sufficient to achieve these purposes. Estimates beyond a two- to three-year outlook, on the other hand, become increasingly uncertain, and it seems undesirable to give any official status to such projections.

The expenditure planning process, however, should not be confined merely to the production of official forward estimates. For technical planning purposes (e.g., examining the debt implications of different expenditure paths), it will be useful to extend the time horizon to five, 10, or more years. These projections may be used to support particular decisions that are embodied in the official estimates. From time to time, it may also be useful to make such long-term studies available as public documents. The purpose of these studies should, however, be clearly distinguished from that of the forward estimates.

CONCLUSIONS

In the introductory section of this paper, the questions were posed as to whether it was either desirable or feasible to promote expenditure planning in DCs as a means of improving expenditure control and achieving structural adjustment targets. While no definitive answer can be given, the lessons both of experience and analysis of the systemic requirements of expenditure planning highlight the difficulties of achieving such a goal. Most DCs lack both the political commitment and the administrative capacity to establish a sufficiently disciplined system of expenditure planning to achieve the system objectives described earlier. It must be added that expenditure planning per se has not been shown to be an effective instrument of expenditure control; though in the appropriate environment and supported by other measures, it can help to achieve this objective.

Expenditure planning is, logically, an essential component of an overall expenditure management system and, therefore, should be included in programs to improve budget management. It is critical, however, that efforts to establish expenditure planning be conceived as part of a broader program—not a "technical fix" for all expenditure management problems. While rather less than a strategy for implementing expenditure planning, a number of "dos and don'ts" emerge from the preceding discussion:

- Political commitment to controlling public spending should be established as a prerequisite to any technical program of budget reform.
- The administrative capacity to carry out all elements of expenditure planning and other supporting measures must be carefully assessed and realistic targets established for improving the budget process in phases.
- First priority should be given to establishing a basic capacity for formulating and monitoring public expenditure in a macroeconomic framework.
- Partial approaches to expenditure planning, such as sectoral "expenditure plans," should be avoided unless these are formulated in the context of a clear overall budget and macroeconomic framework. Essentially, such approaches amount to earmarking of revenues, and they can introduce arbitrary restrictions on fiscal flexibility.
- Similar reservations with regard to partial planning apply to PSIPs, although these have been widely established and, in general, are prepared in the context of a macroeconomic plan. In many cases, however,

governments still do not make realistic provision for the recurrent costs of their investment programs.

- The ministry of finance (or its equivalent) should be responsible for expenditure planning and for financial oversight of any sectoral or investment plans.

ACKNOWLEDGMENTS

I am grateful for comments received on an earlier draft from a number of colleagues. I owe particular thanks to A. Premchand of the IMF and Michael Stevens of the World Bank; many of their comments and suggestions have been incorporated in the final version of the paper.

NOTES

1. See survey of practices in selected OECD countries in Premchand. Axelrod (1988) also comments on practices in several OECD countries.

2. The literature on implementation of PES is extensive, and the references cited in this paper are by no means exhaustive. A review of the PES and subsequent developments of the expenditure control system is given in Henley (1989) and Thain and Wright (1992a, 1992b), a description and review of the experience from 1961-1972 is found in Pollitt (1977), and expenditure control issues in the 1970s are discussed in Wright (1977). Comparative discussion of the PES and other systems are given by Premchand (1983, pp. 206-208)—in the context of an examination of the relevance of expenditure planning to DCs—and Axelrod (1988, pp. 278-280).

3. A description of the main elements of the system and its historical development is given in Keating and Rosalky (1990). An important parallel with the development of the U.K. system is the way in which the system was molded into an effective instrument of expenditure control after 1983. A second similarity is that this development occurred alongside a package of PEM reforms, the Financial Management Improvement Program (FMIP) with similar aims to the FMI.

4. A survey of the structural features of 25 IMF-supported programs by Huyser (1988) indicated that 13 of these countries planned to develop "rolling expenditure planning" as part of their structural adjustment program.

5. A number of articles describe and analyze the Kenyan system of expenditure management. These include Roe (1986) and Lacey (1989). Pinckey, Cohen, and Leonard (1984), in discussing the use of microcomputers in the ministry of agriculture, provide a useful discussion of the system and the impact of budget cutting by treasury on an operational ministry. A summary of experience in expenditure control and the pressures on the budget is given in the *Financial Times Survey* January 8, 1992.

6. See Allan and Hinchliffe (1982) for a description of the early evolution of the system. Lacey (1989) also gives a brief description and suggests reasons for its eventual failure.

7. Thain and Wright (1992b) in assessing the PES identify five principal functions: planning, allocating, monitoring, controlling, and evaluating public expenditure. Planning, allocating, and evaluating are here subsumed as contributing to the resource allocation objective.

8. A variety of these issues are discussed in more detail in Chu and Hemming (1991); see, particularly, "Public Expenditure Management," Chapter V by Hemming, and "Fiscal Activities of Public Institutions," Chapter XXV by Lorie and Miranda.

9. The National Audit Office investigated 20 percent of scrutinies conducted between 1979 and 1983 to assess their contribution (see U.K. 1986). A brief review of the U.K. scrutiny program and the (shorter-lived) application of the technique in Australia is given in Australia Senate Standing Committee on Finance and Public Administration (1989).

REFERENCES

Allan, W., and K. Hinchliffe. 1982. *Planning, Policy Analysis, and Public Spending: Theory and the Papua New Guinea Practice.* Gower, UK.

Australia Senate Standing Committee on Finance and Public Administration. 1989. *Review of the Efficiency Scrutiny Program.* Canberra: AGPS.

Axelrod, D. 1988. *Budgeting for Modern Government.* New York: St. Martin's Press Inc.

Chu, K., and R. Hemming. 1991. *Public Expenditure Handbook: A Guide to Public Policy Issues in Developing Countries.* Washington, DC: International Monetary Fund.

Else, P.K., and G.P. Marshall. 1979. *The Management of Public Expenditure* XLV(580).

Henley, D. 1989. "Central Government." Pp. 56-91 in *Public Sector Accounting and Financial Control,* 3rd ed., edited by D. Henley, C. Holtham, A. Likierman, and J. Perrin. London: Chapman and Hall.

Huyser, W.S. 1988. "Improved Government Financial Management Is Essential to Effective Fiscal Policies." *International Monetary Fund Survey* (June 13), pp. 201-203.

International Monetary Fund. 1986. *A Manual on Government Statistics.* Washington, DC: International Monetary Fund.

Jonsson, G. 1990. "Government Accounting in Sweden." Pp. 275-291 in *Government Financial Management: Issues and Country Studies,* edited by A. Premchand. Washington, DC: International Monetary Fund.

Keating, M., and D. Rosalky. 1990. "Rolling Expenditure Plans: Australian Experience and Prognosis." Pp. 72-97 in *Government Financial Management: Issues and Country Studies,* edited by A. Premchand. Washington, DC: International Monetary Fund.

Lacey, R.M. 1989. "Managing Public Expenditure: An Evolving World Bank Perspective." World Bank Discussion Papers No. 56, World Bank, Washington, DC.

Likierman, A. 1988. *Public Expenditure.* London: Penguin.

________ . 1990. "Government Accounting in the United Kingdom." Pp. 307-325 in *Government Financial Management: Issues and Country Studies,* edited by A. Premchand. Washington, DC: International Monetary Fund.

Nunberg, B. 1990. "Public Sector Management Issues in Structural Adjustment Lending." World Bank Discussion Papers No. 99, World Bank, Washington, DC.

Pinckey, T.C., J.M. Cohen, and D.K. Leonard. 1984. "Kenya's Use of Microcomputers to Improve Budgeting and Financial Management in an Operating Ministry: An Updated Report." Mimeo, Harvard Institute for International Development, Development Discussion Paper No. 169, Harvard University, Cambridge, MA.

Premchand, A. 1983. *Government Budgeting and Expenditure Controls: Theory and Practice.* Washington, DC: International Monetary Fund.

________ . 1990. "Expenditure Controls: Institutional and Operational Issues." Pp. 98-127 in *Government Financial Management: Issues and Country Studies,* edited by A. Premchand. Washington, DC: International Monetary Fund.

Pollitt, C. 1977. "The Public Expenditure Survey." *Public Administration* 55 (Summer): 127-142.

Roe, E.M. 1986. "The Ceiling as Base: National Budgeting in Kenya." *Public Budgeting and Finance* 6 (Summer): 87-103.

Stevens, M.L.O. 1985. "The Management of Recurrent Costs." Pp. 84-101 in *Recurrent Costs and Agricultural Development*, edited by J. Howell. London: Overseas Development Institute.

Thain, C., and M. Wright. 1992a. "Planning and Controlling Public Expenditure in the UK, Part I: The Treasury's Public Expenditure Survey." *Public Administration* 70 (Spring): 3-24.

———. 1992b. "Planning and Controlling Public Expenditure in the UK, Part II: The Effects and Effectiveness of the Survey." *Public Administration* 70 (Summer): 193-224.

United Kingdom. 1961. *Control of Public Expenditure* (Plowden Committee Report), Cmnd. 1432. London: HMSO.

———. 1969a. *Public Expenditure: A New Presentation*, Cmnd. 4017. London: HMSO.

———. 1969b. *Public Expenditure 1968-69 to 1973-74*, Cmnd. 4234, London: HMSO.

———. 1986. *Report by the Comptroller and Auditor General: The Rayner Scrutiny Programmes 1979 to 1983*. London: National Audit Office, HMSO.

Von Hagen, J. 1992. "Budgeting Procedures and Fiscal Performance in the European Communities." Economic Papers No. 96, Commission of the European Communities, Directorate General for Economic Affairs, October.

Wallace, L. 1990. "Reshaping Technical Assistance." *Finance and Development* (December): 26-30.

Wright, M. 1977. "Public Expenditure in Britain: The Crisis of Control." *Public Administration* 55 (Summer): 143-169.

FINANCIAL REFORM IN KENYA:
IMPLEMENTING A PUBLIC INVESTMENT PROGRAM IN LINE MINISTRIES

Stephen B. Peterson

ABSTRACT

Kenya's agriculture ministries have overloaded development budgets. Projects are not promptly implemented and the composition of expenditure is distorted. To solve this problem, the government introduced a public investment program (PIP). The PIP has two roles: information and allocation. This chapter provides recommendations for improving financial information, but the principal recommendations concern the allocation role of the PIP. Allocation reform must promote three changes: incentives for government and donors to adopt a long- rather than a short-term approach to investment, incentives for government not to overload portfolios, and incentives to fund O&M costs. The current reform uses a *project* strategy of specifying a core set of projects and fully funding them. We recommend a *portfolio* strategy that would gradually reduce the resource envelope. The latter strategy not only promotes the changes listed above but would manage the intense conflict involved in restructuring and reducing expenditures. The paper concludes with some observations on the process of financial reform.

Policy Studies and Developing Nations, Volume 3, pages 115-140.

ISBN: 1-55938-190-6

Kenya's agriculture ministries have overloaded their development budgets. Projects are not promptly implemented and the composition of expenditure is distorted. To solve these problems, the government introduced a public investment program (PIP). The principal objective of a PIP is to concentrate public resources on the most critical activities to maximize the return on investment (Ministry of Planning and National Development 1992, pp. 2-3; Office of the Vice President and Ministry of Finance 1992; for an overview of public investment programs, see Baum and Tolbert 1985, pp. 55-66; Kavalsky 1986). This objective requires reducing the size of the project portfolios to a level that can be fully funded, promptly implemented, and adequately supported with recurrent costs.

What is the potential of the PIP to redress the overload problems of the budgets in the Kenyan agriculture ministries? The portfolios of these two ministries pose four challenges to the PIP. First, since they serve a critical economic sector, a basic question is raised of how their share of the budget should be determined? Second, their development budgets are sizable and largely funded by donors. Reducing the portfolio is complicated and involves renegotiating donor commitments. Third, there is a serious imbalance between recurrent and development expenditures. Finally, the projects are complex, and many are multi-sectoral, so that the sector is difficult to rationalize.

Over and above these problems is the role of donor funds in financing public expenditures. The recurrent budget in Kenya is wholly financed by government but in recent years has become principally a payroll budget. (For FY 1992-1993, 59.5% and 58.6% of the recurrent budgets of the MOA and the MOLD were devoted to salary.) For the agriculture sector, the development budget is financed primarily by donors and provides capital investment and operating and maintenance (O&M) support. The agricultural ministries rely on the donor portion of the development budget for approximately 35 percent of their total O&M requirements (Peterson and Kiragu 1990, Tables 1.1, 1.3). The donor-funded portion of the development budget thus provides a subsidy for ministry-wide operations that government should fund through the recurrent budget. In short, the largely donor-funded development budget is the *real* budget, for it is the sole source of stable funding. Rationalizing and especially reducing this vital source of funding through any reform program is bound to be of great concern to the line ministries.

PROGRAM DESIGN

The Objectives of the PIP

The Treasury contends that the PIP will "strengthen the *planning* functions of the forward budget" and provide "a more comprehensive instrument for the planning of public expenditure."[1] The PIP has six objectives:

1. Strengthen the *project cycle*, namely the identification, design, appraisal, implementation, monitoring, and evaluation of projects [with] the application of standard criteria to the selection of public investments;
2. Be an instrument of *economic management* used to monitor public sector capital formation targets and to ensure that sectoral strategies are translated into projects and programs;
3. Be a tool for better *aid coordination* to assist in matching of Government investment needs with donor financing opportunities;
4. Strengthen *public expenditure management* overall by sharpening departmental priorities, improving the phasing of projects, and relating their total implementation costs and subsequent operating costs to recurrent and development budget ceilings;
5. Be used to monitor the investment plans of state corporations that may directly or indirectly impinge on the government's finances; and
6. Allow more accurate forecasting of future recurrent expenditure demands on financial resources (Office of the Vice President and Ministry of Finance, Budgetary Supply Department 1991, p. 2).

The PIP has two roles: information and allocation. The information role is critical because financial management within the agricultural ministries is hampered by a lack of data on project financing and expenditure. Data on physical progress is very poor. But the allocation role is far more difficult and contentious because the PIP seeks to reduce the level of the development budget.

Each ministry and state corporation must prepare three documents for the PIP: a policy statement and list of priority activities, project briefs, and a project list (Office of the Vice President and Ministry of Finance 1992a, pp. 14-15).[2] The policy statement and the list of priority activities include the description of functions, strategy, objectives, and investment priorities of each ministry (Office of the Vice President and Ministry of Finance 1992, p. 14). The list of priority activities is compared with government policy priorities for the sector. The second PIP document is a project brief. Briefs are to be completed for all projects and include the following data: summary financial data, description of project objectives and activities, implementation to date, future implementation, project financing, and forecast of recurrent cost requirements at completion. The third document is a project list that categorizes all projects into four types: core, high priority, medium priority, and others. Under the PIP guidelines, only one-quarter of the projects can be classified as high priority from which only one-third can be classified as core (Office of the Vice President and Ministry of Finance 1992a, p. 14). Thus, only one-twelfth of a ministry's portfolio can be categorized as core, that is, the most important activities in the ministry to be fully funded.

The PIP documents are prepared at the beginning of the financial year during the preparation of the forward budget. The line ministries submit a draft to the Ministry of Planning and National Development (MPND) which reviews the PIP for accuracy and substance (Office of the Vice Pesident and Ministry of Finance 1992a, p. 20). The substantive review is to ensure that the core and high priority projects accord with the policy statement and investment priorities established in national planning documents. The PIP is revised to reflect the MPND review and is submitted to the treasury as part of the ministry's forward budget. The treasury will not consider a ministry's forward budget if it is not accompanied by a PIP which has been satisfactorily reviewed by the MPND.

To summarize, the PIP has both an information and allocation role. Its objective is to categorize the existing portfolio of projects so only the most important projects will be funded. The reform is also meant to ensure the support of existing capacity by adequately funding recurrent costs.

THE PIP'S IMPACT ON IMPROVING INFORMATION

The primary information objective of the PIP is to provide financial data that demonstrate the level and composition of project expenditure. A second objective is to improve data on physical implementation. This section reviews the PIP's performance in improving the agricultural ministries' financial and physical implementation data. There are three types of financial data collected by the PIP: total estimated cost of a project, cumulative expenditure, and recurrent costs.

Improving Total Estimated Cost of Projects

The linchpin of the PIP is the total estimated cost (TEC) of a project. The TEC is needed to budget the full cost of a project and future recurrent costs. Except for a few recent projects, the ministries have been unable to locate the financing agreements for most of their donor-funded projects.[3] Efforts have been made to retrieve these documents from the treasury's External Resources Division (ERD) with little success.

In a recent exercise, the MOA could only locate 12 donor financing agreements (out of 56 projects), and of the 12, only four clearly specified the distribution and scheduling of funding to the ministry (Peterson 1991; on the limitations of project data in both the MOA and the MOLD, see Eskeland 1989). The MOLD has only 21 out of 43 project agreements. The MOA's and the MOLD's summary financial data in the PIP project briefs continue to be inaccurate. Without an authoritative financing agreement that provides the TEC of a project, the ministries estimate this figure from three sources: scattered expenditure data, the current year's budget, and future expenses based on the three years of the forward budget. (Past expenditure data for direct payments made by donors is particularly inaccurate, thus understating expenditure and the TEC.) If a project is long-term and continues beyond the third year of the forward budget, the outlying years are excluded, and the TEC is understated. When the exercise is repeated in later years, the total cost of the project goes up by the amount of the previous outlier year that is now included as the third year of the forward budget. Under this method, the TEC of a project becomes variable and not constant.

An accurate figure for the TEC is crucial. The principal objective of the PIP is to improve the level and composition of expenditure. Neglecting the outlying years means that future investment flows and their recurrent cost requirements will be incorrect. Further, the TEC is essential to good budgeting of projects. If divisions and ministries can make submissions without an authoritative financing agreement, they can tie up the budget and put pressure on the treasury to cut legitimate and fully-funded commitments.

Since neither the ministries nor the treasury have a comprehensive file of financial agreements for donor projects that clearly disaggregates project financing by ministry and by year, the PIP exercise should locate and catalog these documents. The summary financial form of the PIP also should be expanded to include the schedule of disbursements (both government and donor). This form should be attached to all future project agreements between donors and the government. This would ensure that the financial information in project agreements is clearly stated which will help finance officers in the ministries and the treasury. A "Summary of Financial Commitment" form would clarify a project's level and schedule of funding. It would be useful if this document listed the recurrent cost implications of the project. Government and donors should both understand the full financial implications of a project *before* signing the agreement.

Treasury should take the lead in maintaining TEC data for donor-funded projects and clarifying the procedures for translating donor financial agreements into budget commitments. Two issues need to be clarified: whether to use current or constant prices and the procedures for converting exchange rates. The use of current prices in the PIP is appropriate for budgeting but not planning (Bird and Stevens 1992, p. 7).

The project brief should include a balance of the donor commitment in the foreign currency of the commitment. This balance should be updated each year and would provide a better picture of financial absorption particularly as it relates to exchange rate fluctuations. The MOA and the MOLD are often criticized for failing to absorb their development allocations. One cause has been the increased value of donor projects due to the declining Kenya shilling.

The External Resources Department (ERD) should place the TEC figures in a data base and release them to the ministries in preparation of the PIP. Amendments to project financial schedules require approval of the treasury's External Resources Department (ERD) so the data base should be kept current. Such a data base would be invaluable for budgeting to ensure that ministry submissions stay within the donor ceilings.

The PIP should collect two additional pieces of financial data: future outlays and a schedule of expenditure and schedule of replacement capital. The PIP requires ministries to submit a project list that indicates the cumulative expenditures through the end of the current financial year and the outlays likely to be incurred during the three years of the forward budget. While the current project list provides a four-year investment frame, it would be useful to have a schedule of the outlying years to allow phasing of capital investment and recurrent support.[4] Effective management of O&M requires "over-the-horizon" budgeting. The current O&M crisis in Kenya's ministries is in part due to the budgeting process that does not limit current commitments to the availability of future recurrent support. While the objective of the PIP is to ensure an effective composition of expenditure, it takes a static view of this composition. The PIP assumes that an initial tranche of capital will be supported upon completion of a project ad infinitum by recurrent costs. For example, the artificial insemination (AI) services in the MOLD estimates that the useful life of its vehicles is two years. The PIP project brief for AI services is misleading for it does not indicate this large and rapid capital depreciation. The PIP should provide a schedule of capital replacement, and it should indicate whether new capital is for additional capacity or for rehabilitation of existing capacity. If capital is for rehabilitation, it should not require new recurrent cost support.

Improving Information on Past Expenditure

Expenditure data is essential to the PIP, for it indicates the progress in financially implementing a project. Underabsorbtion of donor funds has been a problem for both ministries, and funding flows need to be carefully monitored.[5] The PIP project list and project brief both require cumulative expenditure data. Expenditure is defined as cumulative expenditures through the beginning of the current financial year added to the current year's budget. Both ministries find it difficult to provide accurate expenditure data. First, donor direct payments are difficult to track, and many of these expenses never flow through the government accounting cycle (on the reform of accounting procedures for donor direct payments, see Peterson 1990; Peterson and Kiragu 1990, pp. 26-29). Second, some projects are divided into sub-projects, and it is difficult to allocate expenditures between them. The accounts are not computerized nor are project expenditure summaries maintained so providing cumulative expenditure data is a painstaking manual process.[6] Some of the projects are old, so providing expenditure data requires going back manually through many years of expenditure records and extracting the data.[7]

The PIP project brief should provide data on financial absorption. Data should be calculated by taking the percentage of actual expenditure to revised expenditure for the proceeding years of the project. Listing this data in Section 5 of the Project Brief ("Review of Project Financing") would highlight low absorption.

Improving Information on Future Recurrent Costs

The PIP seeks to improve the composition of expenditure at the macro-level by rationalizing government-wide investment expenditure to limit capital investment to a level that can be supported by recurrent costs. The PIP reform requires forecasts of project recurrent costs. In Section 7 of the project brief, salary, personnel allowances, and non-wage operating expenses (O&M) are forecast based on the termination date of the project. But the PIP has not provided adequate guidance or analytic techniques for government staff. The task is not simple. One impediment is the lack of cost center budgeting which links an activity with a budget head and then links both the capital and the recurrent expenditure. But the budget structure has not been rationalized. One finds capital and recurrent investment in both the development and recurrent budgets with little or no link between the two budgets for the same activity. One outcome of the PIP reform may be the reform of the budget into current and capital accounts.[8] Without cost center budgeting, it is difficult to determine the adequacy of current budgetary O&M allocation for a particular investment.

The centerpiece of the PIP is full funding of a set of core projects. What is full funding of recurrent costs? Is the forecast based on current budget allocations, on a project workplan, on actual expenditures, or on what is ideally needed? It would help if the project proposals and agreements for government and donor-funded projects respectively included a forecast of recurrent cost and supporting explanatory notes.

Forecasting Personnel Costs

Forecasting personnel requirements (salary and allowances) for a specific project is difficult because the budget does not accurately allocate staff among activities. There has been a tendency for staff to be lumped under one or two budget heads and not be disaggregated. A further complication is that field staff may serve on a variety of projects. Apportioning headquarters staff as overhead also needs to be done. Personnel data is poor although the two ministries have recently taken significant steps to improve and modernize personnel management. Assuming one can disaggregate staff to specific project activities, should the forecast be based on in-post or authorized establishment levels? For projects that will extend beyond five years of the latest civil service pay raise, an inflation factor has to be used to account for a potential salary raise.

While the PIP uses salary rather than complement data (numbers of staff), it would be helpful to know the distribution of staff needed to implement the project. It is commonly assumed that Kenya's ministries are overstaffed. This does not mean that the composition of staff is appropriate. The agricultural ministries are bottom heavy in subordinate staff but face shortages in the technical and managerial cadres. While such details are not appropriate for a project brief, they should be in a project work plan (discussed later). Even if the project can be accommodated in the budget, there may not be appropriate staff available to implement the project. Adequate and appropriate staff are a major constraint to effective implementation of projects. The PIP assumes that *financial* composition is the primary constraint to effective implementation. Full funding of projects has to be accompanied by full staffing.

Forecasting O&M Costs

Forecasting O&M costs is more difficult than forecasting personnel expenses because there is greater uncertainty in prices. Although difficult, it is possible to construct O&M norms by ministry and by sector that would provide a "rule of thumb" to ensure that adequate O&M is provided.[9] As a condition precedent to the ASAO II program, the MOA and the MOLD developed O&M norms that indicated, for each major service and by line item, the level of funding required (Peterson and Kiragu 1990). The O&M norms developed by the MOA and the MOLD were based on ratios using personnel as a base. Since the two ministries are overstaffed with subordinate staff and the PIP seeks to rationalize capital investment with available O&M support, it would be more appropriate to develop O&M norms based on capital stock (see Peterson 1992a, appendix; Wilson, Barber, and Milne 1992). While capital stock norms may be more appropriate, such norms are difficult to develop due to the complexities associated with determining original stock levels, calculating investment flows, and assigning depreciation.[10]

The project brief requires recurrent cost data only when a project ends. It does not require ongoing recurrent cost data. This is a serious oversight. Because of the deterioration in O&M support to line ministries, ministries should confirm to the MPND and the treasury the level of O&M currently budgeted. The source of O&M financing should be indicated. It is particularly important that the risk be indicated. Government sources of O&M, especially user fees, should be noted. The composition of expenditure has declined in recent years because the government has not met its contributions and has relied upon risky sources of recurrent cost financing (e.g., user fees).

To improve the composition of expenditure requires analytic techniques that can determine the proper balance of human, investment, and working (O&M) capital. The use of these techniques in the agriculture sector (or in any other government sector) is in its infancy and has yet to be applied to budgeting.

The impact to date of the PIP on improving recurrent cost data is not encouraging. The staff from the ministries' development planning division have attempted to update the recurrent cost data. Unfortunately, the chiefs of the technical divisions have not been forthcoming with new data. The recurrent cost data in the MOA's project briefs was calculated two years ago using the author's O&M norms.[11] The data is based on formulas rather than the actual costs submitted by the technical divisions. While these norms may be accurate, it would be useful for the technical divisions to review them considering prevailing costs. The MOLD project briefs do not provide recurrent cost data and simply refer to the current budget allocation as the recurrent support available. This error was not queried by the Ministry of Planning and National Development.

Improving Information on Physical Implementation

In addition to financial information, the project brief requires data on physical implementation. Specifically, it requires data on implementation to date and a forecast of project implementation over the next three years of the forward budget. Like project TEC, this data has been extremely poor. Both ministries have weak monitoring and evaluation (M&E) systems (a government wide problem), and the ministry lacks current and accurate data on physical implementation (see Peterson 1991; Thompson 1991). There are several explanations for this situation. First, the M&E sections are woefully understaffed and are only now starting to receive adequate resources.[12] Second, the M&E section has not developed a concise method of recording physical implementation of projects. Third, the ministries have not accorded a high priority to M&E.

A strong M&E system is essential for effective project management. It will take longer to improve M&E than to improve expenditure systems. The data is difficult to quantify, is dispersed at field level, and there are no reporting standards. Until the M&E reporting procedures are improved, we would recommend that the PIP exclude this data. Priority should be given to improving the financial data, and information on physical implementation can be developed later.

Project Work Plans

The project brief should not be viewed as a comprehensive document but rather as a summary. Project briefs, however, should be backed up by more comprehensive project work plans which would form the basis of the budget submission. Surprisingly, the government does not require that projects have fiscal year work plans that clearly specify physical targets and financial resources to achieve these targets. Fiscal year project work plans should be required that link resource levels and schedules with physical objectives. Given financial uncertainties, the work plans would propose physical objectives based upon varying funding scenarios. Work plans should have three parts. The first part would be the resource structure of a project listing the level of donor and government funding required and the linkage between resources in the development and recurrent budget (staff, O&M, capital investment).

The second part would link funding scenarios (both level and schedule) to physical objectives (e.g., with *X* level of funding provided on *Y* schedule, *Z* targets would be met). The third part would be an annex which details the costing and interrelationship between staff, capital investment, and O&M support for the project.

Project work plans would provide three benefits. First, they could improve the composition of expenditure by focusing on the recurrent cost requirements of a project and promote an appropriate balance of capital, O&M, and staffing expenditure. Second, they could improve the management of financial uncertainty by planning projects based on funding scenarios. Third, they would facilitate project monitoring by linking physical targets with funds flow. The PIP should be an *abstract* of a project work plan. The work plan should be based on the project proposal (for government projects) or project agreements (for donor-funded projects) which authoritatively establish the level and schedule of funding.

Summary of Improving Information

The first role of the PIP should be to improve financial information. While the PIP project brief is a first step in retrieving this information, more effort is needed. The PIP should first concentrate on acquiring the TEC of projects. Expenditure and recurrent cost data should then be improved. The PIP should focus first on financial data and include physical implementation data only after the financial data is adequate.

The "rock bottom basics of a project profile," according to Bird and Stevens (1992), is "an informative project title, a ten line thumbnail sketch, the total cost of the project and its annual phasing, and incremental recurrent costs" (p. 18). We concur with this prescription but would add three data: the current schedule of recurrent funding and its financing sources, the schedule of capital replacement, and the percentage of financial absorption. The project brief should not be overloaded. In its initial stages, the PIP should provide the minimum data needed to illustrate the composition of public expenditure.

THE PIP'S IMPACT ON IMPROVING THE ALLOCATION OF RESOURCES

The Allocational Dilemma

The composition of expenditure in the two ministries (as well as many other ministries) has dramatically deteriorated over the past decade (Peterson and Kiragu 1990; World Bank 1989). Personnel expenditures are excessive, capital investment is excessive, and O&M is underfunded.[13] During this period, personnel costs increased in real terms 10 percent for the MOA and 17 percent for the MOLD. O&M funding declined in real terms per annum by 8 percent and 10 percent, respectively, for the MOA and the MOLD (Peterson and Kiragu 1990, Tables 1.2, 1.4). The decline is due to a short-term perspective of investment which overloads project portfolios and underfunds O&M costs.

Public investment is a long-term process. Unfortunately, government and donors take a short-term view. For government, it is the result of too few resources and too many commitments. Commitments always exceed resources, for they are driven by political as well as economic needs. Government has attempted to meet its commitments by overloading the development budget with too many projects and overloading the recurrent budget with too many staff.

Overloading the development budget is rational. Overloading promotes financial security for it ensures a full queue of donor projects. Overloading maximizes access to O&M funds of donor projects that are typically top heavy in capital goods and underfunded in O&M. With government overstaffing and underfunding of O&M, ministries rely on donor projects to provide these vital operating expenditures. Overloading is an appropriate response to an inefficient procurement system that can delay project implementation for several years.[14] Overloading is also an appropriate strategy for coping with treasury's budget cuts. The larger the number of projects, the larger the base of the budget assuming there is a minimum size for a project to be viable. Overloading is caused in part by institutional growth and fragmentation. Institutional identity is defined by access to resources. The expansion of these two ministries coupled with the demand by donors to invest in the sector has led to overloading.

Overstaffing in the recurrent budget is an example of short-term government financial policy and is the primary cause of an imbalance in the composition of expenditure. Staff salaries reduce the funds available for O&M which in turn must be found from donor projects since government cannot afford these outlays.

Donors also have a short-term outlook on public investment. Within the donor community, there is a strong incentive to design projects and "move money" but not to oversee the thorny task of implementation.[15] The capital composition of donor projects has a short-term bias. Capital goods are stressed which have a high national content whether they are appropriate or not. Limited complementary O&M means that the capital will quickly deteriorate and require expensive rehabilitation. The reluctance of donors to completely fund O&M costs for the establishment phase of a project (when capacity is being put in place) underscores the short-term perspective.

Why does government underfund O&M? Many donor projects require government to fund a high proportion of operating expenditures. Government views these contributions as optional and frequently delays or reneges on payment. Experience has shown that donors will not enforce the project agreements, so government proceeds to spend the donor portion of the O&M

and limit or ignore its own commitment. O&M expenditures such as fuel, spare parts, and materials often have a high foreign exchange content.

Donors also underfund O&M costs. First, they are fungible and difficult to monitor. Donors prefer capital goods that are easier to track. Second, O&M has a high local content, and donors prefer to fund their own goods. And third, donors take a short-term perspective on investment and are less concerned about long-term implementation.

The composition of public expenditure in the agricultural ministries is distorted because capital is exogenous, personnel are inexpensive and involve no foreign exchange, while O&M is costly. Government rationally uses more capital goods and staff and rations O&M. Donors rationally provide capital goods and rations O&M.

The deterioration in the composition of expenditure is due in large part to the excessive government staffing.[16] Excessive staffing in the recurrent budget reduces the headroom for O&M funds needed to support capacity in the development budget. Excessive staffing will continue to siphon off scarce O&M funds from the development budget, further impeding project success. Without a civil service reform that reduces the salary burden on the recurrent budget, the scope for improving allocation reform is limited. Recognizing the political difficulties of reducing staff, however, it is understandable that the government is addressing the development budget first. However, it must be clear that allocation reform will be limited and will have two short- to medium-term implications. First, improving the composition of the development budget without rationalizing the recurrent budget means a strategy of donor financing of O&M recurrent costs. Government funds in the recurrent budget will be tied up with salaries leaving little or no funds for O&M. Second, projects will have to limit diversion of O&M funds.

Strategies of Allocational Reform: Project Versus Portfolio

To improve investment allocation in the agriculture ministries (and government-wide), three steps are needed. First and most important, incentives are needed for both the government and the donors to adopt a long- rather than a short-term approach to investment. Second, incentives are needed for government not to overload portfolios. Third, incentives are needed for donors and government to completely fund O&M costs.

The PIP Project Strategy

The PIP promotes a *project* strategy of rationalizing allocation. A core set of projects are to be identified and fully funded while the remaining projects are financed as funding permits. This approach does not provide incentives for either the government or the donor to adopt a long-term approach to investment. Projects are by definition short- not long-term investments. Nor does it provide incentives to fund completely O&M costs, since full funding does not eliminate the need to overload portfolios.

Overloading occurs because the ministries are strapped for O&M funds and because donor-funded projects provide a subsidy to wider ministry operations. These pressures will not lessen with a set of core projects. Indeed, they will intensify, for the pressures to divert resources will focus on a smaller set of projects. Also, a project approach will not alter the donor's reluctance to fund completely O&M expenditures in the short-term. With fewer projects, the pressures to divert project resources to ministry-wide operations is increased. There are additional problems with the project approach to rationalizing public investment.

What Is a Project?

Defining a project is arbitrary. In the MOA, one core project, the Second Agricultural Adjustment Operation (ASAO II), has four separate sub-projects yet is considered a single project—different tasks, same project. (The four components of ASAO II are: policy analysis, budget management, monitoring and evaluation, and fertilizer monitoring.) In contrast, the IDA-funded National Extension Project II (NEP II) and the IFAD-funded Farmers Group and Community Support Project (FGCSP) are supporting extension services in different parts of the country—same task, separate projects. NEP II and the FGCSP have been classified as core and high priority projects, respectively. Does it make sense to fully fund one part of the country's extension services and not the other? Similarly, many of the agriculture ministries' projects are multi-sectoral. The PIP has not provided a mechanism for coordinating the classification of these projects. What may be a core project for the MOA may be low priority for the Ministry of Cooperative Development.

Concentrating on a Few Donors

Reducing the number of core projects to a fraction of the total portfolio, five and four for the MOA and the MOLD, respectively, increases the influence of a few donors. For FY 1992-1993, all four of the MOLD's core projects are IDA funded.[17] For MOA, three of the five projects are IDA funded, and IDA funding is 86 percent of the total core funding. The PIP is being promoted by the World Bank and the IDA which has the majority of core projects. Concentrating on a few donor projects limits the flexibility of the ministries and increases the influence of those donor projects. Such influence is especially sensitive in the areas of policy.

Full Funding: Allocation and Cash

The PIP allocation reform involves a simple tradeoff: line ministries will designate a small portion of their projects as core and treasury will fully fund them. The PIP offers the promise of a stable floor of expenditure for a small set of projects. Currently, treasury issues uncertain ceilings that are certain to be reduced, underfunded, or eliminated. We must distinguish between full *allocation* and full *funding* of a project. Full allocation is including the total project budget in the annual government budget. Full funding is supplying the total project budget with cash when required. One of the principal reasons for erratic project implementation and underabsorbtion of donor funds by the agriculture ministries has been the uncertainty and low levels of cash release from the treasury. Cash releases affect donor projects, for they delay or reduce government contributions and restrict the use of donor revenue funds where liquidity prevents government from initiating payments. (Donor projects funded by revenue require government to spend first and claim reimbursement.)

How is full funding of a project to be determined? Without well-developed work plans, is it what the division chiefs submit to the line ministry finance divisions? These submissions are often well-padded because the technical staff expect them to be reduced. Should full funding be dictated by the level of O&M which can be conservatively mobilized for the current year or at the project's termination? Should full funding be determined by the capacity of the ministry to fully implement? Without work plans (supported by project agreements) that provide details on resources, schedules, and objectives, full funding has little meaning.

Since the PIP began, neither the MOA nor the MOLD has received full funding for their core projects. In FY 1991-1992, the MOA had 22 core projects, and they received a smaller proportional allocation in the budget than non-core projects. Core projects received 65.8 percent of the amount originally submitted by the technical divisions. (The percentage is based upon the supplementary budget.) In the same year, the 10 core projects of the MOLD received 49.4 percent of the technical division's submission. This also was a lower allocation than non-core projects. Why did the core projects fare so poorly? Core projects are often the largest loan-funded projects in a ministry's portfolio and frequently have large government contributions. When reducing the government contribution to the development budget, these large government contributions are natural targets for treasury's cuts.

For FY 1992-1993, the allocations for core projects look significantly better. There are several differences between the two years. First, the number of core projects has been drastically reduced from 22 to five for the MOA and from 10 to four for the MOLD. Second, one of the core projects for both ministries is the Second Agricultural Adjustment Operation (ASAO II). ASAO II has as a condition, the full funding of core projects. The pressure on the treasury to comply with this condition precedent of the final tranche of the adjustment has meant that full funding is taken seriously. Two months into the financial year, both ministries were requested to submit budgets for their core projects that reflected full funding of activities. There was considerable discussion about what constitutes full funding, and considerable bargaining between the treasury and the agriculture ministries ensued. The result was an allocation that was far more generous than what was in the development budget. The allocation, however, still fell short of full funding. Again, the principal constraint was availability of government funds. The MOA received only 35.2 percent and 60.7 percent, respectively, of the government and donor funding required. The MOLD received 72.5 percent and 77 percent, respectively, of the government and donor funding required. While these additional allocations were welcome and unexpected, they are only commitments on paper. Core projects are not exempt from the austerity measures taken in February 1993. Stable funding of the development budget by protecting the core does not hold.

Treasury's additional allocation to the MOLD to fund its core projects is generous. The funds did not provide full funding and did not cover the pending bills owed by the core projects. After the pending bills are catered for, the MOLD has only 35.4 percent of the necessary government funds. The PIP program has not addressed the issue of pending bills for core or non-core projects. Government accounting regulations are clear—pending bills take precedence over new commitments. Until these carryovers are catered for, projects will not be fully funded with cash.

A final point about cash—cash flow management is the essence of the financial management in the line ministries. Cash for non-salary expenditures is a scarce and precious commodity. It is used to tap donor funds that are revenue financed, it is used to match donor contributions, and it is used for government development and recurrent expenses. There is never enough to cover past and current commitments. An astute undersecretary of finance knows how to stretch this limited resource to cover the essential needs just in time. The logic of the PIP would limit fungibility. Core projects should receive priority in cash releases, and such funds could not be reallocated to other purposes even if the core project was delayed. In the short- to medium-term, this system would be disastrous for it would hamstring the finance staff. Fortunately, the PIP has not extended the logic of core projects to the release of cash. If treasury wants to give the core concept meaning, it will have to tie cash release to the core projects.

Experience has shown that there is a de facto list of core projects, but it is not based on treasury's elaborate formulas. Financial not technical viability determines whether a project is core, meaning that it is fully accommodated in the budget and fully funded with cash throughout the financial year. Financial viability has three aspects: concessionary quality of funding (grants vs. loans), conditionalities of funding (whether government contributions are required), and the mechanism of funding (is release of funds unencumbered). Currently, the actual core projects are grant funded, require no government contributions, and are released outside of government budget and accounting procedures. The problem in Kenya has been that the World Bank has promoted the PIP financial reform yet its projects are precisely the type which are difficult to accommodate for they are loan funded, involve large government contributions, and have complex payment procedures that involve both government and World Bank accounting systems.

Project Selection Criteria

Selecting five and four core projects from a portfolio of 50 and 44 projects from the MOA and the MOLD, respectively, has been a difficult task. Senior staff often believe that the PIP's allocation formula (one-twelfth of the portfolio of non-fully funded non-grant projects) is arbitrary and inappropriate for the sector. They do not understand the rationale of the formula. They argue persuasively that the sector is vital, all projects are priorities, and that the sector is underfunded (agriculture's portion of total government expenditures has declined despite the increasing size of the population and the declining growth rate of agriculture).[18]

Donors, including the World Bank which is promoting the PIP, contend that the formula is too restrictive. The small allotment would exclude many important projects including several funded by the World Bank. To protest the core formula, the MOLD's initial submission of core and high priority projects completely excluded World Bank-funded projects! To add to the confusion, when the PIP was first introduced in FY 1990-1991, the World Bank was also implementing the Second Agricultural Structural Adjustment Operation (ASAO II). As a condition precedent of the ASAO II, the agriculture ministries were to select a set of core projects. A much higher number of core projects was allowed under the ASAO II (22 rather than five for MOA and 10 rather than four for the MOLD). Reducing the number of core projects has caused both confusion and resistance.

The heart of the PIP allocation reform is the ranking of projects into core, high priority, medium, and other. What criteria are used? The treasury has provided broad methods of ranking core projects: they should be of highest priority and be in an advanced stage of implementation (Office of the Vice President and Ministry of Finance 1992a, p. 14). In addition, the treasury has developed several project selection criteria under the Budget Rationalization Programme (BRP).[19] The BRP provides three broad selection criteria: (1) fewer projects completed sooner, (2) efficiency and potential for economic growth, and (3) provision of additional funds for operating expenses of existing capacity (Office of the Vice President and Ministry of Finance 1989, p. 12). The BRP also outlines five features projects should have: (1) immediate contribution to increasing production, (2) increasing employment and income generating opportunities, (3) assisting the poorer groups, (4) earning or saving foreign exchange, and (5) increasing revenue from beneficiaries to pay for recurrent costs (Office of the Vice President and Ministry of Finance 1989, p. 12). Finally, projects are to be assessed by the Ministry of Planning and National Development (MPND) by five criteria: economic viability, financial structure, social impact, institutional requirements, and environmental impact (Office of the Vice President and Ministry of Finance 1992a, p. 17).

To classify projects under the PIP, the treasury and the MPND have provided no less than 15 criteria: two broad PIP criteria, three broad BRP criteria, five features of projects under the BRP, and five criteria from the MPND. The criteria are too numerous and some are even contradictary. Some are simply inappropriate or ineffective. For example, the broad BRP criterion that projects should be completed as quickly as possible is inappropriate. This criterion is biased toward capacity expanding rather than more appropriate capacity supporting projects given the lack of recurrent cost support. Capacity supporting projects should be as many and long-term as possible. The broad BRP criterion of a project's "efficiency and potential for promoting economic growth" is ineffective since most projects can easily satisfy it.

A critical issue is whether cost benefit techniques should be used to rank projects. To date, such analyses are not a government requirement. Experienced observers of the PIP process in other countries argue that cost-benefit analysis will not be effective (Bird and Stevens 1992, p. 22). It is the rare project that could not be couched to hurdle stringent investment criteria. The sector's portfolio is a product of local and donor interests, and stringent objective investment criteria will not exclude most projects that have strong political backing. The experience of the Ministry of Planning and National Development in applying objective investment criteria to rural development projects has not been encouraging (Gaile 1988, 1994, p. 10).

At present, the government does not require that projects be vetted with project appraisal techniques. As a planning instrument, the PIP would not need project appraisal data. As a budgeting instrument it does. As Stevens and Bird note:

> Formal project appraisal techniques are thus more likely to be used to test alternative designs, to demonstrate the viability of a project to an external aid agency, or *to protect the annual budget from doubtful schemes*, than they are to determine the composition of a PIP (1992, p. 22, emphasis added).

The recent review by the MOA of the PIP is instructive of how project ranking is done. The review had representatives from most of the divisions, although several divisions were absent. Few division chiefs attended. While several ranking criteria were discussed, they were not rigorously applied in reviewing the 50 projects in the ministry's portfolio. There was a strong tendency to rank a project as high priority, and if the divisional representative pressed for such a ranking, it was often given. Virtually no objective data were used to support project classifications. Concern was also expressed about rating a donor project as either medium or low priority. Donors have already complained about their low rankings. Fully grant-funded projects are awkward because they are likely to be funded yet still need to be ranked. To save room for other high priority projects, the grant-funded projects are listed as either low or medium priority. This sends misleading signals to the donor.

Project size was the most important criterion in determining whether a project was core. The national extension program, which is the largest division and activity in the ministry, was selected as a core without question. Three of the five core "projects" were formed by clustering projects together. The ASAO II project has four sub-projects. The National Extension Project had the IDA-funded NEP Phase II project combined with the IFAD-funded Farmers Group and Community Support Project (which has seven components). And a third core project simply listed the donor (IFAD) and has nine sub-projects. The five core projects comprise 46 percent of the gross development allocation in the forward budget for FY 1993-1994.

Inappropriate Project Structures

By stipulating a few core projects, large projects are emphasized while smaller projects may be better suited to the management constraints of ministries. The large project bias of the PIP limits including experimental projects that may have a very high rate of return yet should be kept small. Second, the PIP investment criteria give preference to fully grant-funded projects.

Under the PIP, all fully grant-funded projects are to be implemented like the core projects.[20] The willingness of the treasury to consider additional fully grant-funded projects beyond the current year's budget ceiling indicates the short-term perspective of government (Office of the Vice President and Ministry of Finance 1992b, pp. 22-23). Fully grant-funded projects are desirable. They are fully funded, and they expand the size of the portfolio which increases the potential number of core projects. To maximize the size of its guaranteed portfolio, a ministry should acquire as many small grant projects as possible and select the largest loan (revenue-financed) projects as the core. The allocation rules of the PIP provide a strong incentive to disaggregate grant projects and aggregate loan projects.

By allowing all fully grant-funded projects to be implemented, the treasury is using financial not programmatic criteria to select projects. Optimal sectoral tradeoffs should determine the size of a ministry's portfolio, not the ministry's grantsmanship ability. While the financial structure of a ministry's portfolio should be irrelevant, this is not true of government as a whole.[21] Government needs to maximize grant and minimize loan and government of Kenya payments. Government also needs to determine the optimal sectoral tradeoffs. Treasury needs to be more active in acquiring grants and fungible funds so sectoral tradeoffs can be determined and funded. The PIP's position on fully grant-funded projects erodes the credibility of sectoral allocation criteria and promotes inappropriate grantsmanship. Fully grant-funded projects are not gifts. They are public expenditures like loans, and they add to the public sector's share of expenditure as a percentage of GDP. Fully grant-funded projects require government contributions in personnel, facilities, utilities, and scarce management. Unchecked growth in grant-funded projects can create unsustainable capacity. Lenient project appraisal of fully grant-funded projects can distort the portfolio. Do grant-funded projects complement existing activities or do they divert the ministry's scarce resources, particularly skilled managers?

The Project Strategy of Investment Reform: A Summary

A project strategy of investment reform does not promote a long-term view of investment, it does not solve the O&M shortage, and by rigidly reducing the number of projects to a core set, it addresses the symptom but not the underlying causes of overloading. There are four problems with the project approach. First, it assumes full funding of core projects, yet government cannot even manage this objective. Second, it assumes that financial targeting will improve implementation. The delays of a cumbersome procurement system, inappropriate staffing, and poor management are not altered by designating a handful of projects core. Third, the core concept limits the absorption of donor funds to availability of government funds. If implemented, such a practice would drastically reduce the funding available to the sector diminishing the large investment in staff. Fourth, the core concept introduces rigidity into budgeting and cash management when the scarcity of resources demands flexibility.

AN ALTERNATIVE APPROACH TO PUBLIC INVESTMENT REFORM: BUDGETING BY SECTORS

An alternative approach to investment reform would promote a long-term view of investment through budgeting by sectors. A resource envelope for each ministry would be specified, rigidly adhered to, and reliably funded.[22] The ministries would select the projects and could overload. As part of their annual budget submission, the ministries would prepare a plan that explained sectoral objectives and the expected financing sources. Rationalizing the portfolio would be through a gradual and systematic reduction in the portfolio ceiling (e.g., a 6% per annum reduction).

This approach has several advantages over the PIP project strategy. It manages conflict, it promotes long-term economic and financial planning, and it improves the composition of resources. It lessens conflict with donors because it does not make invidious distinctions between projects and their donors. It lessens bureaucratic conflict because divisions do not have to champion their projects. It is realistic, for it recognizes the common practice of diverting project resources to ministry-wide operations.

The reform would promote long-term inter- and intra-sectoral planning that the project approach ignores. A major objective of the sectoral strategy is to link economic and financial planning. Financial planning would promote the involvement of the donors and would attempt to coordinate long-term financial commitments to the sector (Peterson 1992b, p. 8). Division chiefs would have a strong incentive to see the planning system work. They would want their division's activities represented, and they would want to reverse the decline in allocation to the sector. While the long-term benefits of economic and financial planning are large, the impact of the reform would not be wholly contingent upon improvements in planning.

An investment reform based on the envelope approach would improve the composition of resources. First, to manage the transition of an allocation reform requires discipline and flexibility. Reducing the portfolio while continuing to overload it increases upfront access to donor funds and delays even further the use of government funds. Second, the reform provides a gradual timetable and incentives for donors to change their investment strategy. With a declining resource envelope, donors will have to reduce their investment in the sector. Most important, a reduced portfolio means reduced capital spending. If donors seek to maximize their share of investment in the sector, they will have to switch from financing oversupplied capital goods to undersupplied O&M support. If necessary, O&M funding can be reprogrammed from balance of payments support. If donors increase O&M funding without staffing reductions, they will demand improved financial controls. Strengthening key administrative systems would improve implementation.

A major benefit of an envelope approach would be the development of budget norms on a ministerial and sectoral basis. By viewing the resource envelope as a whole (both development and the recurrent budgets), it would be possible to set indicative targets for capital, O&M, and labor. These norms could be used to reshape the composition of the portfolio. This approach would address a major budgeting problem that Kenya and many other developing countries face, an inability to budget or fund the future recurrent costs of a development expenditure. These costs are "over the horizon," and even forward budgeting systems do not adequately cater for them. By viewing expenditure composition on a portfolio rather than a project basis, these costs can be better provided. Financial planning would involve maintaining investment ratios for the envelope (e.g., 50% staff, 35% O&M, 15% capital goods).

A smaller portfolio is easier to fund and lessens the risk of donor retrenchment and the need to overload. A smaller development budget also will illustrate the overstaffing of the sector and the need for reducing the recurrent budget. Evaluating the resource requirements of a ministry, and eventually a sector, may eventually lead to a coordinated reduction of both the development and recurrent budgets.

With a declining development budget, a sectoral economic and financial planning process in place that promotes stable funding to the sector, with O&M fully funded and controls that limit its diversion, the ministries would have little incentive to overload their portfolios. Government and donors could take a long-term view of the sector and finance a portfolio which is fully funded and promptly implemented.

LESSONS OF FINANCIAL REFORM

The preference of the envelope approach to the project approach to investment reform suggests several lessons:

- Allocation reform should be disciplined and flexible, not rigid (e.g., one approach would specify a percentage reduction of a portfolio, not a specific number of projects).
- Allocation reform should be incremental, not drastic, to allow time for both donors and governments to adjust—time for donors to reduce their funding levels and change the composition of their funding, time for governments to reduce the number of projects.
- Allocation reforms are political. They cannot be achieved simply by a technique. What is needed are incentives to change existing behavior of governments and donors.
- Allocation reforms often involve improvements in financial information. The primary benefits of this information may be administrative and information reforms that underpin allocation, but they do not directly reform the allocation.
- To reduce the political pressures associated with financial reforms, allocation decisions need to be shared (e.g., the size of the reduced portfolio is determined by treasury, while the composition of the reduced portfolio is decided upon by donors and ministries).
- Additional resources are necessary to manage the process of allocation reforms (e.g., donors funding O&M expenditures in the short- and medium-term which reduces government's tendency to overload the portfolio). Kenya's financial reforms have overemphasized allocation reform relative to budget execution reforms (see Peterson 1992).

APPENDIX SAMPLE PIP PROJECT BRIEF: THE NATIONAL EXTENSION PROJECT II

PIP 1992/93 - 1995/96 PROJECT NO. 025

PROJECT BRIEF

Ministry: AGRICULTURE Department: AGRIC. EXTEN. SERVICES

Name of Project: NATIONAL EXTENSION PROGRAM - PHASE II

Project Priority: CORE

Poject Status: on-going Implementation Period: 7 Years

Year Project started: July 92

1. SUMMARY FINANCIAL DATA:

(In K #'s)

	GOK	DONOR	TOTAL
1. Total Estimated cost of Project:	3070000	22611000	2568100*
2. Expenditures Already Incurred: (Projection up to 30/6/96)	786000	3393000	4179000
3. Balance Required to Complete:	2284000	19218000	21502000

*From project document.

2. BRIEF DESCRIPTION OF PROJECT OBJECTIVES

1. Improvement and strengthening of the extension service of the Ministry of Agriculture at all levels and in all major agricultural zones of the Country, and achieve sustained increases in agricultural production
2. Creation of Management system based on a systematic program of farm visits and staff training.
3. Development of relevant technology by researchers and passing of the same technology to farmers by the extension staff.
4. Enhancement of the professional knowledge of specialists in extension, crop and livestock production through monthly workshops where field level problems are discussed and solutions evolved, and formation of strong extension research linkages.
5. Establishment of a network of on-farm trills jointly planned and managed by researchers and extention staff.
6. Focus extension activities on field and horticultural crops, livestock production and activities of rural women farmers through women groups and Home Economic staff.
7. Provision of additional transport and improvement of mobility of Frontline staff to facilitate regular and timely visits to contact farmers and groups.

3. BRIEF DESCRIPTION ON PROJECT ACTIVITIES:

1. Training is the major component of the project. These include orientation training, inservice training (upgrading, monthly work-shops, fortnightly training sessions and communication training).
2. Transport provided by the project include:-
   Four Wheel Drive vehicles, Cars, Mopeds and bicycles.
3. Civil Works, that is, Construction of prefabricated buildings to be ued as offices and for training in some districts and divisions.
4. Farm Demonstrations and farm trials.
5. Monitoring and Evaluation.

4. REVIEW OF IMPLEMENTATION SO FAR:

National Extension Program Phase II (NEP II) is a continuation of NEP I which came to an end in December, 31st 1990. NEP II commenced in July 1991. NEP I commenced in 1983

(*continued*)

Appendix: (*Continued*)

and was supposed to end in 1987 but due to a slow rate of expenditure the project was extended to December, 31st 1990. By the end of the project period, all 30 Districts will continue to implement NEPII and additional nine districts will be included. From January to July 1991, NEP II was operating on pilot basis in Embu and Elgeyo Marakwet districts. The main activity was retraining of agricultural staff in livestock production aspects and livestock staff in agricultural production aspects.

5. REVIEW OF PROJECT FINANCING

NEP II has just commenced (in July, 1991.) However, NEP I experienced delays in disbursements of project funds, that is, delays in procurement arrangement during the initial years of project implementation, budgetary ceilings and delayed submission of Ministry's Final audited accounts to the Bank for disbursement.

6. PROJECT IMPLEMENTATION SCHEDULING FOR 1992/1993-1995/1996

January 1991-July 1991: Pilot phase in Embu and Elgeyo Marakwet

July 1991/July 1992: Commencement of NEP II phase one. This involves 12 districts (ten additional districts to the ones in pilot phase)

July 1992: Commencement of full fledged project implementation, with coverage of 39 districts.

Work Plan is being prepared.

7. RECURRENT COST REQUIREMENTS

Date of Completion - 1999

Salary Costs at Completion .... K# 8,236,666

Allowance Costs at Completion .... K# 1,781,411

Non-wage Operating Expenses at Completion .... K# 8,031,061

8. OTHER COMMENTS ON THE PROJECT

- The project places a lot of emphasis on Research-Extension linkages
- Unlike NEP I, a lot of emphasis is also placed on group approach in the provision of extenstion services.
- To ensure the smooth operation of NEP II, various committees will be formed at the District, Provincial and headquarter level (DDC, PSC, and NSC).
  These committees will help in coming up with a structure that will ensure the workability of the program.

Date of last update June 2, 1993

ACKNOWLEDGMENTS

The author thanks Joe Magari, Claudio Schuftan, Clive Southey, Mike Stevens, and Sam Wilson for their comments on an earlier draft of this paper.

NOTES

1. Kenya has a forward budget that is prepared in the first quarter of the new financial year. For a description and critique of the forward budget see, Lehmann (1986), Office of the Vice President and Ministry of Finance, Budgetary Supply Department (1991, p. 1), Peterson (1992), Office of the Vice President and Ministry of Finance (1992), and Office of the Vice President and Ministry of Finance (1992), Ministry of Finance (1989).

2. The PIP applies to both projects of line ministries and state corporations. This chapter ignores the investments of the agriculture state corporations. Only a few of these state corporations are funded through the ministry's budgets, and those that do simply receive a subvention. Neither ministry can monitor their state corporations, and only the treasury's Government Investments Department can effectively monitor performance. Bird and Stevens (1992, p. 3) contend that reducing government interference in state corporations means that they should not be in the PIP.

3. Project financing agreements *sometimes* provide details on the TEC and the scheduling of expenditure. There is a computerized list of donor commitments to projects managed by the External Resources Department (ERD) of the treasury, but it is often erroneous. More important, the ERD list does not provide details on government commitments by item so the government commitment cannot be adequately budgeted.

4. Bird and Stevens (1992, p. 5) argue that a PIP should ideally have a "main" period of from two to five years when the investment is put into service and a "tail" period in which the recurrent expenditures for the main period are listed. They recommend a two- to three-year tail period.

5. Underabsorbtion of donor funds is not entirely the fault of the line ministries. The treasury has imposed restrictions on the use of revenue funds (prefinancing) of donor projects and has placed spending freezes on loan-funded projects. Donors also contribute to the problem by making direct payments that do not pass through the government accounting system and by off-budget financing.

6. Expenditure data is provided to the line ministries by the treasury's accountancy services in the form of a monthly ledger. This ledger is typically two to three months behind, and the ledger shows monthly and cumulative expenditures. The ledger does not disaggregate by projects so a project total has to be manually calculated.

7. In 1991, the MOA conducted an exercise of extracting expenditure data for the project lists going back to FY 1983-1984. While the exercise found considerable data, the gaps were striking and principally involved donor funds.

8. Some observers have argued that under the Budget Rationalization Programme the budget structure should have been reformed by replacing the dual structure with a unitary budget see the World Bank (1989, p. 34).

9. To improve the composition of government-wide expenditure, the World Bank in 1985 recommended that such norms be developed (World Bank 1989, pp. 28-29).

10. Recurrent cost norms have been developed for various sectors including agriculture. Heller of the World Bank has worked extensively on recurrent cost (*r*) coefficients and contends that the agriculture and livestock sectors' *r*s are 10 percent and 14 percent, respectively (Heller 1979, p. 176). There are three problems with Heller's indexes. First, there is a wide variation in his coefficients within each sector. Second, within a sector Heller does not disaggregate the categories of O&M such as transport and maintenance. Third and most important, Heller's coefficients include both personnel and O&M costs. A high coefficient may mask deteriorating O&M support when it reflects, as in the MOA and the MOLD in Kenya, a high proportion of personnel expenditure (Heller 1974).

11. The recurrent cost data for the MOA is based on the O&M norms developed by Peterson in Peterson and Kiragu (1990). The norms were based on the O&M requirements for each major division by line item (e.g., transport, traveling, maintenance, materials, all others). To determine the level of recurrent support, the O&M norms (which are determined by emolument levels) were multiplied by the budgeted project salary.

12. Under the ASAO II program there is a component to strengthen the monitoring and evaluation section for both the MOA and the MOLD. Resources are provided for technical assistance, training, vehicles, computers, and operating expenses for staff at both headquarters and the field.

13. On personnel expenditures being too high, see World Bank (1992, pp. 44-65). The argument that capital investment is increasing relative to staff is made by Wilson of the Long Range Planning Unit, Ministry of Planning and National Development. Wilson's work is preliminary, and he concedes that much of the investment increases could be due to infrastructure (e.g., roads and buildings) which have low depreciation rates and padded costs. Indeed, it is useful to categorize

capital into infrastructure and machinery (e.g., vehicles, pumps). On the underfunding of O&M, see the World Bank (1989) and Peterson and Kiragu (1990).

14. The National Extension Programme I (NEP I), which is the largest and arguably most important development project in the MOA and the MOLD, was seriously delayed by the cumbersome procurement system. It took more than 18 months to procure vehicles. More recently, several projects under the Second Agricultural Adjustment Operation (ASAO II) have had to delay key activities because the computers have taken over a year to procure.

15. Indeed, the World Bank has recently instituted procedures designed to change this incentive system. Staff who bring projects to board presentation have to supervise their projects for at least three years.

16. Naturally, senior staff in the two ministries feel that they are understaffed. They disagree with the argument that overstaffing occurs in the lower administrative cadre. It is accepted that understaffing exists in the skilled upper technical cadre. The MOA and the MOLD are overstaffed relative to the O&M support available (see Peterson and Kiragu 1990, pp. 15-16).

17. Only the Veterinary Laboratory Surveillance component of the Animal Health Rehabilitation Project in the MOLD has a small (K£s 40,000) portion of UNDP funding. The rest of the core programme is funded by IDA.

18. In the 1970s, the agricultural sector (MOA and the MOLD) received 9.1 percent of total government expenditures; yet in FY 1990-1991, it has declined to 3 percent. Agricultural growth in the 1970s was 3.7 percent and has declined to 3.4 percent in 1990. At the same time, population pressures have increased with growth rates going from 3.4 percent in the 1970s to approximately 4 percent in 1990 (see Peterson 1991, Table 1, p. 3).

19. On the budget rationalization program, see Ministry of Finance and Planning, Taskforce on Budget Rationalization (1985). For a critique of the program, see World Bank (1989, pp. 26-29; 1992, pp. 37-39), and Peterson (1992).

20. By fully grant-funded, we mean that the total is funded by donor grant and that the funding is direct payment rather than revenue. Revenue funding is when government spends and claims reimbursement. The principle of automatic inclusion of fully grant-funded projects has been a practice in budgeting for some time. When the PIP core projects were introduced under the ASAO II program in FY 1990-1991, the treasury and the World Bank agreed that projects should be categorized as core, a-in-a (appropriation in aid or direct payment) grant, medium priority, and low priority. The current PIP categories have omitted the fully grant-funded category.

21. The irrelevance of the capital structure of development projects is analogous to the Miller-Modigliani (M&M) thesis in corporate finance that capital structure is irrelevant to the financing decision of the firm. What matters is not whether an investment is financed by debt or equity but whether the investment has an appropriate rate of return (Modigliani and Miller 1958).

22. Ideally, you would want to specify the resources required by a sector and not simply define the "ministerial" requirements. A sector approach may promote the reorganizations needed as part of civil service reform.

REFERENCES

Baum, W.C., and S.M. Tolbert. 1985. *Investing in Development: Lessons of World Bank Experience.* New York: Oxford University Press.

Bird, A., and M. Stevens. 1992. "Preparing a Public Investment Programme CPIO," (*ECPS/EDA Training Brief*). The World Bank, April 22.

Eskeland, G. 1989. "Budget Rationalization: Issues and Options." Report prepared for the Eastern Africa Office of the World Bank, November 8.

Gaile, G.L. 1988. "Choosing Locations for Small Town Development to Enable Market and Employment Expansion: The Case of Kenya." *Economic Geography* LXIV: 242-254.

———. 1992. "Thought for Food: Model and Policy Approaches for increased Agricultural Productivity and Food Security in Africa." Pp. 7-21 in *Ending Hunger in Africa*, edited by D. Griffith and J. Newman. Syracuse: Syracuse University Press.

Heller, P. 1974. "Public Investment in LDC's with Recurrent Cost Constraint: The Kenyan Case." *Quarterly Journal of Economics* 88 (May): 251-277.

———. 1979. "The Underfinancing of Recurrent Development Costs." *Finance and Development* Vol 26, No. 1 (March): 176.

Kavalsky, B. 1986. "Reviewing Public Investment Programs." *Finance and Development* (331, March): 37-40.

Lehmann, G. 1986. "Kenya's Experience With a Forward Budget." EDI Training Materials, The World Bank, July.

Ministry of Finance. 1989. "Ways and Means of Improving the Quality and Effectiveness of Public Expenditure Programming in Kenya."

Ministry of Finance and Planning, Taskforce on Budget Rationalization. 1985. "Budget Rationalization Programme and Guidelines for Programme Review and Forward Budget." July.

Ministry of Planning and National Development. 1992. "Preparation of the Public Investment Programme 1993/94-1995/96." Circular No. 1, July 10.

Modigliani, F., and M.H. Miller. 1958. "The Cost of Capital, Corporation Finance, and the Theory of Investment." *American Economic Review* 26(1, June): 261-297.

Office of the Vice President and Ministry of Finance, Budgetary Supply Department. 1991. "Public Investment Programme." June.

Office of the Vice President and Ministry of Finance. 1992. "Public Investment Programme Project Briefs of the Ministry of Agriculture." April.

Office of the Vice President and Ministry of Finance. 1992a. "The Public Investment Programme." Discussion Brief No. 2/92 prepared for the Forward Budget Workshops, August 19-20, Nairobi, Kenya.

Office of the Vice President and Ministry of Finance. 1992b. "Budgeting for Externally Aided Projects." Discussion Brief 3/92 for the Forward Budget Workshop, August 19-20.

Peterson, S. 1990. "Improving Financial Management in the Ministries of Agriculture and Livestock Development." November 7.

———. 1991. "Project Financial Monitoring." Paper prepared for the Workshop on Project Monitoring, Lake Naivasha, Kenya, February 20-22.

———. 1992. "Financial Reform in Kenya: The Allocational Bias." May 14.

———. 1992a. "Methodological Issues in Analyzing Recurrent Costs." Pp. 000-000 in *The Recurrent Cost Crisis in Development Bureaucracies*.

———. 1992b. "Proposed ASMP II Strategy for Strengthening the Institutional Response to the Agriculture Sector." Prepared for the project design of the Second Agricultural Sector Management Project (ASMP II), June 19.

Peterson, S., and K. Kiragu. 1990. "Recurrent Cost Issues in the Ministry of Agriculture and the Ministry of Livestock Development." Report prepared for the Ministry of Agriculture and the Ministry of Livestock Development in preparation for the Second Agriculture Adjustment Operation, May.

Thompson, R.H. 1991. "Background to M&E and Overview of Current Monitoring Systems." Paper prepared for the Workshop on Project Monitoring, Lake Naivasha, Kenya, February 20-22.

Wilson, L.S., G. Barber, and W. Milne. 1992. "Capital Stock Estimates for Kenya by Industry and Asset: 1972-1992." Technical Paper 92-02, Long Range Planning Unit, Ministry of Planning and National Development, July.

World Bank. 1989. "Kenya Public Expenditure Issues." East Africa Department, Report No. 7508-KE, April 14.

World Bank. 1992. "Kenya: Re-Investing in Stabilization and Growth through Public Sector Adjustment." East Africa Deparment, Report No. 9998-KE, January, 10.

THE ROLE OF PROJECT DATA BANKS IN PUBLIC INVESTMENT PROGRAMING

Katrina Sharkey

ABSTRACT

The quality of public investments is usually an indicator of the soundness of national planning and budgeting and of macroeconomic management in general. The pre-investment process should facilitate the assignment of investment resources to those projects which make the most contribution to national development and to determine the impact of their costs on the national budget. Several problems, however, have been evident in public investment planning and management in several countries. To address them, project data banks have been set up to improve public sector investment management, support pre-investment planning and programing, and allow for project supervision. This chapter reviews experience of project data banks in three Latin American and Caribbean countries.

Policy Studies and Developing Nations, Volume 3, pages 141-150.

ISBN: 1-55938-190-6

INTRODUCTION

This paper is based on the proceedings and final reports of two seminars on "Project Data Banks and Public Sector Investment Programing" held November 20-22, 1991, and January 14-15, 1992, in Kingston, Jamaica, and Santo Domingo, Dominican Republic, respectively. Both seminars were sponsored by, among other agencies, the Economic Development Institute (EDI) of the World Bank, the Economic Commission for Latin America and the Caribbean (ECLAC), and the Latin American Institute for Economic and Social Planning (ILPES). The original report for the Jamaica seminar was prepared by Eduardo Aldunate (ILPES), Barbara Scott (Government of Jamaica), Francisco Mejia (National Planning Department of Colombia), and Maria Teresa Hamuy (Ministry of Planning and Cooperation in Chile). A compendium of documents and presentations from the Dominican Republic seminar was prepared by ILPES.

PROJECT DATA BANKS AND PUBLIC INVESTMENT PROGRAMING

The growth rate of a country depends, among other factors, on good public investments. In fact, the quality of a country's pre-investment process is usually an indicator of the soundness of national planning and budgeting and of macroeconomic management in general. The contribution of the pre-investment process to economic development lies mainly in facilitating the assignment of investment resources to those projects which make the most contribution to national development. In order to achieve this goal, it is necessary to obtain and make efficient use of information about the contribution that a given project can make to the national economy.

National economic policy is translated into projects during the pre-investment process. In addition to enabling government to assess the contribution of a given project to the goals contained in the national economic plan, the process also requires that sound project costs be established, not only to allow an appraisal of the specific project but also to determine its impact on the national budget.

A well-founded pre-investment process alone is not a sufficient guarantee that resources are going to be deployed efficiently or effectively. A "good" project can go astray if insufficient precautions are taken to ensure its completion within the schedule and budget estimated at the pre-investment stage. It is therefore important to implement a project follow-up and supervision system. Such a system should give timely warnings about projects that are having implementation problems in order to enable the executing and/or funding agencies to adopt appropriate and timely corrective measures.

Several problems, however, have been evident in public investment planning and management in many countries. The most pervasive among these problems are:

- absence of the appropriate institutional and legal environments,
- lack of projects ready for financing,
- delays during implementation,
- emphasis on large infrastructure (often highly visible) projects,
- postponements of projects in the social sectors, and
- inadequate financing for operation and maintenance of projects.

Such problems often relate to poor institutional and human capacity, nonstandardized project appraisal methodologies, lack of timely information, poor accountability, deficient (or sometimes absence of) procedures, or poor selection criteria. Other important characteristics include: (1) a lack of political commitment throughout the administration and (2) an absence of meaningful dialogue between the political and administrative directorates.

Project data banks (PDBs) were born as filing systems to standardize and organize relevant information about public sector investment projects. Over time, these filing systems were computerized and became more complex due to the increased volume of information.

The PDB aims to improve public sector investment management, support pre-investment planning and investment programing, and allow a detailed and timely supervision of public sector projects as integral components of the national budget. It should facilitate pre-investment planning, support investment programing, improve supervision and control, support project ranking, provide information for ex post evaluation, allow analysis of alternative scenarios, clarify the relationships among projects, improve inter-institutional coordination, support negotiation of loans or grants, facilitate follow-up of multiple project programs, and provide an invaluable tool for decentralization. The PDB is complemented with project appraisal methodologies, training in project appraisal, and training in project supervision and control.

Public investment management is like a productive process in which resources are transformed through given processes. For example, through pre-investment, studies are produced; through capital investment, physical infrastructure is gained; and through expenditures, human capital in the country is increased. Public investment management also includes macroeconomic projections, follow-up and budgetary control systems, systems for allocation of the current budget, systems for allocating social expenditure, and systems for developing investment programs. These elements are held together by a public sector management investment system which has four components:

1. methodologies for the formulation and appraisal of projects, pre-investment planning, investment programing, and ex post project evaluation;
2. a training program covering project identification, formulation and appraisal, and project administration and operation of the system;
3. assignment of institutional responsibilities for development of methodologies, administration, training, and procedures for periodic update of the information, distribution of reports, and access to the system; and
4. the PDB which collects data throughout the project life cycle.

THE INSTITUTIONAL FRAMEWORK

Many countries in the world today are going through transition or structural adjustment, whether they be in Eastern Europe, Asia, or Latin America and the Caribbean. For the management of the transition, government officials charged with its implementation need to have at their disposal a set of rules known in advance, which elected bodies, the executives, and the public at large will accept and adhere to. These officials also need to possess the requisite skills and motivation in order to translate plans into practice. Experience shows that certain (1) institutional, capacity, and political factors—which together constitute the institutional framework—are likely to determine a country's success in implementing the programing of public investments, and (2) in the same context, the utility of a tool such as the PDB will be influenced by the extent to which a government gives attention to those factors.

The factors include:

- the extent of genuine political commitment to implement and sustain changes in public finance management practices,
- level of awareness and commitment by government to the need for institutional strengthening and capacity building for public servants,
- the legal status of the public sector investment plan,
- public sector salaries and their comparability with those offered in the private sector,
- public policy on the dissemination of information to the public,
- in-service training for public servants,
- extent of the country's dependence on technical and financial cooperation from the donor community, and
- the level of development of management information systems within government institutions.

Some of the countries participating in the seminars which are the subject of this chapter are going through adjustment and have already or are currently attempting to improve their public sector investment management. Their experience to date will demonstrate how the factors described previously have influenced their ability to carry through with their plans.

THE PROJECT DATA BANK

The project bank may be structured as a centralized or decentralized information system. In the centralized model, one main computer terminal or smaller personal computers are connected on dedicated lines to the mainframe. The advantages of this approach are greater control, non-duplication of information, and easy access. Among the disadvantages are higher investment and running costs, greater opposition to the system, and widespread impact of system failures. A decentralized system needs one database with a copy of all the information and local data bases in line ministries or regional planning offices to manage all information related to the region or ministry. The advantages are lower investment and running costs and greater acceptance of the system. Problems are that data are not updated simultaneously in all databases and that there can be duplication of information.

The project data bank is broken up into modules, including a pre-investment module, a project follow-up and supervision module (allowing physical and financial follow-up of projects), and a technical assistance module in which information about technical assistance projects and donor profiles are registered. Special applications such as macro-impacts and investment programing may also be incorporated.

Implementation of project data banks requires diagnosis of the current public investment management system, design of data capture forms, elaboration of procedures, preparation of training programs and pedagogical materials, development of project appraisal methodologies, calculation of shadow prices, software programing, development of manuals, acquisition of hardware, and initial loading of the information into the project data bank.

One of the main conditions for success is sustained political support. Also needed are a comprehensive long-term training program, adequate funding and staffing, and active involvement of final users. The total cost of implementation is likely to be high. The new systems may encounter resistance to change at all levels, and the work load of involved ministries will initially increase. Nevertheless, several countries, including Belize, Bolivia, Colombia, Chile, the Dominican Republic, Guatemala, Jamaica, Trinidad and Tobago, and Venezuela, have developed project data banks. The rest of this chapter reports on experience in Jamaica, Colombia, and Chile.[1]

Jamaica

The government of Jamaica decided to use the project cycle to develop and implement projects for its PSIP. The aims were to provide (1) a system for macroeconomic management and for measuring the impact of macroeconomic policies, (2) an integrated approach to the implementation of the public sector investment program to enable coordination of projects at all stages of the project cycle, and (3) a system for the control, review, analysis, and assessment of the investment program to ensure efficient allocation of scarce resources.

The Project Management System and Public Sector Investment System are essentially managed by three agencies: the Planning Institute of Jamaica (PIOJ), the Ministry of Finance (Budgets Division), and the Project Analysis and Monitoring Company Ltd. (PAMCO). The PIOJ focusses on projects at the pre-investment stage while the Ministry of Finance and PAMCO focus on projects at the investment stage. The PDB is decentralized and modular. It is a distributed data base, with modules installed at the PIOJ, the Ministry of Finance, and PAMCO. Basic information on projects is registered at PIOJ. Information on financial support and project supervision is entered at the Ministry of Finance and PAMCO, respectively. There is also a technical assistance module located at the PIOJ which registers and tracks technical projects.

Data for the PDB is captured on 10 data forms which collect information on project and program summary, external financing, implementation scheduling and project supervision, and technical assistance (not in the capital investment program). The software generates the following reports:

A. Pre-investment module: (1) a listing of projects registered in the PDB and sorted by different criteria, (2) a short profile or summary of all projects, (3) a capital budget impact report, (4) a report on recurrent budget implications of selected projects, and (5) an aggregate impact of projects on selected indicators.

B. Follow-up module: (1) an implementation schedule of selected projects, (2) the current or expected status of projects sorted by different criteria, (3) jeopardies reports listing projects for which cost overruns or delays are greater than acceptable levels, and (4) an implementation efficiency report.

C. Additional reports as required by the user. For example: (1) a report on aggregate annual operating and maintenance costs covering all projects in the PSIP, (2) geographic distribution of capital investment in the public sector on a sectoral basis, (3) detailed information on project description and objectives, (4) a listing on project indicators, (5) performance of individual contractors and the number of contractors employed on a sectoral and regional basis, and (6) the total number of funding sources and funding portfolios of each.

There have been several difficulties in implementing the PDB. It was decided to begin with all externally-financed ongoing projects and then move on to projects supported solely by government funds, but these have proven to be a large undertaking. A major problem has been a lack of personnel, since staff in the PIOJ, PAMCO, and the Ministry of Finance could not be relieved of their other responsibilities. It has also taken time to acquire necessary hardware. Within the sector ministries and agencies, some of the project managers, though conceding the necessity of the PDB, felt the forms were an added burden, given the resource constraints which they also face, resulting in tardy submission of forms to the PIOJ. Forms have sometimes also been incorrectly or inadequately completed, requiring their revision, and further delaying the data collection process.

Colombia

The enactment of the New Budget Law (Law 38 of 1989) marked the start of a long and gradual process designed to enhance the efficiency of public investment management in Colombia. A fundamental component of this process is the National Bank for Investment Projects (BNPI) established in 1990.

The BNPI was intended to support improved allocation and utilization of public investment resources in all institutions receiving financing or co-financing from the national budget, including national, regional, departmental, and municipal levels. Administration of the BNPI is the responsibility of the Operation and Systems Division and the Methodologies Division of the National Planning Department (DNP).

Although at the time of writing implementation was still at an early stage, the approach to the data bank was already defined. In the sectoral area, ministries and government departments will manage the information generated in any one of their dependent institutions on both proposed and ongoing investment projects. Each agency must send specific information on fixed dates or regular intervals to the DNP. In addition, institutions at the national level may consult the BNPI at DNP to obtain information on the investment projects of territorial government agencies.

Each institution belonging to the DNP will have its own database to record the projects for which it is responsible. All the databases can exchange information using diskettes or communication lines. Those institutions where installation of a computer is not feasible or justifiable will access the BNPI through the government agency to which they are attached. It is expected that the direct cost of the project will be over $2 million (U.S.) and that it will take two years to develop and implement. Finally, it is thought that full operation will require three or four more years.

Much emphasis is being placed on methodologies for estimating costs and benefits of projects. The general methodology consists of seven modules. The first two—institutional framework and project cycle—present basic information for presentation of the methodology. The remaining five—project identification, project preparation, project appraisal, project financing, and project sustainability and viability—consist of formats designed to guide each step of project preparation and appraisal. In addition, cost/efficiency and cost/benefit analysis will be used to select projects in specific sectors.

The BNPI is designed to exchange data with related systems such as the Ministry of Finance's budget monitoring system which monitors all projects financed by the national budget and the credit monitoring system of DNP's International Technical Cooperation Division's system for recording and monitoring international technical cooperation activities.

In Colombia, there is still a long way to go, since most of the institutions surveyed do not possess information systems and methodologies for identifying, appraising, and monitoring investment projects. The path will also be a difficult one because of the large number of institutions at territorial level and the institutional weaknesses of most of them.

However, several benefits are anticipated:

- the development of project appraisal methodologies and the training of many civil servants in the centralized and decentralized agencies in their standard application to ensure that projects wholly or partially financed by the national budget will produce a positive socioeconomic rate of return;
- the availability of updated information on projects proposed by institutions at the national and territorial level to improve substantially inter-institutional coordination;
- the ongoing physical and financial monitoring of project implementation to facilitate the timely adoption of measures for ensuring that each project achieves its objectives;
- the fact that the BNPI contains a group of well-formulated and efficiently appraised projects to facilitate the negotiation of international loans for co-financing projects in the centralized and decentralized sectors;
- the BNPI would provide institutions at the national level with immediate information on the needs of the regions, departments, and municipalities; similarly, it would provide municipalities, departments, and regions with timely information on projects to be implemented in their various geographical areas by national institutions so that they can express their options.

Chile

In Chile, public investments are managed through the National Investment System (SNI). The basic objective of the SNI is to achieve an efficient allocation of scarce resources to the most profitable investment alternative.

The SNI is divided into two sub-systems: The Technical Economic Analysis Subsystem is in charge of formalizing and coordinating the process of allocation of funds and the execution of the public sector's budget. The Budgetary Formulation Subsystem is in charge of coordinating the process of allocation of funds and the execution of the public sector's budget.

The national planning organization (MIDEPLAN) examines studies and projects submitted by the investing institutions, prepares and appraises projects, and updates the integrated project bank for the public sector (BIP). The Ministry of Finance is required to obtain technical reports from MIDEPLAN on investment proposals submitted by public agencies. Planning offices in the public agencies identify and formulate projects.

Chile's BIP was among the first project data banks to be introduced in Latin America. The country's public investment system is currently going through a modernization and adjustment process which includes a series of activities still being implemented to standardize, organize, and systematize the investment process.

In 1982, within the framework of regionalization and decentralization, a system of 13 regional project banks (BRP) was implemented. Later, a second stage was put into operation, with sectoral project banks. These systems were subsequently consolidated to form the public sector's integrated project bank (BIP).

The BIP is part of an effort to improve methodologies for the formulation, submission, and appraisal of projects; establish systems for the selection, monitoring, and evaluation of projects; and introduce permanent training for public officers in public investment management.

The BIP is an information system for investment projects including studies, projects, and programs of the public sector at national, regional, and county level. Its main objective is to support the public investment decision-making process, providing information on the SNI as a whole and on each one of the institutions involved; to give detailed information about each project and its effect on macroeconomic variables; to simplify programing and execution in pre-investment and investment through the delivery of timely information; and to link the institutions participating in the SNI using the BIP system as a tool for inter-institutional coordination.

More than 500 organizations participate in the public investment system. The BIP allows for the supervision of projects through their life cycle (pre-investment, investment, operation, idea, profile, prefeasibility, feasibility, design, and execution). Each project's information structure is organized according to the following information modules: (1) identification module, (2) stage pre-investment module, (3) submission to financing module, and (5) contracts module. The BIP is used for technical-economic analysis of projects, the budgetary formulation process, and the budgetary execution process.

CONCLUSION

The overview of the interim outcomes from the experience of three countries demonstrates (1) the complexity of the task involved in improving public investment management and (2) the useful role which a project data bank can play in the process *if* properly implemented and maintained. It is clear that the countries in the Latin America and Caribbean region have made some progress over the last five years in putting new programing systems into place, although considerable efforts remain to be made if the reform of public investment management is to be achieved. Improvement of existing institutional frameworks, sectoral allocation of capital spending, economic appraisal of projects, and upgrading of management information systems are areas requiring concerted attention. These are the necessary conditions if programing instruments like the PDB are to function effectively and if the underlying links which connect pre-investment, the public sector investment plan and the budget are to guarantee that public investment choices are as satisfactory as possible.

NOTE

1. The government of the Dominican Republic undertook to prepare a comprehensive PSIP with an integrated PDB 10 years ago. The system was not maintained, however, due to a lack of political interest and poor institutional and human capacity in local institutions. The current government has recently decided to start anew, seeking external financial and technical assistance to build a new system including a PDB.

PART IV.

PUBLIC EXPENDITURE MANAGEMENT

BUDGET MANAGEMENT AND BUDGETING:

THE SINGAPORE APPROACH

Joon Chien Doh

ABSTRACT

Singapore adopted program budgeting in the late 1970s, carefully adapting it to its needs. In 1988, it implemented a Block Vote Budget Allocation System (BVBAS), making budgetary decision making more decentralized and specialized. The system also includes extensive five yearly reviews by the Auditor General's Office, as well as annual reviews by the Ministry of Finance. Budgeting is now facilitated by a computerized Budget Operations Support System (BO≡).

Singapore has a mind of its own. It believes in shaping its own political and economic destiny. Ideologically, the government is nondogmatic; it has some socialistic ideals (Lim and associates 1988, p. 61), but it practices market economy and does not believe in social welfare through subsidy. This independent frame of mind is also reflected in budget management and budgeting, a subset of the overall approach to development in Singapore.

Policy Studies and Developing Nations, Volume 3, pages 153-174.

ISBN: 1-55938-190-6

THE BUDGET SETTING IN SINGAPORE

Government policies are framed in a setting influenced by its tough start, clear sense of direction, strong political leadership, and political integrity.

Tough Start

Singapore is a city republic with hardly any natural resources. It has a small land area (620.2 sq. km) and a small population (in 1990, 2.69 million).

When the country gained self-government from the British in 1959, its biggest challenge was economic survival. The private sector was weak; there was "little economic growth, massive unemployment, wretched housing and inadequate education" (p. 61) As an entreprot, industrial experience was lacking. The government had the unenviable task of generating rapid economic growth, creating an abundant supply of jobs to enable the people to work and meet the basic needs.

Clear Sense of Direction

The policy decision adopted by Singapore was a simple but economically effective one: Let the world contribute to Singapore's well-being. It was therefore essential to provide a favorable climate for foreign investment on the basis of free trade. In retrospect, Singapore was economically successful because it was able to develop an economic infrastructure: political stability, political integrity, industrial peace, efficient administration, skilled and productive labor force, efficient communication and telecommunication systems.

In the 1960s and the early 1970s, the multinational companies, in the context of a fast growing world economy, were attracted by the low cost of Singapore as a base for labor-intensive manufacturing activities. By the late 1970s, unemployment had dropped from a high of 8.9 percent in 1966 to a low of 3.4 percent in 1979 (Lim and associates 1988, p. 7). In the 1980s as labor shortages became serious, capital-intensive activities and service industries requiring higher skill and enjoying higher value added began to replace labor-intensive ones. To provide a conducive environment, the government invested heavily in technical and vocational manpower training and infrastructure development with the consequent upgrading of telecommunication and international transportation facilities (Yeo 1990, p. 2).

During this period (1960-1984), the GDP enjoyed an average annual growth rate of 8.9 percent, while the per capita GNP at current market prices jumped from $1,330 to S$15,000 surpassing even a number of industrial economies of Western Europe (Lim and associates 1988, p. 7). However, the republic encountered a serious recession in 1985 when the GDP turned negative (− 1.2%). A review of the economy by an Economic Committee in 1986 resulted in a new direction: the objective was for Singapore to become a developed nation by the 1990s "with a margin of advantage.... We must offer the opportunity for a higher rate of return, and a more conducive environment for business, than the OECD countries" (Singapore Ministry of Trade and Industry 1986, pp. 11-12). This goal was to be achieved by the two strategies of turning Singapore into an international total business center and an exporter of services. Since 1987 the economy has recovered, and between 1987 and 1990 enjoyed a robust average growth of 9.5 percent.

Strong Political Leadership

Singapore has had strong political leadership. The People's Action Party or PAP has been in power with an overwhelming majority in parliament since the country's independence. This stability has facilitated the governmental style of central direction in developing the economy toward high technology industries, financial services, tourist related industries, and so on. Because of the lack of a strong private sector and the necessity to achieve economic results quickly at the time of independence, the government has been heavily involved in enterprises such as airlines, shipping, manufacturing, trading, and banking. Only since 1986 has the government committed itself to a policy of reducing the role of the public sector and moving toward the privatization of state enterprises.

Political Integrity

Singapore has practiced political integrity from its founding with salutary effects. Thus, it has been said:

> Integrity on the part of the political leadership has a towering influence over the political, administrative, and social fabric of society. Leadership integrity in the political system provides the value system which permeates the entire government helping it to gain respect, confidence and support (Doh 1990, p. 7).

CHARACTERISTICS OF BUDGET MANAGEMENT

Budget management in Singapore has certain characteristics of its own which form a distinct pattern.

Balanced Budget

The budget philosophy of the Singapore government has the quality of traditional virtue. The refrain, "Expenditure should not exceed revenue," has been echoed throughout the financial history of the republic (see Table 1).

Table 1. Revenue and Expenditure (in millions of Singapore dollars) Singapore 1965-1990

Year	*Revenue*[1]	*Expenditure*[2] *Total*	*Current*	*Development*	*Surplus Deficit (-) (%)*
1965	538.2	507.8	439.5	68.3	6.0
1966	622.6	593.1	477.8	115.3	5.0
1967	710.2	673.6	553.8	119.8	5.4
1968	857.0	716.7	585.2	131.5	19.6
1969/70 *	1,364.4	1,075.0	920.4	154.6	26.9
1970	1,333.0	1,084.5	935.4	149.1	22.9
1971	1,680.6	1,294.0	1,079.5	214.5	29.9
1972	1,877.6	1,491.3	1.257.4	233.9	25.9
1973	2,426.6	1,626.6	1,417.7	208.9	49.2
1974	2,802.6	2,017.9	1,734.1	283.8	38.9
1975	3,398.6	2,386.1	1,981.4	404.7	42.4
1976	3,581.2	2,818.6	2,200.1	618.5	27.1
1977	4,083.5	3,292.8	2,582.8	710.0	24.0
1978	4,351.0	3,542.9	2,752.3	790.6	22.8
1979	4,694.2	3,978.2	3,054.1	924.1	18.0
1980	5,936.6	5,036.9	3.651.0	1,385.9	17.9
1981	7,344.6	5,550.8	3,936.3	1,614.5	32.3
1982	8,989.5	6,687.9	4,736.9	1,951.0	34.4
1983	10,612.6	7,865.2	5,726.4	2,138.8	34.9
1984	11,250.7	9,614.9	6,034.4	3,580.5	17.0
1985	10,829.4	9,942.3	6.678.3	3,264.0	8.9
1986	10,970.4	10,916.5	6,281.9	4,634.6	0.5
1987	10,470.9	14,014.2	8,465.9	5,548.3	-25.3
1988	13,775.9	10.837.6	7,202.3	3,635.3	27.1
1989	15,508.9	11,797.8	7,681.9	4,115.9	31.5
1990	16,424.7	13,032.0	9,036.8	3,995.2	26.0
	Average				21.9

Notes: [1] Revenue refers to receipts credited to the Consolidated Revenue Account, Development Fund Account, and Sinking Fund Account but excludes capital receipts.

[2] Current expenditure refers to payments from the Consolidated Revenue Account but excludes contributions to the Development Fund, Revolving Fund, Sinking Fund, and repayment of loans. Development expenditure excludes loans to statutory boards and enterprises.

* In 1969, the FY instead of ending on Decener 31, 1969, was changed to March 31, 1970.

Source: Department of Statistics (1975, 1980, 1989, 1990).

For the entire period of 26 years, with the exception of 1987, total government revenue was more than sufficient to finance both recurrent and development expenditure. The average annual surplus was 21.9 percent.

Conservative Revenue Estimates

Balancing the budget annually appears to have been facilitated by a conservative approach to revenue estimation. From 1966 to 1990

Table 2. Difference Between Actual and Estimated Revenue of the Consolidated Revenue Account 1965-1990, Singapore

	Actual revenue (in millions of Singapore dollars) (1)	*Estimated revenue (2)*	*(1) / (2) + or − (%)*
1965	419.8	339.6	23.6
1966	595.2	537.0	9.0
1967	663.0	590.6	12.3
1968	803.0	646.7	24.2
1969/70	1,261.2	1,015.6	24.2
1971	1,266.5	1,041.3	21.6
1972	1,468.5	1,307.2	12.3
1973	1,749.3	1,449.1	20.7
1974	2,219.2	1,874.9	18.4
1975	2,556.9	2,323.0	10.1
1976	3,092.2	2,647.5	16.8
1977	3,156.2	3,107.6	1.6
1978	3,555.5	3,362.4	5.7
1979	3,738.8	3,668.2	1.9
1980	4,603.0	3,884.9	18.5
1981	5,903.5	4,113.0	43.5
1982	7,862.2	6,334.8	24.1
1983	9,128.4	7,638.8	19.5
1984	10,631.8	8,871.2	19.8
1985	10,059.2	9,969.3	0.9
1986	13,058.2	10,620.7	23.0
1987	13,010.1	14,552.9	-10.6
1988	11,085.9	10,804.8	2.6
1989	11,051.9	10,762.0	2.7
1990	13,803.6	11,459.7	20.5
	Average		14.7

Source: Republic of Singapore, *Financial Statements,* 1965-1990.

(see Table 2), leaving aside the transition year of independence (1965), actual revenue of the Consolidated Revenue Account was higher than the estimates except in 1987 when actual revenue fell short of the estimates by 10.6 percent. (The shortfall was due mainly to a much smaller revenue from the sale of government lands and from income tax as the economy was just getting out of the 1985-1986 recession.) For the span of 24 years, the average annual excess of actual overestimated revenue was 14.7 percent. The same pattern of revenue underestimation also holds true for the other major government funds. One might surmise that this conservatism in revenue estimation also reflected a conscious or unconscious strategy of ensuring that expenditure would not get out of hand.

Low Public Debt

Since the government policy of adhering to a balanced budget has also given rise to the annual accumulation of surpluses in the Consolidated Revenue Account and the other government accounts, there has been no need for expenditures to be financed through borrowing. External borrowngs, in particular, have been extremely low in comparison with other countries. Table 3 provides an insight into the public debt situation in the republic.

The overwhelming bulk of the average annual public debt for the period, 1965-1990, was domestic (93.8%). The external component was very low (6.2%) and has declined even further since the mid-1980s. Thus, the debt servicing ratio (i.e., the external public debt service as a percentage of exports of goods and services) was also small (1.0%). This obviously puts Singapore in an

Table 3. Public Debt of Singapore, 1965-1990 (in milions of Singapore dollars)

Year	*Total*	*Domestic (percent)*	*External (percent*	*Debt Servicing Ratio percent*
1965	578.0	89.1	10.9	n.a.
1966	700.2	91.0	9.0	n.a.
1967	1,024.3	95.7	4.3	n.a.
1968	1,636.6	95.6	4.4	n.a.
1969	1,753.4	94.1	5.9	0.4
1970	2,016.6	91.4	8.6	0.6
1971	2,734.0	91.0	9.0	0.6
1972	3,483.2	87.6	12.4	1.0
1973	3,757.6	87.4	12.6	0.6
1974	4,522.4	89.1	10.9	0.6
1975	5,698.1	90.5	9.5	0.7
1976	7.318.2	91.0	9.0	0.8
1977	9,132.9	89.2	10.8	0.8
1978	10,692.6	90.5	9.5	2.3
1979	12,396.5	92.1	7.9	1.3
1980	14,669.4	93.6	6.4	1.0
1981	17,138.2	94.8	5.2	0.8
1982	20,730.4	95.8	4.2	0.8
1983	25,031.5	97.3	2.7	1.3
1984	28,077.3	97.7	2.3	1.0
1985	32,164.44	98.1	1.9	2.4
1986	33,793.1	98.7	1.3	2.3
1987	38,274.3	99.2	0.8	1.3
1988	41,830.7	99.4	0.6	0.4
1989	46,209.7	99.7	0.3	0.7
1990	51,425.6	99.9	0.1	0.2
	Average	93.8	6.2	1.0

Source: Department of Statistics (1975, 1980, 1987, and 1990); Singapore Ministry of Trade and Industry (1989, p. 155).

Table 4. Official Foreign Reserves of Singapore, 1965-1990

Year	*Official Foreign Reserves (in million Singapore dollars)*	*Growth Rates (percent)*	*Ratio to Merchandise Imports (Months)*
1965	1,224.4	n.a	n.a.
1966	1,399.4	24.3	n.a.
1967	1,669.2	21.4	n.a.
1968	2,186.6	31.0	n.a.
1969	2,530.5	16.0	4.86
1970	3,097.9	22.4	4.93
1971	4,094.8	32.2	5.67
1972	4,929.9	20.4	6.20
1973	5,800.1	17.7	5.56
1974	6,502.9	12.1	3.82
1975	7,486.0	15.1	4.66
1976	8,261.5	10.3	4.42
1977	9,022.9	9.2	4.24
1978	11,473.8	27.2	4.65
1979	12,562.4	9.5	3.93
1980	13,757.7	9.5	3.22
1981	15,491.1	12.6	3.19
1982	17,917.9	15.7	3.57
1983	19,755.3	10.3	3.98
1984	22,768.0	15.3	4.47
1985	27,070.9	18.9	5.62
1986	28,157.5	4.0	6.08
1987	30,441.7	8.1	5.34
1988	33,276.6	9.3	4.53
1989	38,607.2	16.0	4.78
1990	48,521.3	25.7	5.30
Average		17.7	4.68

Source: Department of Statistics (1974, 1980, 1990).

enviable position compared with nations with high external debts and a crushing debt servicing burden. In 1988, for example, debt service as a percentage of exports of goods and services was a weighted average of 17.0 percent for low income economies, 21.6 percent for middle income economies, and 19.7 percent for upper income economies. Unfortunately, no figure was available for high income economies including the OECD ones (see World Bank 1990, pp. 224-225).

High Official Foreign Reserves

With surplus accumulating as an annual ritual from the national budget and statutory board sources and a negligible external public debt, the Official Foreign Reserves (in the form of gold and foreign exchange, special drawing rights, and reserve position with IMF) have accumulated continuously over the past 26 years (see Table 4). From 1966 to 1990, the Official Foreign Reserves grew at an average annual rate of 17.7 percent; the average annual reserves were equivalent to 4.68 months of merchandise imports for the period 1969-1990, much higher than elsewhere including OECD countries. (In 1988, the gross international reserves in months of import coverage were 3.7 of weighted average for low income economies, 2.9 for middle income economies, and 3.3 for high income economies including OECD ones; see World Bank 1990, pp. 212-213). The reserves reached a total of $48,521.3 million by 1990 and constituted 75.9 percent of the year's GNP.

Substantial Investment Income

Because of the accumulated annual budget surpluses of prior years, Singapore is in a unique position. It has enjoyed a substantial investment income (in the form of interest, dividends, contributions by statutory boards, currency surplus, income and interest from Development Fund, etc.) (see Table 5). For the period of 11 years (1980-1990) (see Department of Statistics 1990, p. 254; only the investment incomes for the years 1980-1990 are included because a common classification starts only from 1980), the average annual contribution of

Table 5. Investment Income of Singapore in Relation to Total Government Revenue, 1980-1990+

Year	*Investment income*xx (*in million of Singapore dollars*) (1)	*Total revenue*x (2)	(1) / (2) (*percent*)
1980	1,071.7	5,936.6	18.1
1981	1,138.4	7,344.6	15.5
1982	1,721.6	8,989.5	19.2
1983	2,432.8	10,612.6	22.9
1984	2,581.0	11,250.7	22.9
1985	3,054.8	10,829.4	28.2
1986	4,483.4	10,970.4	40.9
1987	4,141.6	10.470.9	39.6
1988	4,612.3	13,775.9	33.5
1989	4,755.3	15,508.9	30.7
1990	4,111.0	16,424.7	25.0
Average			27.0

Notes: +The investment income of years prior to 1980 is not included as it was classified on a different basis.
xTotal revenue refers to receipts credited to the Consolidated Revenue Account, Development Fund Account, and Sinking Fund Account but excludes capital receipts.
xxInvestment income includes currency surplus.

Source: Department of Statistics (1990, p. 254).

investment income to total government budget revenue was 27.0 percent. So significant was investment income that in five (1985-1989) of the 11 years, it was the largest contributor to total revenue, while in the other six years, it was the second largest. This must be a rare achievement for a non-fuel producing country.

Policy Flexibility and Budget Initiatives

As a net surplus nation, Singapore is in an enviable position in terms of policy flexibility and budget initiatives involving a large amount of expenditure. For the fiscal year 1991, for example, even though it was anticipating a domestic economic slowdown (arising from factors like the Gulf War, political instability in the Soviet Union, collapse in the GATT negotiations, recession and slow growth in the major economies of the world), the Singapore government was still able to continue investment in infrastructure and implement a policy of setting aside money for R&D by increasing direct development expenditures by nearly 60 percent over the previous fiscal year to $2.2 billion (Singapore Ministry of Finance 1991a, p. 10). This is in contrast to the United States which has become a net debtor nation since 1985 (Miner 1989, p. 21) and which now harbors worries about its ability to use "discretionary fiscal policies to stimulate the economy" (Miner 1989, p. 30) in a recession situation so as not to aggravate its debt to GNP ratio; or to the Canadian case, which is "in an era of contraction (not) in an era of new initiatives" (Savoie, 1990, p. 71).

Funding availability has also enabled the new prime minister, Goh Chok Tong, to exercise budget policy initiatives. In order "to maximise and equalise opportunities for Singaporeans to improve themselves" (*The Straits TImes* 1990), he announced the establishment in 1992 of an EduSave Fund, a government endowment fund, with an initial capital of $1 billion but reaching $5 billion over the next eight to 10 years assuming 6 percent annual economic growth. Proceeds from the fund, targeted at $500 per year per child, would be credited to the EduSave account of every school-going child between ages 6 and 16. The money could be utilized to pay for any enrichment program for the child's education, such as music, ballet, or other extra-curricular courses. Any residue would be transferred to his Central Provident Fund account (*The Straits Times* 1991).

Another initiative with budgetary implications is the proposal to create a Medifund, an endowment fund, to ensure that all Singaporeans have access to health care (*The Straits Times* 1991). The scheme, however, has not been finalized.

BUDGETING

In the field of budgeting, the 1960s and 1970s were the heyday of budgetary innovation and reforms. Performance budgeting (as it was known to the

American originators) was popularized in the 1960s by the United Nations as program and performance budgeting through its manual on the system; the United States evoked a sense of short-lived euphoria with its planning-programming-budgeting system (PPBS) in the 1960s and zero-base budgeting (ZBB) in the 1970s.

Many countries in the developing world, under the persuasive influence of technical advisers from aid agencies or international organizations, were unwilling either to be left out of the benefits of budgetary reforms or the glamour associated with them and took swift steps to jump on the bandwagon by participating in the romanticism of budgetary innovations, especially performance budgeting (Doh 1990, pp. 4-6). Possibly the first country to introduce the budget system outside the United States was the Philippines, which passed the Revised Budget Act in 1954 authorizing the introduction of performance budgeting. By the early 1960s, 16 countries (10 of them in Latin America) were already listed by Waterston as having experimented with or introduced the system (Dean and Pugh 1989, p. 15). A number of other countries in Asia, Latin America, and Africa also followed.

Realities, such as the necessity for technical know-how, adequate qualified staff and expertise, supportive leadership and a conducive bureaucratic culture and environment, soon began to emerge and frustrate the reform efforts. Generally, much hoped for benefits failed to materialize. Enthusiasm soon turned into disillusionment, and in many of the countries, the reforms were either fossilized or abandoned.

What is the status of budgeting in Singapore? Have budgetary reforms taken place? Has disillusionment occurred as in other countries, or is reform something still ongoing?

Characteristics of Budgeting

While not unaffected by developments internationally, budgeting in Singapore has a dynamic of its own. Three aspects will be highlighted: timing of reforms, momentum of reforms, and computer technology.

The Timing for Budgetary Reforms

Singapore determined its own timing for budgetary reforms. Unlike the zeal of many countries in the 1960s which launched programs of budgetary reform as a high profile event, Singapore was hardly touched by the romanticism underlying budget modernization. For the republic, it was first things first. Looking back, it would appear that the line of thinking of policymakers, consciously or unconsciously, ran something like this: "budget innovations can wait; economic and social priorities of overcoming unemployment, providing housing and education have to take precedence." The pace of budgetary reforms has thus been a cautious and unhurried one.

From the British colonial administration, Singapore inherited the line-item system of budgeting. With its focus on objects of expenditure, the system, despite its limitations, was useful for the narrow purpose of controlling expenditure. In fact, Seah (1973) had concluded that "the present classification is relatively adequate to meet the requirements of the bureaucracy, the political leadership and the society" (p. 29). With the government preoccupied with major socioeconomic issues in the early years of the country's independence, the treasury continued with the line-item approach to budgeting for the first 10 years. The government not only lacked staff with formal training in budgeting, but the accounting system and financial procedures were also inadequate to support any major change in the budget system.

The treasury, however, was not unaware of the weaknesses of the budgetary system, especially in meeting the demanding needs of a government undergoing rapid expansion in the provision of public services and the increase in expenditure. Two improvements were made in the direction of providing more meaningful expenditure information. The first, in the 1960s, entailed the introduction of a functional classification for budget expenditure along the lines advocated by the United Nations (1958). The second, not long after, involved the implementation of a standardized format for use in classifying and coding objects of expenditure. The coding and standardization of expenditure data facilitated budget preparation and the eventual computerization of the entire budget process.

By the early 1970s, Singapore had already made considerable economic progress. During the period 1965-1971, per capita GDP at current market prices grew at an average annual rate of 12.9 percent (Department of Statistics 1975, p. 3) while per capita GDP itself more than doubled (from $1,567 in 1965 to $3,233 in 1971) in just six years (p. 1). The government was in a better position to direct attention to other areas of concern.

The budgetary system began to gain some attention in 1972 when the government engaged the services of a United Nations expert (Eric Danecke) to look into the usefulness of introducing a program approach to budgeting. While Danecke urged a hurried approach to implementing the system, the government adopted a cautious stance. The Sports Council was chosen in mid-1974 by MOF for experimentation. While no published information is available as to the rationale for the choice of the agency, one might surmise that the apparent quantifiability of its outputs and the smallness of its size might have accounted for the decision. Arising from the budget exercise, it was found that, while it was not difficult to establish a program structure, program evaluation was not an easy task owing to the problem of determining objective criteria and indicators.

Meanwhile, a certain amount of pressure for budgetary reforms was building up from the Estimates Committee of Parliament. Its 1975 report expressed concern over the soundness of budget evaluation procedures used by the treasury for assessing estimates from the ministries, the restrictions pertaining to virement, as well as inadequacies present in the budget formulation and the evaluation of expenditure estimates. The report also suggested that each ministry should include in its budget estimates a review of its performance in the past year highlighting any variation from targets/objectives and any significant changes in policies and priorities.

While the above developments were going on, the treasury must have considered that the time was ripe to initiate a major budgetary reform. The first move came in 1976 when a small cell of two budget officers was formed in the Budget Division of the Ministry of Finance to guide the implementation of program and performance budgeting in the operating ministries. The first chosen was the Ministry of Labor, like the Sports Council, possibly because of the relative ease with which its output could be quantified. A program structure was developed for the ministry on the basis of programs identified. Each program consisted of a number of activities. The objective of each program was also defined. Over the next few years, PPB was implemented in other ministries, and by FY 1978, the system was extended to the entire government. With the change in the budgeting system, program structures replaced line-item structures as the main organizing framework for presenting government budgets.

Little scholarly work on budgeting in Singapore has been done. Fortunately, Prasad, who was for many years closely involved in the implementation of PPB, did write about it. In his 1982 article, he identified the emphasis of PPB in Singapore as structural, analytical, and control oriented. For the convenience of discusssion, the analytical aspect will be dealt with last.

Structural aspect. The focus of the structural aspect was on the identification of programs and activities that would contribute to the achievement of goals, objectives, and targets of a ministry. Prasad mentioned realities in the development of program structures: those which were logical for expenditure and performance analysis did not necessarily suit the needs of financial and operational control. The outcome was a combination of program structures: those which cut across departmental lines and those which did not. No serious problem was mentioned in relation to the structural aspect.

Pugh, writing two years later, gave the impression that substantial progress had occurred in the structural aspect. He gave the example of the Ministry of Labor which had six programs; each program was subdivided into a number of activities, and each activity grouped together related items of expenditure. There was a statement of objective for each program and a description of each of the activities which supported the program (Dean and Pugh 1989, pp. 95-96).

Control aspect. As explained by Prasad, the aim was to provide greater flexibility to operating ministries in using their funds. Until the introduction of PPB, all virements had to be approved by the treasury. In line with the management orientation in the new system of budgeting, a certain amount of decontrol was initiated, and the rules governing the use of virement were somewhat relaxed. Ministries were given the authority to make transfer of funds (virement) between objects of expenditure within each activity without first having to gain the approval of MOF. To Prasad, the change had the salutary effect of speeding up the response of ministries to changing needs as well as reducing paperwork.

Analytical aspect. Prasad summarized the analytical aspect as:

> Each ministry formulating its annual expenditure requirements using objective critieria such as performance and workload statistics; Budget Division evaluating expenditure requirements of ministries using cost- effectiveness, cost-benefit and input-output criteria; periodically monitoring and evaluating on-going programs (Prasad 1982, p. 2).

To him, this aspect was crucial; without making headway in this direction, the new budget system would be just another exercise in accounting or budget classification or another set of budget rituals.

The problems he noted included non-measurability of output, increase in workload and paperwork, and shortage of trained staff in analytical techniques. He was, however, optimistic and considered the whole exercise of budgetary reform a worthwhile one as the bulk of government programs had outputs which were quantifiable and thus subject to analysis, the paperwork could be reduced once a computerized budget system was implemented, and staff expertise could be developed by both formal and on-the-job training.

Pugh had difficulty in reaching any precise conclusion regarding the progress in the analytical aspect as published data were inadequate. He was, however, of the opinion that the information needs of the main users including the Budget Division and the Auditor-General would have been better met through the generation of data on program and activity costs and performance indicators. In view of conceptual difficulties in performance measurement and the problems in training staff in the development and use of analytical data, he ventured to guess that the analytical aspect had made "only moderate progress in Singapore" (Dean and Pugh 1989, p. 99). His overall assessment of PPB was that its infrastructure was established, but how useful it was and what its final form would be were still unknown.

The recession of 1985 in Singapore had its impact on budgeting. Owing to the need to hold down recurrent expenditure, the treasury made it mandatory for ministries and statutory boards to undertake a five-year revenue and expenditure forecast before the formulation of their budget estimates.

Thus, the timing of the first major budgetary reform in Singapore was the outcome of internal dynamics. The government embarked on a program of budgetary reform only when the treasury considered that the time was ripe. The introduction of five-year forecasting of revenue and expenditure was also to meet its own requirements arising from changes in the economic scene.

During the first 20 years of Singapore's history, budgeting and budget innovations were primarily treasury oriented. Data generated by the operating ministries were basically the outcome of treasury initiatives to meet its own needs, although in the process some of the information requirements of the Prime Minister's Department, the Auditor-General, the Parliament, and the public were also met. To a limited extent, the delegation of financial authority to the ministries, in the form of easing of virement rules, also occurred. The dominance of the treasury in both budget formulation and execution was, however, evident.

Keeping the Momentum of Reform Going

While the enthusiasm for budget innovations has died in most countries, Singapore has maintained the momentum for reform. Fiscal year 1989-1990 marked an important beginning toward ministry-oriented budgeting. The changes, in a way, also reflect the changing concept of management and the recognition of the necessity for decentralized decision making. Under the new orientation, the role of ministries in budget execution and in generating information primarily to serve their own management purposes began to become much more significant. The change was heralded by a radical shift in the Budget Division's perception of its own role from that of control to that of facilitator as may be seen in its new mission statement:

> To *assist* ministries and statutory boards select and efficiently administer programs and projects... (Singapore Ministry of Finance 1989a, p. 6, emphasis added).

The Finance Circular of the Treasury in 1988, on the preparation of the budget for FY 1989-1990, announced the introduction of the Block Vote Budget Allocation System (BVBAS). With the implementation of this system, budgetary decision making has become much more decentralized and specialized. The treasury no longer towers over and dominates the entire budgetary process.

Macro-Policy Decision Making

Under BVBAS, the role of the treasury and the operating ministries in budgeting has become much better delineated. A form of specialization has emerged with each party playing the role which it is best suited. The treasury focuses attention on macro-policy decision making.

Briefly, the preoccupation of the treasury is on the following.

The size of the budget. Historically, budget formulation was a bottom-up approach; ministries had a chance to have their voice heard through their budget proposals in the form of expenditure estimates submitted by them to the treasury. While the treasury had the final say in advising the cabinet, the ministries did have their case heard beforehand. Under BVBAS, this is no longer the practice as budget formulation has become a top-down approach. A pre-preparation phase precedes the annual budget preparation during which decisions are made on both the size of the government-wide budget and how the aggregate government expenditure is going to be shared by the ministries.

The rationale for BVBAS (presumably including also the top-down approach) has been given by the treasury as:

- ensure a balanced budget;
- contain government expenditure and manpower as a proportion of GDP and the workforce;
- help ministries respond speedily to changing priorities; and
- improve the effectiveness and efficiency of government operations (Singapore Ministry of Finance 1989b, p. 2).

An important consideration in capping aggregate government expenditure and hence the top-down approach has to do with the desire of MOF to make budgeting less contentious and less arbitrary than was the case under the bottom-up approach when the ministries keenly competed for a bigger slice of the budget resources, and the Treasury had to make arbitrary cuts to match expenditure with the financial resources available. Inspiration for the new system could also have come from the practice of the Ministry of Defence, which had for many years been receiving appropriations as a fixed percentage of GDP as well as the Canadian Envelope System introduced in 1979, which tied expenditure increases for sectors of government with growth in GNP (Savoie 1990).

Since it was the policy objective of the government to have an overall balanced budget under BVBAS, the treasury is concerned to ensure that the expenditure target is in line with the revenue estimates. Determination of the size of the budget is relatively easy, since for the five-year planning period 1989-1993 government revenue has been projected in excess of 25 percent of nominal GDP: expenditure should be comfortably targeted at 25 percent of GDP as well.

Allocating Budget Expenditure to Ministries. Once total budget expenditure is determined, the treasury will allocate this share of the projected GDP to the operating ministries for both their recurrent and development expenditure. The allocation is on the basis of the treasury's own predetermined financing formula (each ministry is accorded a fixed share of GDP) which takes into account national priorities, past expenditure patterns, as well as the long-term development plans of the ministries.

After accounting for recurrent expenditure, the balance of the ministry's share of GDP is available for development expenditure. In fact, for the five-year planning period, FY 1989-1993, each ministry was given the tentative allocations supported by the MOF for the entire duration. The target allocations are, however, subject to annual revisions on a rolling five-year basis.

Thus, with the top-down approach, macro-policy decision making related to both the aggregate level of budget expenditure and its distribution to the ministries become primarily the preserve of the MOF.

Returns from ministries. Upon receipt of the preliminary allocations, it is the task of the ministries to distribute the funds among programs, activities, cost-centers, and line-items of expenditure in the manner they deem will serve the best interest of their own organizations in their budget proposals to the MOF. They are, however, also required to include the following in their submissions:

a. *Expenditure trend:* An overview of the expenditure trend for the past five years and for five years into the future.
b. *Five-year new development plan:* An expenditure estimate of new development projects planned for the next five years.
c. *Performance indicators:* Performance indicators for the past year, the current year and the budget year.
d. *Policy issues:* Response to policy issues raised by the MOF (Singapore Ministry of Finance 1990, pp. 3-4).

Micro-Management Decision Making

With BVBAS, the management in each ministry assumes responsibility for managing its own budget during the execution stage. Since FY 1989, the operating ministries have been in a position to plan and allocate financial and personnel resources on the basis of their own organizational priorities. This is in contrast to the inherited British colonial practice in which centralizes finance in the hands of the treasury and manapower in a central personnel agency leaving a ministry's management responsible for the implementation of the budget with inadequate authority over both finance and personnel.

Manager's budget. With the change in management philosophy on the part of the MOF, "Permanent Secretaries are given complete discretion in deciding on the detailed distribution of their ministry's annual recurrent expenditure allocation among programs, ..." (Singapore Ministry of Finance 1989, p. 3) and make any necessary variations on their own during budget execution without having to refer the changes to the MOF as long as they do not spend more than the total provisions for the ministry. As for personnel matters, permanent secretaries have been delegated with the authority to deploy their staff in the manner best suited to the needs of their organizations, whether this involves the transfer of posts, the redeploying of staff, and the regrading of posts from one scheme of service to another as long as this does not result in an increase in the wage bill. The only constraint is that they have to keep their staff strength at the actual December 1986 level as the government has committed itself to a zero-growth manpower policy.

In the case of development expenditure, permanent secretaries are empowered to make variations within the approved development plans subject to a maximum variation of $5 million for each project. Approval of the minister concerned would be necessary when the sum is in excess of $5 million.

Support for Manager's Budget. To facilitate efficient management of budget resources, the original plan was to provide the ministries with three types of management support:

1. *Management accounting system:* To enable ministries to ascertain the cost-effectiveness of their services, products, or activities, external consultants would help develop management and cost accounting systems appropriate to their specific needs so that costs could be traced and analyzed. This would facilitate the task of the ministries in identifying and taking remedial action in relation to poor performance, inefficiencies, and waste. As a supplement to the existing cash accounting system, the government has installed a Fixed Assets System (FAST) for the purpose of recording the stock of government's capital assets and computing depreciation expenses. It thus becomes possible for the government to know more accurately the funds required for replacing the capital assets. The implementation of Phase 1 of the management accounting project covering five ministries (finance, education, health, national development, and environment) has already begun; another five ministries have been included in Phase 2 scheduled to start in the FY 1991. The plan is to extend the management accounting system to all ministries by FY 1993.
2. *Training:* Training was regarded as essential in the implementation of BVBAS. Briefings and training of staff of ministries on BVBAS have become an ongoing activity. A module on BVBAS has already been included in the course on financial management conducted by the Civil Service Institute.
3. *Financial and management services units:* The original plan was to post trained accountants and management services officers to each ministry for the purpose of setting up a Financial and Management Services Unit in order to enable the ministries to establish control and review systems and undertake in-house financial and management reviews of their operations. This plan, however, has been modified; the ministries

now have to deploy staff to undertake the function without setting up new organizational units.

Performance Control

With the budget orientation of the operating ministries shifting from supplying data useful to the treasury for the purpose of expenditure control to generating data for their own internal management purposes, the role of the treasury has also become much more sophisticated. It no longer spends time in developing detailed guidelines for the ministries; instead it focuses attention on broad guidelines only. In this way, it frees itself from the details of expenditure control to a broader view of the performance of ministries. There are a number of reinforcing elements in this approach.

Management review. A zero-base review of the organization and operations of each ministry or statutory board would be undertaken every five years for the purpose of weeding out outdated practices and procedures. Initially, the review was undertaken by the Management Services Department in the Ministry of Finance; however, since its corporatization in July 1990, the duties have been assigned to the Auditor-General's Office, which has already set up a Zero-Base Review Division to implement the added responsibilities. So far such reviews have been done for the Ministry of Community Development and the Ministry of Communications and Information, while a review on the Ministry of Home Affairs has begun. Other ministries and organs of state (central agencies) would come under reviews in due course (Singapore Ministry of Finance 1991, p. 12).

Comprehensive financial systems audit. Each ministry and statutory board would be subject to a comprehensive financial systems audit by the Auditor-General's Office every five years. Since the introduction of BVBAS, five ministries (communications and information, law, labor, environment, and health) have undergone such auditing on a comprehensive basis.

Annual review of selected policies and programs. Each year the Budget Division of the Ministry of Finance would undertake a review of the cost-effectiveness of a number of chosen policies and programs.

Performance measurement. Workload and performance indicators of ministries have been published in the annual budget documents since the FY 1989. At this stage of development, it would appear that the main purpose has been to provide information to Parliament and the general public about the performance of the ministries. Hopefully, this would provide an added incentive to ministries to improve their performance further.

Use of Computer Technology

Because of rapid economic growth, Singapore has been facing an acute shortage of labor. Since the FY 1989/1990 budget cycle, budgetary reforms have taken full cognizance of the environmental reality. A computerized support system has been operating smoothly for the past two years. A brief description of the operating aspects of the system follows.

The computerized system, Budget Operations Support System (BO$$), incorporates the budget allocation rules which compute what percentage share of the GDP should go to which ministry and how on the basis of the centrally controlled financing formula; this allocation should be shared between recurrent and development expenditure. BO$$ would then produce draft budget spreadsheets for each ministry by splitting its aggregate allocations down to cost-center and account code levels. Once this is completed, the Budget Division of MOF will, at the beginning of the budget cycle, distribute diskettes containing the following to each ministry:

1. Its detailed actual expenditure for the past two financial years.
2. Its appropriations and the revised estimates for the current year.
3. Its preliminary provisions for the budget year (Singapore Ministry of Finance 1991b, p. 1).

Each ministry will then decide how the provisions should be distributed most appropriately among programs, activities, cost centers, and line-items of expenditure. The individual ministry will then upload its proposed budget to the MOF through BO$$ which will check whether the target allocations have been exceeded and highlight any significant variations. The highlighted aspects of the ministry's proposal will then be analyzed and reviewed by the budget officers as the basis for preparing their reports for the annual budget review meetings between the MOF and the permanent secretaries of ministries. Once the budget recommendations of the MOF have been approved by the cabinet, BO$$ will do the printing of the budget documents for offsetting by the Singapore National Printers.

SUMMARY AND CONCLUSIONS

It has been said that in investment the contrarian wins. This may smack of conventional wisdom. Conventional wisdom or not, it has its own grains of truth when it comes to the Singapore's approach to budget management.

In budget management, the tradition of Singapore coincides with the views of the classical economists that "outlay should not exceed income,. . . " (Bastable cited in Borna and Mantripragada 1989, p. 40). This is contrary to the popular practice of governments elsewhere, including those in the OECD countries, during the past few decades.

Arising from this difference in fiscal philosophy, balancing the annual budget became an institutionalized routine reinforced by the tradition of making a conservative revenue estimates annually. The prudent approach to budget management has certainly been one of the factors which has helped to produce a financial outcome most gratifying to Singaporeans: a low external public debt, high official reserves, a substantial annual investment income, and room for policy flexibility and budget initiatives on the part of the government.

In budgeting, Singapore has not followed the path adopted by many other countries. This is reflected in three ways:

1. The timing of budgetary reforms was determined more by internal factors than by external stimuli.
2. The republic has kept the momentum of budgetary reforms going by implementing BVBAS in FY 1989-1990 as an element in its own management development.
3. Its budgetary system has made extensive use of computer technology to conserve manpower and improve administrative efficiency so that there is no mismatch between budgeting and environmental reality.

The introduction of BVBAS in conjunction with BO$$ has given rise to a number of benefits (So far, no systematic empirical research on BVBAS has been undertaken by anyone. The observation can thus only be of a tentative nature.)

By separating macro-policy decision making from micro-management decision making, budgeting has become less contentious at the civil servant level as fund allocation for ministries has become the policy decisions of the cabinet acting on the recommendations of the treasury. It is the researcher's impression, gained from talking to civil servants, that this approach of throwing major budget decisions to the cabinet has worked better in Singapore than elsewhere, such as in Canada (see Savoie 1990), because of conducive factors specific to the republic:

a. The ruling party, the People's Action Party, has a rigorous selection process in putting up candidates to stand as members of Parliament and in making cabinet appointments. Members of the cabinet has a common orientation; there is a strong element of homogeneity in philosophy and thinking among them.
b. A major policy, whether it is transportation, housing, or education, evolves over time; it is debated and a consensus is forged before the cabinet makes the final decision. There is thus consensus over priorities at the highest level in government.

c. Being a small island republic, the benefits of development are spread to all parts of the republic and all sectors of society. With the country enjoying a high rate of growth, no minister feels that his ministry is denied adequate resources.
d. This type of context facilitates consensus in decision making. Thus, the initial decision on the slicing of the GDP among the public and the private sectors and the slicing of the budget among the ministries was supported by the entire cabinet. Budgeting becomes a relatively straightforward provisioning exercise to implement policy decisions of the cabinet.

Ministries can now plan on a more confident basis each year as they have advance knowledge of the size of the budget allocations available to them. Paperwork has been much reduced, so has time and the cost of budget preparation with the introduction of BO$$.

ACKNOWLEDGMENTS

The author would like to thank Low Sin Leng, Deputy Secretary (Budget), Ministry of Finance; Ajith Prasad, Director of Housing, Ministry of National Development; and Dr. Lance Eric Brannman, School of Accountancy and Business, Nanyang Technological University, Singapore, for their valuable comments and suggestions on the initial draft of the paper. The author alone, however, is fully responsible for the paper.

REFERENCES

Borna, S., and K.G. Mantripragada. 1989. "Morality of Public Deficits: A Historical Perspective." *Public Budgeting and Finance* 9(1): 00-00.

Department of Statistics. 1975. *Yearbook of Statistics: Singapore 1974/75*. Singapore: Author.

Department of Statistics. 1980. *Yearbook of Statistics: Singapore 1979/80*. Singapore: Author.

Department of Statistics. 1987. *Yearbook of Statistics: Singapore 1987*. Singapore: Author.

Department of Statistics. 1989. *Yearbook of Statistics: Singapore 1989*. Singapore: Author.

Department of Statistics. 1990. *Yearbook of Statistics: Singapore 1990*. Singapore: Author.

Dean, P., and C. Pugh. 1989. *Government Budgeting in Developing Countries*. London: Routledge.

Doh, J.C. 1990. "Budgeting With Special Reference to Singapore." Paper presented at the Conference on the Fiscal System of Singapore: Trends, Issues and Future Directions, National University of Singapore, February 8-10.

Lim, C.Y., and associates. 1988. *Policy Options for the Singapore Economy*. Singapore: McGraw-Hill Book Co.

Miner, J. 1989. "The Reagan Deficit." *Public Budgeting and Finance* 9(1): 15-32.

Prasad, A. "Developments in Government Budgeting." *Management Development* (35): 1-3.

Pugh, C. 1989. "Budget Innovation in Singapore." Pp. 95-99 in *Government Budgeting in Developing Countries*, edited by P. Dean and C. Pugh. London: Routledge.

Savoie, D.J. 1990. "Reforming the Expenditure Budget Process: The Canadian Experience." *Public Budgeting and Finance* 10(13): 63-78.

Seah, C.M. 1973. "The Budgetary Process in Singapore Bureaucracy: Some Observations." *The Singapore Manager* 7(1): 25-29.

Singapore Ministry of Finance. 1989a. *Act 2: A Budget Division Manual.* Singapore: Author.

Singapore Ministry of Finance. 1989b. "Finance Circular No. 3/89." April 1.

Singapore Ministry of Finance. 1990. "Finance Circular Minute No. M8/90." May 8.

Singapore Ministry of Finance. 1991a *Budget Statement 1991.* Singapore: Author.

Singapore Ministry of Finance. 1991b. "Finance Circular Minute No. M2/91." May 9.

Singapore Ministry of Trade and Industry. 1986. "The Singapore Economy: New Directions." Report of the Economic Committee, February.

Singapore Ministry of Trade and Industry. 1989. *Economic Survey of Singapore.* Singapore: Author.

The Straits Times. 1990. December 18.

The Straits Times. 1991. August 12.

United Nations. 1958. *Manual for the Classification of Government Transaction by Economic and Functional Categories.* New York: Author.

World Bank. 1990. *World Economic Report 1990.* Washington, DC: Author.

Yeo, Philip. 1990. "Economic Development—Strategic Thrusts for the 1990s." Pp. 000-000 in *Singapore 1990*, edited by XXXX. Singapore: Ministry of Communications and Information.

THE RECURRENT COST CRISIS IN DEVELOPMENT BUREAUCRACIES

Stephen B. Peterson

ABSTRACT

While public sector bureaucracies in developing countries attempt to implement ambitious economic reform programs, their daily operations have been brought to a standstill by low and uncertain levels of basic operating and maintenance resources. Governments and donors share responsibility for this state of affairs. This chapter reviews the deterioration of recurrent cost support in Kenya's critical Ministries of Agriculture and Livestock Development. It recommends several reforms that could improve the utilization of public sector resources: more stringent personnel policies and stronger financial management by government and a shift from capacity-expanding to capacity-supporting projects by donors.

A persistent problem in developing countries is the underfunding of the operating and maintenance (O&M) recurrent costs of capital expenditures. While donors fund capital investments in development budgets, existing projects often founder because of lack of resources to support their

Policy Studies and Developing Nations, Volume 3, pages 175-203.

ISBN: 1-55938-190-6

maintenance and supplies. For decades, dismayed observers have noted the vicious cycle of abandonment of capital or a need for costly rehabilitation programs. This chapter examines the crisis in recurrent O&M cost financing in two ministries in Kenya and suggests possible solutions.

THE LEVEL OF RECURRENT COST FUNDING

As in many developing countries, the agriculture and livestock sectors in Kenya employ the majority of the work force. The Ministries of Agriculture and Livestock Development, therefore, should be a critical focus for development efforts. Yet, their financing does not reflect their significance. For the Ministry of Agriculture (MOA), the total allocation (recurrent plus development budget) in FY 1980-1981 was 2.1 percent of total government expenditure and averaged 2.6 percent of total government allocation from FY 1980-1981 to FY 1990-1991. For the Ministry of Livestock Development (MOLD), the total allocation in FY 1980-1981 was 2 percent and averaged 1.7 percent from FY 1980-1981 to FY 1990-1991.

Allocations to recurrent O&M expenditures indicate an even more serious situation. The recurrent O&M budget of the MOLD in FY 1990-1991 in real and operational terms is one-twenty-sixth of what it was in FY 1980-1981- the last year in which the chiefs of the technical divisions contend they received an "acceptable" budget. In FY 1990-1991, the MOA also received a minuscule recurrent O&M cost allocation, one-tenth the size of the "acceptable" level of FY 1980-1981.

The resources that would be needed to restore the O&M balance to effective levels based on norms from the 1980-1981 financial year are staggering. For FY 1990-1991, the MOA would have required an additional allocation of 52 million Kenya pounds ($41.6 million) or 10 times the revised net recurrent O&M budget (see Table 1). The needs for the MOLD in FY 1990-1991 were even greater at 90.9 million Kenya pounds ($72.7 million) which is 26 times the revised net O&M recurrent budget (see Table 2).

The problem is that personnel expenditures continued to increase while critical O&M expenditures experienced a decline in real terms. For the MOA, the annual average real increase for personnel emoluments between 1980 and 1989 was 10 percent while for the same period the average annual expenditures for transport, traveling, and maintenance all *declined* by 8 percent. For the MOLD, total personnel emoluments increased 17 percent annually in real terms between 1980 and 1989, while for the same period the average annual expenditures for transport, traveling, and maintenance all *declined* by 10 percent. Tables 4 and 5 illustrate the deterioration in the composition of recurrent cost support. Using recurrent cost norms based on personnel emoluments, the tables show the projected levels of support based on norms

Table 1. The Current O&M Shortfall for Agriculture

Analysis of the Non-Wage Operating Expenditure Shortfall to Allocations for the FY 1990-1991 Revised Estimates (in Kenya pounds)

LINE		(A) Amount Projected by Norm	(B) Amount Allocated in 90/91 Revised Estimates	(C) Shortfallin Allocation: (Column B less Column A)	(D) Revised Estimates as a Percent of the Norm Projection
	Transport	19,992,570	2,398,198	(17,594,372)	12.0%
	Traveling	14,936,229	1,897,499	(13,038,730)	12.7%
	Maintenance	14,908,293	2,692,097	(12,216,196)	18.1%
	Materials	3,017,444	1,074,786	(1,942,658)	35.6%
	All Others	10,894,880	3,440,513	(7,454,367)	31.6%
(1)	*Total Shortfall*				(52,246,323)
	Gross 1990-1991 Revised Recurrent and Development Budgets:				63,394,942
(2)	Shortfall as a percent:				82.4%
	Gross 1990-1991 Revised Recurrent and Development Budgets less personnel expenditures:				34,515,221
(3)	Shortfall as a percent:				151.4%
	Gross 1990-1991 Revised Recurrent Budget less personnel expenditures:				7,232,467
(4)	Shortfall as a percent:				722.4%
	Net 1990-1991 Revised Recurrent Budget less personnel expenditures:				5,152,029
(5)	Shortfall as a percent:				1014.1%

Note: *Personnel expenditures include personnel emoluments and the following expenses: house allowances, passage and leave expenses, etc.

adjusted for inflation (Section 1 of Tables 4 and 5). Section 3 of Tables 4 and 5 show the actual level of recurrent support as a percent of projected norm support.

What should be the appropriate level of O&M recurrent cost funding? Whatever the ideal position might be, budget constraints suggest that the appropriate size of a ministry should be those activities which can be fully funded in terms of staff, capital equipment, and O&M support. Current budgeting practice is first to fully fund personnel (defined narrowly as simply covering their salaries and allowances), then fund capital expenditures, and residually fund recurrent O&M support. It would be preferable to constrain the overall scale of the ministries' activities by the extent recurrent O&M cost funding is available to support *fully* the requisite staff and equipment. Personnel in particular should be determined by the availability of marginal recurrent cost financing.

Table 2. The Current O&M Shortfall for Livestock Development

Analysis of the Non-Wage Operating Expenditure Shortfall to Allocations for the 1990-1991 Revised Estimates (in Kenya pounds)

LINE		*(A) Amount Projected by Norm*	*(B) Amount Allocated in 90/91 Revised Estimates*	*(C) Shortfall in Allocation: (Column B less Column A)*	*(D) Revised Estimates as a Percent of the Norm Projection*
	Transport	37,632,594	3,125,775	(34,506,819)	8.3%
	Travelling	14,026,920	1,249,875	(12,777,045)	8.9%
	Maintenance	8,091,572	542,182	(7,549,390)	6.7%
	Materials	36,208,493	5,382,444	(30,826,049)	14.9%
	All Others	7,552,516	2,224,156	(5,328,360)	29.4%
(1)	Total Shortfall				(90,987,663)
	Gross 1990-1991 Revised Recurrent and Development Budgets:				54,452,622
(2)	Shortfall as a percent:				167.1%
	Gross 1990-1991 Revised Recurrent and Development Budgets less personnel expenditures:				30,234,519
(3)	Shortfall as a percent:				300.9%
	Gross 1990-1991 Revised Recurrent Budget less personnel expenditures:				10,619,361
(4)	Shortfall as a percent:				856.8%
	Net 1990-1991 Revised Recurrent Budget less personnel expenditures:				3,500,271
(5)	Shortfall as a percent:				2599.4%

Note: *Personnel expenditures include personnel emoluments and the following expenses: house allowances, passage and leave expenses, etc.

But in Kenya, the issue of funding levels is complicated by the balance between the operating budget (the recurrent budget), financed by the government of Kenya, and the development budget, financed primarily by donors. In FY 1990-1991, donors funded 89 percent and 87 percent of the respective development budgets of the MOA and the MOLD, but the donor-funded portion of the development budget funded vital O&M recurrent costs of projects and thus ministry activities. The government funded recurrent or "operational" budget was virtually a payroll. For FY 1990-1991, salaries and benefits comprised 77 percent and 70 percent of MOA's and MOLD's respective recurrent budgets. Table 3 illustrates for both ministries the extent to which expenditures in the development budget were used to fund recurrent O&M costs.

Table 3. The Amount of O&M Funded Through the Development Budget

Development Budget Expenditures as a Percent of Both Development and Recurrent Budget Expenditures
(percent, in constant 1975 prices, 1980-1981 FY base)

The Ministry of Agriculture

	1980-1981	*1983-1984*	*1984-1985*	*1985-1986*	*1986-1987*	*1987-1988*	*1988-1989*	*1989-1990*	*1990-1991*
Transport	40.2%	49.5%	44.6%	50.5%	55.3%	44.1%	50.8%	44.3%	43.2%
Traveling	23.6%	39.4%	35.8%	35.8%	38.1%	32.2%	47.5%	39.7%	39.1%
Maintenance	67.8%	75.1%	39.1%	61.3%	68.6%	57.6%	50.4%	45.1%	33.1%
Materials	32.4%	13.7%	25.7%	71.0%	15.3%	28.0%	6.4%	4.2%	4.6%
All Others	6.8%	4.9%	4.6%	3.9%	4.6%	10.6%	10.2%	11.7%	12.8%
The Ministry of Livestock Development									
Transport	37.3%	45.0%	30.0%	26.0%	20.4%	34.8%	29.5%	28.6%	24.0%
Traveling	36.5%	53.4%	49.5%	38.4%	25.8%	45.6%	39.5%	39.2%	32.2%
Maintenance	61.3%	75.9%	54.1%	38.7%	16.6%	34.2%	47.8%	26.7%	27.3%
Materials	49.0%	48.4%	45.1%	52.1%	51.3%	47.9%	53.8%	49.9%	24.8%
All Others	8.6%	13.3%	4.8%	1.3%	4.1%	3.1%	7.0%	8.4%	10.1%

WHY HAVE O&M EXPENDITURES DETERIORATED IN KENYA

The O&M crisis is a result of both government and donor practices, and its solution will require the coordinated effort of both.

Government Practices

While the principal culprit in the decline of O&M support has been excessive personnel recruitment which has absorbed the bulk of the recurrent budget, several other factors have contributed to the problem.

Weak Financial Planning

Multi-year financial planning through three-year forward budgets has failed to meet the problem of providing recurrent O&M funding in the long-term.[1] The three-year timeframe of the forward budget is too short to cover the period after new donor projects end and O&M support of those projects funded through the recurrent budget should begin. Both ministries have donor-funded projects in the development budget where the donor is providing virtually all the O&M support (e.g., National Extension for the MOA and Animal Health Rehabilitation for the MOLD). Ministry staff do not budget for replacement of donor resources, much less recurrent O&M support for the projects, because the requirements far exceed the ministry's existing and potential resources. In any case, the forward budget is primarily a "forward draft" of the annual budget, and the two outlying budget years are virtually ignored and are not taken seriously as a means of projecting future recurrent costs of capital investments. Projects often deteriorate or collapse because government O&M funds are not available when donor support ends.

Lack of Coordination Between the Development and Recurrent Budgets

A major weakness in government budgeting is the failure to link the recurrent and development budgets. Activities are not treated as cost centers making it difficult to identify capital and O&M expenditures in the recurrent and development budgets with a particular activity. The structure of the budget thus makes it difficult to determine the level or adequacy of O&M support for particular activities.

Poor Cost Budgeting

Effective budgeting requires accurate costing of line items. Except for the donor projects in the development budget which often have project documents

Table 4. The Trend in O&M Support for Agriculture

Deterioriation of the Non-Wage Recurrent Cost Support for MOA: 1980-1990
(Percent of Non-Wage Operating Expenses to Personnel Emoluments)

	1980-1981 (Norms)	*1983-1984*	*1984-1985*	*1985-1986*	*1986-1987*	*1987-1988*	*1988-1989*	*1989-1990*	*Printed Estimates 1990-1991*	*Revised Estimates 1990-1991*
(1) Projected Levels of Support Based on 1980-1981 Norms*										
Transport	17.8%	33.3%	37.6%	46.1%	53.9%	59.9%	63.9%	77.6%	85.9%	85.9%
Traveling	13.3%	24.9%	28.0%	34.4%	40.2%	44.7%	47.7%	57.9%	64.1%	64.1%
Maintenance	21.5%	37.4%	39.3%	43.8%	46.5%	50.3%	53.2%	59.1%	64.0%	64.0%
Materials	4.4%	7.6%	8.0%	8.9%	9.4%	10.2%	10.8%	12.0%	13.0%	13.0%
All others	15.7%	27.4%	28.7%	32.0%	34.0%	36.8%	38.8%	43.2%	46.8%	46.8%
(2) Actual Levels of Support										
Transport	17.8%	15.7%	15.3%	14.1%	13.0%	9.4%	13.2%	12.1%	12.3%	10.3%
Traveling	13.3%	8.7%	8.2%	8.2%	6.0%	5.6%	9.4%	8.1%	8.3%	8.2%
Maintenance	21.5%	33.3%	9.2%	14.2%	20.2%	10.6%	9.6%	8.9%	12.3%	11.6%
Materials	4.3%	2.4%	2.5%	8.2%	4.4%	3.4%	3.8%	5.1%	5.2%	4.6%
All others	15.7%	12.7%	17.0%	23.7%	13.1%	11.4%	16.8%	14.3%	15.3%	14.8%
(3) Actual Support as a Percent of Projected Norm-Based Support**										
Transport	100.0%	47.2%	40.7%	30.5%	24.0%	15.6%	20.6%	15.6%	14.4%	12.0%
Traveling	100.0%	35.1%	29.2%	23.8%	14.8%	12.6%	19.6%	14.0%	12.9%	12.7%
Maintenance	100.0%	88.9%	23.4%	32.4%	43.4%	21.0%	18.1%	15.0%	19.2%	18.1%
Materials	100.0%	31.1%	31.3%	93.2%	46.7%	33.0%	35.3%	42.3%	40.4%	35.6%
All others	100.0%	46.5%	59.1%	74.0%	38.5%	31.1%	43.3%	33.2%	32.7%	31.6%

Notes: *Projected norms use the 1980-1981 percentage level of support (e.g., 17.79% for transport) multiplied by a deflation factor given in Table 7. This percent multiplied by the nominal emolument for the respective FY year provides the nominal value of the norm determined level of support.

**Calculated by dividing the percents in Section 2 by the respective percents in Section 1.

Table 5. The Trend in O&M Support for Livestock Development

Deterioration of the Non-Wage Recurrent Cost Support for the MOLD: 1980-1990
(Percent of Non-Wage Operating Expenses to Personnel Emoluments)

	1980-1981 (Norms)	*1983-1984*	*1984-1985*	*1985-1986*	*1986-1987*	*1987-1988*	*1988-1989*	*1989-1990*	*Printed Estimates 1990-1991*	*Revised Estimates 1990-1991*
(1) Projected Levels of Support Based on 1980-1981 Norms*										
Transport	41.1%	77.0%	86.8%	106.5%	124.6%	138.4%	147.8%	179.4%	198.5%	198.5%
Traveling	15.6%	29.3%	33.0%	40.5%	47.4%	52.6%	56.2%	68.3%	75.5%	75.5%
Maintenance	15.0%	26.1%	27.4%	30.5%	32.4%	35.0%	37.0%	41.1%	44.6%	44.6%
Materials	63.5%	110.5%	116.0%	129.1%	137.1%	148.4%	156.9%	174.4%	189.0%	189.0%
All Others	13.4%	23.3%	24.4%	27.2%	28.9%	31.3%	33.0%	36.7%	39.8%	39.8%
(2) Actual Levels of support										
Transport	41.1%	24.5%	21.7%	22.9%	21.5%	10.6%	15.1%	20.0%	17.6%	16.4%
Traveling	15.6%	8.7%	6.9%	8.0%	7.8%	4.8%	5.6%	6.8%	6.8%	6.5%
Maintenance	15.0%	12.3%	5.7%	3.6%	2.7%	2.1%	3.0%	2.9%	2.8%	2.8%
Materials	63.5%	58.7%	53.9%	56.0%	56.3%	14.4%	40.9%	63.4%	35.6%	28.2%
All Others	13.4%	4.5%	8.4%	11.7%	10.0%	5.1%	6.4%	11.4%	10.8%	11.6%
(3) Actual Support as a Percent of Projected Norm-Based Support**										
Transport	100.0%	31.8%	24.9%	21.5%	17.2%	7.6%	10.2%	11.2%	8.8%	8.2%
Traveling	100.0%	29.8%	21.0%	19.7%	16.4%	9.1%	10.0%	9.9%	9.0%	8.6%
Maintenance	100.0%	47.1%	21.0%	11.8%	8.3%	5.9%	8.2%	7.0%	6.4%	6.4%
Materials	100.0%	53.1%	46.4%	43.3%	41.0%	9.7%	26.1%	36.4%	18.8%	14.9%
All Others	100.0%	19.5%	34.5%	43.0%	34.7%	16.4%	19.5%	31.0%	27.2%	29.2%

Notes: *Projected norms use the 1980-1981 percentage level of support (e.g., 17.79% for transport) multiplied by a deflation factor given in Table 7. This percent multiplied by the nominal emolument for the respective FY year provides the nominal value of the norm determined level of support.

**Calculated by dividing the percents in Section 2 by the respective percents in Section 1.

Table 6. Deflators Used to Create the O&M Norms

	80-81	*83-84*	*84-85*	*85-86*	*86-87*	*87-88*	*88-89*	*89-90*	*90-91*	*91-92*
Personnel Deflator	1.0000	1.1452	1.1935	1.2419	1.2984	1.3548	1.4194	1.4839	1.5484	1.6129
Transport Deflator	1.0000	2.1453	2.5196	3.2179	3.9330	4.5587	5.1006	6.4749	7.4749	8.3687
Goods and Services Deflator	1.0000	1.9939	2.1818	2.5273	2.8061	3.1697	3.5091	4.0788	4.6121	4.9818

Notes: 1. All three deflators are determined by 1975 prices with a 1980 base.
2. The personnel deflator is based on the per annum increase of government salaries from 1975 to 1991 which was 4.43 percent. In determining the average per annum increase, a weighted average of the job groups was used based on the assumption of a constant composition of job groups and using the 1990-1991 distribution as the base.
3. The transport deflator is from the Nairobi Consumer Price Index of the Central Bureau of Statistics and is the "transport and communications" index for middle income groups.
4. The goods and services deflator is from the Nairobi Consumer Price Index of Central Bureau of Statistics and is an equally weighted average of four of the indexes: (1) fuel and power, (2) transport and communications, (3) miscellaneous goods and services, and (4) furniture, furnishings, household equipment, and household operation.

Table 7. Adjustment Factors Used in Creating the O&M Norms

	80-81	*83-84*	*84-85*	*85-86*	*86-87*	*87-88*	*88-89*	*89-90*	*90-91*	*91-92*
Transport and Traveling	1.0000	1.8733	2.1110	2.5910	3.0291	3.3647	3.5936	4.3635	4.8275	5.1886
Maintenance, Materials, all Others	1.0000	1.7412	1.8280	2.0349	2.1612	2.3395	2.4723	2.7487	2.9787	3.0887

Note: The adjustment factors are based on the deflators of Table 6 and "adjust" the percentages of the norm year (e.g., 17.79% for the MOA in 1980-1981) to the following years. The adjustment factors are calculated by dividing the personnel deflator by the transport or the goods and services deflator. The inverse of this quotient is the adjustment factor.

prepared in detail by consultants, accurate costing is not the norm. This is particularly true of the government-funded recurrent budget which in principle is to provide long-term recurrent support. Lack of discipline in budget costing is in part explained by the incremental budget process. Ministry budget staff rightfully know that meticulous preparation of the budget is futile since the budget notes accompanying their submissions are ignored by the treasury. In the end (and if they are lucky), the allocation will simply be an increment based on last year's budget. Incrementalism undermines efforts to increase the analytic content of budgeting.

Divisible and Vulnerable Nature of O&M Expenditures

O&M expenditures have deteriorated, in part because they are divisible and easier to cut than lumpy capital investments in the development budget. They are particularly vulnerable in the context of Kenya's incremental budgeting process. Unlike high profile development projects that have champions both in and out of government, O&M expenditures have few if any proponents.

Given the choice, even the most enlightened senior officer would increase personnel rather than improve operating expenses. O&M allocations have been vulnerable to the treasury's cuts because they are deemed to be "controllable" expenditures which are abused and can and should be cut when budgets require trimming. In a decade of declining public resources relative to need, budgeters have had to prune with mirrors. The mirror has focused on O&M expenditures on the assumption that they can be finessed with donor funds through the development budget.

Inability to Fund the Government Contribution to Development Projects

A major cause of the decline in the level of O&M support has been the high government contribution required by donors for the operating expenses of development projects. The government contribution ranges as high as 60 percent for some projects, and it is not uncommon for it to average between 30 percent and 40 percent. Since donor projects comprise the largest component of the development budget, government contributions to these projects are quite sizeable. In recent years, the treasury has resorted to trimming government contributions to donor projects to reduce its deficit while allowing the donor grant or loan portions to be fully funded. The result, of course, has been an imbalance in capital investment relative to recurrent cost support. Even where the treasury has not cut or reduced the government contribution, in recent years it has encouraged the ministries to implement projects with only the donor portion and not fund the government contribution. This practice not only underfunds O&M but is very disruptive to the smooth supply of operating goods and services.

Erratic Release of Funds

Because of the difficulties of the Ministry of Finance (MOF) in forecasting and collecting revenues and in balancing various interests in allocating funds, the lack of stable cash flows to the ministries has impaired effective management of scarce O&M resources. O&M support is delayed at the beginning of the financial year when carryovers are paid and is often reduced midway through and at the end of the financial year when the MOF imposes cuts and freezes due to revenue shortfalls or donor conditionality. Both practices tend to involve reduction of vital O&M expenditures. The cutbacks imposed in FY 1990-1991 virtually eliminated the remaining allocations for transport, traveling, and maintenance.

For operating ministries in Kenya, as in most developing countries, the critical financial management issue is not the allocation in the budget books but the cash that has been released from the exchequer. The heart of budgeting as well as O&M management in developing countries is cash flow management. The demand by donors for relatively high government contributions to support project expenditures leaves governments with the problem of supporting O&M expenditures without adequate cash. In recent years, the government has resorted to three tactics, all of which worsen the situation. First, the Authority to Incur Expenditure (AIE) is delayed so spending cannot begin. For FY 1992-1993, the government delayed for eight weeks the release of both ministries' Authority to Incur Expenditure (AIEs) for the development budget, thus stopping the use of development funds (for both recurrent and capital support) for one-sixth of the financial year (Office of the Vice President and Ministry of Finance, Budgetary Supply Department 1990). Second, the cash to pay for the debts incurred by the AIEs is delayed. Exchequer releases often cover only the absolute minimum expenditures (salary) thereby delaying payment of debts incurred by the AIEs often to the next financial year. Third, partial payments of debts incurred under donor development projects are encouraged. The donor-funded portion of the debt is paid, but the government portion is delayed.

Tactics 2 and 3 result in partial and delayed payment to suppliers. The cumulative effect of these tactics has been highly disruptive to the prompt and cost-effective delivery of services. Suppliers respond by inflating prices, demanding cash payments in advance of delivery, withdrawal of services, and even expensive legal actions. The credit worthiness of the government is so low that field officers have to circumvent accounting procedures to obtain needed services (e.g., purchase fuel with cash advances raised through temporary imprest).

Because of the erratic delayed release of development expenditures to recurrent cost support, donor funding takes on added importance. As Table 3 indicates, donors provide a substantial portion of the total O&M funds (roughly 40% for MOA and 30% for MOLD). In many ways, the development budget is the "core" budget because of the reliability of donor funding, much of which is composed of direct payments.[2] Thus, even though the donor share of the critical O&M items is less than half, the donor share is often more reliable because much of it involves direct payments which can be made promptly when needed and is not constrained by government liquidity.[3] Government funds are frequently frozen toward the end of the financial year, and donor funds become particularly crucial at these times.

For those projects that require a substantial government contribution to O&M items, donor funding is a mixed blessing, for it creates unsustainable capacity and entices government to commit to operational expenses it can only partially pay with donor funds. This practice quickly creates a large unfunded operational debt.

Financial instability has several negative effects on ministry operations. First, it disrupts implementation. Second, it skews the pattern of implementation, for staff spend quickly on the assumption that funds will not be forthcoming during the second half of the financial year. Third, cutbacks are often made late in the financial year when the ministry has already made commitments thereby creating excess votes and carryovers to the next financial year. Finally, cutbacks and freezes often occur in the second half of the financial year which is particularly crippling for the MOA because this is the time when farmers prepare their crops and when the ministry's extension service can have maximum impact.

Financial Leverage of User Fees

Both ministries are required to collect user fees for their services, known as appropriations-in-aid (A-in-A) in the recurrent budget. In essence, A-in-A *leverages* a ministry's financial position, for it must raise a portion of its recurrent budget from the services it provides. To the extent that user fees do not generate the expected revenues, the overall recurrent budget is reduced and the shortfall reduces the O&M expenditures of the recurrent budget but not salaries which are fully funded.

A-in-A collection is a particularly serious problem for the MOLD, for it has been required to collect on average 12.5 percent of its gross recurrent budget from A-in-A over the past decade (FYs 1980-1981 to 1990-1991). During the same period, the MOA has been required to collect 4.3 percent of its gross recurrent budget in fees. Collection rates for the two ministries have varied considerably over the period but have averaged 70 percent, although in recent years the MOLD's collection rate has dropped significantly reaching a low of 40.2 percent in 1988-1989. On average, the MOLD has suffered a 3.6 percent reduction in its gross recurrent budget due to undercollection of A-in-A.

The explanation for the decline in A-in-A collections varies by institution. The treasury claims that these collections are conservatively estimated and are reasonable. Lack of collection then is simply a failure of the respective ministries to adequately manage the collections. The ministries contend that the levels are arbitrarily set with little regard to the capacity to provide the service and thereby collect the fees. The ministries feel that the instability and inadequacy of recurrent cost funding has crippled their ability to provide reliable services for which farmers are willing to pay.[4] The failure to collect A-in-A fees in turn *reduces* the recurrent funds available, creating a vicious cycle of diminishing recurrent O&M cost support. Ministry staff involved in managing A-in-A services point out that simply raising the fees of a service does not automatically increase revenues. Given the mixed performance of government in providing services, the steep hikes in user fees in recent years have led to a *decline* in collection in part due to the elasticity of demand.

Failure to Use Donor Funds Earmarked for O&M Support

Recent experience in Kenya suggests that improvement of the recurrent cost position of sectoral ministries is difficult to achieve through balance of payments support. For FY 1991-1992, the treasury did not meet the conditionality of the recently negotiated IDA-funded Second Agricultural Structural Adjustment Operation (ASAO II), for it refused to allocate to the MOA and the MOLD the supplementary funds for recurrent cost support specified as part of conditionality.[5] The O&M supplements which the ASAO II program were to provide were modest but still significant. The O&M provision would have met 5.3 percent of the MOLD's O&M deficit and 10 percent of MOA's deficit. Instead, the treasury retained the funds which came as part of balance of payments support. Not only did the treasury violate conditionality by not providing the mandated incremental recurrent cost support, it worsened the problem by providing a recurrent budget to both ministries which was *under* the proposed ceilings.

Expenditure Accounting

The problem of declining O&M resources is exacerbated by inadequate accounting systems. The appropriations accounts that provide data on expenditure do not allow for an accurate accounting of O&M resources because they only list donor appropriations in aid and do not separate donor from government revenue payments.[6]

Political Factors

With growing budget deficits and other pressing commitments, government increasingly is leaving the vital agriculture and livestock sector to the donor marketplace. Compared to other public investments that provide the government more immediate political support (e.g., the military and, to a lesser, extent education), this sector has been and will continue to be neglected. The neglect is rationalized by the knowledge that donors will not abandon the sector as demonstrated by their continued investment. Kenya is not alone in its shifting priorities—governments throughout Africa are diverting their attention away from the agricultural sector (Gray and Martens 1983; Lim 1983; Peterson 1986).

Donor Practices

While primary responsibility for the decline of O&M support on balance rests with government, donors have contributed to the deterioration. The following practices have worsened the O&M situation.

Promotion of New Rather Than Existing Capacity

Donors prefer to fund new projects rather than support existing capacity, although supporting existing capacity through direct O&M support is often a far better investment. First, the rate of return is often much higher on maintaining rather than introducing capital. Second, this approach provides for more stable and better managed services. Third, it promotes institutionalization of services managed by government departments rather than the temporary management (often by expatriates) of project enclaves.

An alternative to maintaining capital is to replace it with new capital, which is both expensive and unreliable. The expense is obvious—O&M is a marginal cost compared with new capital. The strategy is unreliable because there is no guarantee that O&M resources can or will be released. Donor projects are "lumpy"; and it is difficult first to get them into a ministry's budget, and then it is difficult to release their funds particularly if the funds require an accompanying government contribution.[7]

Failure to Accept Government's Financial Limitations

Donors exhibit a myopia in understanding the government's financial limitations. Donors hamstring their projects by two practices: requiring large government contributions and government pre-financing. The government often trims its contributions in the development budget and delays or reduces the cash available to make the government-funded payments which have to be budgeted.

Once a project is in the budget, the donors are persistently frustrated when government matching funds are not released. The consequence of these donor pressures is a development portfolio with too many projects that cannot be fully funded in the short-term much less sustained in the long-term. This problem is not confined to Kenya. A study by the World Bank showed "that in six out of ten of the Bank's borrowers, underfunding of both the construction of ongoing projects and the maintenance of completed projects assumed serious proportions" (Baum and Tolbert 1985, p. 54).

Promotion of Self-Contained Projects

Recognizing the deteriorating conditions of ministry resources, donors often design projects to be relatively self-contained to ensure their objectives are met. While this is a rational response to a poor project environment, it has negative consequences. The "self-contained" projects fragment the budget. All costs except those for personnel are funded through the development budget and the recurrent O&M costs—which are initially covered by the donor but which must eventually be covered by government—are virtually "invisible" in the government's recurrent budget. Thus, these expenditures are not integrated within the government budget process. As such projects near completion, it is also difficult to shift them onto the recurrent budget. Off-budget financing of projects is another practice which weakens financial management, for it erodes accountability with the result that government does not understand the full costing (including O&M) of a project.

RECOMMENDATIONS FOR IMPROVING O&M SUPPORT

Government Reforms

Down-Sizing the Ministries

One approach to improving the composition of funding would be to "downsize" the ministries by reducing the number of staff. Using the personnel emolument data for FY 1990-1991, the MOA alone would have to reduce personnel emoluments by 31 percent to bring them in line with O&M allocations. The MOLD would have to reduce emoluments by a staggering 55 percent to bring them in line with O&M expenditures. There have never been government mandated reductions in staffing levels, and such action with current levels of high unemployment is not politically acceptable. Over the past three years, however, the agriculture ministries have implemented a painful and difficult policy of not recruiting the graduates of the sector's professional disciplines.

While downsizing the ministries through personnel cutbacks is unlikely, it is possible to improve the composition of recurrent O&M support through rationalization of services. Rationalization might be either inter-ministerial (specialization between the MOA and the MOLD), intra-ministerial (consolidating divisions), or both. Inter-ministerial rationalization focuses on the production extension services of the two ministries which in terms of staff is the largest division in the MOA and the third largest division in the MOLD. Since both extension services reach the same farmers in the majority of areas where there is both crop and livestock production, the World Bank has proposed that these two services specialize and not duplicate efforts. This proposal has caused considerable conflict between the two ministries and has particularly rankled the MOLD because extension services are viewed as the "core task" of a field ministry. While rationalization of services through inter-ministerial cooperation has been notoriously ineffective in Kenya, intra-ministerial rationalization is possible, though there are significant internal bureaucratic politics and donor interests to overcome. Each ministry would need to rank order its priorities.

Assuming that reducing personnel is not feasible in the short- to medium-term, the criteria for prioritizing *services* should be (in rank order) economic productivity, level of the recurrent cost burden, and support for existing ministerial staff.[8] Those services which have a marginal impact on productivity (or could be achieved by less costly means), consume a disproportionate share of O&M support, and support a limited number of staff should be cut. A good example of such a service is MOLD's Artificial Insemination (AI) program which in FY 1988-1989 supported 3 percent of the ministry's staff yet consumed 30 percent of the ministry's transport budget. Some experienced observers have argued that the quality of livestock might be improved more cheaply and efficiently by other means (e.g., the use of local grade cattle).[9] Emphasis should be placed on prioritizing *services* not *projects*, though the former is far harder for it entails organizational restructuring.

Staffing Levels Tied to Budgeting Norms

In response to the dramatic increase in personnel recruitment over the past decade, the treasury has for the past three years refused to allow the ministries to recruit either administrative staff or new professional staff. It has also introduced a salary ceiling into the annual budget which for the past three years has only allowed for the annual increment awarded all civil servants as they move through their grades. While these measures are significant and have been difficult to implement, the treasury might go further to authorize recruitment only if *marginal recurrent costs* of additional staff can be funded. Based on norms of recurrent O&M cost support prevailing in FY 1980-1981 and adjusting for inflation, for FY 1990-1991 the MOA and the MOLD would need to have budgeted 71 percent and 145 percent, respectively, for the recurrent O&M costs of each increment of salary (Peterson and Kiragu 1990, p. 19).

Recruitment should also be based on budgeting norms which determine the appropriate level of human capital in terms of the material capital available and the recurrent investment needed to support it. Such budgeting norms need to be developed for the major services of each ministry. Heller of the World Bank has worked extensively on recurrent cost (r) coefficients and contends that agriculture and livestock's r is 10 percent and 14 percent, respectively (Heller 1974, 1979, p. 176). There are three problems with Heller's indexes. First, there is a wide variation in his coefficients within each sector. For example, livestock has an overall coefficient of 14 percent, yet veterinary services is only 7 percent. The coefficients for rural development (which both ministries are engaged in) vary enormously from 8 percent to 43 percent. Second, within a sector Heller does not disaggregate the categories of O&M such as transport and maintenance (for an analysis of the categories of O&M expenditure by service for these two ministries, see Peterson and Kiragu 1990). For example, for FY 1980-1981 in the MOLD, veterinary services needed 5.2

percent of personnel emoluments to be allocated to transport while the range management services needed 46 percent (Peterson and Kiragu 1990, Annex I, pp. 53, 55).

The major problem with Heller's coefficients, however, is that they *include* personnel costs. Thus, a high coefficient may mask deteriorating O&M support in cases where it reflects, as in these two ministries, a high proportion of personnel expenditure.

While it is relatively easy to construct budgeting norms based on the ratio of O&M expenditure to personnel costs, as in Tables 1 and 5, it is much harder to determine budget norms for O&M support to capital stock. The difficulty of using budget coefficients with a capital stock base is that estimates of capital stock are historical and inherently imprecise[10] because of poor data on initial inventory, relevance of depreciation schedules, and accuracy of the deflating index which relates capital stocks to current capital investments. Unfortunately, there is no accurate time series on public sector capital stocks in agriculture and livestock though preliminary work in this area has begun (Barber, Milne, and Wilson 1991; Peterson and Kiragu 1990, pp. 62-68).

Improved Budgeting

The *instability* of O&M support has been as much of a problem as its declining *level.* Its improvement is not easy. It requires that the MOF resist weak claims on the budget that have strong political support, accurate projection of revenue, and vigorous collection. Stable allocations may require *lower* but more accurate estimates that ministries can trust and thus plan on. What is needed are budgets with *floors* not ceilings.

Prompt Release of Cash

Budgeting alone is not enough. It is essential that *cash* releases from the exchequer *support* the allocations printed in the budget books.

Better Management of User Fees

Improving the management of user fees deserves a separate paper, but a few brief recommendations may be noted.[11] First, a ministry's user fees should be based on conservative and historically established collection rates. Second, the incentives for field staff to collect should be increased. Districts should be able to retain excess collections, and the burden of undercollection should be borne by the *field* and not the headquarters as is currently the case.[12] Perhaps the most ambitious recommendation which the MOLD is currently working on is to privatize virtually all services which involve the generation of fees (e.g., artificial insemination, veterinary health services, livestock dipping) (Kenya Veterinary Association 1986).

Improved Financial Planning

Once budgeting is strengthened, multi-year financial planning needs to be improved. Despite impressive attempts to reform financial management, notably the Budget Rationalization Program and more recently the Public Investment Program, financial planning remains weak.[13] The forward budget has too short a timeframe to provide meaningful financial planning and is primarily a budgeting not a planning exercise. The newly introduced Public Investment Program requires the line ministries to submit briefs on each project and rank projects as core, medium, or low priority. However, with its short three-year timeframe, it is doubtful that it will improve financial planning. Kenya still lacks an effective financial planning instrument of adequate duration to allow an analysis of capital investment and recurrent cost support. Botswana's five-year project planning framework could serve as a useful model for Kenya *once* budgeting is strengthened (for a discussion of Botswana's system, see Stevens 1985, p. 92; World Bank 1984, p. 33).

While it is important to establish investment priorities and establish a longer-term timeframe for planning, it is even more important to secure stable and full funding of core projects. Stable funding promotes trust from which budget reform can proceed and planning and project cycles strengthened.

Full funding of a set of high priority core projects could provide a budget floor. Core projects, those which support only the most essential tasks of the ministry, should have detailed work plans which reflect the level and schedule of O&M expenditure required to facilitate management. For the core approach to work, the treasury needs to guarantee funding, and the ministries need to manage carefully and monitor their progress. The core classification was only recently introduced (FY 1990-1991), but the line ministries have not made a realistic list of priority projects, and the treasury has not guaranteed funding.

More effort is needed in examining the recurrent O&M cost requirements of the existing portfolio of projects. This would have four major benefits. First, it would force a link between the recurrent and development budgets. Second, it would involve an explicit analysis of the tradeoffs between capacity-supporting and capacity-expanding investments. With the present underutilization of capacity, such analysis could demonstrate the high returns to funding recurrent cost support for existing capacity or rehabilitation projects and the relatively low returns of capacity expanding projects. Such analysis could help discredit the commonly held assumption that recurrent expenditures are "consumption" and should be cut, whereas capital expenditures are "investments" and should be increased. The third benefit of financial planning based on O&M recurrent costs is that it would greatly reduce the number of capacity expanding projects because the availability of recurrent cost resources would determine the absorption of new projects. Capacity supporting projects, particularly those that are grant financed, would not be limited. Finally, the most important benefit of such planning would be the promotion of an effective balance between personnel and capital expenditures.

Improved Expenditure Management

Donors will not provide O&M support without a careful accounting of funds, but O&M support is fungible and thus difficult to manage. While Kenya has taken steps to strengthen budgeting, little attention has been given to improving expenditure management. More effective financial management information systems are one way to improve the monitoring and reporting of line ministry expenditures (Lacey 1989, pp. 31-32; Peterson 1990). It should be noted that both the MOA and the MOLD have embarked on an ambitious program to upgrade their expenditure control systems involving procedural reforms and automation (Peterson 1991b).

Donor Reforms

Donor Funding of Recurrent Costs

Should donors fund O&M recurrent costs? There are three arguments against donor financing of recurrent costs. First, donor financing compounds the original problem of overstaffing by providing the funds for operating expenses thereby enabling government to use its own O&M funds to hire more staff. The quid pro quo of recurrent cost financing by donors has to be government restraint in recruitment.[14] Such restraint is extremely difficult in the face of strong social and political pressures to provide employment in government.

Second, it is imprudent to use short-term capital for long-term obligations. Such criticism generally overlooks several issues. The reality of development in an aid-dependent country is the longevity of foreign assistance. A critical sector such as agriculture and livestock will continue to attract foreign assistance. The donor project portfolio may vary but is unlikely to decline significantly and will certainly not end. At the project level, projects are frequently extended over many years: thus, direct financial support for a particular activity often *is* long-term. It may also be argued that it is the *capital* investment and not the O&M recurrent cost support which is the long-term obligation financed with short-term funds. Further, capital investment in the sector is itself often relatively short run. Vehicles, for example, are considered to have a depreciable life of only five years; yet, they are one of the major "capital" goods in a field service such as agriculture and livestock.[15] Clearly, support for vehicles would be short run in terms of the life of the asset yet would contribute considerably to the productivity of the ministries' core task—support of extension staff.[16] Moreover, capacity-supporting projects consistently demonstrate a higher return than capacity expanding projects.[17]

In practice, donors are already funding recurrent costs through a very expensive strategy of capital *replacement* rather than capital *maintenance*. Short project cycles (two to three years) followed by new phases or "rehabilitation" projects phases are replacing the capital that was not maintained.

The third argument against donor funding of recurrent costs is that the practice tends to fragment the budget. Fragmenting the budget is a far lesser evil than the current practice of wasting scarce capital due to lack of marginal recurrent investments. Indeed, one of the primary sources of financial stability for the government is project financing, though the treasury's recent arbitrary cuts of MOA's fully grant-funded projects indicates that even this sanctuary is not safe from reductions. It is true that by recommending increased donor involvement in recurrent cost financing one is promoting project-based financing of ministry budgets (assuming donors do not provide ministries program funding). But this practice will be beneficial if it leads to fully funded and promptly implemented projects.

Promote Capacity Support not Expansion

Donors need to implement capacity supporting not expanding projects. The ideal configuration of a capacity supporting project is one of relatively long duration (four to five years) with a modest but bimodal investment of capital (investment in the beginning and at the end). The schedule of investment would be as follows. In the first year, capital would be rehabilitated or replaced. Over the next three years (assuming a five-year life), the project would support the capital to bring it to full utilization.[18] In the fourth year, the donor and government would equally support the project, with the donor simply matching government contributions. In the fifth year, government would provide the entire support for the project. The level of support demonstrated in the fourth and fifth year would determine the final tranche of capacity investment by the donor as well as a schedule of government (and perhaps donor) recurrent cost support. Implicit in this approach is the establishment of the investment "carrying capacity" of a ministry. The above recommendation relates primarily to projects with smaller capital (rehabilitation) investments stretched over longer periods of time, yet the model is applicable to most of the government's ministries.

The longer timeframe of capacity supporting projects would have several advantages. First, the donor would carry the recurrent costs for longer. Second, government would have more time to analyze the specific recurrent cost requirements of a project and prepare for their absorption into government's recurrent budget. Third, the donor would have a longer timeframe to build government's institutional capacity to manage the project and thus the recurrent costs. Fourth, more time would be available for potential benefits to be reaped which, in turn, would generate additional growth and revenue for government to support the project's recurrent cost. A fifth advantage of this type of project is that recurrent costs at the end of the project would be reduced because the capital stock would be replaced by donors at a level which government (and donors) could support.

The "new style" of project recommended earlier is in accordance with one of the tenets of the Kenya government's Budget Rationalization Programme (introduced in 1985)—that projects should "provide additional funds for operating expenses of completed development projects and for existing physical infrastructure and facilities" (Ministry of Finance and Economic Planning, Task Force on Budget Rationalization 1985; for a further description, see Ministry of Finance, Budgetary Supply Department 1989a). It violates, however, another tenet of budget rationalization—that fewer projects should be completed sooner (Ministry of Finance, Task Force on Budget Rationalization 1985). The ideal project outlined previously would be of *longer* duration and, if grant financed and capacity supporting, then there should be as many as the budget ceiling can absorb. Capacity-supporting projects should have as long a time horizon as possible, as distinct from capacity-expanding projects where the investment should be implemented as quickly as possible. A major weakness of the Budget Rationalization Programme has been its emphasis on capacity-*expanding* rather than *-supporting* projects.

There are some projects in Kenya that approach this ideal model. The Kisii Integrated Development Project (KIDP) fits many characteristics of the project design outlined above. The KIDP is grant financed, as a two tranche four-year project and provides recurrent cost support to both the MOA and the MOLD (Kisii Integrated Development Programme 1989). It "fits in" with existing operations and alleviates the critical resource bottlenecks (principally O&M recurrent costs) which confront field staff. It also requires staff from the two ministries to prepare jointly an annual work plan which is discussed and, if approved, funded. The direct link between the work plan and resources makes district level planning more effective. The project has also promoted collaboration between the two ministries in sharing scarce resources such as vehicles. Ironically, a recent evaluation of the KIDP was critical of KIDP's overemphasis on recurrent cost support, particularly the provision of critical transport operating expenses.

Capacity Support Should Be Fully Donor Funded

To arrest the rapidly deteriorating situation in the agriculture and livestock sector, capacity-supporting projects in the short-term should be fully funded by donors to overcome the delays and liquidity problems caused by the failure of government to contribute its share. If possible, such projects should be grant rather than loan funded to ease absorption in the budget.

Coordinate With Other Donors

Capacity support requires funding that is fungible and available to support a variety of ministry activities. Once the ministries establish their priority projects, donors will have to accept funding of other donor and government initiatives. Funding tied to rigid and uncoordinated donor agendas undermines ministry planning and the principle of capacity building.

Strengthen Financial and Personnel Management

Donors are concerned about funding recurrent costs because they are fungible and difficult to monitor. Improved expenditure monitoring by government is an essential quid pro quo for donor funding of recurrent costs (on the constraints and solutions to project financial monitoring in the Ministry of Agriculture, see Peterson 1991a). Ironically, despite the many projects and large sums spent in the MOA and the MOLD, few of these resources have been used to improve financial and personnel management. Viewed as costly overhead, the administrative divisions of finance, accounts, supplies, and personnel are often denied the resources and training opportunities that the technical divisions receive. This neglect results in administrative departments starved of resources and staffed by personnel whose morale is very low.

What needs to be done? The first step is for the donors to understand their *own* weaknesses in this area. The World Bank recognizes the complexities of the "institutional dimensions of public expenditure management" and admits that even most bank staff do not have enough "expertise in the practicalities of public expenditure management" to advise governments (Lacey 1989, p. ix). Strengthening public expenditure management takes time. Reforming financial control procedures cannot be done overnight, and government is prudent to be cautious in reforming such *systems*. It is inappropriate to tie such reforms to quick disbursing structural adjustment loans or even traditional sector loans.[19] Like the capacity-supporting projects described previously, such technical assistance should be long-term. Lacey of the World Bank has made a fruitful suggestion for promoting financial institutional development.

> Finance a time-slice of the country's public investment programme (on a sector by sector, but preferably on an aggregate basis) to support not only a more appropriate size and composition of the program itself, but also institutional and procedural reforms in the the process by which public expenditures are prepared and implemented (Lacey 1989, p. xii).

The outlines of the necessary technical assistance needed to strengthen financial management in the line ministries deserves another chapter. Briefly, the World Bank has cataloged many of the ills: "scarcity of technical and financial competence, poor management, inadequate training programs, . . . and a lack of entrepreneurial spirit" (Baum and Tolbert 1985, p. 55). Several steps are indicated, including promoting professionalism among the finance and accounts staff through training and funding professional training and certification *for accountants*. Middle and senior finance staff need training in financial analysis, especially project appraisal.[20]

CONCLUSION

This chapter argues that O&M shortfalls in Kenya's agricultural sector should be corrected. Increasing the *level* of resources will require continued government restraint in recruitment. Improving the *composition* of funding will require the donors to fund a greater share of the O&M costs. If donors choose to invest *prudently* in the sector, they must for the short- to medium-term fund the bulk of O&M costs. Improving the *stability* of funding will depend on reforms in the Ministry of Finance. The more difficult task, however, will be to improve the management of *all* resources including O&M.

APPENDIX

Methodological Issues in Analyzing Recurrent Costs

This chapter uses budget coefficients to examine the trend in recurrent cost support.[21] A budget coefficient is a relationship between expenditure items which is used to determine if the composition of expenditure is appropriate. For example, budgeting coefficients would specify for transport the marginal maintenance costs of additional investment.

There are four approaches to constructing budgeting coefficients in terms of the base used (the expenditure item upon which all other ratios are based): (1) staffing levels, (2) personnel emoluments, (3) capital stock, and (4) combining either emoluments and staffing with capital stock. For Kenya, developing a time series using staffing levels as a base is not appropriate because the data is inaccurate. Even figures for current staffing levels are inaccurate. Personnel emoluments is far more accurate for accurate audited accounts can be used for the entire time series. Using personnel emoluments as a base, capital and recurrent expenditures are viewed as a proportion of each unit of expenditure (in this case the Kenya pound). A third approach to analyzing financial balance uses capital stock as the base and other O&M expenditures as a proportion of each financial unit of stock. A fourth approach combines the second and third approaches by using personnel emoluments to determine the appropriate level of capital stock which in turn is used as a base to determine the appropriate level of O&M support.

The principal dilemma in constructing budgeting coefficients norms is whether to use personnel emoluments or capital stock as the base for determining O&M support. Capital stock is often preferred because it is seen to serve as a resource "constraint" on absorption of additional staff. Some believe that budget coefficients based on personnel levels do not constrain additional staffing. This argument is weak, however, since coefficients using a staffing base indicate the marginal costs of additional staff and, if judiciously applied, should act as a fiscal brake on recruitment.

Personnel emolument data was used rather than staffing levels to measure the personnel base of the coefficients because the staffing levels indicated in past budget estimates reflect the authorized establishment rather than the actual in-post complement. Emolument expenditure data is far more accurate than staff levels. One difficulty with using personnel emolument data is that it includes administrative personnel who do not require as much recurrent support as do field staff (e.g., transport).

Having selected personnel emoluments as the base of the coefficient, the magnitude of the coefficients has to be determined. This is, of course, the most difficult task, for it involves specifying what is the correct relationship between expenditures. The study adopted an "acceptable allocation" approach by which senior staff in the ministry were asked to comment on when they felt (if ever) their divisions had received adequate allocations within the past 15 years. The longevity of division heads in the two ministries allowed this approach, for virtually all had been the head of division or very senior in the division for the period in question. Senior staff unanimously agreed that FY 1980-1981 was the last year the allocations were acceptable. A norm for O&M support, indeed any budget norm, is necessarily subjective because it raises the fundamental allocation question, "how much is enough?" A budgeting norm, however, cannot be a wish list but rather an authoritative assessment of what is a *reasonable* level of support for a service. From the judgement of the senior technical staff, budget coefficients based on FY 1980-1981 are assumed to provide an adequate level and balance of support.

Two methodological issues remain: the assumption of a constant "mix" in the ministries' capital-labor ratios and the indexes used to make the time series constant. This study assumes that there is a constant ratio of labor to capital and a constant composition of labor throughout the time series. That is, if transport costs increase faster than personnel costs (as the transport deflator in Table 6 indicates), it is not assumed that a ministry would substitute labor for transport. These assumptions are supported by the rigid bureaucratic roles that prevail in the Kenyan bureaucracy.

A far more thorny issue is the indexes used to create a constant time series. Tables 6 and 7 detail the deflators and the adjustment factors which were applied to the nominal data to construct a constant time series. The personnel deflator used was the per annum increase in government salaries from 1975 to 1991 which was 4.4 percent. The transport and goods and services deflators were derived from the Nairobi Consumer Price Indexes of the Central Bureau of Statistics. "Adjustment factors" were derived from these deflators and were calculated by dividing the personnel deflator by the respective transport or goods and services deflator and then taking the inverse of this quotient. The adjustment factors were corrected to a base of 1 for the 1980-1981 norm year. From Table 6, it is clear that the cost of transport and goods and services increased substantially more than personnel costs over this period. Given this disparity and the imprecision of indexes, there is some inaccuracy in our statistics of recurrent cost support. However, given the magnitude of the imbalance as illustrated in Tables 1-2 and 4-5, the study's major conclusion about the erosion of the balance of support is upheld.

To analyze the trend of expenditure, expenditure data from the appropriation accounts was entered into computer spreadsheets for the following financial years: 1980-1981, 1983-1984, and 1988-1989. Expenditure data for 1988-1989 data from the draft unaudited appropriation accounts was also entered. Data was entered item-wise by budget head, and the heads were then aggregated into the major respective services of the two ministry's services (e.g., extension or disease and pest control). Subventions to parastatals were excluded since they do not support the staff reflected in the personnel emoluments. Recurrent expenditure items were extracted from both the recurrent budget and the development budget and then combined into a consolidated recurrent section. From this nominal time series, a constant series was created by using three deflators for personnel, transport, and goods and services (see Tables 6 and 7).

The time series treated the Ministry of Livestock Development as a separate ministry throughout by separating expenditure items which related to the ministry's current activities. The time series established a consistent pattern of activities for the two ministries based on their current activities. For example, the research function of the two ministries which was transferred to the Ministry of Science and Technology was excluded from the analysis.

A final methodological note. Entry of nine years of expenditure data by item is a large and complex task which is prone to error. Some small errors in the expenditure data remain. Cross-checking has determined that the magnitude of these errors is well under 1 percent of the total expenditure *by item* in any particular year. The data errors therefore do not significantly affect the results.

ACKNOWLEDGMENTS

The author would like to thank Naomi Caiden, Clive Gray, Michael Roemer, and Jennefer Sebstad for their comments on an earlier draft of this paper. A previous version was presented at the National Workshop on "Capacity Building in Policy Analysis and Economic Management," Lake Naivasha, Kenya, September 16-19, 1991.

NOTES

1. Even the Ministry of Finance recognizes the weakness of the forward budget exercise as being overly concerned with ceilings and fine tuning of allocations (see Ministry of Finance, Budgetary Supply Department 1989). A critique of the forward budget is found in Lacey (1989, pp. 55-58).

2. Analysis of the 1988-1989 Exchequer Releases for the MOA indicate that development vote releases were very late. After six months, only 31.6 percent of the first tranche was released. Similarly, in 1988-1989 MOLD received only 48.9 percent of the first tranche within six months.

3. Donor *revenue* payments are constrained by government liquidity, for in this mode of support the government spends funds and then claims reimbursement. In contrast, with direct payments donors provide the funds directly without reimbursement.

4. During FY 1989-1990, the MOLD lacked acaracides for over four months which seriously impaired its ability to charge for dipping services. Acaracide shortages lasting several months has occurred for the past three years.

5. Though modest, the World Bank's incremental funding of recurrent costs under ASAO II was 14.4 percent and 16.3 percent of the 1990-1991 net recurrent budget for the MOA and the MOLD, respectively.

6. In Kenya's budget, there are two forms of payment—appropriations in aid (direct payment by donors) and revenue which is either provided by donors (government spends then claims reimbursement) or government.

7. Virtually all donor projects require a government contribution in kind (e.g., staff, office facilities, utilities); in addition, they often require a modest but direct project contribution (often about 15% of a line item though contributions range up to 35% and 50%).

8. The Ministry of Agriculture has developed five major project criteria under the Agricultural Sector Adjustment Operation II. The five criteria are economic viability assessment, financial structure analysis, social impact analysis, institutional requirements assessment, and environmental impact assessment (see Ministry of Agriculture, Finance Division and the Development Planning Division 1990). These criteria have been adopted by the treasury for the nationwide Public Investment Programme (see Office of the Vice President and Ministry of Finance, Budgetary Supply Department 1991, p. 11).

9. This observation is from Ted Alexander, senior adviser to the Kisii Integrated Development Project (KIDP), who has over 23 years of field experience in livestock production in both Kenya and Uganda.

10. On the methodological difficulties of capital stock analysis based on budget expenditure data, see Peterson and Kiragu (1990, pp. 62-68). For a treatment of capital stock analysis using national accounts data, see Barber, Milne, and Wilson (1991).

11. See Peterson and Kiragu (1990) for a preliminary discussion of the factors needed to reform user fees. A more detailed discussion is in Gitu and Wambugu (1989) and Gitu (1985).

12. Undercollection of field level user fees reduces the recurrent allocation available to the headquarters. Districts are funded directly by the district treasuries which are under the Office of the President. In contrast, headquarter payments are discretionary and are based on the exchequer release from the treasury. Thus, there is no disincentive to the field for undercollection of user fees.

13. The Budget Rationalization Programme is explained in Ministry of Finance, Budgetary Supply Department (1989a). The new Public Investment Programme is described in Office of the Vice President and Ministry of Finance, Budgetary Supply Department (1991, 1992).

14. Gray and Martens (1983) contend that the two principal factors which preempt Sahelian government budgets and prevent adequate support for recurrent costs are recruitment and subsidization of state enterprises (p. 112).

15. Field staff from both ministries cite lack of transport as the major resource constraint they face in carrying out their work. See Peterson and Kiragu (1990).

16. The critical importance of investing in equipment rather than structures in promoting growth has been demonstrated by De Long and Summers (1990).

17. This argument is supported by Gray and Martens (1983), but they also caution that many development projects are poorly designed and should not be "bailed out" with recurrent cost support (p. 115).

18. Gray and Martens (1983) make the distinction about "establishment" and "operation" recurrent costs. Establishment recurrent costs are the *working capital* to place an investment in operation. Only after this investment is it possible to determine what the long operational costs are (p. 104). In terms of our proposed project scheduling, the donor would provide "investment" capital and hopefully one year of the operational recurrent costs. The problem in budgeting operational recurrent costs is that many projects never complete the "investment" recurrent cost phase.

19. The MOA and the MOLD are implementing expenditure reforms under a quick disbursing structural adjustment operation—ASAO II. The expenditure reforms were started, however, before the ASAO II program under the Technical Assistance II Project. It has taken at least two and a half years to get these expenditure reforms moving. See Harvard Institute for International Development (various years).

20. For a discussion of training programs for strengthening financial management in the MOA and the MOLD see Peterson (1990). Under the World Bank-funded Second Agricultural Adjustment Operation (ASAO II) the Ministries of Agriculture and Livestock Development are benefitting from a project which aims to strengthen their financial management capacity. See Harvard Institute for International Development (1992).

21. This paper uses "percentage" norms to determine the adequacy of recurrent cost support. For a detailed discussion of this approach as well as an "absolute" and "unit cost" norms, see Stevens and Bird (1991). See also Hinchliffe (1986).

REFERENCES

Barber, G., W. Milne, and L.S. Wilson. 1991. "Capital Stock Estimates for Kenya by Industry and Asset." Paper prepared for the Technical Sub-Committee, Long Range Planning Unit, Ministry of Planning and National Development, January 30.

Baum, W.C., and S.M. Tolbert. 1985. *Investing in Development: Lessons of World Bank Experience*. New York: Oxford University Press.

De Long, J.B., and L.H. Summers. 1990. "Equipment Investment and Economic Growth." National Bureau of Economic Research, November.

Gitu, K.W. 1985. "Financing Public Expenditures in Agriculture." Development Planning Division, Ministry of Livestock Development, April.

Gitu, K.W., and P.N. Wambugu. 1989. "Cost Sharing with Beneficiaries: The Case of the Agricultural and Livestock Services." Paper prepared for the Technical Sub-Committee, Long Range Planning Unit, Ministry of Planning and National Development, May.

Gray, C., and A. Martens. 1983. "The Political Economy of the 'Recurrent Cost Problem' in the West African Sahel." *World Development* 11(2): 109-112.

Harvard Institute for International Development. 1992. "Technical Proposal: ASAO II Budget Management Project."

Harvard Institute for International Development. Various years. "Semi-Annual Reports for the Technical Assistance Pool II (TAP II)." Reports ν29, ν30, ν31, ν32 (July 1990-July 1992).

Heller, P. 1974. "Public Investment in LDC's with Recurrent Cost Constraint: The Kenyan Case." *Quarterly Journal of Economics* 88 (May): 251-277.

_______ . 1979. "The Underfinancing of Recurrent Development Costs." *Finance and Development* (March): 176.

Hinchliffe, K. 1986. "Development of Recurrent Expenditure Norms for the Ghanaian Education Sector." School of Development Studies, University of East Anglia, October.

Kenya Veterinary Association. 1986. "Animal Health Project Report."

Kisii Integrated Development Programme. 1989. "Annual Report: 1988-89."

Lacey, R.M. 1989. "Managing Public Expenditure: An Evolving World Bank Perspective." Policy, Planning and Research Working Paper No. 56, World Bank.

Lim, D. 1983. "Instability of Government Revenue and Expenditure in Less Developed Countries." *World Development* 11(5): 447-450.

Ministry of Agriculture, Finance Division and the Development Planning Division. 1990. "Agricultural Sector Adjustment Operation II: Present Project Preparation Guidelines and Suggested Future Selection Criteria for Agricultural Projects and Programmes." September.

Ministry of Finance, Budgetary Supply Department. 1989. "Ways and Means of Improving the Quality and Effectiveness of Public Expenditure Programming in Kenya."

Ministry of Finance, Budgetary Supply Department. 1989a. "Management of Financial Resources in Sector Ministries: Budget Rationalization Programme."

Ministry of Finance, Task Force on Budget Rationalization. 1985. "Review of Externally Aided Projects." July.

Ministry of Finance and Economic Planning, Task Force on Budget Rationalization. 1985. "Budget Rationalization Programme and Guidelines for Programme Review and Forward Budget." July.

Office of the Vice President and Ministry of Finance, Budgetary Supply Department. 1990. "Austerity Measures and Expenditure Adjustments," Treasury Circular No. 14, November 16.

Office of the Vice President and Ministry of Finance, Budgetary Supply Department. 1991. "Public Investment Programme." June.

Office of the Vice President and Ministry of Finance, Budgetary Supply Department. 1992. "Public Investment Programme." April.

Peterson, S.B. 1986. "Neglecting the Poor: State Policy Toward the Smallholder in Kenya." Pp. 59-83 in *Africa's Agrarian Crisis: The Roots of Famine*, edited by S.K. Commins, M.F. Lofchie, and R. Paine. Boulder, CO: Lynne Rienner Publishers, Inc.

_______ . 1990. "Improving Financial Management in the Ministries of Agriculture and Livestock Development." Finance Divisions, Ministries of Agriculture and Livestock Development, November 7.

_______ . 1991a. "Project Financial Monitoring in the Ministry of Agriculture." Paper prepared for the Ministry of Planning and National Development's Workshop on Project Monitoring, Lake Naivasha, Kenya, February 20-22.

_______ . 1991b. "Strengthening Financial Management in the Ministries of Agriculture and Livestock Development: Technical Assistance for Public Finance Under the Second Agriculture Sector Adjustment Loan." Finance Divisions, Ministries of Agriculture and Livestock Development, January 14.

Peterson, S.B., and K. Kiragu. 1990. "Recurrent Cost Issues in the Ministry of Agriculture and the Ministry of Livestock Development." Report prepared for the Ministry of Agriculture and the Ministry of Livestock Development in preparation for the Second Agricultural Sector Adjustment Operation (ASAO II), May.

Stevens, M.L., and A. Bird. 1991. "Budgeting Operations and Maintenance Costs: The Application of Standard Cost Analysis." Paper prepared for the World Bank's Public Expenditure Management Seminar.

Stevens, M.L.O. 1985. "The Management of Recurrent Costs." Pp. 84-101 in *Recurrent Costs and Agricultural Development*, edited by J. Howell. Nottingham, UK: The Russell Press, Ltd.

World Bank. 1984. "World Bank Approaches to Economic Planning and Financial Management in Borrowing Countries: A Survey of Issues With Suggested Guidelines for Future Intervention." Projects Policy Department, Public Sector Management Group, November.

REFORMING PUBLIC BUDGETING IN ZIMBABWE

Jonathan N. Moyo

ABSTRACT

In many developing countries, budgets are nothing but fiscal year statements formulated by bureaucrats behind the scenes and announced in legislative assemblies at the behest of powerful executives unaccountable to their electorates. In Zimbabwe, the introduction of a market economy has been accompanied by growing expectations that there will be a liberalization of the budgetary process to allow for greater citizen participation in resource allocation decisions. This chapter critically assesses the budgetary process in Zimbabwe and makes some suggestions for its improvement.

It is now a truism that a critical area of public policy in the life of a modern nation-state is public budgeting. All public decisions, in one way or another, ultimately reflect budgetary decisions. Thus, public budgeting was one of the most basic traditional management functions captured in the now classical acronym, *POSDCORB* (planning, organizing, staffing, directing, coordinating, and budgeting). However, in the early periods of modern management,

Policy Studies and Developing Nations, Volume 3, pages 205-214.

ISBN: 1-55938-190-6

public budgeting did not play an important managerial role, and in most of these classical works, public budgeting was seen merely as an accounting procedure for assuring that public monies were spent in ways that had been approved by the policymakers. This basic accounting approach to public budgeting remains important today, but the political process of public budgeting has become much more important than its accounting counterpart. Through its political component, public budgeting has attained the status of being perhaps the single most important managerial function of the modern public manager.

A budget is now seen as a work or operating plan and a policy evaluation instrument which gives direction to the execution of public policies by expressing the values of the decision makers. Rather than being simply a technical accounting tool used to balance revenues and expenditures, public budgeting now involves answering fundamental political questions about who gets what, how, and when. Such questions are dealt with under conditions of competing interests, uncertainty, and usually conflicting values. As the work of Wildavsky shows (e.g., Wildavsky 1988), the contemporary budgetary process is replete with dynamic issues of interchange between politics and administration. These issues involve balancing competing private interests and balancing these against conflicting views of the public interest. Beyond this, the politics of budgeting have become a means for redistributing national wealth and income and for promoting national development. How this happens varies from country to country, depending on the culture, values, and economic structure of the particular country under examination.

BUDGETING IN DEVELOPING NATIONS

Notwithstanding the pervasive influence of public budgeting as a critical function in public policy, many developing nations continue to give their budgetary process scant public policy attention. In many developing countries, budgets are nothing but fiscal year statements formulated by bureaucrats behind the scenes and announced in legislative assemblies at the behest of powerful executives unaccountable to their electorates.

Not surprisingly, most literature on budgeting in developing countries tends to be "accounting" oriented with little if any critical examination of fundamental political questions (Beyer 1971; Dean 1989). This is understandable because of a variety of background issues behind the existence of developing countries as nation-states in the modern world. For example, developing nations are frequently caught in a cycle of authoritarian and even totalitarian rule dominated by the personality of incumbent leaders. This cycle has the effect of diminishing the possibility for openness and accountability in the political budgetary process.

An instructive approach to understanding budgeting in developing nations is still found in the classic work on planning and budgeting in poor countries by Caiden and Wildavsky (1974). Despite the importance of public budgeting, it is somewhat surprising that since the publication of this work there have not been other equivalent sustained studies of public budgeting in developing nations except for the "accounting" or "how-to" methods designed to transplant *techniques* from developed to developing countries. Absent from the literature are the needed studies of the underlying problems of public budgeting as a fundamental political process in developing nations.

That there are major differences between budgeting in developed and developing countries is now a generally accepted proposition. What is not always clear is (are) the reason(s) which account for the differences. A major explanatory factor is found in cultural theory. Yet, there are very few studies which have examined public budgeting from the standpoint of cultural theory.

Wildavsky (1986, p. 334) developed a model useful for formulating but not testing hypotheses built on the cultural theory that different political regimes cause different budget behaviors. Wildavsky's model points to the existence of four types of cultural regimes: fatalist, hierarchy, market, and sectarian. The model is based on the consideration that there is no one culture which is viable on its own. (Wildavsky 1986, p. 333). No culture is sufficient unto itself. The implications for public budgeting lie in the ways governments can manage their revenues and expenditures. Wildavsky lists the following possibilities:

1. Governments can manage neither their expenditures nor their revenues.
2. Governments can manage their expenditures but not their revenues.
3. Governments can manage their revenues but not their expenditures.
4. Governments can manage both their expenditures and their revenues.

Of course, the possibilities are not either nothing or everything propositions. But their significance lies in the fact that they map out the various extreme possibilities within which governments actually operate. Wildavsky (1986, p. 343) notes that the actual operations of governments within the four extreme possibilities are carried out with reference to five basic strategies. These are:

1. Do nothing.
2. Decrease spending.
3. Increase revenues.
4. Increase revenue and increase spending.
5. Decrease revenue and decrease spending.

The cultural hypothesis developed by Wildavsky is that the five strategies listed above define any government's ability or inability to manage income related to culture. In political terms, this means that the essential relationships between revenue and expenditure vary with the type of regime. The public budgetary process in the United States, for example, approaches that of a market regime, while Zimbabwe's is largely of the hierarchy type.

PUBLIC BUDGETING IN ZIMBABWE

In Zimbabwe, the financial year begins on July 1 and ends on June 30 the following year. The public budgeting process, however, starts well before July 1 for any financial year. The Ministry of Finance, Economic Planning and Development (henceforth referred to as "treasury") sends an estimates (budget development) circular to other government ministries in October of the preceding year. The purpose of the policy circular is both to obtain and provide the following information:

- The level of desired activity during the forthcoming fiscal year, that is, whether services should be expanded or contracted or maintained at their existing level.
- The global (total) allocation for the ministry.
- The required form and layout of the ministry estimates.
- Hints on compiling the preliminary estimates.
- The date by which the ministry is expected to submit its estimates (usually in mid-January).
- Ministries are also given the date on which they will be called to discuss their estimates with the treasury.
- The circular also includes information on how to avoid inconsistencies and how to clear estimates with the minister, how to schedule vacant posts, how to include annual bonuses paid during the year (November/ December), how to copy estimates to Public Service Commission establishment expansion, and how to formulate a general shopping list, among other considerations.

When the estimates circular has been sent to each government ministry, the next stage of the budgetary process is one of assessment. The assessment phase follows the stipulated deadline for receiving the responses which contain bids from sectoral ministries. This phase involves a systematic examination of budget requests. This usually occurs in the first week of February when government ministries meet with treasury officials to discuss their bids.

During these meetings, each government ministry is asked to explain and justify its budgetary bid. This allows the treasury to examine whether public revenues would be effectively and efficiently utilized and to assure, as far as possible, uniformity in the allocation of funds in accordance with the existent five-year development plan. During this process, treasury officials operate within parameters set by the cabinet under very specific instructions from the president (his influence on public budgeting is not publicly known). For their part, representatives of government ministries, who usually are not privy to the parameters set by the president and his cabinet, use the meetings to get as much as they can from the treasury to finance their projects.

These discussions continue daily until about April/May. During the meetings, bids of each government ministry are also examined by invited delegates, usually foreign experts seconded from multilateral agencies such as the World Bank and the United Nations Development Program (UNDP), who go through the bids thoroughly to check whether they meet their stated objectives, whether they are in line with government policy, and also to assess their overall economic and political implications within the context of the global economy.

After the bids of all government ministries are assessed and making the necessary amendments, treasury officials then consolidate the bids and the recommended allocations into a comprehensive government policy statement which is presented to the Minister of Finance, Economic Planning and Development for his assessment, after which he takes the policy document to the president for final approval. Subsequently, it is forwarded to Parliament as a policy statement in a "blue book" (the estimate of expenditure) and in a "white paper" (the estimate of revenues). This is done by the Minister of Finance, Economic Planning and Development in July.

Parliament then is supposed to debate, vote by vote for each ministry, the estimated allocations proposed by the treasury. Thereafter, Parliament passes the Finance and Expenditure Bills. The Minister of Finance, Economic Planning and Development then presents the Appropriations Bill (for expenditures) which becomes the Appropriations Act providing moneys for services to the public as presented in the *Government Gazette*. This publication allows ministries to proceed with the implementation of their projects as approved by Parliament. The other bill is enacted by Parliament as part of the budget process is the Finance Act which levies taxes, duties, charges, and fees on the nation.

The foregoing budget process is summarized diagrammatically in Figure 1.

REFORMING ZIMBABWE'S BUDGETARY PROCESS

Public budgeting is not only an accounting procedure for ranking governmental priorities, activities, and programs but is also an arena for political and cultural compromises, with outcomes reflecting the relative strengths of competing groups and the nature of the compromises reached among the competing values of a democratic society. A budget is an important link between material resources, policy behavior, and human values.

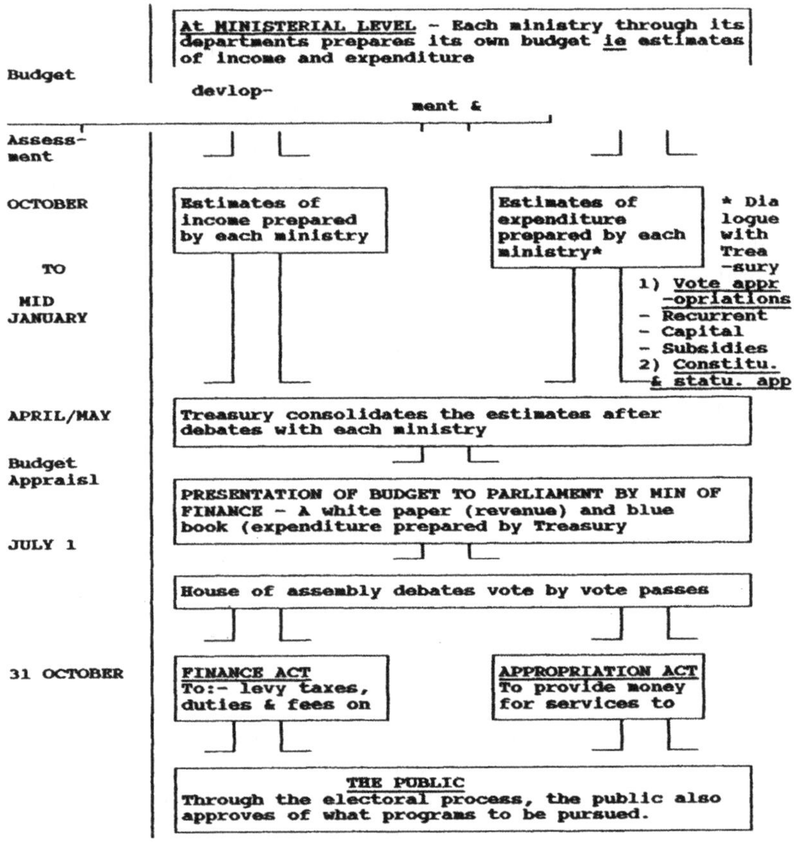

Note: Budget Execution: Implementation of public policies

Figure 1. Flow Chart of the Zimbabwe Public Budget Process

Viewed this way, the socio-political pattern is one in which different groups in society rise and fall relative to their influence in the political arena. The pattern is a function of the extent to which a given group commands national policy issues and of the extent to which the groups set the national policy agenda through the budgetary process.

Thus, public budgeting can be viewed from a highly quantitative, financial management point of view wherein fiscal policy issues like taxation, analysis of revenues and expenditures, redistributive justice, and others are examined with great detail. Or public budgeting can be seen in terms of its political and management processes, wherein the focus is on *process*. Focusing on process raises questions about how things get done and why. In this case, more attention is given to value premises as well as cultural considerations and less to specific cash flow analysis (as tends to be the case in Zimbabwe's budgetary process).

Focusing on process facilitates the examination of the management actors, as custodians of the public realm, in terms of what they do, how they do it, and why they do it in relation to their responsibilities to society at large.

In Zimbabwe, however, public budgeting shows little attention to such standards as it is still very much steeped in politics, in the guise of accounting through and by the Ministry of Finance, Economic Planning and Development. Thus, there is a need for reform in the Zimbabwean budgetary process, to create a process which will be sensitive to Zimbabwean cultural values, and which will also be practical and sensitive to the demands of effective and efficient public policy within the dynamics of changing and competing interests. Such an adjustment would need to deal with the problems in Zimbabwean political culture.

One rather obvious problem in the Zimbabwean budget process is that its political content tends to be decidedly unidimensional, driven by a top-down approach with politicians basically telling everyone what they think is good for the country. In the corresponding budgetary milieu, bureaucrats in government ministries, particularly in the Ministry of Finance, Economic Planning and Development, tend to adopt an "office boy" mentality wherein they view their budgeting role as merely an accounting process of facilitating and implementing cabinet wishes without raising or considering fundamental critical questions essential for the viability of a democratic society.

Of even greater concern is that Parliament, which is supposed to represent the people has, at least over the first decade of independence between 1980 and 1990, played a minimal if any *political* role in the *formulation* of the national budget. Its role has been akin to a toothless watch dog which barks after the robbery. Members of Parliament, including government ministers, wait until the ritualistic budget day when the veil of budget secrecy is removed by the Minister of Finance, Economic Planning and Development; then, they sit in stoic ignorance and amazement at the budget speech.

One is tempted to conclude that Zimbabwe's budgetary process still has a long way to go in incorporating democratic norms. The people, either directly through the supposedly decentralized planning structures from the cell to the province or indirectly through their elected representatives in Parliament, do not participate in deciding important allocative questions of who will get what, how, when, and why. This practice belies the concept of a national budget as probably the single most important policy statement of any government.

In Zimbabwe (which happens to have the second highest tax levels in the world after Israel), taxpayers have been treated as having the money but not the voice when it comes to public budgeting. They pay much more in the form of taxes but get much less in services for their money, and they have virtually no political say in the matter. The quality of public services in the hitherto heavily subsidized areas such as education and health leaves much to be desired. The quality of teachers and the absence of requisite implements in most public schools, particularly in high density townships and rural areas, is appalling. Instead, the bulk of the money allocated to education appears to pay salaries and administrative costs for bureaucrats who hardly justify their roles. The same is true with defense spending. Notwithstanding the Renamo menace in Mozambique and Zimbabwe's commitment to the security of Mozambique's Beira Corridor, the huge defense expenditure throughout most of the first decade of independence appears hard to justify beyond the simple provision of unproductive employment.

In 1990, the Zimbabwean government joined the long queue of developing countries attempting to embrace the World Bank-sponsored market-based programs for restructuring their now ailing, previously state-run economies. Whether these programs will succeed is an open question. In the meantime, there are growing expectations that, whatever its contradictions, the introduction of the market economy in Zimbabwe should be accompanied by a liberalization of the budgetary process in order to allow for greater citizen participation in resource allocation decisions.

For democracy to really fully obtain in the new Zimbabwe, it must be reflected in the budgetary process. Over the first decade of independence, the Zimbabwean status quo created the spurious impression that public budgeting is only an economic process dominated by bureaucratic accounting of the political wishes of the president working under the cloak of his cabinet. But the 1989-1990 budget, for example, showed that budgetary considerations can be different in an environment of real politics, one with opposition. The taxation concessions announced by the Minister of Finance, Economic Planning and Development on July 27, 1989, were directly related to the then growing political opposition to the ruling Zimbabwe African National Union-Patriotic Front (ZANU-PF) rule spearheaded by the Zimbabwe Unity Movement (ZUM), then enjoying growing popularity. That opposition, which later dwindled following internal squables within ZUM, forced ruling politicians to be sensitive to the taxpayer, even though the concessions may not have been sufficient.

However, and this is the point emphasized here, the budgetary process need not be driven into democracy by external opposition. The process should be inherently democratic by design. Four immediate policy considerations need to be given serious attention. First, the process should be open rather than shrouded in secrecy. Before independence, colonial regimes hid the budgetary process from the masses for obvious reasons; now, there is no good reason why there should be fear of popular participation in the budgetary process of an independent Zimbabwe. The notion that public discussion of the budget might encourage practices such as the hoarding of goods (which might cause prices to skyrocket in anticipation of budget price hikes) is tantamount to vulgarizing public budgeting. The national budget should be subjected to public debate *prior* to adoption.

Second, Parliament should be actively and substantively involved in the formulation of the budget. The house of laws should not be reduced to rubber stamping the agenda of the executive branch. Matters such as price increases, tax increases, or tax initiatives of any kind should be subjected to informed parliamentary debate and vote so as to give the electorate a basis for wisely choosing its representatives. Important matters should not be adopted by executive decrees. The cabinet should not be allowed to make laws; it should implement laws enacted by Parliament.

Third, there is a need to establish a Public Budgeting Commission in Zimbabwe. There are two functions in public administration, budgeting and personnel, which are so pervasive in every aspect of democratic government as to require independent existence from a particular government ministry. It is for this reason that, in theory, the Public Service Commission is an autonomous body provided for in the constitution. Similarly, there is a need for an autonomous Public Budgeting Commission, especially now that Zimbabwe is going through a pro-market economic structural adjustment program. Subsuming public budgeting under the Ministry of Finance, Economic Planning and Development is as untenable as subsuming the civil service under the Ministry of the Public Service.

Fourth, and related to the third consideration above, Zimbabwe's Executive Presidency must assume full and unambiguous responsibility for the national budget through the proposed Public Budgeting Commission. Under the 1987 Constitutional Amendment Act, No. 7, which made the president the head of both the state and government through the Executive Presidency, it is ironic that the responsibility for such an important function as public budgeting still falls on the shoulders of one government minister. That in 1987 the concerned minister was given a "senior" designation, presumably ranking him above other ministers, is simply beside the point. He is still one minister. Given that public budgeting is the single most important annual policy statement of the government, it is imperative that the president take full and direct responsibility and present the budget to the people through Parliament for discussion and debate before it is finally voted on.

The failure to make the president directly and personally responsible for the budget means that his office will continue to be seen in public as purely ceremonial. Presently, the president takes responsibility for giving speeches at such ceremonies as New Year's Eve, Independence Day, Africa Day, and Heroes' Day. While the symbolic importance of these days to the national heritage cannot be overemphasized, they are only symbolic.

The policies which dominate the daily lives of individuals are announced and made concrete on budget day. The tragedy is that they are made public by a government minister rather than the president. The responsibility of the president in the national budget should not be oblique via delegation. He should take direct and full responsibility for the budget, of course with some advice from his Minister of Finance, Economic Planning and Development. The proposed Public Budgeting Commission should assist the president in formulating and implementing the budget. Members of Parliament should debate a president's budget speech and not the general address he traditionally gives during the opening of Parliament and the State of the Nation address he gives at the end of the calendar year.

Indeed, since the presidential election in Zimbabwe is now separate from General Elections, the national budget is the one concrete platform from which any sitting president or any presidential hopeful can run for election or re-election. In this regard, the success or failure of a president should be measured by (1) the kind of budget he presents to Parliament and (2) his ability to convince the nation through Parliament that his budget is morally, politically, and economically sound, and thus worthy of national support and sacrifice. For such a scenario to occur, Parliament should be necessarily and sufficiently insulated from the institution of the Executive Presidency, an institution with separate powers. Unfortunately, part of the challenge facing Zimbabwe or any nation is that such a scenario is not possible in a personalistic political system which thrives on patronage politics in circumstances lacking checks and balances.

REFERENCES

Beyer, J.C. 1973. *Budget Innovations in Developing Countries: The Experience of Nepal.* New York: Praeger.

Caiden, N., and A. Wildavsky. 1973. *Planning and Budgeting in Poor Countries.* New York: Wiley.

Dean, P.N. 1989. *Government Budgeting in Developing Nations.* London and New York: Routledge.

Sarfraz, N. 1961. *Problems of Budgetary Reform in Pakistan.* Karachi, Pakistan: Institute of Development Economics.

Wildavsky, A. 1975. *Budgeting: A Comparative Theory of the Budgetary Process.* Boston: Little, Brown and Company.

———. 1988. *The New Politics of the Budgetary Process.* Boston and London: Scott, Foresman and Company.

PART V.

PRIVATIZATION

PRIVATIZATION OF PUBLIC ENTERPRISE IN ASIA:

CURRENT PATTERNS AND EMERGING ISSUES

James Leigland

ABSTRACT

Public or state-owned enterprise is pervasive in the developing countries of Asia, but since the mid-1980s, many of these governments have begun to reconsider the appropriate role of government in enterprise activities. This paper focuses on efforts to privatize public enterprise, which are now underway formally or informally in nearly every Asian country. The goal of this paper is to present case studies of current privatization efforts and derive from them patterns—what these efforts do and do not have in common—as well as identify emerging issues of concern to public officials. In general, it appears that privatization contributes most to economic development when it is a part of a broader sequence of steps toward economic liberalization and is used to nurture competition and sustain growth, rather than when it is used out of desperation to reduce deficits or debt burdens.

Policy Studies and Developing Nations, Volume 3, pages 217-246.

ISBN: 1-55938-190-6

INTRODUCTION

Public enterprises often play dominating roles in the economies of developing nations, but there is widespread agreement that the performance of these entities generally has been disappointing. In the developing world, public enterprise statistics typically show low or declining profitability and low or negative return on investments. These enterprises tend to achieve the noncommercial, "social" goals set for many of them only at great cost or with perverse social consequences. They also tend to impose heavy financial burdens on parent governments, not only in terms of losses that must be supported with operating subsidies and injections of new equity but also in terms of negative impacts of enterprise borrowing on the credit standing of parent governments. Public enterprises have long been recognized as major contributors to heavy accumulations of foreign debt afflicting governments in much of the developing world (see Gillis 1980; Short 1984).

In the developing countries of Asia, public enterprise is pervasive. Despite impressive achievements in industrial development and economic growth, particularly in East Asia, most of these countries still allow large numbers of public enterprises to operate as "self-sustaining budgetary subsystems," beyond the effective control of central budget authorities (Caiden 1985, p. 33). But since the mid-1980s, the Asian approach to public enterprise has undergone change. For a variety of reasons, and in ways not always consistent with the orthodox prescriptions of the World Bank and the IMF, these governments have begun to reconsider the appropriate role of government in enterprise activities. This is the case in virtually every Asian country, from Kazakhstan in the West to Papua New Guinea in the East, Indonesia in the South and Mongolia in the North. In some countries, like Thailand and Malaysia, these kinds of questions have been subject to wide and intense public debate. In others, like China and Vietnam—and some of the other Asian command economies possibly on the verge of extensive economic liberalization—such questions are under consideration by government officials, but public debate is much more restricted. Such questions are also being asked in countries like South Korea, Taiwan, and Singapore, which have already achieved a considerable degree of economic development despite years of defying orthodox prescriptions regarding the state's appropriate economic role.

A central issue being considered in Asia, as in other parts of the developing world, concerns how public enterprises can be more effectively managed or controlled by parent governments. But efforts to limit or control the independence of public enterprises face a dilemma: tight controls over these entities by outsiders are seemingly at odds with the independence and flexibility—and other perceived advantages of this widely used government form—thought to be required for "business-like" enterprise activities.

Privatization of public enterprise is often viewed as a solution to this problem, one that is favored by many international economists and development specialists. Advocates of privatization hold that the most efficient "controls" are those associated with the incentive structure of the marketplace, that even social goals can be more effectively pursued with the profits from successful, competitive enterprises that survive careful pruning by government officials and market forces. Indeed, over the last decade, the promotion of marketplace efficiency has been a dominant concern in public enterprise oversight reform efforts sponsored by the World Bank, the International Monetary Fund, and other international aid donors (see, e.g., World Bank 1983).

This paper focuses on efforts to privatize public enterprise in the developing countries of Asia. The objective here is to present case studies of current privatization efforts and derive from them patterns—what they do and do not have in common—as well as to identify some emerging issues of concern to public officials. The emphasis is on particular countries and particular enterprises rather than abstract theory, which has been carefully surveyed in many other publications.

In keeping with the broad gauge, empirical nature of this survey, "privatization" is used just as the countries involved use it—to cover a wide range of activities that attempt in some way to shift elements of industrial, commercial, public utility, or other public service delivery responsibilities from government to non-government entities. It therefore includes divestiture, management contracts, privatization of service delivery, and liquidation. Efforts to liberalize the competitive environment in which public enterprises operate are sometimes carried out as preparation for privatization, are used as alternatives to privatization, or are simply referred to as privatization. As such, they seem to constitute a legitimate focus of this study.

ASIAN ECONOMIC PRIORITIES

The goals of each privatization program in Asia as elsewhere are determined by the economic development priorities of the government administration involved. These countries vary tremendously in size, wealth, and other social and economic indicators (see Table 1). However, for the purposes of reviewing the effects of national economic priorities on privatization efforts, they can be roughly grouped into two general categories.

The first category includes the four newly industrializing countries (or NICs) that lead the region economically: South Korea, Taiwan, Hong Kong, and Singapore. Economic growth indicators are relatively high in these countries, and inflation and debt relatively low (see Table 2). These four are followed

Table 1. Basic Social and Economic Indicators For Selected Asian Countries

	Population (millions) 1990	*Area (thousands of square kilometers)*	*GNP Per Capita (US$) 1990*	*Life Expectancy at birth (years) 1990*	*Adult Illiteracy (percent) 1990*
Philippines	61.5	300	730	64	10
India	849.5	3,288	350	59	52
Pakistan	112.4	796	380	56	65
Indonesia	178.2	1,905	570	62	23
Malaysia	7.9	330	2,320	70	22
Thailand	55.8	513	1,420	66	7
China	133.7	9,561	370	70	27
Hong Kong	5.8	1	1,490	78	<5
Singapore	3.0	1	11,160	74	<5
S. Korea	42.8	99	5,400	71	<5

Source: World Bank (1992).

closely by Malaysia and Thailand with average annual percentage GDP growth rates of over 9 percent from 1989-1991. In all of these countries, economic development is an enduring high priority of central government officials, and all have developed export-oriented economies with reasonably flexible and accurate pricing systems. Together, these six countries account for half of all developing countries' exports of manufactured goods, according to the 1992 year-end economic outlook published by the Organization for Economic Cooperation and Development (OECD).

All six of the countries mentioned previously appear likely to continue making the principal contributions to what the World Bank expects to be East Asia's leadership in world economic growth at least into the late 1990s and possibly for much longer. But all six countries must struggle to keep productivity growing faster than real wages or the cost of land. For South Korea, Taiwan, Hong Kong, and Singapore, this is increasingly difficult as their products become more complex and short-lived. Their efforts to develop brand names and domestic technology face considerable challenge from Japan. Malaysia and Thailand require better educated work forces to meet the rising costs of production and to remain competitive with lower cost countries such as China, and perhaps eventually Vietnam, Bangladesh, and other countries. To encourage continued foreign and domestic investment, they also require stronger systems of commercial law, as well as fair and consistent enforcement of such law.

China and Indonesia complete this first category of Asian countries engaged in privatization efforts. These two trail the others economically, but both appear able to sustain average annual percentage GDP growth rates of

Table 2. Economic Development Indicators For Selected Asian Countries

International	*Avg. Ann. GDP Growth Rt. (percent) 1965-1990*	*Total Govt. Revenue/ Expenditure Balance % of GNP 1990*	*Average Annual Inflation (GDP deflator) 1980-1990*	*Total External Debt as % of GNP 1990*	*Gross Reserves* 1990*
Philippines	3.78	-3.5	14.9	69.3	1.5
India	4.28	-7.3	7.9	25.1	1.9
Pakistan	5.64	-7.2	6.7	52.1	1.2
Indonesia	6.40	-2.1	8.4	66.4	3.2
Malaysia	6.52	-2.8	1.6	48.1	3.5
Thailand	7.42	4.9	3.3	32.6	4.4
China	7.88	..	5.8	14.4	7.4
Hong Kong	8.00	..	7.2	..	..
Singapore	8.56	10.5	1.7	..	4.8
S. Korea	9.82	-0.7	5.1	14.4	2.2

Note: * In months of import coverage.

Source: World Bank (1992).

6 percent to 7 percent (and perhaps higher as has been the case recently in China). Like Thailand and Malaysia, Indonesia began to deregulate its economy after the commodity collapses of the mid-1980s. With continued political stability, deregulation of the economy, and large foreign investment, Indonesia's growth should continue, particularly if the government can control its foreign debt and make adequate investment in education and infrastructure. Like Malaysia and Thailand, Indonesia also needs to update and consistently enforce its system of commercial law. All of this can also be said of China, where recent economic reforms and growth have been dramatic. But Chinese officials have the added burden of pursuing economic reform while preserving an ideological commitment to central planning, state ownership of the means of production, and other tenets of state philosophy.

All of the leading economies of Asia (with the possible exception of Singapore) need to finance massive investment in all forms of public works infrastructure to maintain growth. Partly to make private sector participation in such infrastructure investment possible, all of these countries also need deeper and far more efficient capital allocation systems, including deeper and better regulated stock and bond markets.

The remaining Asian countries constitute a second category for the purposes of this study. These countries have not experienced the kind of economic growth, combined with relatively low inflation, exhibited by the countries above. Since the restoration of democratic institutions under the Aquino administration, the Philippines has struggled with budget deficits, a heavy burden of national debt, inflation, and many other problems that have severely limited national economic growth. In India, a long-term commitment to socialism, combined with cycles of political and social unrest, and many other problems have inhibited growth. Pakistan, Bangladesh, Sri Lanka, and Nepal have all recorded very modest economic growth or decline through the 1980s and early 1990s.

This category also includes a variety of countries that have transformed themselves from totalitarian state control to some form of democratic capitalism or may be on the verge of such a transformation—but for whom economic liberalization has not yet resulted in the kind of dynamic growth experienced by China in the early 1990s. This group includes Myanmar, Cambodia, Laos, Vietnam, North Korea, Mongolia, and the central Asian republics. International agencies such as the World Bank and the IMF suggest that most of these economies suffer from years of mismanagement. Many of these countries have experienced recent economic crises precipitated by disruption of traditional export markets, as well as foreign aid cutoffs, resulting from the political turmoil in Eastern Europe. Among other economic policy reforms, all of these countries have been urged to free pricing systems, remove barriers to international trade, create sound financial systems, and of course balance their national budgets.

CASE STUDIES IN ASIAN PRIVATIZATION

Virtually all of these Asian countries have privatization programs underway, and each program reflects the kinds of development priorities outlined earlier. Countries with stronger, growing economies tend to carry out highly deliberate privatization programs geared to strengthening competition within sectors or the competitive position of strategic firms. Access to capital needed for enterprise expansion is often a specific purpose of limited privatization in these countries with a secondary consideration being the strengthening of capital markets. In most cases, these privatization efforts are not designed to precipitate economic "takeoff" but rather to help sustain growth. There is also considerable evidence among these countries of privatization efforts that are designed to involve private business in infrastructure development and other activities that traditionally have been the responsibility of public enterprise. These kinds of privatization priorities seem to characterize programs in the first category of countries outlined previously: Taiwan, South Korea, Hong Kong, Singapore, Malaysia, and Thailand, and to a lesser extent in Indonesia and China.

Privatization programs in the Asian countries with much weaker economies tend to be geared toward relieving budget deficit problems by capturing sales income or at least ridding the state of unprofitable enterprises that must be supported continually with subsidies and injections of equity. Another typical concern is the shifting of enterprise debt from the public to the private sector. Again, strengthening of capital markets and overall economic liberalization are secondary goals of these privatization efforts, but the lack of reasonably mature capital markets and other free-market economic institutions sometimes seriously inhibits privatization progress. These programs sometimes seem more visible and somewhat more ambitious than those in the more advanced Asian countries and are also sometimes characterized by highly personalized leadership as well as vocal opposition. Countries with these kinds of privatization programs include the Philippines, India, and Pakistan.

The highly centralized command economies of Asia with announced privatization programs are also driven by the need to balance budgets and are often proceeding with privatization out of economic desperation despite strong traditional ideological disincentives. The almost complete lack of capital markets or banking systems contributes to slow progress in these countries, such as Vietnam, Myanmar, and Laos. Some progress is being made, if only because of widespread agreement that radical action is required for national economic rescue. Mongolia and the Central Asian Republics have already abandoned their ideological commitments to command economies and have expressed enthusiasm for privatization. But their lack of experience and institutions necessary to support such efforts has slowed progress considerably.

Taiwan

Although Taiwan launched an extensive privatization campaign in the late 1980s, the country achieved tremendous economic growth while maintaining strict state control over many companies in strategic sectors. Beginning in the late 1950s, Taiwan sustained growth through consistent and effective price-level and interest rate policies and general promotion of the non-state sector. Despite only a few successful attempts at privatization (during the 1960s), the share of industrial assets owned by public enterprises dropped from 90 percent in 1952 to 20 percent by the early 1990s; value-added in manufacturing accounted for by state firms dropped from 55 percent to 10 percent over the same period (*The Economist* 1992a, p. 11).

Taiwan began a program in 1989 to divest itself of 22 public enterprises, including industrial enterprises and banks. The program was expected to raise as much as $20 billion, but the basic goal of privatization according to government officials was the improvement of management efficiency and competitiveness of the firms involved. In particular, officials expected that the role of state banks in allocating capital to private businesses would be strengthened if banking regulations were first formalized, then the large state banks privatized in order to lessen the influence on their affairs of the Provincial Assembly, the banks' majority shareholder. The banking laws were strengthened and formalized in 1989, but the Provincial Assembly refused to sell its shares in the banks largely because they provided both reliable income and patronage appointments (see Friedland 1992, p. 72). In 1991, the Ministry of Finance proceeded with plans to cut its share in the three largest state-owned commercial banks, the original targets of the privatization program. In the same year, the government also liberalized competition in the banking sector by licensing 15 new private banks.

Slow progress has been achieved in other efforts at privatization. A 20 percent share of a subsidiary owned by the state oil monopoly was sold to the public in May 1991 as a prelude to further privatization, but many legislators objected to further divestiture of so profitable a government asset. In June 1992, the government offered shares in China Steel Corporation, but because of a severe stock market slump only 38 percent of the offered shares were purchased. The entire privatization program was officially postponed later in 1992 because the stock market appeared unable to absorb further share issues. However, bureaucratic delays and opposition by government officials and labor unions were also clearly important factors in the decision.

The government announced a resumption of the program in December 1992 with a public offering of 60 percent of a government-owned construction firm, one of the nation's largest. The sale would have marked the first time since the 1960s that a public enterprise was transferred to majority private ownership. But less than 15 percent of the offered stock was purchased. Again, the market slump, exacerbated by uncertainties after the December 1992 national elections, was blamed for the poor sale results. The government pledged that privatization would proceed, through private placements of stock if necessary, and indicated that shares in two other large public enterprises, a petrochemical firm and a machinery manufacturer, would be offered before June 1993. In January 1993, the government announced that foreigners would be allowed to bid for shares in upcoming privatizations.

Singapore

As an independent island-state with concerns for national security as well as social and economic development, the government of Singapore has played a large and continuing role in the nation's economy. Singapore's initial lack of local entrepreneurs and small size prompted government efforts to "jump start" the economy by protecting and promoting specific sectors of the economy identified by government planners as capable of rapid growth. The result has been a public enterprise system that is more extensive and complex than in any other noncommunist Asian nation. Forty wholly owned "statutory boards" provide a variety of social and recreational services and maintain a number of public infrastructure facilities, including housing, port facilities, rapid transit, and communications. Over 500 "government-linked companies" (or GLCs) are active in manufacturing (everything from steel to high technology) and various service areas including financial services. GLCs include a variety of government ownership arrangements, ranging from minority stakes to 100 percent ownership. Restrictions on the release of information regarding GLC performance and little oversight or control by the Singapore Parliament make this a sometimes confusing multilevel network of holding companies and subsidiaries.

In the mid-1980s, the government initiated a modest privatization program. From 1985-1988, the government divested itself completely of shares in 13 GLCs while significantly reducing its stake in 10 others, including Singapore Airlines. More recently, the government has also proceeded with plans to partially privatize some statutory boards, including the telecommunications monopoly (Telecom) and the Public Utilities Board. More extensive privatization was scheduled for 1993, including boards involved in mass transit, gas, and electric utilities. Most of the proceeds from these sales go to a wholly-owned GLC, Temasek Holdings, which is charged with implementing the government's strategy of helping to sustain Singapore's economic development by making direct investment abroad.

The government has consistently claimed that virtually all of these enterprises are profitable and self-financing. The reason most often given for privatization is that it will help reduce the administrative burden of government officials. The government also clearly hopes to strengthen the Singapore Stock Exchange, which lost considerable ground in the early 1990s to other Asian exchanges. Although the government has often denied that the extensive use of public enterprise has retarded the growth of local private sector entrepreneurship, the privatization program appears to be motivated at least in part by the need to respond to this kind of criticism (see Yuan and Low 1990, pp. 143-175).

Privatization of GLCs also clearly seems aimed at increasing the ability of Singapore companies to compete in the international marketplace at a time when the government has determined that continued economic growth depends heavily on the success of such competition (see Balakrishnan 1991, pp. 55-62). The privatization of Singapore Airlines and Telecom are expected to help each company in negotiations for more business abroad. The government may also be concerned about the quality of management in some GLCs, especially when measured against international competition. Almost all GLCs are managed by current or former civil servants or ministers. Losses in international high-risk ventures of more than $245 million, announced in 1992 by government holding company Singapore Technologies Holdings underscored the importance for GLCs of professional business management.

South Korea

Many aspects of South Korea's economic policies and financial structure have been modeled on Japan, including its policies with regard to public enterprise. Defying the recommendations of the IMF and the World Bank in the 1960s, South Korea focused on the development of heavy and chemical industries in order to create a solid industrial base for further development. Public enterprises were used when the government found it necessary to protect or nurture industrial activities. By the 1970s, 12 of the largest 16 enterprises were owned by the state (Jones 1975, p. 200). Korea's successes in promoting automobile and steel industries have been well documented.

In the late-1970s, however, government mistakes in promoting heavy industry raised questions about the nature of state involvement in the economy. Involvement in the form of enterprise ownership was not particularly large by Asian standards. By 1981, the public enterprise share of nonagricultural employment in Korea was 2.5 percent, as opposed to 17.7 percent in India and 14 percent in the Philippines (Shirley 1983, pp. 95-97). The productivity of this labor was also high relative to labor in other Asian countries. Few Korean enterprises required direct subsidies from the government. Laws had already been established stipulating that enterprises retain surplus revenues for investment purposes rather than paying dividends to the government.

Nevertheless, growing doubts about economic efficiency, as well as questions about what some critics charged were overlapping control structures, accelerated efforts to at least partially privatize some enterprises. In the early 1980s, the government began a series of divestiture efforts involving Korea Oil Company and the Korea Telecommunications Authority, in which a minority of shares were sold after the entity was corporatized. In 1982 and 1983, the government sold shares in all of its commercial banks, but these sales were characteristic of the government's attitude toward public enterprise and privatization. Individual share holdings were limited to 8 percent, leaving the Finance Ministry as the controlling shareholder in most cases. Tight government supervision of bank decision making regarding personnel and policy continued into the 1990s, with government approval necessary for the appointment of bank managers (often recruited from among former officials of the Finance Ministry and central bank) and lending policy also guided by the government. In exchange, the government protected its privatized banks from insolvency, providing them with low-interest loans when necessary.

By the late 1980s, the Korean government owned majority stakes in 25 enterprises. Although there were some plans for additional privatization, the process was slow, particularly due to a stock market slump exacerbated by growing political and economic uncertainties. Market recovery in the 1990s is likely to mean an acceleration of share sales of government companies as the government begins implementing a massive new infrastructure development program and seeks to strengthen the competitive positions of its enterprises in the international economy. Like Korea's private sector corporations, public enterprises suffer from a lack of access to capital rather than high debt burdens or unprofitability. The government also has significantly improved its oversight and control of these entities according to recent analysis by the World Bank (Shirley 1989). In addition to share sales, the government also plans to use build-operate-transfer (BOT) contracting and other types of concession arrangements to involve private management expertise and private capital in what have traditionally been public sector project activities.

Hong Kong

As a British colony, Hong Kong relies on Britain for defense and foreign affairs, and the colonial government devotes itself to issues of law and order and minimal regulation of economic activity. With a small civil service, it routinely privatizes government functions and plays a minor role in public enterprise activities (it has few essential or strategic industries that require ownership by the colonial government for protection). For example, despite the finding of an official commission in 1964 that the government should acquire the two companies that supply the colony's electricity, government officials decided instead to adopt regulatory "schemes of control" that would keep the companies private but limit profits. The colony's third major private utility, Hong Kong & China Gas, remains unregulated.

Hong Kong does have government-owned corporations, such as the Mass Transit Railway Corporation and the Provisional Airport Authority, which administers the colony's huge and controversial Chek Lap Kok airport development project. But the government has taken steps to limit its involvement in such projects. In the late 1980s, the Tuen Mun Light Rail Transit project used a turnkey contract between the government and a private developer to arrange for the design, construction, and commissioning of a light rail transit system. With the Chek Lap Kok project, the colony has encouraged even more private sector involvement. Over half of the $21 billion project is to be financed and built by private sector firms, which would operate the facilities for a specified period before relinquishing ownership to the government. This kind of build-operate-transfer (BOT), or concession, arrangement is similar to arrangements increasingly used in other Asian countries and is typical of Hong Kong's ongoing efforts to contract out government services.

Thailand

Recent efforts at privatization in Thailand began in the mid-1980s with government concern that public enterprises were relying too heavily on foreign borrowing, creating debt service problems, and contingent liabilities for the central government in the process. A ceiling on the use of sovereign loan guarantees was applied collectively to all public enterprises in 1985, and plans were announced to begin limited privatization, beginning with the sale of shares in Thai Airways, the state-owned national airline. Divestiture of enterprises was seen as a way of increasing their efficiency and decreasing their reliance on foreign borrowing.

But it was not until 1992 that 7 percent of Thai Airway's shares were finally sold. Actual divestiture in all sectors proceeded slowly. In general, Thai enterprises are not unprofitable—only 5 of the 63 national level state companies were reported to have lost money in 1989—and enterprise unions and managers and many central government bureaucrats resisted the state's efforts to relinquish such valuable assets (Handley 1991). The military also slowed some privatization efforts. Acting and retired military officials traditionally have played important roles in enterprise activities, as members of boards of directors and sometimes directly or indirectly as suppliers or subcontractors. In 1991, the military junta that briefly held power lifted the ceiling on foreign borrowing for Thai Airways, presumable to delay the long-scheduled privatization plans. At that time, military officials held seven of the 15 Thai Airways directorships, including the board chairmanship.

But by the early 1990s, the thrust of Thai privatization had shifted from a concern about too much debt to a concern that these enterprises might not have access to enough capital to meet the rapidly rising demand for their goods and services. The high levels of economic growth that the nation had begun to achieve in the late 1980s focused attention on ways of sustaining growth. Although still not generally unprofitable, public enterprises were increasingly unable to meet the nation's development needs in areas such as transport, communication, and power. By the end of 1991, a number of large public enterprises in addition to Thai Airways started preparing share sales, public-private joint ventures, or other kinds of arrangements to contract out their activities. These included the Electricity Generating Authority of Thailand and the Petroleum Authority of Thailand. Many smaller enterprises, such as the Port Authority of Thailand and Thai Maritime Navigation, were also forced to give up monopoly advantages and compete with the private sector.

The need to continue promoting rapid development also led central government officials to pull back or moderate some privatization efforts, particularly in the area of large development projects. The rush to privatize many of these activities in the mid-1980s led to project delays due to lengthy negotiations and political infighting, as well as charges of corruption. With large and growing budgetary surpluses in the late 1980s and raised limits on foreign borrowing, the government began to move back to a leadership role in project design and implementation. In late 1991, the government proposed new rules for project development and management, substituting more public-private cooperative arrangements, including carefully designed BOT contracts, for the outright transfer of public sector activities to private businesses (Handley 1992).

Malaysia

In 1984, Malaysia began what became one of the most ambitious of Asian privatization programs. Between 1984 and 1990, the government sold minority shares in 22 enterprises and turned 10 large public projects (road construction and other public works) over to private companies. During the same period, local state development corporations sold nearly 200 smaller government-owned businesses (Tsuruoka 1990). The government judged these efforts to be successful because of profit increases at some privatized companies as well as large government profits from some of the sales. The total capitalization of the Kuala Lumpur Stock Exchange was increased considerably by the listing of nine former state corporations, including an airline, a shipping firm, a television station, and the sole distributor of the locally made Proton Saga automobile. As the stock market deepened, the Malaysian investment community gained considerable experience in handling large share issues.

But the program was also controversial. The government was criticized for continuing to provide tax incentives and loans from the state-owned central bank to many of the privatized enterprises and for allowing most of the enterprises to retain the monopoly status they enjoyed as government companies. The government's claim to have shifted the debt of these enterprises to the private sector was also questioned because the government still held majority shares in most cases. Critics also questioned the procedures used in privatizing some companies after an official admitted in 1990 that the program had been used as part of the national effort to nurture bumiputra (indigenous Malay) businesses. Finally, critics suggested that many of the indigenous private sector companies that benefited from the sale of government enterprises and the shift of large public works projects to the private sector appeared to be linked to the business empire run indirectly by the ruling United Malay National Organization (UNMO) (Tsuruoka 1990).

In December 1990, the government extended the program and shifted its objectives. In an effort to increase the efficiency and competition in the economy and expand the role of the private sector the government planned to privatize as many as 246 state companies worth $5.9 billion (Richardson 1990). The government's action program called for the sale of 15-20 enterprises each year, including at least one of its "flagship" companies. The program proceeded steadily but more slowly than anticipated. From 1990-1992, a number of large state-owned companies accounted for large new offerings and listings on the stock exchange, including the national power monopoly, Tenaga Nasional, and the national telecommunications company, Telekom Malaysia. In April 1991, Telekom issued $190 million in convertible debt securities, the first such issue by a privatized company. With its Sixth Malaysia Plan (1991-1995), the government also made clear that it intended to reduce its assistance to indigenous entrepreneurs in favor of more broad-based economic development. In December 1992, the government lifted its limit on foreign share holdings in privatized auto maker Proton Saga and extended the move to other enterprises. By the end of 1992, the government's economic planning unit was keeping pace with the original 1990 plan as it identified 57 government agencies and services that were to be privatized by 1995.

Indonesia

The collapse of oil prices in the mid-1980s triggered consideration in Indonesia of measures to stimulate the economy through deregulation. At that time, pubic enterprises played a large role in the economy, with 222 enterprises operating at the national level and hundreds more at regional levels (Tjokroamidjojo 1990, p. 247). They were particularly important in the industrial sector but also in agriculture in the form of large state plantation enterprises. With the exception of a few firms in mining, cement production, and a few plantations, almost all of these firms were unprofitable and represented significant drains on budgetary resources and credit. In the early 1980s, the nonfinancial enterprises were responsible for 90 percent of all domestic credit outstanding (Shirley 1983, p. 15). Because they were allowed to borrow internationally without central government oversight, public enterprises also contributed significantly to the country's rapidly growing foreign debt burden.

In 1988 and 1989, ministerial decrees were issued which provided a framework for reviewing the performance of public enterprises and determining what kinds of central government interventions might be called for, including divestiture, liquidation, and liberalization of competition. At that time, the Ministry of Finance announced plans to partially privatize 52 national-level enterprises by selling shares on the Jakarta Stock Exchange. But the exchange had become a fully functioning stock market only in 1989 and was still far too small, too illiquid, and poorly regulated to handle what for it were large share issues. In June 1991, a government cement company, Semen Gresik, sold 23 percent of its equity as common stock worth $144 million in what was to be the country's first major effort at privatization. But when the shares appeared in the stock market a month later, they dropped 20 percent in value during the first hour of trading. The government later acknowledged that any further privatization would face considerable delays.

Three years after the performance evaluation program was announced, government documents show that five enterprises had been merged, 14 liquidated, and shares in two sold (one via private placement, in addition to the Gresik sale). A number of oversight and control measures also had been put in place in an effort to improve enterprise efficiency. Enterprises were required to prepare annual budgets and five-year plans, and enterprise employees were no longer allowed the employment protection of civil servant status. The government also allowed enterprises to enter into joint ventures with private firms and encouraged the use of BOT and other concession arrangements to increase the participation of the private sector in business areas traditionally dominated by public enterprises. In September 1991, enterprises were no longer allowed to engage in overseas borrowing without central government approval.

A series of statements by government officials in 1992 indicated that the privatization program would continue but at a deliberate pace. The government described privatization as a way to help maintain the high annual GDP growth that followed economic liberalization in the 1980s by making public enterprises more competitive and easing their access to capital. But the government also indicated its awareness of public concern that privatized firms might fall into the hands of non-indigenous, or ethnic Chinese, entrepreneurs—already a dominant and resented force in the economy. In July 1992, the minister of finance announced that the government was preparing 52 public enterprises, including seven state banks, for the sale of minority equity shares, subject to the ability of the stock market to handle the sales. He pledged that the government would maintain control of these enterprises so as to avoid a "free-for-all market" (*Jakarta Post* 1992, p. 8). In the meantime, public enterprises began issuing bonds to raise capital, and the government moved to facilitate this process by easing restrictions on bond sales and encouraging the development of a secondary bond market so that investors could actively trade their holdings.

China

China's massive economy has undergone a series of reforms since Deng Xiaoping's groundbreaking initiatives in 1978. From 1978 to 1990, the share of industrial output accounted for by public enterprises fell from 78 percent to just over 50 percent, but almost all of this change was due to increased productivity of the private sector, particularly to the success of private rural enterprise rather than to divestiture of public enterprises (*The Economist* 1992a, p. 8). For ideological reasons Chinese officials have resisted selling state firms. The current five-year plan reaffirms the government's intention to maintain public ownership of the means of production. Central government officials have instead pursued a "marketizing" program, a moderately successful effort to make enterprises more accountable for their profits and losses and less dependent on government for loans and subsidies. The government has merged some unprofitable enterprises with profitable ones and has promised to close enterprises if necessary. A bankruptcy law was passed in 1988, but by 1993 it had yet to be applied to any state-owned companies. By the early 1990s, the government had also begun to reconsider enterprise commitments to workers, including the standard promise of life-time employment and the provision of housing, medical care, canteens, and kindergartens, all virtually free of charge.

Despite improvements in efficiency, Chinese public enterprises have continued to lose money and monopolize domestic credit. The huge numbers of these enterprises make such losses difficult to ignore. Government statistics indicate that by 1992 11,500 large state enterprises reported directly to central government ministries, while 105,000 enterprises employing over 45 million workers fell under local government jurisdiction (McGregor 1993, p. 1). Other government reports indicate that one-third of all enterprises are unprofitable, but if standard accounting procedures are used, that figure probably would increase to at least 40 percent and might be as high as two-thirds (until the implementation of accounting reforms announced in late 1992, state companies accounted for loans as revenues). The government has traditionally supported the system with massive subsidies but has been able to hold its subsidies down to 14 percent to 15 percent of its budget—and its total budget deficit to 2 percent to 3 percent of GNP—only by forcing the banking system to extend billions of dollars worth of credit each year to unprofitable enterprises (*The Economist* 1992b, p. 90). In 1990 and 1991, the sector was hit by larger than usual total losses, more than double the 1989 figure.

In 1992, privatization of public enterprise began in China at the local level. Under pressure to increase economic efficiency and unwilling to wait for explicit central government authorization, these officials began to sell off unprofitable companies under the guise of joint venture arrangements. A Hong Kong company became the first foreign firm to purchase a majority share in a Chinese state-owned company when it purchased a 51 percent stake in the Wuhan No. 2 Printing and Dyeing Works from the city of Wuhan in Hubei province. The first large sale of this kind took place in August 1992 in the city of Quanzhou in Fujian province when the controlling interest in 40 state factories was sold to another Hong Kong company. A typical arrangement allowed the foreign firm to buy a factory outright or the rights to its land. The factory was then either renovated or demolished to make way for new private businesses. Some of the proceeds from these sales were usually reserved to support laid-off workers. By the end of 1992, such sales were reported to be proceeding in many parts of China (Chen 1992, p. 1).

By early 1993, central government officials still hesitated to sanction outright privatization, but a number of reforms were already clearing the way for privatization efforts at the national level. Officials moved quickly to develop the country's two stock markets with the clear intention of using them for mixing foreign and local capital, merging firms, and selling shares in state enterprises. In late 1992, the government announced that it would adopt international accounting standards for public enterprises in order to attract foreign investors. In January 1993, the government announced a large expansion in the number of private firms that would be allowed listings on the stock markets and indicated that private firms would be allowed to compete with government companies in most of the industrial and manufacturing fields previously occupied exclusively by public enterprises. Planning began in 1992 to open the nation's airlines to private and foreign investment, and in early 1993 the government announced that 10 state firms would seek listings on foreign stock exchanges.

The Philippines

Six years of democratic political renewal under the Aquino government did little to alter the basic structural problems of the Philippine economy. Three decades of protectionist policies created a small, import-dependent domestic industrial sector, a weak export sector, and recurrent balance of payment crises. By the end of the 1980s, manufacturing contributed only about 25 percent of GDP. Underlying socioeconomic problems, as described by the World Bank, were said to include oligopolistic control of the economy by vested industrial and agricultural interests that had succeeded in organizing themselves into a complex structure of monopolies and cartels. Powerful political allies of these interests have been effective in blocking efforts to make the economy more competitive and have contended with bureaucrats and unions to manipulate government privatization efforts for their own purposes.

Public enterprises have long been a feature of the economy. Under the state interventionist policies of Marcos, including his efforts to nationalize some industries, the role of public enterprises and their negative effects on the national budget grew precipitously—from 32 enterprises in 1972 to 94 parent firms with 149 subsidiaries in 1985 (Galang 1985, p. 66). The government takeover of Philippine Airlines in 1978 resulted in chronic mismanagement and operating losses. During the nation's foreign debt crisis in 1983, the central bank was forced to assume huge liabilities of a number of public enterprises (as well as the debts of some favored private companies). By the late 1980s, losses by the central bank, as well as other state-owned companies such as the National Power Corporation, were contributing to huge deficits in the government's consolidated budget. By 1992, the government reported that subsidies and other payments to cover losses of nonfinancial public enterprises accounted for 28 percent of the consolidated budget deficit. If losses of the central bank were included, the public enterprise share of the deficit rose to 83 percent or over 3 percent of GDP (Tiglao 1992, p. 66).

A privatization program was initiated by the Aquino administration in 1987 to reduce the deficit by eliminating subsidies and realizing some profits from share sales. A secondary motive was the strengthening of the capital market, one of the most underdeveloped in the region. But the program proceeded more slowly than hoped and had little effect on the deficit, raising concerns at multilateral aid agencies such as the IMF. A cornerstone of the program was the privatization of Philippines Airlines (PAL). Mounting losses and management problems delayed the sale while government officials, assisted by the World Bank's International Finance Corporation, restructured debt and shifted managerial assignments. A sealed bid auction in early 1992 resulted in a sale of 67 percent of PAL shares to a consortium led by one of the most powerful business families in the Philippines. The government retained 46 percent of the shares through direct ownership and indirectly through its ownership of a holding company. But by early 1993, the government's methods for screening bidders and structuring share sales were brought into serious question after financial maneuvering threatened to shift PAL management control to a banker and long-time business associate of former President Marcos, something that government officials had structured the sale precisely to avoid (MacDonald and Carey 1993, p. 1).

Other aspects of the privatization program have shown mixed results. In 1989, Philippine National Bank became one of the Manila stock market's few "blue chips," and investor interest in the market appeared to grow after the government sold 30 percent of its shares in the bank. (In early 1992, the government proceeded with plans to sell its remaining shares in the bank.) In the spring of 1991, the government encountered complex legal and technical problems negotiating the sale of the bankrupt Philippine Phosphate Fertilizer Corporation, the largest fertilizer plant in Southeast Asia and a huge drain on the national budget. In early 1992, the privatization of a $130 million telephone network was blocked by the Philippine Justice Department after congressional committees refused to grant the purchaser the appropriate franchise. By late 1992, the finance secretary admitted that privatization efforts had failed to accelerate under President Fidel Ramos (MacDonald 1992, p. 20).

But more privatization was promised, and in January 1993 President Ramos approved the sale of 65 percent of Petron Corporation, the gasoline sales and distribution arm of Philippine National Oil Company. Government reports indicate that, from the initiation of the privatization program in 1987 to December 1992, the program had raised $2.23 billion in total sales. However, 58 percent of that total was generated by the sale of previously private assets that had been foreclosed by government banks. The remaining $1.29 billion was generated by the sales of shares in 75 government-owned or controlled enterprises.

India

The economic turmoil of Eastern Europe and the collapse of the Soviet Union deprived India of its principal source of foreign aid and trade. This, combined with annual government budget deficits averaging almost 12 percent of GDP in the early 1990s, brought the country close to default on its foreign debt. Impending economic disaster caused the nation's leaders to reconsider the government's long-time use of central planning and direct controls to guide industrial development. The Eighth Five-Year Plan was prepared in 1991, but the focus of government investment was on social welfare and infrastructure rather than on industry, and government leaders claimed finally to be willing to leave the allocation of economic resources to private enterprise and market mechanisms.

Traditionally, India's state companies have been thought of as a way of socializing some of the profits of modern industrial enterprise—but much of the system has long been highly unprofitable. By the end of 1991, 244 firms were owned by the federal government, of which over 100 were acknowledged to be chronic money losers. In 1989 alone, these firms cost the government $784 million in support—no consolidated statistics exist on companies owned by state governments, but their deficits were estimated at more than $1.5 billion in 1987 (Desmond 1991, p. 34). Unions, often associated with political parties as well as individual politicians who benefit from patronage opportunities presented by public enterprise, successfully blocked attempts at extensive privatization until impending economic collapse ruled out any other alternative.

As a key part of its efforts to reform the economy begun in July 1991, the federal government began a modest program to privatize some public enterprises, although the term "privatization" is carefully avoided. Under what became known as the government's "exit" policy, 58 of the most unprofitable enterprises were referred for rehabilitation or liquidation to the Board of Industrial and Financial Reconstruction, originally a private sector oversight body whose purview had just been extended to include the public sector. At the same time, the government prepared a "disinvestment" program to offer company shares for sale. Because of the weakness of the national stock market and the desire to conclude sales as quickly as possible, sales were carried out through special-invitation auctions.

For the first auction held in October 1991, bids were restricted to eight state-owned mutual funds. The government offered for sale 825 "baskets" or mixed collections of shares in 31 profitable public enterprises. No more than 20 percent of any one company's shares were included. For the second sale held in February 1992, the cabinet raised the limit for private ownership from 20 percent to 49 percent. Shares in only 16 of the original 31 companies were offered, and the number of invited bidders was increased from eight to 40, as more government-owned financial institutions and their subsidiaries were allowed to participate.

In a third auction held on October 14, 1992, the government opened bidding on eight of the government's "blue chip" firms to private sector participants, but the response was poor. Only one private firm made a bid, and in all the government accepted only one-third of the bids submitted, deeming the rest to be too low. Critics pointed out that bidders had no access to basic accounting and financial documentation, such as statements of accounts, asset valuations, and corporate plans (Penna 1992, p. 7). In the last sale of the year, held on December 25, the government lowered the minimum bid, but only state-own companies—in financial services, mutual funds, insurance, and banking—actually purchased shares.

As 1993 began, the government admitted that it would be forced to sell more shares and hold sales more often than originally planned in order to meet revenue targets for the fiscal year ending March 31. The average equity share per company sold during the year was 13 percent, considerably below the 49 percent allowable (Dubey 1992, p. 8). Critics from opposition parties charged that shares were being sold at prices that were suspiciously low and called for investigations. The government also had been criticized for avoiding the stock market and not making shares readily available to the general public, but plans were announced late in 1992 to sell shares directly to public enterprise workers.

The government's stated purpose in proceeding with the privatization program was to use proceeds from the sales to help cut the operating deficit to 5 percent of GDP—a condition imposed by the IMF for the provision of badly needed credit. However, by the end of 1992, it appeared that public enterprise sales were having little effect on the deficit, still running at approximately 8 percent of GDP, up from 6.5 percent in the previous fiscal year.

Pakistan

Declining U.S. foreign aid, failure to meet IMF and World Bank conditions for assistance, sharply rising debt, and increasing budget and current-account deficits all contributed to a decision in late 1990 by the new administration of Prime Minister Nawaz Sharif to sponsor an extensive package of economic reform measures. As part of the program, the government declared that 90 percent of its business activities would be transferred to the private sector. The Denationalization and Deregulation Commission was created in January 1991 to recommend companies for disposal, and by the spring it had identified 160 enterprises, 90 of which were wholly owned by the government. The list included companies that had been nationalized in the early 1970s as well as scores of companies created by the government. The government also announced plans to allow private businesses to compete with public enterprises in industries previously closed to them.

The prime minister proposed that all sales be completed by the end of 1991, but a series of factors delayed the process considerably, including long-entrenched opposition to privatization among unions and government bureaucrats, as well as fear that privatization would simply turn companies over to the large business families that have dominated the Pakistani economy since the 1960s (Ali 1991). Because the stock market was considered underdeveloped and the domestic savings base weak, the government decided to use an auction system for the sales with minimum prices established through government evaluation.

By the end of August, no firms had been sold, and only 30 had been advertised. Of the bids received, most were far below the minimum price fixed by the government. Some potential bidders argued that minimum prices were set too high. Others claimed that they were not allowed to see accounting records of enterprises on sale. The government's requirement that all enterprise employees were to be retained for at least one year after a sale may also have discouraged some potential bidders. (Employees who chose to quit were to be compensated at the rate of five months' salary for each prior year of service to the company.) Government officials admitted that many of the firms for sale were seriously overstaffed.

In late October, the government sold 24 enterprises after a new auction was held for 101 of the firms for sale. Most of the bids were below minimums set by the government, and 12 firms attracted no bids. But government officials and donor agencies were encouraged that a major sale finally had been achieved. The government proceeded with efforts to privatize some of its more unprofitable companies by re-advertising some, floating others on the Karachi Stock Exchange, and liquidating others. The government also began to progressively offer shares in more profitable and strategic government industries. By the end of 1992, the government reported that it had earned $145 million from total sales of shares under the privatization program. Companies involved included those engaged in the production of automobiles, cement, engineering goods, chemicals, and pharmaceuticals. The figure was well below the $600 million that some officials had expressed hope in achieving from the sales by June 30, 1992.

Vietnam

After the end of the Vietnam War in 1975, the Soviet Union became Vietnam's largest aid donor and largest single trading partner. The collapse of the Soviet Union and the U.S.-led effort to isolate Vietnam economically as well as politically triggered economic crisis in the country in the early 1990s. In response, government leaders decided to extend a comprehensive economic reform program that had begun focusing on the nation's 12,000 public enterprises in 1986. In order to control inflation, the government moved to reduce the budget deficit, much of which was caused by subsidies and low interest loans to public enterprises—they accounted for almost 87 percent of all bank credit in the early 1990s (Hiebert 1992, p. 22). In late 1991, the government summarily abolished all such subsidies. In early 1992, seven state-owned shareholding companies created the Saigon Finance Company, which was designed to provide a variety of financial services to the public enterprise sector, including advising on conversions to shareholding status as well as market making for those shares.

In the spring of 1992, the Council of Ministers identified seven state-owned companies that would issue shares on a trial basis, including a soap factory, a match-making plant, and an animal-feed processing unit. (The share-issuing process has been referred to as "equitization" or "stockization" rather than privatization.) The government expected to use auctions to sell shares to foreign investors but planned to retain state ownership of at least 30 percent of the shares. Opposition to the sales arose immediately, and protests by managers and workers led to the removal of four firms from the program. The government quickly added nine more candidates to the list and began a long process of liberalizing rules affecting foreign investment in the country.

By the end of 1992, Vietnam was negotiating with the World Bank regarding prospects for a structural adjustment program that would include a privatization component. The program was to be finalized after the U.S.-led economic embargo of the country was lifted. By 1993, however, it was clear that considerable ambivalence toward the privatization program still existed among some members of the central committee, responsible for approving all privatization arrangements. This lack of a strong ideological and legal commitment to privatization raised questions about the continuing willingness of foreign investors to participate in the process (see Conboy 1993, p. 6).

Laos

Crop failures and the loss of aid from the Soviet Union prompted Laos officials in 1991 to begin new efforts to control inflation, stabilize exchange rates, and reduce budget deficits. A significant step in controlling inflation involved a halt in central bank credit to money-losing enterprises. Officials also initiated an ambitious privatization program that resulted in the sale or lease of 105 of the government's 604 enterprises by August 1992 (Hiebert 1992, p. 15). But a lack of transparency in the process led to protests by bidders. Some complained that foreign businesses were being informally excluded from buying many of the nonstrategic, but potentially profitable, enterprises. In some cases, the government also refused to divulge terms of sale, business plans, or the names of firms making successful bids.

Myanmar (Burma)

Since it took power in 1988, Myanmar's ruling military junta has been widely accused of doing little better managing the economy than the 26-year socialist dictatorship that preceded it. The country is classified among the world's least developed nations, with high rates of inflation, thriving black market activity, huge budget deficits, and endemic poverty. But Myanmar's leaders declared 1992 to be the Economic Year and promised a series of reforms to strengthen private enterprise. Among them has been a new policy of privatizing state enterprises, most of which are characterized by insufficient electric power, a lack of foreign exchange with which to buy spare parts, and huge subsidies from the central government—despite the fact that most operate at less than 40 percent capacity (Wain 1992, p. 1).

Although government announcements imply that any of the nation's nonstrategic enterprises may be purchased by foreign or domestic buyers, the mechanics of the process, including who will handle the sales, are vague. Government requirements that any purchaser must retain all existing employees are likely to further discourage potential buyers.

Mongolia

In 1990, Mongolia became the first Asian communist country to embrace popular rule. By 1991, the country's economy was on the verge of a collapse precipitated by the breakup of the former Soviet Union, Mongolia's traditional (and almost exclusive) trading partner and long the source of its critically needed budget subsidies. By the spring of 1991, the country began an extensive privatization program that the government described as the most ambitious of any former communist country. The national legislature quickly passed a law giving vouchers (worth approximately $250) to each Mongolian citizen, entitling them to buy shares in state enterprises. However, program officials immediately encountered problems in explaining the process to the public, almost half of whom are pastoral nomads. Five months after the program began, fewer than 20 percent of the vouchers had been claimed.

By March 1992, although most of the government's 340 companies remained in state hands, a good deal of progress had been made in privatizing smaller enterprises. The government claimed, for example, that it had sold 90 of the government-owned stores in Ulan Bator, the nation's capital. Farming cooperatives, not burdened by complicated vouchering systems, were reported to have privatized 60 percent of their livestock—usually by simply giving away the animals to the herdsmen who tended them (*International Herald Tribune* 1991, p. 6).

By the end of 1992, multilateral aid officials were openly critical of what they considered to be inconsistent efforts at economic reform in the country. Despite a small but functioning stock market and public claims that 80 percent of state assets would be in private hands by the end of 1993, the privatization program had made little progress. Loans to state enterprises increased precipitously in 1992, contributing to an expansion of credit that pushed annualized inflation to almost 250 percent (Hannam 1992, p. 71).

Other Asian Privatization Programs

A number of other Asian countries have recently introduced privatization programs of one sort or another. In 1992, Bangladesh began offering for sale industrial units of public enterprises as part of a plan to sell 40 such units by June 1993, but the World Bank urged that the pace of privatization be accelerated. In 1992, the government of Sri Lanka sold a hotel and a powdered-milk packager, corporatized several other enterprises in preparation for sale, and announced a "peoplization" plan to break up two holding companies operating over 500 tea plantations. Of the five central Asian republics, Kazikhstan and Kirgyzstan have experimented with programs to privatize agricultural land and equipment, but large plantation-style farming is so entrenched in the region that progress has been very slow. All five of the republics also fear that disputes over land may incite discontent among the region's many ethnic groups. Finally, after the October 23, 1991, agreement designed to bring peace to Cambodia, officials of the Phnom Penh government were said to have sold factories and government buildings and kept the proceeds. In December 1991, angry enterprise workers held violent demonstrations to protest their loss of jobs. Feared in Eastern Europe as "spontaneous privatization," these sales were reported to have been widespread (Thayer 1992, p. 11).

CONCLUSIONS: PATTERNS AND EMERGING ISSUES

Privatization to Sustain Growth

Most of the dynamic economies of Asia, including Taiwan, Singapore, South Korea, Thailand, Malaysia, and Indonesia, have initiated formal privatization programs. (Hong Kong has few public enterprises to privatize and routinely contracts out government services; China's privatization program is still informal.) All of these programs are small-scale in character, with the exception of Malaysia. None of them has produced large number of divestitures, and the sale of minority stakes in public enterprises has been the rule in all of these countries.

All of these programs have been in place since the 1980s. But privatization in the 1990s tends to be viewed by officials in these countries primarily as a way of helping to nurture competition and sustain growth, rather than as a method for reducing deficits or debt burdens. Even in Indonesia and China the desire to raise investment capital and improve economic efficiency—rather than the considerable unprofitability of their public enterprises—appears to have been the primary motivation behind government efforts to proceed with limited privatization in the face of institutional shortcomings and ideological resistance.

Perhaps more important is the fact that, with the exception of Hong Kong, these countries have achieved economic growth despite considerable numbers of public enterprises—public enterprise was a key part of the growth strategies of Taiwan, South Korea, and Singapore, the most developed economies of the group. This lends support to the position taken by some Japanese aid officials that the experience of Japan and Asian NICs with public enterprise argues in favor of a more cautious and deliberate approach to privatization in some countries than that sometimes attributed to the World Bank and the IMF (see Overseas Economic Cooperation Fund of Japan 1992, pp. 17-18; for an study showing that, in terms of actual development assistance, both the World Bank and IMF have been far less dogmatic on the subject of privatization than their critics suggest, see Babai 1988). It also raises questions about the direction and pace of reform in Russia and Eastern Europe, especially whether privatization is as critical in the early stages of economic liberalization as has been assumed. Government officials in countries such as Singapore, Thailand, and Taiwan have described the value of public enterprise for guiding and sustaining some stages of economic development in terms not unlike those used recently to describe the "dedicated capital systems" of Europe and Japan, in which long-term owners of significant corporate shares help to optimize long-term social, as well as private, returns (see Porter 1992).

Privatization for Relief From Deficits and Debt

Most of the rest of the Asian countries engaged in privatization of public enterprise do so in order to reduce budget deficits by ending subsidies and accruing sales revenue or to reduce heavy debt burdens (or both). In most of these countries, improved competition and efficiency via economic liberalization are secondary considerations. To what extent are such objectives being realized?

In the first place, privatization is making headway in some of these countries, usually because of strong leadership roles played by key government officials. The large, highly visible privatization campaigns in India and Pakistan were created by—and have depended for crucial support on—the prime minister/finance minister teams in each country (Rao and Singh in India and Sharif and Aziz in Pakistan). The lack of such leadership in the Philippines may be a significant factor in the slow progress of privatization in that country.

One reason for the critical role played by individual leaders is the extent and intensity of opposition to privatization in each of these countries. In the absence of immediate convincing evidence that their economics can prosper as a result of increased competition and other liberalization measures, workers, managers, bureaucrats, and opposition politicians typically view privatization in terms of narrowly defined benefits (jobs, patronage opportunities, etc.) that will be reduced through layoffs and corporate restructuring necessary to make these enterprises profitable. Significant opposition to privatization also exists in countries like Taiwan and Thailand, but public enterprises in these countries tend to require much less radical restructuring; the social disruption associated with privatization is less and the opposition of managers and workers less intense. In countries such as Vietnam, Laos, and Myanmar, privatization efforts seem to be sustained in part by the force of example rather than by crusading leaders. Officials in these countries clearly have been impressed by the reform-led economic growth in China and are at least generally informed about the massive privatization campaigns mounted by their former trading partners in Eastern Europe.

In the second place, virtually all of these programs have raised relatively small amounts of revenue, at least much smaller than expected, while transaction costs associated with these programs tend to be unexpectedly high (although no country makes comprehensive cost-benefit calculations available to the general public). In no case are these programs close to realizing revenues necessary to have a significant impact on budget deficits. In many cases, governments have found to their surprise that investors are unwilling even to bid for unprofitable enterprises without extensive managerial and financial restructuring already in place. The assumption by government of public enterprise debt also has been necessary in some cases to interest investors in enterprise shares, but this of course works against the government's ultimate purpose in making such sales.

The achievements of secondary objectives, such as liberalized competition and economic efficiency, are even harder to assess, but a tentative judgment seems possible. To some extent, the maximization of sale proceeds is achieved at the expense of future competition. Governments hesitate to deprive their public enterprises of the characteristics, such as monopoly status, that make them attractive to investors, if numbers of sales or sale proceeds are measures of privatization success. Divestiture in monopoly sectors may also lead to a weakening of the informal regulation associated with 100 percent government ownership, and formal and explicit regulatory modes are often not in place (see Heald 1992). These governments also may be neglecting necessary reforms in the management and oversight of enterprises that remain in government hands in favor of impressive privatization sales.

Finally, haste in pushing these programs forward often leads to a sacrifice of transparency and, ultimately, lower sales revenue than might otherwise be the case. Goals and procedures associated with programs may remain vague as sales begin, leading to confused bidders and charges of irregularities. Bidders may be denied access to enterprise accounts and other essential data, or the terms of sales may not be announced, discouraging many potential investors from participating. Transparency problems seem to plague the less dynamic Asian economies, where stock markets are too underdeveloped to provide a regulated, public environment within which large share sales can take place.

All of this suggests the possibility that, not only do these kinds of privatization programs not contribute to economic liberalization, but in some cases they may work directly against it. This is the kind of reasoning behind much of the criticism of Russia's "shock therapy" privatization program (Passel

1992, p. 6). Again, the case for carefully sequencing steps toward economic liberalization seems to be supported (for a more detailed discussion of this, see McKinnon 1991).

BOT: Privatization or Public Sector Expansion?

Build-operate-transfer (BOT) and other kinds of concession arrangements are spreading rapidly across Asia, as mechanisms for involving private sector companies in the design, financing, construction, and operation of facilities, especially public works projects, that might otherwise be considered the responsibility of the public sector, including public enterprises. But the complexity of these arrangements and their long-term implications for privatization efforts raise almost as many questions as the technique serves to answer.

Developed by the World Bank and the Asian Development Bank, the BOT contract allows private firms, particularly foreign firms and foreign-domestic joint ventures, to finance their design and development work through eventual ownership and operation of the completed projects. After an agreed period of time necessary for the private companies to recoup their investment with some specified level of profit, they relinquish ownership to the public sector. The technique can be attractive to developing countries where domestic capital markets are weak and the level of external debt tends to deny access to foreign capital markets. The Philippines recognized the potential of the technique in 1990 when it passed a law allowing extensive use of BOT contracting in a variety of different kinds of public works projects.

BOT has been used perhaps most visibly in the Anglo-French Channel Tunnel project, but since the late 1980s it has been used across Asia in connection with a variety of projects, including bridges and airports in Hong Kong, power and railways in China, highways and airports in Malaysia, mass transit and telecommunications in Thailand, power and port expansion in Indonesia, mass transit and power in the Philippines, highways in Vietnam, and telecommunications and power in Pakistan. At $1.8 billion, Pakistan's Hub River thermal energy project involves BOT arrangements that are second in size and complexity only to the Channel Tunnel project (Rowley 1992, p. 53).

The legal negotiations required for such projects sometimes take years to conclude, as complicated risk allocation and sharing arrangements among many project participants are worked out. Contractor proposal preparation alone may cost millions of dollars. The failure of government officials to carefully identify their interests and coordinate their participation in the development process can lead to contract terms that subsequently may be viewed as highly disadvantageous for the government. The Thai government discovered this in connection with some large telephone BOT contracts concluded in 1990. The evaluation of BOT possibilities clearly requires an assessment of advantages and disadvantages not usually incorporated into traditional project cost-benefit analysis (see Gurwitz 1992).

In addition, although these arrangements are often discussed under the heading of privatization, they are designed ultimately to have the opposite result. BOT contracts do in effect privatize many aspects of project design, construction, and operation. But the long-term result is an expansion of the public sector when the concession period ends and ownership reverts to the government. By the early 1990s, most of the large Asian BOT projects underway had not yet even finished construction, much less been transferred to government ownership (typical concession periods range from 10-50 years). It remains to be seen if the current wave of BOT financing will result ultimately in the need to undertake new privatization efforts of various kinds.

ACKNOWLEDGMENT

Sources of information for this study include published studies of public enterprise and privatization efforts in developing countries, official government documents, interviews conducted in Indonesia, Singapore, Thailand, and Japan, as well as scores of published news accounts.

REFERENCES

Ali, S. 1991. "Privatise or Bust: Pakistan Plans Rapid Asset Disposals to Avert Economic Crisis." *Far Eastern Economic Review* (April 18): 58-60.

Babai, D. 1988. "The World Bank and the IMF: Rolling Back the State or Backing Its Role?" Pp. 254-285 in *The Promise of Privatization: A Challenge for U.S. Policy*, edited by R. Vernon. New York: The Council on Foreign Relations.

Balakrishnan, N. 1991. "Lion on the prowl: Singapore Looks Outwards to Sustain Rate of Economic Growth." *Far Eastern Economic Review* (May 23): 55-62.

Caiden, N.J. 1985. "Comparing Budget Systems: Budgeting in ASEAN Countries." *Public Budgeting and Finance* 5 (Winter): 23-38.

Chen, K. 1992. "Hong Kong-China Venture Overhauls State-Run Firms." *Asian Wall Street Journal* (December 22), p. 1.

Conboy, K. 1993. "Vietnam Divided Over Capital Markets." *Asian Wall Street Journal*, (January 15-16), p. 6.

Desmond, E.W. 1991. "India: Dogma on the Run." *Time* (October 7), p. 34.

Dubey, S. 1992. "Latest Public-Sector Equity Sale in India Brings in $413 Million." *Asian Wall Street Journal* (December 28), p. 8.

The Economist. 1992a. "China Survey." (November 28): 11.

The Economist. 1992b. "China's Financial System: Still in the Middle Kingdom." (December 12): 90.

Friedland, J. 1992. "Customers Come First: New Entrants in Taiwan Shake Up Stuffy Industry." *Far Eastern Economic Review* (May 7): 72.

Galang, J. 1985. "The Philippines Prepares for Massive Auction." *Far Eastern Economic Review* (July 25): 66.

Gillis, M. 1980. "The Role of Public Enterprises in Economic Development." *Social Research* 47 (Summer): 248-289.

Gurwitz, A. 1992. "Privatization in a New Key." Pp. 828-835 in *Handbook of Municipal Bonds and Public Finance*, edited by R. Lamb, J. Leigland, and S. Rappaport. New York: New York Institute of Finance.

Handley, P. 1991. "Privatised Parts: Thai Government Slowly Opens Up State Monopolies to Freer Competition." *Far Eastern Economic Review* (June 27): 48-52.

———. 1992. "Call to Wise Men: Thailand Aims to Clean Up Project Procedures." *Far Eastern Economic Review* (January 9): 47-48.

Hannam, P. 1992. "Donors Turned Off: Mongolia's Aid Honeymoon Is Over." *Far Eastern Economic Review* (October 29): 71.

Heald, D. 1992. "How Much Privatization Should There Be in Developing Countries." *Annals of Public and Cooperative Economics* 63 (April-June): 229-269.

Hiebert, M. 1992. "Crisis Management: Party Abolishes Subsidies to Loss-Making State Firms." *Far Eastern Economic Review* (February 12): 22.

———. 1992. "Barriers to Lao growth." *Far Eastern Economic Review* (August 6): 15.

International Herald Tribune. 1991. "Road to Privatization Is Slow in Mongolia." (October 18), p. 6.

Jakarta Post. 1992. "Government Will Retain Control of State Enterprises." (July 15), p. 8.

Jones, L.P. 1975. *Public Enterprise and Economic Development*. Seoul: Korea Development Institute.

MacDonald, L. 1992. "The Asian Economist: An Interview on Regional Economic Issues." *Asian Wall Street Journal* (December 17), p. 20.

MacDonald, L., and S. Carey. 1993. "Control of PAL May Be Shifted To Marcos Ally." *Asian Wall Street Journal* (January 12), p. 1.

McGregor, J. 1993. "China's State Enterprises Think Private." *Asian Wall Street Journal* (January 8-9), p. 1.

McKinnon, R.I. 1991. *The Order of Economic Liberalization: Financial Control in the Transition to a Market Economy*. Baltimore, MD: Johns Hopkins University Press.

Overseas Economic Cooperation Fund of Japan (OECF). 1992. "Issues Related to the World Bank's Approach to Structural Adjustment—Proposal From a Major Partner." OECF Occasional Paper No. 1, Tokyo.

Passel, P. 1992. "Slow Reform to Save It, Russians Are Now Advised." *International Herald Tribune* (October 14), p. 6.

Penna, A. 1992. "India Rethinks Privatization After Failed Auction." *Jakarta Post* (October 26), p. 7.

Porter, M.E. 1992. "Capital Disadvantage: America's Failing Capital Investment System." *Harvard Business Review* (September-October): 65-82.

Richardson, M. 1990. "Managing Malaysia's Selloff." *International Herald Tribune* (November 1), p. 12.

Rowley, A. 1992. "Banking in Asia: Footing the Progress Bill." *Far Eastern Economic Review* (September 24): 53.

Shirley, M. 1983. "Managing State-Owned Enterprises." World Bank Staff Working Paper No. 577, Washington, DC.

———. 1989. "Improving Public Enterprise Performance: Lessons From South Korea." Policy, Planning and Research Working Papers, WPS 312, World Bank, Washington DC.

Short, R.P. 1984. "The Role of Public Enterprises: An International Statistical Comparison." Pp. 110-181 in *Public Enterprise in Mixed Economies: Some Macroeconomic Aspects*, edited by R.H. Floyd, C.S. Gray, and R.P. Short. Washington, DC: International Monetary Fund.

Thayer, N. 1992. "Plunder of the State: Corrupt Officials Thrive in Political Vacuum." *Far Eastern Economic Review* (January 9): 11.

Tiglao, R. 1992. "Economic Monitor: Philippines." *Far Eastern Economic Review* (August 20): 66.

Tjokroamidjojo, B. 1990. *Public Administration in Indonesia.* Jakarta: Lembaga Administrasi Negara.

Tsuruoka, D. 1990. "Privatized Patronage: Malaysia's Ambitious Effort to Sell State Assets Likely to Accelerate." *Far Eastern Economic Review* (December 20): 42-46.

Wain, B. 1992. "Burma's Junta Does Little To Mend Ailing Economy." *Asian Wall Street Journal* (December 23), p. 1.

World Bank. 1983. *World Development Report.* Washington, DC: Author.

Yuan, L.T., and L. Low. 1990. *Local Entrepreneurship in Singapore: Private and State.* Singapore: Institute of Policy Studies.

PRIVATIZATION IN LATVIA:

MARKET, POLITICAL, FINANCIAL, AND SOCIAL FACTORS

David O. Porter and Gundar J. King

ABSTRACT

Privatization is not a straightforward process, and it has many implications for public budgeting. While the countries of Eastern Europe are not usually thought of as developing, they share many of the problems of countries that are trying to transform their economies and societies. This chapter enumerates some of the hurdles faced by countries which are trying to privatize quickly and the conditions necessary for support of privatization.

After waiting over 50 years to regain their independence, many Latvians are not quite sure what to expect from their new market democracy. Will it empower their families politically and economically as it has for their Western European and American counterparts? Will the Latvian economy work as well? Will Latvia's elected leaders be more responsive and effective?

Policy Studies and Developing Nations, Volume 3, pages 247-261.

ISBN: 1-55938-190-6

The answers to these questions, in the broadest sense, are that Latvia can expect to settle between Scandinavian-style politics and prosperity and Latin American-style politics and low incomes. If franchise and income are broadly distributed, market democracies provide the vast majority of their citizens with opportunities to choose leaders they can trust and buy the food, shelter, and other necessities they want. But if franchise and income distribution are restricted, most political and economic choices will be illusory for those segments of the population who are disenfranchised.

Ownership of private property is an essential element in an effective market democracy. This paper focuses on the first year of privatization in Latvia. Our investigation is based on careful conversations with many Latvians, detailed visits to farms and factories, discussions with new entrepreneurs, and interviews with government officials. Our study included people from local and national levels.

We found a few situations where privatization had proceeded easily and quickly and others that remain essentially the same as they were under the Soviet rule. Overall, however, we found that privatization proceeds at a halting, rather slow pace. Most of the causes appeared to be beyond the control of anyone in Latvia. Others were not. Any expectations for quick and extensive privatization are unrealistic and naive.

We analyze our findings under three rubrics—market factors, political and financial factors, and cultural and social factors. We begin with an analysis of market factors because of the centrality of buying and selling to the process of privatization. Second, we analyze political and financial factors because any sales must take place with the political and financial frameworks available in Latvia. Finally, we cover some of the overarching cultural and social factors which are affecting business activities in Latvia and then suggest some of their impacts on privatization.

MARKET FACTORS AND INSTITUTIONS

A market, stripped to its bare essentials, consists of transactions between sellers and buyers. There must be goods and services offered for sale on one side of each transaction; there must be willing buyers with money on the other side. If there are problems on either side of the transaction the market will not function properly. Our investigations in Latvia identified a number of substantial problems on both sides of the market transactions, that is, the nature of properties being offered for sale and the lack of interested buyers with money, suggesting to us that privatization will proceed more slowly than may be desirable. This section first describes the properties that are for sale and then identifies potential buyers.

Quantity and Quality of Properties Available Glut on the Market

Curiously, few people the authors talked with in Latvia mention what is perhaps the most obvious and important impediment to privatization. There is an unbelievable amount of property for sale in Eastern Europe. Virtually all economic enterprises, agricultural assets, and residential property in 21 formerly communist countries and republics are for sale.

Prices, Listings, and Title

Within the former communist countries, there are special problems when it comes to establishing prices, listing available property, and establishing clear title to land that is being offered for sale. There are so many assets on the market in these countries that reasonable offers are nearly impossible to establish. Relatively few of the properties have been listed and described in a manner useful (and essential) to buyers with specific location, facility, and equipment needs. Terms for purchase are sometimes cluttered with provisos which may require the new owner to employ all or most of present workers and/or restrict the controlling ownership to citizens of the country in which the property is located.

Blight and Neglect

In Latvia, most of the assets are in poor condition. Their infrastructure in electricity, roads, rail terminals, heating plant, water supply, and waste disposal has not been maintained. Also, the design of these infrastructure facilities is usually inappropriate for use by Western manufacturers. Building codes and the quality of construction since 1940 tend to be far behind standards in Western Europe.

Employee Resistance to Private Purchase

Many larger state enterprises have been approached with offers for purchase. The offers run the gamut from the ridiculous to the sublime. In a few cases, the current management has tried to manipulate employees into accepting below market offers and thereby save their jobs. More realistic offers have been made by international investors. Some of each kind of offer have been accepted, most refused.

The employees and present managers in Latvian enterprises are as leery of having new bosses as the employees and present managers in the United States. Efforts to purchase companies are frequently resisted in the United States, prompting a struggle for a "hostile takeover." In Latvia, these very natural concerns about what a new boss will do are sometimes heightened by a knowledge that the proposed new owners accumulated their funds through illegal activities.

Distrust is aggravated by lack of employment opportunities in a distressed economy. There is wide understanding that most production facilities in Latvia are seriously outdated and that products are of inferior quality to competitive Western goods.

Commodity Markets

Many if not most commodities with good potential for export must compete in worldwide markets. Forest products are a good example. There is currently an oversupply of wood fiber in Western Europe and prices are low. At first glance, the oversupplied wood fiber market should not affect Latvia because its producers prefer to export finished wood products and thereby provide local employment. But Latvians do not, as yet, have connections with Western wholesalers to buy their finished wood products. Further, Latvian firms do not have the capacity to produce in the quantity and quality required for large wholesale contracts, and their production methods are relatively inefficient in use of raw material and labor compared with Western European and North American companies.

Neglecting the Commons

Most common resources are not being fully utilized because of uncertainties in ownership, loss of markets, or political uncertain ties. Incentives provided through the Soviet system discouraged personal initiative and gave few rewards for extra effort. The result of 50 years of such policies has been that common activities have been systematically neglected in favor of personal interests. Evidence of this phenomenon can be found almost everywhere, from the foyers in apartment buildings to the fields of the former collective farms. Large collective fields of vegetables are choked by weeds. Small, personally farmed plots of vegetables are extremely well tended. Making matters worse, with the confusion of the transition from the socialist system to private ownership, much agricultural land lies fallow, even abandoned. Vast agricultural areas have been reclaimed by brush and forest.

POTENTIAL BUYERS OF LATVIAN PROPERTY

Resident Latvians

The people most interested in becoming owners of Latvian's economic assets and residences, the resident Latvians, have no money. What capital there is to be found in Latvia was obtained, it is almost universally believed by Latvians, through illegal activities and corrupt practices by former officials in the Communist Party. To allow the holders of such caches of wealth to purchase the productive assets is abhorrent to most citizens. Many of the policies and legislation related to privatization include provisos which attempt to exclude the holders of illegally-gotten capital from purchasing property.

Latvian Money From Abroad

Expatriate Latvians share with their resident relatives the same intense interest in the purchasing of economic and residential assets in Latvia. They are returning to purchase property and/or reclaim assets which were seized in 1940, 1941, 1945, and 1948. Complex, yet incomplete, legislation regulating the reclaiming of urban assets especially has discouraged many former owners from assuming ownership of their previous properties. A combination of high taxes, rent controls, and a responsibility for maintenance and repairs has made the privatization of most urban property nearly impossible.

Investments by Collectives and State Enterprises

A surprisingly productive group of investors are the corporate farms and state enterprises. The leadership of the farms and enterprises had relatively more flexibility in their investments during the Soviet occupation than individual citizens and so gained experience in evaluating them. On collective farms, for instance, there is considerable evidence of locally-based decisions to build such things as a brewery, add a new line of processed food, or open additional retail outlets. Some state enterprises had similar levels of discretion.

In discussions with emerging small businesses, one of the most frequently mentioned sources of venture capital was corporate farms and state enterprises. Funds which had earlier been used by the farms and enterprises to invest in their own expansion and equipment are being invested in new enterprises. The uncertainties of the privatization process on corporate farms, in particular, has encouraged them to look outside of the farm for opportunities to invest. Farm lands have been returned to pre-Soviet owners much more rapidly than other assets. Even though some of the large and vertically-integrated collectives are perceived to be more efficient than the smaller acreage of the previous ownership patterns, there is little objection to quick privatization of agriculture.

There is a perception on the part of some government officials that farms and enterprises are "hoarding" their revenues, not turning them over to the government which needs the funds desperately to finance its activities. This frustration on the part of government surfaced repeatedly. Officials in local government are angry with the national government's decisions to retain control of the more productive enterprises, thereby denying the local governments of the revenues, materials, and potential capital which will be derived from future sales. Conversely, municipal managers are disturbed with governments dumping unprofitable properties.

Opportunists

Short-term opportunity seekers fill the bars of Latvia's hotels each night. They are hustlers of marginal means and even fewer scruples. Most have few Latvian connections or relatives. They often collaborate with organized crime.

International Organizations and Capital Markets

Western governments and international monetary organizations—the European Economic Community, the Scandinavian governments, the United States, the World Bank, and the International Monetary Fund—are providing modest amounts of direct and indirect aid. Little of this money is available for use in the privatization process. Generally, with all of Eastern Europe emerging from socialist systems almost simultaneously, resources from Western governments and international organizations are thinly spread out among many countries.

Further diminishing the pool of international investment capital is the fact that most Western economies have been in a prolonged recession. An unusually large number of properties and assets in developed economies are for sale as corporations, and investors adjust to lower earnings. Potential international investors are stressed and cautious. Governments and international financial institutions have adopted policies of retrenchment, tight credit, and domestic economic stimulation. The Nordic countries of Finland, Sweden, Denmark, and Norway are privatizing many state-owned enterprises and assets themselves.

Many of the funds which may have been available to Latvia have been directed toward countries in the first group of post-Communist states, especially Poland and the previous German Democratic Republic. Many German families lived hundreds of years in the Baltics and would probably have directed more resources from the Federal Republic of Germany into Latvia were it not for the huge obligations that country has assumed as they rebuild eastern Germany and relocate Soviet soldiers. The German Treuhandanstalt is well financed and aggressive in its privatization programs and has soaked up much of the private capital from Germany and Europe.

Given these circumstances, it is surprising that so many joint ventures with Western businesses are underway. The most numerous of these ventures are undertaken by Finnish, Swedish, Danish, and Norwegian interests.

POLITICAL AND INSTITUTIONAL FACTORS

Before significant numbers of international investors would consider Latvia, a number of political and financial conditions would need to be in place. A short list of these conditions and institutions include:

1. Long-term political viability,
2. A financial system which accepts deposits, provides loans to business, and completes international and domestic transactions in a standard and timely manner,
3. Clear legislation regulating property and economic activities,
4. Unhindered opportunities for international investment and ownership of major assets,
5. A justice system which respects and enforces contracts,
6. Safety of persons and property, and
7. A convertible currency.

Long-Term Political Viability

Relative to other former Soviet republics, Latvia has been stable and free from internal violence. While the probability for continuation of a peaceful and stable democracy in Latvia is high, there are three possible sources of political disruption and instability.

Russian Troops

There is deep bitterness among Latvians about the forceful occupations of their country by the Soviet Union in 1940 and 1944. Few Latvian families escaped without losing family members to Soviet repressions. Property was confiscated. Civil liberties were abolished. Hundreds of thousands of non-Latvian colonists (mostly Russians) were relocated into Latvia. As a small country with limited land and resources, Latvians are especially angered about having large numbers of immigrants brought into their country. It is, therefore, not surprising that the issue of citizenship in the new Republic of Latvia is the most important issue on the political agenda. The granting of citizenship to any immigrants directly associated with the Soviet occupation is controversial and emotional.

About two-thirds of the Latvian population, including about half the ethnic Russians, voted for parliamentary candidates supporting Latvian independence. But there has also emerged a group perhaps best called Imperial Loyalists, who have close ties with Russian armed forces in Latvia and include virtually all top managers of industry and trade. This group is hostile to Latvian independence and frustrated by their personal loss of power from powerful

Soviet officials to Russians without Latvian citizenship and uncertain employment rights.

Each day the Russian armed forces remain in Latvia, feelings between the two neighbors deteriorate. Every politician must aver a determination to get them out of Latvia. And as the rhetoric escalates, more Russians are blamed for more and more black market activity, Communist Party corruption, and clannish conspiracies. In this poisoned atmosphere, policies are debated which would deny most Russians citizenship and/or rights to hold real property in Latvia.

Police Forces

The second potential source of serious political instability is closely related to the growing enmity between Latvians and Russophiles. Police personnel recruited during the Soviet period, not surprisingly, came primarily from non-Latvian peoples. Most of the high level officials in the police services, especially in Riga, speak only Russian and would fail the 1990 requirement to speak Latvian.

In the meantime, Latvian nationalists continue to press for the dismissal of "Russian" police officials. At the local levels of the Latvian National Guard, they are organizing an all Latvian police force.

Ineffective Tax Collections

A third and potentially destabilizing situation is the ineffective fiscal system of Latvian governments at all levels. No government entity was collecting sufficient revenues through taxes to continue operations at what they believed to be the required levels. Two changes will have to be made to correct this situation. First, the number of services and subsidies will have to be reduced or placed on a full cost recovery basis. Second, methods of fair and effective tax collection will need to be put in place.

Under the Soviet system, the republic and its governmental entities were supported through appropriations from Moscow. Since all property and enterprises were owned by the state, funds for their maintenance, utilities, capital expenditures, and staffing were included in city, region, and national budget allocations. Most utilities were not metered. Prices for the necessities—for example, food, shelter, medical care, and air travel—were administratively set at levels far below full-cost recovery. With increased costs of energy alone, local governments and many enterprises are going bankrupt.

Latvian governmental entities, enterprises, and collectives have been scrambling to find revenues. The vast majority of transactions are conducted with cash, leaving few paper trails from which to track profits and/or losses. There is little hope for effective and equitable tax collections prior to the emergence of effective financial institutions and the adoption of Western accounting practices.

Governments at all levels have resorted to relying on revenues generated by the enterprises to which they still hold title. The enterprises, skilled from the Soviet years in keeping substantial portions of their cash out of sight, desperately try to hold back some revenues for new investments.

Peace Dividend

There is one source for considerable optimism in Latvia's revenue picture even though is has been muted by the continued presence of Russian troops in Latvia—a peace dividend.

The peace dividend is, or will be, derived from two sources. First, Latvia was relatively more productive than other republics and, consequently, contributed a disproportionate per capita share to the Soviet system. With independence, all of these revenue collections remain in Latvia. Second, spending on defense within the Soviet Union exceeded 30 percent of GNP. The Scandinavian countries spend between 5 percent and 6 percent of their GNP for defense. Assuming a Latvian defense establishment that is on a par with the Nordic countries, there will be a peace dividend of 20 percent to 25 percent of GNP if and when tensions between the Baltic states and Russia subside.

A partially disguised form of the peace dividend is already being realized as the military provides jobs during the period of economic transition. The numbers and types of military uniforms have multiplied during the last year, in part related to the beginnings of a national Latvian army and in part to provide transitional jobs.

Financial Institutions

Comprehensive financial institutions have been slower to develop than many Latvians anticipated. One reason lies in lack of trust in banks because many older Latvians have personally lost their savings and other deposits in banks several times in recent years, lastly through rampant inflation. Few Latvians trust banks. Western currencies are overvalued on Latvian currency exchanges.

In the absence of a normal banking system, a robust cash economy has emerged. Almost all transactions, including payrolls, are in cash. Western currencies are used as hedges against the devaluation of the Latvian ruble. Goods and weak currencies are easily and legally converted to Western currencies which are stored in private safes and strong boxes. Large volumes of Western currency circulate in Latvia to facilitate these transactions.

One of the most visible and thriving new financial institutions is the currency exchange companies. A remarkable number and variety of locations have mushroomed in Riga—in a corner of a retail store, a camper van parked in a square or on the sidewalk, in kiosks and hotels. The spread between buying and selling is around 5 percent of the total value of each transaction.

Other vested interests in keeping this cash economy have emerged. Chief among them may be the newly created small retailers. With cash transactions and almost no accounting standards, these businesses systematically do not report their tax obligations. Illegal transactions also escape taxation.

Clear Legislation on Property Rights

Many important policies relating to property ownership and other financial relationships are still being formulated. Sufficient legislation has been passed, in most cases, to begin an orderly process of privatization. Land claims for return of nationalized rural properties were due at the end of 1992.

There are still complicating issues. Chronic shortages of apartments and buildings were in large part related to the unrealistically high Soviet subsidies for rent. Very little replacement housing has been constructed in recent years. When pre-1940 owners present themselves to claim buildings which were or have been converted to apartments, it is proving impossible as a practical matter to find alternative housing for present tenants. Private ownership becomes a charade—that is, the privilege to pay high property taxes and be responsible for maintenance but with no opportunity to collect rents which will cover costs. It is often not even possible for the owner to occupy one of the apartments.

Foreign Ownership

Foreign ownership of major corporations and highly visible properties have traditionally been politically sensitive in the Nordic countries. Finland, for instance, is just now considering major reforms in its laws relating to foreign ownership as part of its effort to attract international investors. Latvian legislation appears to be leaning toward allowing long-term leases of land.

Enforcing of Contracts

Recent Latvian experience in observing the terms of contracts was influenced by Soviet practices in which political connections had more influence on the observance of a contract than its terms. Fortunately, the Latvian legal system is adjusting to Western expectations, drawing on experience during independence and on new legislation.

Safety of Persons and Property

Latvia is in the midst of a substantial social and economic transition. Citizens speak of more petty crimes, burglaries, and family violence than they experienced five years ago. Even so, levels of violence against persons and the safety of property are lower than in parts of many American cities.

A Convertible Currency

The Latvian ruble is a transitional currency. It is fully and easily convertible, within Latvia, for Western currencies. Latvian policy is fully committed to developing a stable and internationally convertible currency at the earliest opportunity.

SOCIAL AND CULTURAL FACTORS

It is probably true that Latvia's rich cultural traditions pulled it through the Soviet and the many previous occupations. The collective memory of what it means to be Latvian is kept alive through the festivals, literature, music, poetry, and folk songs. Most of these traditions will be instrumental as Latvia develops a strong and attractive democracy. In fact, it could be argued that these traditions will be the most important factors supporting a successful social and economic transition. But Latvians did not escape the Soviet occupation without some lasting negative effects on their culture and social attitudes which will slow the emergence of a market economy. In this section, we discuss some of the more obvious cultural and social factors which will affect privatization.

Educational Infrastructure

Latvians are well educated. Most communities have several excellent elementary and secondary schools. All of the larger cities have access to a university of some sort. Further, since the mid-1990s, these educational institutions have moved quickly to adopt Western curricula and pedagogical techniques, gradually discarding Soviet practices.

Looking West

Given their choice, Latvians look West, not East, for cultural models. German crusaders colonized Riga in the thirteenth century. Since that time, Swedish, Polish, Lithuanian, and Russian princes have shared with Germans in government, languages, legal codes, commercial practices, philosophies, literature, and music. Although English was not as widely spoken prior to 1940, Latvians recognize its importance in world business and science. Large numbers of Latvians are studying English, German, and French.

Remembering Russian

Almost every Latvian can speak and read Russian. It was the official language of government throughout the Soviet occupation and still serves as the common language when citizens of the former Soviet republics and satellites meet. This widespread ability to speak and read Russian will serve Latvians well if they reassert Riga's historical position as the trading center between West Europe and East Europe. Very few Westerns speak or read Russian, and they will welcome empathetic facilitators as they develop commerce with the large countries which once comprised the Soviet Union.

Leadership, Elite Deficit

Perhaps one of the more serious problems faced by Latvians is the absence of independent, experienced political, intellectual, and entrepreneurial elites. It would be difficult to overstate the impact on Latvia's leadership elites of the ruthless policies of Stalin and Hitler. Beginning in June 1940, hundreds of Latvian political, cultural, and business leaders were rounded up and deported by the KGB. Hitler's Gestapo continued with even more brutal policies of imprisonment and execution, adding Jews, Poles, and Russians as ethnic groups to their lists of Latvian political and intellectual leaders. The reoccupation of Latvia by the Soviets in 1944 allowed the KGB to resume their policies of deporting an entire generation of Latvian leaders of all ranks.

The only avenue Latvians could choose to exercise leadership and gain experience was through the Communist Party. With independence, literally thousands of positions requiring leaders with political and administrative experience must be filled. The number of experienced Latvians who are not compromised in some way by earlier service to the Communists is very small.

Economics, the Unknown Science

It is an ironic twist of history that the citizens of Riga lack understanding of the basic concepts and attitudes intrinsic to a market system. Riga was one of the early Hansa trading cities with its traders and entrepreneurs leaders in European commerce since the thirteenth century. But the generation of Latvians who have grown to maturity in 50 years of Soviet occupation have almost no knowledge of such key concepts as opportunity cost, profit, supply, demand, and subsidy. There is an almost total absence of modern accounting, finance, and marketing. Whole branches of business activity are dismissed as illegitimate or unproductive. Wholesaling and the sourcing of goods appear to most Latvians to be the same thing as illegally hoarded scarce goods for later sale at exorbitant prices. Providing business and financial services as traders, bankers, and accountants—activities at the center of Riga's economy as a Hansa city—are viewed as intrinsically inferior to manufacturing. These attitudes will slow privatization and investment.

Latvians have little recent experience in setting up new business enterprises. They do not recognize opportunities which may be developed into legitimate businesses. When they do, they have no experience in mobilizing the capital to realize the potential that is there.

Blighted by Illegal Markets

The final years of the Soviet system were especially blighted by large numbers of black markets and organized crime. A growing list of goods and services necessary for daily life were available to citizens only through black markets or other illegal channels. Even though citizens became cynical about their constant law breaking, they still believed they were acting normally. The psychological result seems to be a toleration of illegal activity and confusion between what are legitimate business activities in market democracies and what are criminal activities. Many stolen goods are openly circulating in Latvia with respectable citizens buying them. Business does not have a good name in Latvia. The litmus test on this attitude, perhaps, is that we talked with no parent who hoped his or her child would become a business person.

Chronic Shortages

The Soviet system, rooted in the Gosplan, was always characterized by chronic shortages. Long lines for bread, gasoline, clothes, and meat were a way of life. From the viewpoint of the enterprises, there were always more customers than they could or wanted to serve.

In general, the Soviet system of low prices, quotas, and haphazardly distributed raw materials led to a situation where many resources were persistently underutilized, workers became accustomed to a stop and start pace at work. There were too many empty tables and idle waiters in restaurants, too many idle production lines and workers waiting for raw materials in factories, too many clerks standing next to empty shelves in stores. Productivity was low.

Marketing: A New Force

To a large degree, Latvian distribution is still operating on the Soviet model, best characterized as bureaucratic, top heavy, and monopolistic. It performs best in allocating tangible goods. This system is currently undermined by farm corporations selling directly to consumers through their emerging systems of stores. Lacking Western business education, good examples, and relevant experience, the breakup of the old system is slow. It is accelerated by the *nouveau riche* economy. Although this sector is much distrusted by the Latvian population, a new class of affluent traders is supporting new marketing forces and provides appropriate examples and experience. Thus, a Nina Ricci perfume shop stresses impeccable, high quality service to customers. New Western car dealerships even offer very well paid employment to mechanics and service personnel as a trickle down benefit. Office equipment suppliers, such as Rank-Xerox, meticulously follow tested global strategies to build market share with adequate inventories, quick service, and lovely advertising. These market forces are further supported by services catering to Western tourists with special hotel sections and restaurants. Lastly, Western business knowledge is injected into the Latvian economy through the Riga Business School (taught exclusively by Western staff), other training organizations, and the business press (in particular, the *Dienas Bizness*, a joint Latvian-Swedish newspaper venture).

Lack of Initiative

One of the most pernicious effects of a totalitarian system is that it penalizes individual initiative. No one will take responsibility for anything beyond their narrowly defined job.

This attitude contributes to some paradoxical situations. At a series of meetings we attended, all participants agreed the enterprise was failing. An easy consensus emerged that the survival of the enterprise depended on finding personnel to perform a list of essential new tasks. They also discussed, under a slightly different context, a number of personnel at risk of losing their jobs because their tasks were not needed. But they could not solve the problem of finding the people to assign to the vital new jobs. After the meeting adjourned, the participants walked out wringing their hands, deeply worried and wondering what to do. They walked down the hall, dodged physical evidence of essential work left undone, and stepped around workers who were doing nothing or were engaged in low priority activities. Habits of looking only at their assigned duties were so deeply ingrained, however, that administrators and supervisors did not feel an obligation to take personal initiative.

PATIENCE, PATIENCE: A SUMMARY

Although there is abundant evidence that Latvia is making a successful transition to a market democracy, it is unrealistic to expect a rapid privatization of major properties. There is a worldwide glut of real estate on the market. Properties in Latvia are in relatively poor condition. Listings of the real estate are incomplete and inadequate. Legislation governing the transfer of titles is new and untested. Most important, the buyers—most interested Latvian residents—have neither the funds nor the credit to close the deals. And finally, with international investors less able to buy because of the worldwide recession, profiteers from the black market and organized crime are among the few remaining groups in the market for Latvian property.

In the meantime, conditions and institutions to support extensive privatization are improving. Despite many dire predictions, it appears there will be sufficient food and shelter this winter. Also, the university system has responded by expanding enrollments, reforming curricula, and offering specialized, very practical, courses to working executives in government and enterprises.

There is a sense of entrepreneurism in Riga reminiscent of the Hansa city it once was. There are lively discussions and actions on Riga's strategic location as the hub for trade between Western Europe and Russia. The infrastructure for business services and tourism is burgeoning. New shops, refurbished hotels, and new and revitalized restaurants are springing up. The heart of Riga, Old Town, is remodeling and restoring at what would have been an unbelievable pace just 12 months ago. Latvians are learning English, German, and Swedish to supplement their fluency in Russian so they can better serve a facilitating role between the business interests of East and West.

Even some of the more difficult problems seem closer to solution. Thousands of Russian troops remain in the Baltics, but it appears likely they will be ordered back to Russia before the end of 1993. The Latvian ruble, introduced as an intermediate currency between the Russian ruble and the Latvian lat, has been more successful than anticipated. And the pieces of an effective financial system are coming together, slowly but steadily. Additional banking services are added almost monthly.

The government is relatively stable, given the magnitude of the tasks they face and the lack of experience this generation of Latvians has in self-government. But revenue collections are still too uncertain, too chaotic to inspire the confidence of citizens and international investors. There are still too few Latvians with administrative and leadership skills for all the new positions in politics and government, too few Latvians with experience in starting up new businesses.

ACKNOWLEDGMENTS

The authors acknowledge their debt to many Latvians who so graciously shared their time and insights. They are particularly indebted to James Kenney, Program Officer for the United States Information Agency in Latvia. This investigation was supported in part through a grant from the SEED Program of the USIA. All opinions and policies are our own and in no way reflect official positions of the United States government.

PART VI.

ACCOUNTING AND AUDITING

GOVERNMENT ACCOUNTING IN DEVELOPING COUNTRIES

Peter N. Dean

ABSTRACT

This paper presents a method of assessing the quality of government accounts using an index. The index reflects the timeliness and completeness of accounting data submitted by 135 countries to the International Monetary Fund in 1988. Variability of the index appears to be associated with differences in GNP per capita, the region in which a particular country is situated, and the rate of participation of its nationals in higher education. In Africa, it was also possible to analyze the data by the number of accountants per million of population and by the European language inherited from colonial times. Both factors appear to be associated with variations in the index. The article ends with a discussion of possible uses of an index of the quality of government accounts. These include easier identification of the stage of financial management development reached by particular countries, better understanding of their needs and therefore more realistic programs of financial management improvement, and better information on their credit-worthiness as borrowers.

Policy Studies and Developing Nations, Volume 3, pages 265-283.

ISBN: 1-55938-190-6

This chapter is in four parts. It starts with a brief discussion of government accounting, its components, and objectives. The second section deals with government financial management in a developing country environment. The third section proposes a method of differentiating countries, with respect to the development of their government accounting systems. A final section summarizes and concludes the discussion.

GOVERNMENT ACCOUNTING

It is convenient to start with a definition:

> Government accounting is the process of recording, analysing, classifying, summarizing, communicating and interpreting financial information about government in aggregate and in detail, reflecting all transactions involving the receipt, transfer and disposition of government funds and property (Oshisami and Dean 1984).

From such a definition, we can proceed to specify the components of a government accounting system. First, there is the accounting entity: the entity whose transactions are to be subject to accounting, which has to be defined. Second, comes a decision on which events and which aspects of these events are to be recognized in the accounting system. For instance, in a cash and commitment accounting system (the most typical form of government accounting system), expenditure is recognized both when it is committed and when it is paid in cash (or check), while tax revenue is recognized only when it is received in cash (or check). Commercial accounting has a different definition of the events to be recognized. For instance, some items such as depreciation are recognized even though no cash flow takes place at that time; while the liability in connection with money which is owed and the asset representing money which is to be received are always recognized in the form of payables and receivables (as they are in some government accounting systems, too). The decision on which events are to be recognized is known in the West as the choice of accounting policies or standards.[1]

Third, there must be a classification system. This sorts transactions into like compartments and allows them to be aggregated in suitable forms for reporting. This permits control, both budgetary and otherwise. Classification schemes for government accounts usually follow the Manual on Government Finance Statistics (International Monetary Fund 1986). Such schemes generally provide multiple layers of analysis: by economic characteristic, function, and program (and often by program constituent). However, the basic classification scheme is a hierarchical one based on budgetary and organizational responsibility (e.g., votes, sub-votes, heads, subheads, and line-items). Depending on the progress made with program budgeting, a program structure may appear in what we have termed the basic classification scheme. The latter is reflected in appropriation law and is common to government budgeting and accounting. It allows comparison between amounts budgeted and amounts spent or received. It thus provides for budgetary control and, in open systems of government, establishes a basis for public accountability. In some systems (notably the French), the subject of classification is subsumed under the title, Chart of Accounts.

The fourth essential element in a government accounting system is a means of identifying transactions so that they can pass through the classification scheme and be correctly allocated to the appropriate account. This is usually achieved by a coding scheme which records details such as the amount, the nature of the transaction, its date, the originating organizational unit, and all the other information required by the classification scheme. Fifth, the accounting system requires a set of internal controls. These are designed to regulate the quality of information passing through the system. They cover the procedures by which transactions are originated, checked, authorized, and recorded and are usually expressed with the help of an accounting manual and financial regulations.

Finally, the reporting and other parameters of the accounting system must be specified. These cover the content of various types of financial reports (e.g., reports of expenditure, budgetary variance, cash position, payables, etc.), the appropriate level of accuracy (which differs with different types of reports), the periodicity of reports (e.g., annual, quarterly, monthly, etc.), and their distribution. They also cover the regular measures taken to ensure the quality, accuracy, and reliability of the system (e.g., deadlines for the timeliness of reports and for various types of check and reconciliation which have to be carried out regularly to prove the reliability of the system).

Having defined the accounting system and described its major components, we are in a position to consider its purposes. It is often stated that the purpose of an accounting system is to provide relevant information to legitimate users who need that information for reaching informed (and therefore better) economic decisions. According to this formulation, having defined the needs of users, we can proceed to define the accounting system itself. A moment's thought reveals that this is a partial and even misleading point of view: anyone who had to work for an organization whose accounting system provided information but did not provide a pay check would understand why. Thus, the purposes of an accounting system are as follows:

a. To carry out the day-to-day business of the organization at a level of efficiency acceptable to its management and to those with which it conducts financial transactions (e.g., collection of debts, payment of wages, etc.).

b. To promote the financial well-being of the entity and to control its finances so that transactions entered into comply with authorizations and meet quality requirements set by management or others to deter negligence, theft, and corruption.
c. To provide relevant information to those within the organization needing to take financial management and resource management decisions (e.g., with regard to budgetary control, the management of debts, the management of liquidity, etc.).
d. To provide relevant information to those outside the organization, with a legitimate right of access to such information, for them to reach informed economic decisions, for example, relating to financial status and performance. In government, a large part of this objective concerns giving adequate evidence of accountability for the stewardship, control, and management of public resources.

GOVERNMENT FINANCIAL MANAGEMENT IN DEVELOPING COUNTRIES

Treatises are written on the meaning of development and on what constitutes a developing country. It would be inappropriate, here, to enter such discussions. Instead, we treat as developing those countries which the World Bank refers to as low and middle income economies. This is despite two facts: that the indicator which the bank uses for this purpose (gross national product per capita of population expressed in U.S. dollars) is subject to a number of well-known limitations and that some countries thus classified as developing have actually experienced reduced levels of GNP per capita in recent years.[2]

It is common to characterize the government accounts of developing countries as inadequate. For instance, in 1984 the U.S. General Accounting Office examined this issue in relation to U.S. aid programs and concluded that "poor accounting, budgeting and auditing capability in developing countries is eroding the performance of development programs" (p. 1). Holzer and Chandler, writing from an academic perspective about both the public and private sectors (1981), enumerated basic problems including "late closing of accounts (if indeed they are ever completed), poor internal control, absence of management accounting, incomplete and inaccurate records and unauditable systems." They judged these deficiencies "widespread throughout the third world" (p. 23). A paper submitted by the World Bank to a U.N. expert group meeting on the auditing of development programs in 1987 covered the compliance of its borrowers (many of whom are in the government sector) with the financial requirements of the bank. It concluded that "[a]nnual accounts and audit reports are frequently long-delayed and when produced, may be uninformative or even misleading. There is often failure to address, or even to recognize, the implication of basic deficiencies in the standards of accounting and auditing. The maintenance and improvement of accountability is therefore a continuing task in difficult circumstances" (World Bank 1987, p. 197). An IMF adviser, commenting in 1988 on the government financial reporting systems of developing countries, found that a large number were "inadequate for management purposes because they fail to provide policy makers with relevant information on a timely and regular basis" (Blöndal 1988, p. 12). A U.N. report in 1989 on the training of government accountants and auditors reported that "[n]o reliable comprehensive survey of government financial management in developing countries exists. Fragmentary evidence suggests that financial management is often defective" (United Nations 1989, p. 1). Finally, an inspector general, writing in 1991 on the experience of USAID, observed, "It is unfortunate but true that all too frequently, foreign aid progams, systems and projects are characterised by poor perfomance, poor accountability and poor results." Experts who have experience of several government accounting systems, seem to support these views.

If it is true, the picture sketched above is a disturbing one. However, the comments are very general, and one is bound to question their applicability to all developing countries. Surely, the quality of government accounts differs from country to country. One way to test for this would be to evaluate the accounting systems of different countries using a uniform approach. For this, we would need criteria for judging whether an accounting system is performing well. Textbooks provide such criteria. Accounting should be accurate and reliable, responsive and timely, verifiable in the sense, for instance, that transactions and their authorization and classification can be traced and confirmed, and relevant to the needs of those who use it. Such criteria can relate to any of the various components of the accounting system, as described previously. For instance, timeliness might relate to any of the following: to the initial recording of a transaction, to the completion of a transaction, to the carrying out of an accuracy test such as a reconciliation, or to the delivery of a financial report to an information user. Given that the quality of accounting can be judged according to several criteria and that the criteria may be applied to various components of an accounting system, the evaluation of accounting systems can be seen to be a complex task. Moreover, to apply such an approach to a large number of countries would be costly and time consuming. An alternative procedure is to evaluate government accounting systems on the basis of published data. Clearly, the resultant evaluation cannot be as thorough, but it is considerably more convenient and may have advantages from the point of view of uniformity of approach.

DIAGNOSING THE QUALITY OF GOVERNMENT ACCOUNTS

Research Procedure

Each year the International Monetary Fund (IMF) publishes its *Government Finance Statistics Yearbook*. The 1988 yearbook, on which the research is based, presents government finance statistics for 135 countries, most of them members of the IMF in that year. A first section comprising 115 pages presents comparative tables for all countries for which information is available, giving the major aggregates of government expenditure and revenue and their division by sector and type. A further 950 pages are devoted to detail for each country. In 1988, this section started with Argentina and concluded with Zimbabwe. For each country, the relevant statistics of government finance are presented according to uniform formats and definitions established by the IMF. The IMF operates a system of correspondents. One is located in the government or central bank of each member country. These correspondents are trained at annual training courses held in Washington to provide appropriate financial statistics in accordance with IMF requirements. In addition, staff members of the fund visit the countries from time to time to help overcome problems. Thus, the reliability of the data reported in the yearbook is the object of some effort.

Using this information, an index of quality of government accounts was created. It is composed of four separate indexes derived from the IMF yearbook. The first, an index of timeliness, was derived from the main comparative table in the first section of the yearbook titled, "Central Government Major Components." This table shows for each country the year for which its data were submitted. Thus in 1988, Canada submitted 1986 data while Seychelles submitted 1977 data. An index of timeliness was constructed with 1988 equal to 9, 1987 equal to 8, and so on down to zero (for 1979 and before). The second, an index of completeness of data, was derived from the country tables in the second section of the yearbook. As each country has to submit the same array of data in terms of content, format, and classification, the incidence of omissions and the length of a country's entry provide a good indicator of completeness. For each country, the main tables of the latest year for which data were submitted were examined for length in terms of pages of data submitted and completeness in terms of omitted data. From this examination, an index of completeness of data was ascribed to each country, varying between 9 (complete) and 0 (incomplete). To illustrate, the Congo presented four pages of data in 1988, from which almost all items were omitted. It was ascribed a score of 1. On the other hand, Austria provided almost six pages of data in which there were no omissions and was ascribed a score of 9. The third index was based on tables "D," "E," "F," and "G" in the country section of the yearbook. These tables relate to the financing of government debt at the central government consolidated level. They cover the type of debt holder (e.g., internal-external), the type of financing (e.g., short-long), the outstanding debt by type of holder, and the outstanding debt by type of debt instrument. It was assumed that countries with good accounting systems could complete these tables with ease and that those without could not. Therefore, the degree of completeness of the tables would be a good indicator of the quality of this aspect of government accounting. An index value varying between 0 and 9 was ascribed to each country on this basis. For instance Djibouti was ascribed an index score of zero, as the tables did not appear at all, whereas Finland which submitted a full page of data without omission was given a score of 6. Finally, a similar procedure was used to construct an index for table "L" in the country section of the yearbook. This relates to local government financial statistics. Again, the index varied between 0 and 9. To illustrate, Bangladesh had provided no information for this section since 1978 and was ascribed a score of zero. However, Canada submitted very complete data for 1986 and was given a score of 9.

On the basis of the four indexes described earlier, a single index of the quality of government accounts was formulated (Appendix A) which varied between 1 and 9. The procedure was to take the mean of a country's four scores. However, in that countries with small populations may not have highly significant layers of loçal government, countries with a population of less than 3.5 million were subject to a slightly different procedure. In these cases, the index based on local government accounts was omitted from the calculation of the main index, unless its inclusion would result in the same or a higher score on that index.

For instance, New Zealand with a recorded population of 3.3 million in 1988, had the following index scores:

1.	Timeliness	8
2.	Completeness	5
3.	Government Debt	7
4.	Local government	4

Its main index was calculated at 6.7 as a mean of the first three items only.

Findings

Before presenting the detailed findings, we need to consider the quality of the data and of the methods used.

First, is the information published by the IMF reliable? The IMF, as we have seen, has established detailed measures and a system of correspondents in each member country to ensure relevant and reliable information. The fact that it also publishes the information is reason to believe that it is of good quality. Also, we know that some information submitted to the IMF is not published because of doubts concerning its reliability. This leads us to believe that the data published are reasonably reliable. However, there is the possibility of a country submitting good data to the IMF when its accounting system and records are highly defective. Referring back to the discussion in the first section, we have said that an accounting system is composed of as many as six major components. The research considers only one component: what comes out of the accounting system in the form of financial statements. Precisely because unscrupulous managers may produce misleading financial statements, most legal systems require professionally qualified auditors to verify the financial statements of companies. In the present rather different context, governments may also be motivated to provide apparently good quality data even though their government accounting systems may be defective. The IMF tries to guard against this by checking the internal consistency of the data submitted by each country. However, the audit of the accounts is not performed by the IMF but by the government auditors of each country. We have reason to believe that these audits vary greatly in thoroughness.[3] Thus, in some cases the information published by the IMF may be unreliable in an accounting sense, and this is a limitation of the research.

Second, are the methods used to construct the index reliable and valid? In terms of reliability, the four components of the index were calculated by objective methods. If these were repeated by other researchers, they would arrive at very similar results. However, the composition of the index involved personal judgement. Another researcher might adopt a different approach to the elements which should figure in the main index and to its structure. This is clearly something to bear in mind when considering the reported findings.[4]

Table 1. Quality of Government Accounts (Index Score) by Countries' Geographical Region (135 countries)

Geographical region	*Number of countries*	*Number and percentage of countries with index score between 1 and 3*		*Number and percentage of countries with index score of 6 or more*	
		No.	*%*	*No.*	*%*
Africa	44	20	(45)	8	(18)
Middle East	10	4	(40)	2	(20)
Caribbean and Central America	22	8	(36)	5	(23)
Far East	16	5	(31)	7	(44)
South America	11	2	(18)	5	(45)
Pacific	6	1	(17)	3	(50)
Europe and North America	26	2	(8)	19	(73)
	135				

Appendix B presents the main findings of the research in five tables. The first three analyze variations in the index of quality of government accounts according to countries' geographical regions, GNP per capita, and percentage of the age group in higher education.[5] The final two tables relate only to Africa and present variations in the index with respect to English- versus French-speaking countries and with respect to the number of qualified accountants per million of population.[6]

Summarizing the main features of these tabulations:

1. The quality of government accounts, as revealed by the index, varies considerably between the major geographical regions of the world (Table B1). If we take the two extremes of the index, countries with poor quality of government accounts (index score 1-3) and those with good quality government accounts (index score 6 or more), we find an unbroken trend through the major regions of the world. Africa has the highest incidence of poor accounting and the lowest incidence of good accounting. The opposite is true of Europe and North America. The other regions of the world are distributed between these two extremes: The Middle East, the Caribbean, and Central America tending toward poorer accounting and South America and the Pacific toward better quality government accounting.
2. There is also a strong relationship between countries' GNP per capita and the quality of their government accounts (Table B2). For instance, of countries with the lowest GNP per capita (0-149 U.S. dollars), 69 percent have poor government accounts (index score 1-3), and only 8 percent have good government accounts (one country in this group has an index score of 6 or more). At the other end of the spectrum, of countries with GNP per capita of $10,000 (U.S.) and above, only 14 percent have poor government accounts whereas 76 percent have good government accounts (index score of 6 or more). The relationship between GNP and the quality of government accounts is apparent at all levels of GNP per capita: as income rises the incidence of poor government accounting falls and the incidence of good accounting rises.
3. The relationship between the quality of government accounts and the prevalence of higher education (represented by the percentage of the age group in higher education) is also reasonably strong (Table B3). For instance, of 34 countries with very low participation in higher education (i.e., 0-2% of the relevant age groups in higher education), 50 percent had low index scores (1-3), and only 21 percent had high scores (6 and above). However, for countries with 30 percent or more of the relevant age group in higher education, only one country (6% of the group) had a low index score while 14 (88% of the group) had high index scores.

4. It was possible to assign 38 countries in Africa to either the French or English language speaking group. Among the English-speaking group, 25 percent of countries received low index scores (1-3), and 25 percent of countries, high index scores (6 and above). However, the picture for French-speaking countries was different: 64 percent had low scores and only 5 percent high scores (Table B4).
5. For 39 countries in Africa, information was available on the number of qualified accountants per million of population. Table B5 shows that there is a tendency for those with small numbers of qualified accountants to achieve low index scores. Those with larger numbers achieve better scores.

We can summarize the findings as follows: on average, countries in Africa, the Middle East, and the Caribbean/Central America) tend to have relatively poor government accounts, while countries in Europe/North America, the Pacific and South America tend to have relatively good government accounts. Also, the level of a country's national income per head and the percentage of the age group in higher education, appear to be strongly associated with the quality of its government accounts. In Africa, the legacy of colonial language and the number of accountants per million of population are both related strongly to the quality of government accounts.

DISCUSSION, SUMMARY, AND CONCLUSION

In this last section, we turn to the potential significance of the findings and their possible uses. We now discuss these under four headings.

Table 2. Quality of Government Accounts (Index Score) Analyzed by Countries' GNP Per Capita (130 countries)

GNP per capita in US Dollars	*Number of countries*	*Number and percentage of countries with index score between 1 and 3*		*Number and percentage of countries with index score of 6 or more*	
		No.	*%*	*No.*	*%*
0 - 149	13	9	(69)	1	(8)
250 - 499	27	11	(41)	7	(26)
500 - 999	21	7	(33)	5	(24)
1,000 - 1999	23	8	(35)	7	(30)
2,000 - 2999	10	2	(20)	4	(40)
3,000 - 5999	8	-	(-)	4	(50)
6,000 - 9999	7	-	(-)	5	(71)
10,000 +	21	3	(14)	16	(76)
	130				

Table 3. Quality of Government Accounts (Index Score) by Countries' Percent of Age Group in Higher Education (105 countries)

Percentage of age group in higher education	*Number of countries*	*Number and percentage of countries with index score between 1 and 3*		*Number and percentage of countries with index score of 6 or more*	
		No.	*%*	*No.*	*%*
0 - 2	34	17	(50)	7	(21)
3 - 4	9	4	(44)	2	(22)
5 - 9	13	4	(31)	2	(15)
10 - 14	7	2	(29)	2	(29)
15 - 19	10	4	(40)	2	(20)
20 - 24	7	-	(-)	4	(57)
25 - 29	9	2	(22)	6	(67)
30 +	16	1	(6)	14	(88)
	105				

More Informed Discussion

The equation, poor countries:poor accounting, is frequently expressed. The present study establishes a positive relationship between GNP per capita and an index of quality of government accounts (correlation coefficient, 0.51), and this gives some support for this approach. However, the level of the coefficient implies that some richer countries have relatively poor government accounts and vice versa, and this is clearly apparent from an examination of Appendix A. Better facts about the quality of government accounts in different countries should improve analysis and discussion. In the field of government accounting, countries which are classified as developing, but which have good government accounts, may have more in common with many developed countries than had previously been realized. On the other hand, countries classified as developed, but with poor government accounts, may have more in common with many developing countries. Realizing this might help to modify the content of articles, reports, training courses, seminars, and long-held assumptions concerning government financial management in developing countries.

Evaluating Government Credit-Worthiness

Clearly, the results may have some relevance to the evaluation of credit-worthiness. Many governments of developing countries have been heavy borrowers, and this has led to what has been termed the debt crisis. Within market economies, major borrowers are assessed by specialist evaluators who ascribe them appropriate credit-worthiness status. The status ascribed, which is publicly available in tabular form, helps to determine the availability, price, and other terms of credit that may be offered. Arguably, better government

Table 4. Quality of Government Accounts (Index Score) Analyzed by French-Speaking and English-Speaking Countries in Africa (38 countries only)

Country category	*Number of countries*	*Number and percentage of countries with index score between 1 and 3*		*Number and percentage of countries with index score of 6 or more*	
		No.	*%*	*No.*	*%*
English-speaking	16	4	(25)	4	(25)
French-speaking	22	14	(64)	1	(5)
	38				

accounting information would make credit-worthiness assessment more precise and meaningful. This would apply to the quality and content of the general accounting statements of government and to the accounts specifically concerned with government debt (component three of the index). The assessment of credit-worthiness of corporations is significantly concerned with the quality and meaning of their accounts. Perhaps assessments of the credit-worthiness of sovereign states could with advantage be similarly focused. Many developing country governments would then be seen to be very bad risks. Inability to obtain credit would provide a strong stimulus for improved accountability. On the other hand, by continuing to provide credit to borrowers who have no intention of providing proper accountability, lenders not only expose themselves to undue risk but undermine the possibilities of real progress in financial management of the host countries concerned.

Host Country Accountability

Recently, two large donor/lenders have introduced innovations in the field of aid accountability: the World Bank increasingly makes use of revolving

Table 5. Quality of Government Accounts (Index Score) Analysed by Countries Qualified Accountants per Million of Population in Africa (39 countries only)

Qualified accountants per million of population	*Number of countries*	*Number and percentage of countries with index score between 1 and 3*		*Number and percentage of countries with index score of 6 or more*	
		No.	*%*	*No.*	*%*
0 - 4	22	14	(64)	3	(14)
5 - 9	11	4	(36)	2	(18)
10 - 14	2	-	(-)	-	(-)
15 - 19	4	1	(25)	2	(50)
	39				

funds and statements of expenditure and the United Nations Development Programme (UNDP) has introduced the National Execution modality (NEX). Both of these new regimes imply more responsibility for host countries and more accountability from them. Under the statement of expenditure process, statements of eligible expenditure are compiled in the host country and sent without full accompanying documentation to the World Bank for reimbursement. Reimbursement is made immediately. Proofs of eligibility are verified later. The procedure improves cash flow to countries badly in need of resources. It also exposes the bank to risks associated with poor accountability. The NEX modality of UNDP transfers many responsibilities traditionally undertaken by U.N. executing agencies to host country institutions. The objective is to increase host country involvement in its own aid programs and to improve the capacity to be so involved. Besides these positive aspects, it also exposes UNDP to possible accountability risks because NEX transfers to host countries responsibility for accounting for UNDP funds.

The present research is of relevance to initiatives of this sort. A precondition of all international assistance, even that given under emergency conditions, is diagnosis of the host country's capacity to absorb it. Under normal conditions, the capacity to absorb assistance includes the capacity to account for it, for without accountability there are no proper reassurances concerning the actual use of the resources supplied. Under these circumstances, procedures which impose greater accountability duties on host countries must be related to the capacity of these countries to respond. Put simply, this means that governments with very low financial management capacity (in this study, this would correspond with an index score of 3 or less) need fundamentally different reform strategies and assistance from those who have much better financial management capacity (those with an index score of 6 or more). Generally, less would be asked because less can be expected from those with limited capacity. Also, it can be assumed that increasing the accountability responsibilities of those least equipped to discharge them is unlikely to succeed even if government commitment and technical assistance were sufficiently sustained to confront the obvious difficulties. In summary, funding agencies which do not base accountability expectations on accountability capacities are likely to experience accountability failures, which will be damaging to them if made public. In this context, an index of the quality of government accounts could be useful because it would allow donors and lenders to tailor accountability regimes to host countries capacities.

Selecting Reform Strategies

Where government accounting is unsatisfactory or very unsatisfactory, as it seems to be in many but not all developing countries, the question of reform is of interest. The diagnosis of needs must precede prescription. However,

APPENDIX A

Index of the quality of Government Accounts

Country	*Index Score*	*Country*	*Index Score*
Argentina	6.2	Ghana	4.5
Australia	7.2	Greece	6.0
Austria	8.5	Grenada	1.7
Bahamas	5.3	Guatemala	5.2
Bahrain	5.3	Guinea	1.2
Bangladesh	2.7	Guinea Bissau	2.7
Barbados	5.3	Guyana	4.3
Belgium	7.2	Haiti	1.7
Belize	3.0	Hőnduras	1.7
Bhutan	3.3	Hungary	7.7
Bolivia	4.5	Iceland	7.3
Botswana	6.3	India	6.5
Brazil	6.7	Indonesia	7.0
Burkina Faso	2.5	Iran	5.2
Burma	2.2	Ireland	4.2
Burundi	2.5	Israel	7.5
Cameroon	4.5	Italy	6.2
Canada	8.0	Jamaica	2.0
Cayman Islands	5.7	Japan	3.7
Central African Republic	3.0	Jordan	4.2
Chad	3.5	Kenya	6.2
Chile	6.2	Korea	5.7
Colombia	5.2	Kuwait	3.7
Comoros	4.0	Lesotho	4.7
Congo	2.0	Liberia	7.0
Costa Rica	6.0	Luxembourg	8.6
Côte d'Ivoire	3.0	Madagascar	2.0
Cyprus	7.7	Malawi	4.7
Denmark	6.2	Malaysia	5.5
Djibouti	3.7	Maldives	6.0
Dominica	0.7	Mali	4.2
Dominican Republic	6.2	Malta	7.0
Ecuador	1.7	Mauritania	2.0
El Salvador	3.7	Mauritius	7.7
Ethiopia	6.0	Mexico	5.7
Fiji	6.3	Morocco	5.0
Finland	7.2	Nepal	3.7
France	7.5	Netherlands	7.7
Gabon	4.3	Netherlands Antilles	7.7
Gambia	7.0	New Zealand	6.7
Germany, West	8.7	Nicaragua	5.3
Niger	1.7	Turkey	4.0
Nigeria	3.2	Uganda	5.0
Norway	6.5	United Arab Emirates	2.0

(*continued*)

Appendix A. *(Continued)*

Country	Index Score	Country	Index Score
Oman	8.3	United Kingdom	7.7
Pakistan	4.7	United States of America	8.2
Panama	8.3	Uruguay	7.0
Papua New Guinea	4.7	Vanuatu	5.3
Paraguay	6.0	Venezuela	5.2
Peru	1.0	Western Samoa	2.7
Philippines	6.7	Yemen Arab Republic	3.7
Poland	4.7	Yugoslavia	6.7
Portugal	2.2	Zaire	3.5
Romania	4.5	Zambia	3.7
Rwanda	3.0	Zimbabwe	5.7
St. Kitts Nevis	2.7		
St. Lucia	2.7		
St. Vincent	4.0		
Senegal	4.0		
Seychelles	3.7		
Sierra Leone	4.2		
Singapore	6.7		
Solomon Islands	5.3		
Somalia	1.2		
South Africa	7.5		
Spain	7.7		
Sri Lanka	5.7		
Sudan	3.0		
Suriname	5.7		
Swaziland	8.7		
Sweden	8.0		
Switzerland	5.5		
Syria	2.2		
Tanzania	1.7		
Thailand	7.2		
Togo	6.0		
Trinidad and Tobago	5.3		
Tunisia	5.7		

while the need for change is often apparent, the direction which change needs to take is less so. In other words, prescription concerns planning appropriate changes in an appropriate order. Is there an appropriate order for improving government financial management? At the descriptive level, Schick (1966) discerned three stages of budget reform in the United States:

The present author has proposed an evolutionary theory of government financial management based on three stages: regularity and control, financial management, and strategic choice (Dean 1988). This is meant to be more than a descriptive theory, in that it is argued that substantial performance at one stage is a precondition of successful performance at a subsequent stage.

Stage	*Date*	*Characteristics*
Control of Expenditure	1920-1935	Line itemization and functional classification of expenditure. Control by appropriation process.
Management Orientation	1935-1960	Cost accounting, performance budgeting, and evaluation.
Planning Orientation	1960-	Economic techniques used in budgeting; new decision and information technologies; integrating planning and budgeting.

The approach is based on that of Schick (1966) and is consistent with that of Caiden (1980). In the latter work, the author asks: "How can we frame realistic budget advice, which those concerned with budgeting in poor countries, will be both willing and able to follow?" In answer, the author suggests first, a comparative typology of countries (one which would identify groups of countries with similar government budgeting traditions); second, reform efforts which are not simply carbon copies of those used elsewhere but which reflect the different circumstances of the countries concerned; and third, methods for evaluating the government budget performance of different countries. Bearing in mind that government budgeting and government accounting are very closely related, the work presented in Section 3 of this chapter responds either directly or indirectly to all of these points. Moreover, the index scores for quality of government accounts indicate very roughly a country's stage of development in government financial management. For instance, in the author's opinion, those scoring 3 or less are at a very early stage of development. The accounting information which they produce is inadequate, and if financial management reform were contemplated, it would have to start here: that is to say with improvement of the basics of the government accounting system, for it is difficult to see in these cases how any financial management aspect (such as auditing or budgeting) could be improved without first improving accounting.

Summarizing, an evolutionary theory regarding the development of government financial systems coupled with indicators of financial management performance (of which an index of quality of government accounts might be one) would offer several possibilities:

a. Less ambiguous information than is currently available on governments' financial management capacities. This would lead to better diagnosis of their needs for reform.
b. A framework in which the development of financial management systems could be better understood, the necessary order of reforms more easily specified, and the relative development of different countries more accurately gauged.

c. Programs of reform which would correspond more closely to the abilities of countries to profit from them, leading to improved chances of successful reforms.

It is preferable to travel hopefully, even if the destination (good government financial management) is distant and difficult to attain. On the constructive side, now that we have a human development index (see United Nations Development Programme 1991 which provides a human development index) perhaps it is time to construct an index of absorptive capacity. This would tell us about the likely chances of successful development in different environments. Its major use would be to indicate the capacity of different countries to absorb and benefit from outside assistance. In such an aggregate index, an index of the quality of government accounts would be a useful constituent. In the meantime, such an index would be useful in its own right in any of the four contexts discussed at the beginning of this section. The first step is to confirm or improve on the methodology. If as a result a widely acceptable index were to emerge, it might become an important criterion for deciding on external assistance. Countries with good government accounts would attract credit and assistance at lower cost and in more flexible forms than countries with inadequate government accounts because the former would present smaller financial risks. The latter would then have a strong incentive to improve their accounts, and their donors and lenders would have a similar incentive to help them.

ACKNOWLEDGMENTS

While responsibility for the contents and conclusions of the chapter is the author's alone, help is ackowledged as follows: for statistical analysis, Salvatore Favazza (formerly of UNDESD) and for advice on the text, Clay Wescott (UNDP); Cheryl Larsen (UNDESD) and Jonathan Levin (IMF).

NOTES

1. Several countries have adopted or are considering the adoption of government accounting standards which go further than what we have referred to as the typical form. For instance, in 1991 the U.S. Federal Accounting Standards Advisory Board published an exposure draft on accounting for financial resources, funded liabilities, and net financial resources. It concerns items such as accounts receivable, interest receivable, advances and prepayments, investments, accounts payable, interest payable, and funded liabilities. A system based purely on cash and commitment principles would not be able to record these items.
2. Summers (1992), using data from the World Bank Development Report, lists 36 developing countries whose GNP per capita was lower in real terms in 1989 than it was in 1965.

3. The evidence for this assertion is as follows: government audit standards differ widely from country to country, so do the professional capacity and independence of supreme audit institutions. The variations are great enough sometimes for bodies such as the World Bank and Inter American Development Bank to insist on private sector auditors, rather than the supreme audit insitution of the host country, auditing projects which they have funded.

4. When considering the index score ascribed to 135 countries in Appendix A, the reader should also bear in mind that people close to the material have given their opinion on the scores. While in 10 percent to 15 percent of cases they felt a particular score was either too high or too low, their general feeling was that the scores broadly reflected the quality of government accounting in the countries concerned.

5. Details of geographical region, GNP per capita, and percent of the age group in higher education were taken from the World Bank (1989).

6. Estimates for Africa of the number of qualified accountants per million of population were taken from the International Labour Office (1987).

REFERENCES

Blöndal, G. 1988. "Government Financial Reporting Systems in LDCs." *Finance and Development* (September).

Caiden, N. 1980. "Budgeting in Poor Countries: Ten Assumptions Re-Examined." *Public Administration Review* (January/February).

Dean, P.N. 1988. "Government Financial Management Systems in Developing Countries." Pp. 000-000 in *Governmental Accounting and Auditing: International Comparisons*, edited by J.L. Chan and R.H. Jones. New York: Routledge.

Durnil, J.B. 1990. "Accountability and Audit of U.S. Foreign Economic Programs." Paper presented at the expert group meeting on accounting and auditing of aid programs, Vienna, INTOSAI/UNDTCD.

Federal Accounting Standards Advisory Board. 1991. *Financial resources, Funded Liabilities and Net Financial Resources of Federal entities.* Washington, DC: Author.

Holzer, H.P., and J.S. Chandler. 1981. "A Systems Approach to Accounting in Developing Countries." *Management International Review* 21(IV): 23-32.

International Labour Office. 1987. "Dynamics of Accounting Development in Africa." Discussion paper by Management Development Branch, Geneva.

International Monetary Fund. 1986. *A Manual on Government Finance Statistics.* Washington, DC: Author.

International Monetary Fund. 1988. *Government Finance Statistics Yearbook.* Washington, DC: Author.

Oshisami, K., and P.N Dean. 1984. *Financial Management in the Nigerian Public Sector.* London: Pitman.

Price Waterhouse. 1987. "Improving Host Country Financial Management." Report submitted to the U.S. Agency for International Development, Washington, DC.

Schick, A. 1966. "The Road to PPB: The Stages of Budget Rreform." *Public Administration Review* (December).

Summers, L.H. 1992. "The Challenges of Development." *Finance and Development* (March).

United Nations. 1988. *Audit of Major Development Programmes.* New York: Department of Technical Cooperation for Development TCD/SEM.87/1.

United Nations. 1989. *Training of Government Accountants and Auditors.* New York: Department of Technical Cooperation for Development ST/TCD/SER.E/9.

United Nations. 1991. *Accountancy development in Africa.* New York: United Nations Centre on Transnational Corporations.

United Nations Development Programme. 1991. *Human Development Report.* New York: Oxford University Press.

U.S. General Accounting Office. 1979. "Training and Related Efforts Needed to Improve Financial Management in the Third World." GAO ID-79-46, Washington, DC.

U.S. General Accounting Office. 1984. "Financial Management Problems in Developing Countries Reduce the Impact of Assistance." GAO/NSIAD-85-19, Washington, DC.

World Bank. 1989. *World Bank Development Report.* Washington, DC: Author.

AUDITING IN AFRICA:
SOME UNMET NEEDS

Richard E. Zody

ABSTRACT

This article discusses efforts at addressing problems with finances, auditing, and public management in African nations. The problems identified (corruption, mismanagement, and errors resulting from lack of educational or technological opportunities), are linked to problems in government and other institutions in these nations. The lack of viable democracies and the imposition of inappropriate donor standards are identified as possible roots of these problems. The article also discusses possible solutions to these problems, notably how African financial accountability needs to include management and program auditing.

The problems associated with finances and public management in African nations are well-known, but the efforts aimed at addressing these problems have been limited. A few years ago, a World Bank Economic Development Institute (EDI) seminar was held in Nairobi on the relationships of financial

Policy Studies and Developing Nations, Volume 3, pages 285-292.

ISBN: 1-55938-190-6

systems and development in Africa (Callier 1991). Despite its obvious awareness of the problems of mismanagement, corruption, lack of accountability, and political influence which characterize the operations of many African governments, little recognition appeared to be given to the role of auditing in assuring proper financial, managerial, and programmatic accountability. While these considerations were perhaps outside the scope of this particular seminar, it does not justify a continuing inattention to problems of accountability in Africa by donors and the nations themselves. This omission is, unfortunately, not atypical in considering financial systems and effective management in developing areas (a noteworthy exception may be found in efforts underway in Latin America and the Caribbean; see, e.g., Price Waterhouse 1992).

Although this author's exposure to Africa has been limited to only seven relatively short stays (primarily in Kenya and Nigeria) in the past decade, each visit served as a reminder that auditing plays a limited and severely constrained role in its financial management systems. Working with staff training colleges and institutes, teaching in their programs, and interacting formally and informally with students from all levels of government revealed a common perspective of auditing, one limited to, at best, compliance or fiduciary audits undertaken in an environment frequently nonsupportive of audit integrity or in circumstances which often failed to meet even basic auditing information needs.

At times, this author recalled his studies of American government corruption in the late nineteenth century through the mid-twentieth century, his experiences with machine politics American-style, and thought of the similarities to contemporary developing nations (he later found many parallels to his experiences in Klittgaard 1990). He was surprised at the candor of the many financial managers he worked with. They were free in their discussions of the problems noted previously and commonly lamented the lack of "good government." When asked what were the most important problems facing governments in their country, government financial managers, for example, consistently put corruption at the top of the list. Not always implicitly, they would put their valuation in the context of a political structure that was governed by the military or one political party. This writer believes that the characterization is more basic: in much of Africa, there are few governments with truly independent branches of government. If America's struggles to present the best of democraticization are any indicator, then truly independent branches of government are critical to assuring governmental integrity.

Documentation of the legendary lack of governmental integrity in Africa is more difficult than it is in many other areas, but it does occur (see, e.g., *Africa* 1990, p. 10191, 1991b, p. 10554, 1991c, 10515; a number of governments froze or eliminated their aid to Kenya in 1991 due to "widespread corruption and mismanagement"). Recently, for example, another in a series of scandals was exposed in Kenya. The popular press labeled it the "Goldenberg Scandal." In this particular case, it is alleged that, with the collusion and participation of high level government officials, an individual was able to manipulate the government's export subsidization policies (Export Retention Scheme) to realize a gain estimated at more than 2 billion Kenyan shillings from exporting Kenyan gold and diamonds (there are no diamond mines in Kenya and modest gold deposits). The fraud unraveled in 1993 when an auditor in the Central Bank began raising questions about paperwork discrepancies.[1]

Visitors to Nigeria are often impressed by the large number of government buildings started but never finished or left unused. Inquiries reveal that it is common practice for capital project funds to be expended with no verification that project work was completed as specified. One must be suspect when it is reported that the government is building (for over a decade now) arguably the world's most expensive steel mill, one which is still not fully operational (*Africa* 1990).[2] Even greater suspicion is created when the same government has a history of violating commitments to donors, for example, by expending oil-pricing windfall revenues for purposes outside of financial agreements (*Africa* 1991a).[3]

These repeated illustrations point to a pervasive need for more than just fiduciary or compliance accountability without reducing the importance of effective fiduciary or compliance auditing (as illustrated by the "Goldenberg Scandal"). The illustrations also suggest that the full value of such simple accountability in developing nations needs to be reassessed.

The basic purpose of auditing was well-stated by the Comptroller General of the United States:

> A fundamental tenet of a democratic society holds that governments and agencies entrusted with public resources and the authority for applying them have a responsibility to render a full accounting of their activities. This accounting is inherent in the governmental process and is not always specifically identified by legislative provision. This governmental accountability should identify not only the objects for which the public resources have been devoted but also the manner and effect of their application (Comptroller General of the United States 1974, pp. 1-2, cited in Herbert, Killough, and Steiss 1985, p. 5).

While this purpose is essential to viable democracies, it was not written with a developing country with a less than viable democracy in mind. It is a critical distinction.

Donors tend to expect and impose their accounting standards on recipients without regard to their realistic feasibility or the necessary infrastructure. For example, by encouraging fiduciary and compliance standards similar to those of a developed nation, donors may be adding undue costs upon the recipient.

Typically, recipients have neither the trained staff, technology, or information systems necessary to support such standards in a cost-effective manner. As a consequence, it is not uncommon to find significant numbers of accountants, chartered and unchartered, attempting to keep books by the recommended standards (e.g., through pre-audit controls) in a manual environment of hand-written ledgers.

Apart from issues of corruption and mismanagement, errors are more than likely, frequently because the workers have not been advantaged by a developed nation's educational system or technology. Since many of these environments arose out of a colonial tradition, there is a heavy emphasis on exactness. Thus, coupled with a highly centralized system and dependency on poorly-paid and educated public servants, the emphasis tends to be on following all policies and procedures literally, one in which form precedes function. It is a narrow perspective of accounting and a costly one.

What can be done? A number of major steps need to be taken; most are not short-term in realizing operationality. These steps are limited in this discussion to those of expanding the auditing perspective, governmental restructuring, improved information systems, and a pervasive educational emphasis on the requirements for effective democratic government.

As mentioned, the current emphasis in African financial accountability is one of fiduciary and compliance auditing. This auditing perspective needs to be expanded to include management and program auditing. Management auditing focuses on the efficiency (relationships between inputs/outputs or workload) and effectiveness (results of operating policies and procedures) of government operations. Program auditing attends to the effectiveness (results) of programs (Herbert 1979, p. 4; see, also, Fountain, Arrowsmith, and Lockridge 1984, p. 9).

In both types of auditing, training and education must give greater emphasis to non-accounting concepts and behaviors, for example, in the social and management sciences. In both types of auditing, as in fiduciary and compliance audits, a generic mode of control is assumed:

1. establishment of standards,
2. observation of performance,
3. comparison of actual versus planned performance, and
4. taking the necessary actions to assure that the actual performance is consistent with planned performance.

Program audits, frequently called program evaluations, are often the most troublesome for governments because of the rigorous requirement for quantifiable program standards (objectives).

As Wholey points out, "government managers are ambivalent about managing for results," and notes that there are major problems in making it reality: lack of agreement on what constitutes solid results, inadequate management resources, reluctance to take responsibility, inadequate program information, and motivational issues related to improving program performance (Wholey 1983, p. 15).

Although Wholey was writing in the context of the American experience, his observations become even more appropriate when applied to Africa. How can donors expect agreement on what is good performance when good performance is as fluid as the most recent government press release or presidential proclamation? How can managers execute authority when it is centralized? Why should they take responsibility for that which they are denied responsibility? How can they secure adequate program information for sound management when even basic programmatic information is not collected, erroneous, belated, or suppressed? Why should personnel be motivated to improve program performance when program performance is not valued?

In the African situation, as well as similar ones, the answers are complex and not likely to be achieved in the short-term. Governmental restructuring must be a part of any answer. It is more than the common donor recommendation for a reduction in force which denies the reality of the implications, at least in financial areas, of donor accounting expectations on a developing nation. In this instance, it refers to improved pay for public servants and to the relationships between the branches of government. Little needs to be said about the consequences of poorly paid public servants: it is a part of the foundation for corruption (see "First Inter-American Conference on the Problems of Fraud and Corruption in Government: Final Report" 1989).[4] While most African nations have three branches of government, these are rarely truly independent of each other or frequently treated as if they are not. Such independence is critical for responsible democratic government. And, in terms of accounting and auditing, this independence and its decentralization ramifications are essential to improving governmental operations.

When such independence is realized, then one possibility is the creation of legislative audit organizations similar to the legislative audit organizations existing in many U.S. states and the U.S. General Accounting Office. Normally, the state units focus on management and program audits. In Virginia, for example, the Joint Legislative Audit and Review Commission undertakes eight to ten such audits each year, serving as an additional check on the operation of executive branch units. Its staff largely consists of professionals with non-accounting degrees. It is separate from the state's Auditor of Public Accounts (also a legislative agency) which focuses on fiduciary and compliance audits, executive branch agency and state internal auditors (which are beginning to engage in management and program audits), and Virginia's Department of Planning and Budget (which has a unit that focuses on program evaluation). Alternatively, a management and program unit could be placed in the judicial branch (which appears to be somewhat more independent than the legislative branch in many African states). In either situation, executive operating units should also establish their own internal management and program audit units.

While longer-term, it is clear that Africa's developing nations must build a culture of managerial responsibility, one which relates productivity, accountability, and responsibility in a meaningful structure. U.S. governments are attempting to improve their efforts by engaging in strategies that include pay for performance, total quality management, team organizations, and performance accounting and budgeting.[5] These may or may not work, even in the United States. Regardless, decentralization of managerial authority in Africa appears central to such a culture and its effect of improving governmental operations.

While there are efforts underway to improve financial information in Africa, little attention appears to be given to equally essential nonfinancial program management information. This author is of the opinion that this condition appears to be due to the predominance of economic and accounting perspectives among those organizations attempting to effect change in Africa. If other perspectives were to play an equal role in donor efforts, then perhaps the results, informational and otherwise, would be more realistic and effective.

The improvement of governmental information is a long-term undertaking because of the general conditions which characterize many African nations.[6] At a minimum, it involves rethinking the purpose of present information systems, and at a maximum, it requires the linking of that rethinking to technology and managerial capacities. It is directly linked to another long-term reform, one that is primarily educational in nature.

The widespread lack of basic democratic principles valuation appears to be a fundamental problem of the African auditing context. These values include ones of integrity and honesty in public functioning and responsible stewardship in achieving desired results in an economical and efficient manner. These values are both learnable and teachable. The major road to developing these values is education. They must be given greater emphasis in primary through secondary schooling, higher education, and re-emphasized in professional programs at, for example, staff colleges and training institutes. The emphasis needs to focus on democratic principles and their performance, equality before the law and in government policies, and a thorough understanding of democratic ethics and their effective execution. In professional education and training, greater attention needs to be given to these values and their relationships to management and program auditing. Moreover, auditing related matters should not be restricted to accounting/financial professionals but receive substantial attention in both accounting and non-accounting programs. Equally important, the ethics of accounting and auditing need to be more than words on paper; they need to be enforceable and enforced. Professional organizations should play a leading role in assuring that professional integrity is maintained. The effectiveness test for such educational achievements would be that public officials, elected and appointed, adhere to these standards in their performance.

To summarize, the unmet auditing needs of Africa's developing nations are complex and interrelated. They include the development of broader auditing perspectives, governmental restructuring, improved information systems, a governing culture which emphasizes productivity, accountibility, and responsibility, and thorough and extensive related educational policies.

NOTES

1. This incident received widespread attention in all but the government press. The author's photocopies of the story, received from a Kenyan journalist, did not, unfortunately, include citation information.
2. The World Bank decided not to disburse a $500 million (U.S.) loan as a result of its concern about the Nigerian government's continued expenditures for the Ajaokuta steel plant despite its cost overruns and lack of completion after a decade of construction expenditures. At the time, an official of the bank estimated that $4 billion had been spent on the plant, but that another $2 billion would need to be spent before it was fully operational.
3. The matter came to world attention when on-site donor economists ascertained that at least $3 billion was unaccounted for in Nigeria's Central Bank figures. It is believed that the windfall helped pay for Nigeria's involvement in the Liberian peace force, the OAU summit in Abuja, and on the initial construction costs of an aluminum smelter. It was reported that the smelter construction costs were 60 percent to 100 percent higher than those of comparable plants elsewhere in the world.
4. The conference was sponsored by USAID's Regional Financial Management Improvement Project-LAC/RFMIP organized by Price Waterhouse, the project contractor. It, too, noted the negative consequences of problems associated with pre-controls, particularly external ones on effective auditing, corruption in public contracting, and low pay levels for government employees.
5. The reemergence of performance budgeting in the United States may be indicated by the growing attention to performance measures. See, for example, U.S. Congress, Congressional Budget Office 1993).
6. There appears to be hope. The Harvard Institute for International Development is completing a multi-year project directed at improving financial management in Kenya. See, for example, Peterson (1994) and Peterson, Kinyecki, Mutai, and Ndungu (1993).

REFERENCES

Africa. 1990. "Kenya." 27(11): 10190-10191.

Africa. 1991a."Nigeria." 28(6): 10440-10441.

Africa. 1991b. "Kenya." 28(8): 10554.

Africa. 1991c. "Nigeria." 28(8): 10515.

Callier, P. Ed. 1991. *Financial Systems and Development in Africa.* Washington, DC: The World Bank.

Comptroller General of the United States. 1974. *Standards for Audit of Governmental Organizations, Programs, Activities, and Functions.* Washington, DC: United States General Accounting Office.

"First Inter-American Conference on the Problems of Fraud and Corruption in Government: Final Report." 1989. Miami, Florida, December 4-6.

Fountain, R.M., Jr., D.S. Arrowsmith, and R.L. Lockridge II. 1984. *Performance Auditing in Local Government*. Chicago: Government Finance Officers Association.

Herbert, L. 1979. *Auditing the Performance of Management*. Belmont, CA: Lifetime Learning Publications.

Herbert, L., L.N. Killough, and A.W. Steiss. 1984. *Governmental Accounting and Control*. Monterey, CA: Brooks/Cole Publishing Company.

Klittgaard, R. 1990. *Tropical Gangsters*. New York: Basic Books.

Peterson, S.B. 1994. "Budgeting in Kenya: Practice and Prescription." Unpublished manuscript, Harvard University, January 27.

Peterson, S.B., C. Kinyecki, J. Mutai, and C. Ndungu. 1993. "Computerizing Accounting Systems in Development Bureaucracies: Lessons From Kenya." Unpublished manuscript, Harvard University.

Price Waterhouse. 1992. *Latin American and Caribbean Regional Financial Management Improvement Project-LAC/RFMIP*. USAID Contract No. LAC-0658-C-00-9021-00, Washington, DC, June.

U.S. Congress, Congressional Budget Office. 1993. *Using Performance Measures in the Federal Budget Process*. Washington, DC: Author.

Wholey, J.S. 1983. *Evaluation and Effective Public Management*. Boston: Little, Brown and Company.

AUTHOR INDEX

Printed and bound by CPI Group (UK) Ltd, Croydon, CR0 4YY

15/09/2026

14962364-0007